KU-314-362

BIOGRAPHY OF JAMES HUDSON TAYLOR

JAMES HUDSON TAYLOR
From a portrait by an aunt, painted in 1852.

BIOGRAPHY OF JAMES HUDSON TAYLOR

by

Dr. and Mrs. Howard Taylor

LONDON
CHINA INLAND MISSION
Overseas Missionary Fellowship
Agents: Lutterworth Press

Made and printed in Great Britain for
China Inland Mission Overseas Missionary Fellowship
Newington Green, London, N.16
by Billing & Sons Limited, Guildford and London
Trade Agents: The Lutterworth Press
4 Bouverie Street, London, E.C.4

Foreword

FOR about half a century the full standard biography of James Hudson Taylor, founder of the China Inland Mission, was contained in two volumes. Under the sub-titles of 'The Growth of a Soul' and 'The Growth of a Work of God', these two books by Dr. and Mrs. Howard Taylor have run into seventeen editions, and have appeared in at least six European languages. The demand for them has been so steady, and testimonies to blessing received through reading them so numerous, that no question as to whether their publication should continue has arisen. The principles of God's work in and through a human soul, as revealed in the experiences of Hudson Taylor, remain unchanged with the passing of the years. The need for abridgement has been realized, however, particularly as some of the events and personalities mentioned have now disappeared over the horizon of history, and their retention in the narrative tends to confuse rather than to enlighten the readers of later generations.

This new abridged edition has been produced for the centennial year of the Mission's history, and is sent forth with the earnest desire that the inspiration of the founder's life may be conveyed to a new generation.

Contents

CHAPTER 1

Set Apart unto the Lord

(1824–1849)

WHEN Benjamin Hudson, a Methodist minister, was transferred in 1824 to the Barnsley Circuit, it must have seemed like coming home, for his native place lay only a few miles westward on the edge of the great grouse moors. There both he and his wife had been born and bred, and from that Yorkshire valley, running back into the Peak country and many a mile of mountain, dale and moor, had come the artistic temperament and courageous spirit of their children. The minister at the Manse, though not a gifted speaker, was a faithful and devoted minister of the Gospel, and an artist into the bargain. His decided talent for portrait painting was inherited by three at least of his children. His most prominent characteristic, and one that gave him difficulty at times, was an irrepressible fund of humour. This also was passed on in measure to his descendants. Reproved in the Methodist 'Conference' on one occasion for not sufficiently restraining this tendency, he apologized in a reply so witty that the whole assembly was overcome with laughter. But in Barnsley he was on his native heath. Yorkshire folk could appreciate his dry, droll speeches and pointed exhortation.

None, probably, appreciated him more than John Taylor the reed-maker, whose plain but substantial stone house stood on the opposite side of the road to the Manse. As both families had the same number of boys and girls, there was naturally a good deal of intercourse between the households. Amelia, the eldest daughter of the Manse, had a voice so sweet that John Taylor called her 'the nightingale'. As for his son James, apprenticed to a chemist ten miles away, more than usual eagerness winged his feet on his visits home when he came to know for himself the charming singer. The result was inevitable. A warm affection sprang up between the two, culminating in their marriage, after a seven-year engagement, in April 1831.

By this time James Taylor had started up in business on his own, and it was the chemist's home in the Market Place that really saw Amelia shine. There the qualities that made her an ideal wife could not be hidden. In all her husband's work and interest she bore a cheerful part. His class of forty or fifty lads felt the influence of her sympathy and prayers only less than the girls who became her special care, and one of the joys of their early married life was an old-time revival in the Chapel that resulted in the conversion of many of these young people.

In preparing sermons for his preaching engagements throughout the Circuit James Taylor found his wife an unexpected help. When his heart was full and his pen could not keep pace with the thoughts he longed to utter, she would take rapid notes, and write out many a sermon delivered as he paced the little room behind the shop. A gifted speaker, he gave much care to the preparation of his discourses. He was an excellent chemist, too, and as a business man was highly respected. So scrupulous was he in financial matters that he made it a rule to pay every debt the day it fell due.

'If I let it stand over a week,' he would say, 'I defraud my creditor of interest, if only a fractional sum.'

Possessed by a profound conviction of God's infinite faithfulness, he took the Bible very simply, believing it was of all books the most practical if put to the test of experience. On a day his young wife could never forget, in their first winter together, he sought her to talk over a passage that had impressed him. It was part of the thirteenth chapter of Exodus, with the corresponding verses in Numbers:

'Sanctify unto me all the firstborn . . .'

'All the firstborn are mine . . .'

'Mine shall they be . . .'

'Set apart unto the Lord.'

Long and earnest was the talk that followed in view of the happiness to which they were looking forward. Then together they knelt to fulfil as literally as possible an obligation they could not relegate to Hebrew parents of old. Just as definitely the Lord responded, giving them faith to realize that He had accepted their gift: that henceforth the life so dear to them must be held at the disposal of a higher claim, a deeper love, than theirs.

Thus springtime came again touching with tender loveliness those Yorkshire hills and valleys, and on May 21, 1832, this child of many prayers was born, uniting in his name that of both his parents – James Hudson Taylor.

In the course of the years others were added to the Taylor family. One great advantage of the childhood of Hudson and his sisters was that they were so continually under their mother's care. This in itself was sufficient compensation for the limited means that made it necessary. A great deal of sewing had to be done, but she was able to go on with it while they read aloud or wrote from dictation. Many were the hours thus spent over history, literature and travels. She early inspired them with a taste for reading, and to her accuracy and thoroughness may be traced the unusual attention to detail that characterized her son in later years.

Personal neatness she taught them in the same practical way. A work-basket was always ready on their dressing table, and stitches were put in as soon as needed. It became second nature to feel that one must be clean and tidy, however simply dressed. How she managed it no one could tell; but with the entire care and education of the children, cooking to attend to, washing to be done at home, and all the housework, with the help of only one maid, she invariably kept her surroundings neat and attractive.

The little parlour behind the shop, though constantly in use for meals and lessons, needlework and play, was a picture of comfort and good order. With its corner cupboard filled with shining crockery and glass, its little window affording interesting glimpses through the shop to the Market Place beyond, its long, old-fashioned couch and its spacious bookcase, the family living room was a cosy spot.

The chief feature in the room, undoubtedly, was the bookcase, and it had also much to do with the order that prevailed. Over the lower shelves hung a curtain concealing a characteristic device of the mother's household management. Everything in use for meals or lessons, work or play, had its appointed place in sideboard or cupboard, while magazines, books and papers found hospitality upon the ample shelves. But one shelf behind the crimson curtain was unappropriated. Clean and empty, it stood ready for emergencies. Was the room needed for unexpected visitors? The work in hand, whatever it might be, was laid away without embarrassment and just as easily brought out again. Were the older people busy with letters or accounts when the table was wanted for a meal? A place was ready in which ink and papers would be accessible and out of danger. It was a convenient receptacle at tea-time for the mother's sewing or the children's toys. But whatever its uses in the daytime, it was always cleared and dusted before night. Simple as such a plan may seem, it was effective because of the orderly mind that carried it out, and went far toward solving the problem of how to turn one room to so many uses without litter or confusion.

The mother's gentle discipline had much to do with the happiness of Hudson's childhood, and gave rise to a situation that was long remembered. In attending to guests at dinner one day, she overlooked the needs of her little son. The meal went on and still the child said nothing, knowing he must not ask for things at table. At length, however, an expedient suggested itself, and a little voice was heard requesting for salt. That at any rate was permissible.

'And what do you want the salt for?' questioned his neighbour, seeing the empty plate.

'Oh,' he replied, 'I want to be ready. Mamma will give me something to eat by-and-by.'

On another occasion he called attention to his needs by inquiring in a pause in the conversation,

'Mamma, do you think apple pie is good for little boys?'

The children lived in touch with their father almost as much as with their mother, and he felt himself no less responsible for their training. Though he was stern and even quick-tempered at times, the influence James Taylor exerted in the life of his son can hardly be over-estimated. He was decidedly a disciplinarian. But without some such element in his early training who can tell whether Hudson would ever have become the man he was? With James Taylor, to keep the children moderately happy and good-tempered was not the point. He was a man with a supreme sense of duty. The thing that ought to be done was the thing he put first, always. Ease, pleasure, self-improvement, had to take whatever place they could. He was a man of faith, but faith that went hand in hand with works of the most practical kind. His children must be doing their duty, getting through their daily tasks, acquiring habits that alone could make them dependable men and women in days to come.

The importance of punctuality, for example, he impressed both by teaching and example. No one was allowed to be late for meals or any other engagement.

'If there are five people,' he would say, 'and they are kept waiting one minute, do you not see that five minutes are lost that can never be found again?'

Dilatoriness in dressing or undressing, or in making a start when the time came to begin, he also reprehended as a serious waste of time. 'Learn to dress quickly,' he would say, 'for you have to do it once, at least, every day of your life. And begin promptly whatever the work in hand. To loiter does not help, it only makes the task more difficult.'

'See if you can do without' was another of his maxims. This of course applied, among other things, to the simple pleasures of the table. He fully realized the lifelong influence of little habits, and felt he must secure to his children the power of self-control.

'By and by,' he would explain, 'you will have to say "No" to yourself when we are not there to help you; and very difficult you will find it when you want a thing tremendously. So let us try to practise now, for the sooner you begin the stronger will be the habit.'

Family worship he conducted regularly, after both breakfast and tea. Every member of the household had to be present, and the passage read was explained in such practical fashion that even the children could not fail to see its application. He was very particular about giving them the whole Word of God, omitting nothing. The Old Testament as well as the New was taken in regular course, and at the close of every day's reading the date was carefully entered in the family Bible.

He explained to them the necessity for maintaining the life of the soul by prayer and Bible study, as the life of the body is maintained by exercise and food. To omit this was to neglect the one thing needful. He spoke of it frequently as a matter of vital importance, and arranged for everyone in the house to have at least half an hour daily, alone with God. The result was that even the little ones began to discover the secret of a happy day.

James Taylor was sociable and talked freely in congenial company. On Quarter Day, when fellow-workers came to Barnsley from every part of the Circuit, he often improved the occasion by inviting one and all home to tea. It was on those occasions chiefly that the subject of foreign missions came up, and the children were delighted by many a story from far-off lands. China held the first place in their father's sympathies, and he used often to lament the indifference of the Church to its appalling need. It especially troubled him that the denomination to which he belonged should be doing nothing for its evangelization.

'Why do we not send our missionaries there?' he would exclaim. 'That is the country to aim at, with its teeming population, its strong, intelligent, scholarly people.'

Hudson early made up his mind to go to China as a missionary, and his interest in the land was increased by a little book called *China* which he read and reread until he almost knew it by heart. Any hope his parents may have entertained that he would be called to just such a service, however, had been abandoned, on account of his continued delicacy. He was not even sent to school until he was eleven, and his brief career as a schoolboy terminated two years later. It was not a particularly happy period, for although he enjoyed study immensely, hardly a week passed without his having to miss a day or two on account of illness. He was not sufficiently a lover of boyish sports to become a general favourite, and was delighted when it was decided that he should leave to carry on his studies at home, and help his father in the shop on the Market Place. Thus childhood's years passed by, and all unconsciously Hudson Taylor was drawing near the crisis of his life.

Outwardly he was a bright lad of seventeen, with few anxieties or cares, but inwardly he was rebellious and full of unbelief. For a few months he had gone as junior clerk into one of the banks at Barnsley, where most of his new associates were thoroughly worldly. Sceptical views to which he was a stranger were freely discussed among them, and religion was seldom spoken of without a sneer. One of the older clerks in particular, a handsome and popular fellow, took every occasion to laugh at what he called Hudson's 'old-fashioned notions', and did all he could to make him as light-minded as himself. The boy began to long for gaiety and distraction, for money and a horse to go hunting as did some of his companions. He found it weary work to try to keep up the outward forms of Christian life, though he struggled to do so for a time. And when overtime work by gas light brought on a serious inflammation of the eyes and he had to resign his position and return to his father's shop, his unhappiness continued.

Needless to say, this state of things marred the happiness of home and overclouded his naturally sunny disposition. All was not right, and his parents could not but see it. The father tried to help him, but found it hard to be patient with the phase through which Hudson was passing. The mother understood him better, and redoubled her tenderness and prayers. But it was his sister Amelia, though only thirteen years of age, who was nearest to him and best able to win his confidence.

To her he could speak more freely than to older people and his indifference and unhappiness so affected her that she determined to pray for him three times every day until he was really converted. This she did for some weeks, going alone to plead with God for the salvation of her brother, and even making a note in her journal that she would never cease to pray for him until he was brought into the light, and that she believed her petitions would be answered before long.

So, held by the faith and prayers of those who loved him, he came to the day he could never forget, of which he wrote years later,

My mother being absent from home, I had a holiday, and in the afternoon looked through my father's library to find some book with which to while away the unoccupied hours. Nothing attracting me, I turned over a basket of pamphlets and selected from amongst them a Gospel tract that looked interesting, saying to myself, 'There will be a story at the commencement and a sermon or moral at the close. I will take the former and leave the latter for those who like it.'

I sat down to read the book in an utterly unconcerned state of mind, believing indeed at the time that if there were any salvation it was not for me, and with a distinct intention to put away the tract as soon as it should seem prosy.

Little did I know at the time what was going on in the heart of my mother, seventy or eighty miles away. She rose from the dinner table that afternoon with an intense yearning for the conversion of her boy; and feeling that, absent from home and having more leisure than she could otherwise secure, a special opportunity was afforded her of pleading with God on my behalf. She went to her room and turned the key in the door, resolved not to leave the spot until her prayers were answered. Hour after hour that dear mother pleaded, until at length she could pray no longer, but was constrained to praise God for that which His Spirit taught her had already been accomplished, the conversion of her only son.

I in the meantime had been led in the way I have mentioned to take up this little tract, and while reading it was struck with the phrase: 'The finished work of Christ'.

'Why does the author use this expression?' I questioned. 'Why not say the atoning or propitiatory work of Christ?'

Immediately the words 'It is finished' suggested themselves to my mind.

'What was finished?'

And I at once replied, 'A full and perfect atonement and satisfaction for sin. The debt was paid for our sins, and not for ours only, but also for the sins of the whole world.'

Then came the further thought, 'If the whole work was finished and the whole debt paid, what is there left for me to do?'

And with this dawned the joyful conviction, as light was flashed into my soul by the Holy Spirit, that there was nothing in the world to be done but to fall down on one's knees and, accepting this Saviour and His salvation, praise Him for evermore.

Thus while my mother was praising God on her knees in her chamber, I was praising Him in the old warehouse to which I had gone alone to read at my leisure this little book.

Several days elapsed before I ventured to make even my sister the confidante of my joy, and then only after she had promised not to tell anyone. When Mother returned a fortnight later I was the first to meet her at the door and to tell her I had such glad news to give. I can almost feel that dear mother's arms round my neck as she said,

'I know, my boy.'

'Why,' I asked in surprise, 'has Amelia broken her promise? She said she would tell no one.'

My mother assured me that it was not from any human source she had learned the tidings, and went on to tell the incident mentioned above. You will agree with me that it would be strange indeed if I were not a believer in the power of prayer.

Nor was this all. Some time after, I picked up a pocket-book exactly like my own and, thinking it was mine, opened it. The lines that caught my eye were an entry in the little diary belonging to my sister, to the effect that she would give herself daily to prayer until God should answer in the conversion of her brother. One month later the Lord was pleased to turn me from darkness to light.

Brought up in such a circle and saved in such circumstances, it was perhaps natural that from the commencement of my Christian life I was led to feel that the promises were very real, and that prayer was in sober matter of fact transacting business with God, whether on one's own behalf or on the behalf of those for whom one sought His blessing.

It was the month of June, 1849, when this definite apprehension of the atoning work of Christ changed the whole of life for Hudson Taylor. Henceforward he rejoiced in conscious acceptance with God, not on the ground of anything he could do or be, but simply because of what the Lord Jesus is and has done. 'Not I, but Christ' brought freedom, joy and rest. It was the turning point in his experience, the commencement of a new order of things that, little as he realized it at the time, meant for him – China.

The unspeakable value of years of steady discipline in a Christian home now became apparent. He was in a position to make rapid progress. The Bible was no strange book to him, but familiar territory, a land of promise waiting to be possessed. Prayer was no unwonted effort, but the natural outgoing of a heart long accustomed to turn to God. There was much yet to learn, but mercifully there were few habits or memories of evil to erase. The Holy Spirit had, comparatively, a free field in his heart. And at seventeen years of age, all life was yet before him in which to spend and be spent for the Lord he loved.

He longed for some work to do for God, some service that might prove his gratitude, some suffering even. A leisure afternoon gave opportunity for prayer, and with this desire filling his heart he went up to his room to be alone with God. And there in a special way the Lord met him.

> 'Well do I remember,' he wrote long after, 'as in unreserved consecration I put myself, my life, my friends, my all upon the altar, the deep solemnity that came over my soul with the assurance that my offering was accepted. The presence of God became unutterably real; stretching myself on the ground and lying there before Him with unspeakable awe and unspeakable joy, a deep consciousness that I was not my own took possession of me, which has never since been effaced.'

One result of this definite consecration was that he began to care about the welfare of others. If he could not preach as yet, he could at any rate give away tracts and invite people to the House of God. Busy from morning till night in the shop, it was not easy to make time for this work. But he found that by denying himself one of his chief pleasures, the Sunday evening service, he could gain a few hours just when people would be most accessible.

Instead of attending chapel therefore on Sunday evenings, he and Amelia went out as soon as tea was over and made their way to the poorest parts of the town. They became familiar figures, passing from door to door, handing tracts to all who would receive them. Even the poorest lodging-houses were not passed over, though it cost an effort to go down those dark, narrow passages into the crowded kitchens. They were more than rewarded by a sense of their Master's approval.

But the joy in the Lord and in His service was not the only experience as summer passed away. Coldness of heart crept in, forgetfulness, indifference. Somehow there seemed a gap between the power of the Lord Jesus to save 'to the uttermost' and the needs of everyday life in shop and home. The good he longed to do he did not, and the evil he hated too often had the mastery. He did delight in the law of God after the inward man, but there was that other law bringing him into captivity to sin with all its deadening influences. And he had not yet learned to cry, 'Thanks be to God . . . The law of the Spirit of *life in Christ Jesus* hath made me free from the law of sin and death.'

At such times two courses are open to the perplexed and troubled soul. One is to abandon the ideal, and gradually sink down to a low level Christian life in which there is neither joy nor power. The other is just to go on with the Lord, and because of His 'exceeding great and precious promises' to claim complete deliverance not from the guilt only, but also from the mastery of sin.

Nothing less than this could satisfy Hudson Taylor. Conversion with him had been no easy-going assent of the mind to an abstract creed. The Cross of Christ had cut him off for ever from the old life, and from rest in anything the world could give. Nothing could satisfy him now but unbroken fellowship with God. Hence times of spiritual lethargy and indifference were alarming. He could not take backsliding easily. It was nothing less than full deliverance upon which he had set his heart – real holiness, and daily victory over sin.

The conflict lasted all through the autumn, apparently. September brought the first break in the family circle, when Amelia went to complete her education at Barton-on-Humber, where their mother's sister, Mrs. Hodson, had a school for girls and received a few resident pupils under her own roof. Her eldest son, John, was meanwhile apprenticed to his uncle in Barnsley, and it was arranged that the cousins should exchange homes for the time being, without additional expense to either family. With John sharing his room, there was less privacy for prayer and Bible study, more provocation to exuberance of spirits and more tendency to friction in business hours. His father had a somewhat hasty spirit, and all this combined to make things difficult, until early in December it would seem a crisis was reached.

Outwardly things were much as usual, but inwardly he was almost driven to despair. A deadness of soul had begun to steal over him. Prayer was an effort and the Bible devoid of interest. Christmas was close at hand and business correspondingly pressing. There seemed no time for quiet waiting upon God, even had the desire been present. But it was not. At times a terrible fear assailed him, that he was drifting he knew not whither and might miss the purpose of God for his life now, if not hereafter.

Just about that time his attention was arrested by an article in the November *Wesleyan Magazine,* setting forth in glowing terms the very experience he needed. It was entitled 'The Beauty of Holiness', and it quickened again the longing of his heart for victory over self and sin. Then a mission was held in the chapel he attended, that resulted in so real a revival of spiritual blessing that within a few days more than 100 converts were gathered in. And finally a definite promise from the Word of God came home to him with power:

> I will sprinkle clean water upon you, and ye shall be clean: from all your filthiness, and from all your idols, will I cleanse you. A new heart also will I give you, and a new spirit will I put within you: and I will take away the stony heart out of your flesh, and I will give you an heart of flesh. And I will put my spirit within you, and cause you to walk in my statutes, and ye shall keep my judgments, and do them (Ezek. 36.25–27).

B

Sunday morning came, December 2, 1849. He was glad rather than otherwise of a cold which kept him in and gave him time to be quiet and alone. The Lord was consciously with him but things were not right. He had given himself to God without reserve, longing to be always and only His. And yet he could not maintain that attitude.

'I cannot help wishing that instead of a slight cold I had some sickness that would take me to Heaven', was the weary note on which the boy still in his teens concluded a long letter to his sister. 'I have a desire to depart and be with Christ, which is far, far better.'

That night upon going to bed he was deeply troubled. His soul was athirst for God, and yet an intense realization of failure and unworthiness almost overwhelmed him. 'Draw nigh to God, and he will draw nigh to you' is a promise always fulfilled to the sincere and humble spirit, but how often the vision granted calls forth the cry, 'Woe is me! for I am undone; because I am a man of unclean lips.'

Nor was this all.

Absorbed in his own need, the lad was longing for true holiness, the life that is 'no longer I, but Christ' in everything. The Lord with wider needs in view was seeking him for this, but not for this only. In His great purposes the time had come when the Gospel could no longer be withheld from the 'uttermost parts of the earth'. China even must be opened, and its most distant provinces hear the tidings of a Saviour's love. There it lay in agelong darkness, its teeming millions – a quarter of the human race – living, dying without God. It was of China the Lord was thinking, may we not say it reverently, as well as of Hudson Taylor. But the lad was not ready yet to hear the call, 'Whom shall I send, and who will go for us?' The work of the convicting Spirit must go deeper ere he could be fully blessed and brought into harmony with the mind of God. Thus his sense of sin and need became more intense as he wrestled for the deliverance without which he could not, dared not go on.

What was it that kept him from the life for which he longed? What was the secret of his frequent failure and backsliding in heart? Was there something not fully surrendered, some disobedience or unfaithfulness to light? Fervently he prayed that God would show him the hindrance whatever it might be, and enable him to put it away. He had come to an end of self, to a place where only God could deliver, where he *must* have His succour, His enlightenment, His aid. It was a life-and-death matter. Everything seemed at stake. Like one of old he was constrained to cry, 'I will not let thee go except thou bless me.'

And then, alone upon his knees, a great purpose arose within him. If only God would work on his behalf, would break the power of sin and save him, spirit, soul and body, for time and for eternity, he would renounce all earthly prospects and be utterly at His disposal. He would go anywhere, do anything, suffer whatever His cause might demand, and be wholly given to His will and service. This was the cry of his heart; nothing held back – if only God would deliver him and keep him from falling.

Instinctively we pause and turn aside from a scene so sacred. The place is holy ground. Of what transpired further we know no more, save for a few lines written when occasion required it in the following year. For he rarely referred to this experience, though all his life he lived it out.

> 'Never shall I forget', he wrote, 'the feeling that came over me then. Words can never describe it. I felt I was in the presence of God, entering into covenant with the Almighty. I felt as though I wished to withdraw my promise, but could not. Something seemed to say "Your prayer is answered, your conditions are accepted". And from that time the conviction never left me that I was called to China.'

For distinctly, as if a voice had spoken it, the command was given, 'Then go for Me to China.'

As silently as the sun rises over a summer sea, so dawned this new day upon his waiting soul. China? Yes, *China.* That was the meaning of his life – past, present, and to come. Away beyond himself, outside the little world of personal experiences, lay the great, waiting world, those for whom no man cared, for whom Christ died. 'Then go for Me to China.' Your prayer is answered: your conditions are accepted. All you ask and more, far more, shall be given. There shall be deeper knowledge of the Lord; fellowship in His sufferings, His death, His resurrection; a life of inner victory and power. 'For to this end have I appeared unto thee, to appoint thee a minister and a witness both of the things wherein thou hast seen me, and of the things wherein I will appear unto thee; delivering thee from the people and from the Gentiles unto whom now I send thee, to open their eyes, that they may turn from darkness to light, and from the power of Satan unto God.'

> 'From that hour', the mother wrote, 'his mind was made up. His pursuits and studies were all engaged in with reference to this object, and whatever difficulties presented themselves his purpose never wavered.'

For inwardly there was a deep subjection to the will of God, resting upon a profound and unalterable sense of what that will was for him. And with this came new purity and power, a steady growth in grace, and fullness of blessing that carried him through all the testing and preparation of the next few years.

'Faithful is he that calleth you, who also will do it.'

That was what made him and kept him, the real beginning of his walk with God as a man set apart.

CHAPTER 2

The New Starting Point

(1850–1851)

THUS closed the old year and the old life, and with the dawn of 1850 came a new beginning of things for Hudson Taylor. A work of which he still knew next to nothing claimed him; a work that must absorb every energy of his being, and might require the sacrifice of life itself. How to set about it he had no idea. What could he, a chemist's assistant in a provincial town, do for China? But the call of God had come, and there could be no looking back. Whatever might be involved, the future held but one thing for him – to do his Master's will in and for China. So he began at once to pray for guidance and to learn all he could about his future field.

Very little was known about China in the middle of last century. True, five ports had been opened along the coast to the residence of foreigners,[1] and the London Missionary Society, for nearly forty years the only British Mission at work in that land, had been reinforced by several newly organized efforts.[2] But they were all in their infancy; and beyond the Treaty Ports practically nothing was being attempted. In the absence of definite knowledge about the interior, exaggerated rumours were afloat. The wealth and learning of the people and the wonders of their ancient civilization, as reported by some travellers, were only exceeded by the cruelty and ignorance enlarged upon by others. But travellers of any kind who had penetrated beyond the coast were few and far between. Even for books upon the subject Hudson Taylor hardly knew where to turn. One friend might be able to help him, and that was Mr. Whitworth, the founder and superintendent of the Sunday School, who had recently become connected with the British and Foreign Bible Society. He would know something at any

[1] The Treaty Ports of Canton, Amoy, Fuchow, Ningpo and Shanghai, opened by the Treaty of Nanking, which concluded the first opium war with England, in 1842.

[2] The order in which the British Societies commenced work in China, up to this point, is as follows:

1807. The London Missionary Society; sending Robert Morrison to Canton.

After the Treaty of Nanking—

1843. The British and Foreign Bible Society.
1844. The Church Missionary Society.
1845. The Baptist Missionary Society.
1847. The English Presbyterian Mission, whose first representative was the Rev. William Burns.

rate about the circulation of the Bible in China, and might possess a copy of the Chinese Scriptures in whole or part. So to Mr. Whitworth he went.

The visit was encouraging, for his old friend was able to give him a copy, in the Mandarin dialect, of the writings of St. Luke. This was a treasure indeed. From him he may also have heard for the first time of Dr. Medhurst of the London Missionary Society, who had written a book on China which was actually in the library of the Congregational minister at Barnsley. This he was able to borrow, and through it was given guidance concerning the sort of training that he should seek, as he observed the value of medical work on the mission field. Not yet eighteen years of age, he could not embark on that yet, but he could and did start to study Chinese.

Courageous in his inexperience Hudson Taylor set to work, despite the fact that he had neither teacher nor books with the exception of that one little volume of the writings of St. Luke. A grammar would have cost no less than four guineas, and a dictionary could hardly have been purchased for fifteen. Needless to say, he had neither. But hard work and ingenuity accomplished wonders, as may be judged from the fact that within weeks he and the cousin who was with him in the shop had found out the meaning of over 500 characters. Writing to Amelia he explained their method.

> We find a short verse in the English version, and then look out a dozen or more (also in English) that have one word in common with it. We then turn up the first verse in Chinese, and search through all the others for some character in common that seems to stand for the English word. This we write down on a slip of paper as its probable equivalent. Then we look all through the Chinese Gospel for this same character in different connections. It occurs as a rule pretty frequently. And if in every case we find the same word in the English version, we copy the character in ink into our dictionary, adding the meaning in pencil. Afterwards, if further acquaintance shows it to be the true meaning, we ink that over also. At first we made slow progress, but now we can work much faster, as with few exceptions we know all the most common characters.
>
> I have begun to get up at five in the morning, and so find it necessary to go to bed early at night. I must study if I mean to go to China. I am fully decided to go, and am making every preparation I can. I intend to rub up my Latin, to learn Greek and the rudiments of Hebrew, and to get as much general information as possible.

He dispensed with his cosy feather bed at this time also, in order to prepare for a rougher sort of life. And with his practical turn of mind he saw that something could be done, right here and now, in Barnsley, to forward the cause to which his life was given. He could pray and lead others to pray, give and encourage others in giving. The only drawback was that he hardly knew how to communicate with China since, large as the field was, the Methodists had no mission there. Work in the Treaty Ports was being carried on by other societies; but even then Hudson Taylor longed after the vast waiting world of the unreached interior, still destitute of the Gospel.

Just at this juncture a new movement set on foot by Dr. Gutzlaff of Hong Kong came to his knowledge through papers lent to him by Mr. Whitworth. With what joy did he read that a society had been organized in London to do the very work on which his heart was set! Interdenominational in character, 'The Chinese Association', as it was called, aimed at employing Chinese evangelists to co-operate with Dr. Gutzlaff in an enterprise that bid fair to solve the problem of how to send the Gospel to the unreached interior. Quite a number were already working under his supervision, and great was the success that seemed to attend their efforts.

Burning with love to Christ and zeal for the advancement of His cause Dr. Gutzlaff had returned from Hong Kong a few months previously, and had commenced in London as a starting point a missionary crusade of the most remarkable kind. From Ireland to Hungary he passed, proclaiming in the capitals of Europe the duty of the Christian Church toward the unevangelized millions of China. For the first time the need and claims of that great land came home to many a heart, with the result that many were on their knees praying as never before. It was prayer for which Gutzlaff primarily appealed, prayer for the outpouring of the Spirit of God upon China in its age-long darkness. But true prayer, potent in itself, is sure to bring about practical results, and in this case quite a number of organized efforts grew up in London and on the Continent.

Gutzlaff's piety was deep and real, his schemes were large and his optimism unbounded. He was a man of unusual gifts, and as Interpreter to the British Government in Hong Kong occupied a position of influence. So great was his enthusiasm for the spread of the Gospel that he had risked his life repeatedly in daring attempts to reach the interior, as well as in voyages along the entire coast. Wearing Chinese dress, he made seven journeys during the years 1831–35, landing at places as far north as Tientsin. With considerable experience as a sailor he even engaged himself as mate on a Chinese junk, and at another time as cook, in order to visit places to which no foreign vessels sailed, and thus obtained opportunities for making known the truth as it is in Jesus. He lived for one thing only – the extension of the Kingdom of God. To this he devoted his large salary, his remarkable powers of mind and body and all his available time. He wrote and published eighty works in no fewer than eight different languages, including a translation into Chinese of both the Old and New Testaments. He founded 'The Chinese Union', a native missionary society whose members were to carry the Gospel far and wide to every part of the eighteen provinces, and one may almost say he awakened Europe with enthusiasm in support of this cause, everywhere organizing prayer meetings and associations to carry on the work. The new society in London was one of these, and immediately claimed the sympathy of Hudson Taylor.

According to tabulated reports brought home by Dr. Gutzlaff, the evangelists of 'The Chinese Union' inaugurated six years previously had met with amazing encouragement. They now numbered 130 men, engaged in systematic preaching throughout the interior and in the distribution of Christian literature. They had circulated over 10,000 New Testaments, besides many Bibles and countless books and tracts. They wrote long and detailed letters from almost all the provinces of China, telling of journeys even to the borders of Mongolia and Tibet. And last but not least, they had baptized, 'upon examination and satisfactory confession of their faith', no fewer than 2,871 converts. Such results, within so short a time, could not but arouse the deepest interest.

All through the spring and summer these developments were delighting Hudson Taylor. He took from the first an excellent magazine which was commenced in March of this year to supply the latest tidings from Dr. Gutzlaff's workers, as well as missionary information from other parts of the world. The careful study with which he followed it for years formed in itself a valuable education in missionary principles and practice. From its pages he learned of many on the Continent as well as in Great Britain who were engaged in active efforts for the evangelization of China. It informed him also of the varied labours of George Müller of Bristol, who during this and the previous year had expended more than £2,500 on missionary work. God used this well-directed magazine to introduce Hudson Taylor into a new world of Christian enterprise, unsectarian in its character and international in its interests, preparing him while still in his teens for the far-reaching associations of coming years.

The Gleaner was evidently edited by the secretaries of the Chinese Association, a new society in London, and on July 29, 1850, he wrote to one of them, Mr. George Pearse, asking him to forward 'a few circulars or collecting cards, as well as any information, rules, etc., calculated to assist me in introducing the work to my friends'. He little realized to what that modest overture would eventually lead.

Reports meanwhile had begun to reach England of the doubtful character of Dr. Gutzlaff's organization, and the reply from Mr. Pearse was discouraging. Further developments tended only to confirm the fear that, with all his brilliant gifts and rare devotion, Gutzlaff sadly lacked common sense. In a word, he had been systematically swindled, as the German missionary acting as his *locum tenens* in Hong Kong discovered. Few of his so-called evangelists had travelled beyond Canton, and many of their glowing reports had been concocted in opium dens a few minutes only from his own door. It was a painful and almost incredible exposure, and no one suffered more from grief and disappointment than the noble-minded leader, who did not long survive the failure of his work.[1]

And yet – had Gutzlaff failed? His plans miscarried grievously and his projects came to nothing. But prayer and faith cannot fail. 'Even in his last hours,' *The Gleaner* reported, 'all his thoughts were directed to the evangelization of China. He spoke of it with great confidence, and in the delirium of fever frequently expressed bright hopes for the blessing and regeneration of his beloved Sinim. Truly of him it may be said that he departed this life and entered the presence of the Lord bearing the millions of China upon his heart.' And the aims he had never been able to realize, the ideals that seemed to fail, fell as good seed into other hearts.

Long years after, when the China Inland Mission had become a fact in all the inland provinces, its founder loved to refer to Dr. Gutzlaff as in a very real sense the father of the work.

The failure of Gutzlaff's plans was not the only disappointment that came to test the reality of Hudson Taylor's call to China. He was overtaken by trial of a very different kind, that went with him through months and even years, bringing the strongest influences to bear against unquestioning obedience. He had just received a wonderful baptism of love and power. He had come to know the will of God for his future and was entering with unreserved consecration upon his life service. At that very point the tempter met him with suggestions so natural and attractive that a powerful countercurrent set in.

It all began with the Christmas holidays when Amelia returned from school with the young music teacher to whom she had become very attached during the term. Miss V. was decidedly attractive. Bright and gifted, with a voice so sweet it was a pleasure to listen to her, she was happy in the family circle and interested especially in the son of the household. When the little sister, with whom there was much talk over his call to China, discovered that someone else was beginning to take first place in her brother's affections, she rejoiced unselfishly. Life would not be so lonely for him now, she thought, far away from home.

It was Hudson who saw difficulties ahead, though it had not occurred to him that the one he loved might be quite unsuited for the life he hoped to live in China. While sympathizing to a certain extent with his feelings, there was something lacking and she would gladly have held him back. This he did not realize, or if he did feel it intangibly from the first he did not admit it even to himself. What concerned him was his lack of means, prospectively, to support a wife. How he was to go to China he had no idea, for he knew

[1] Dr. Gutzlaff passed away at Hong Kong on August 9, 1851, devotedly labouring among the Chinese until his brief but fatal illness came on.

of no society that sent out unordained men, unless perhaps the Chinese Association. The collapse of Dr. Gutzlaff's enterprise was seriously affecting missionary interest in China. It seemed more than likely that he would have to be a self-supporting missionary, trusting the Lord who sent him to provide. But that precluded any thought of marriage, at any rate for a long time to come. And meanwhile his lips were sealed. Someone else was sure to love her. Everyone must who was near her and free to win her love. No one could care as he did! That was beyond question. And yet, with such prospects or lack of prospects before him he must be silent.

This was the ground, then, on which the conflict commenced: not so much a struggle between love and duty, though it came to that at last, as a long fight of faith with questionings and fears. '*No good thing will he withhold.*' Would it prove really true? Could he leave all in the hands of God and simply trust – nothing but uncertainty ahead?

The year that followed was full of perplexity and pain, in the midst of which his spiritual life was deepening. Sharing a room with his cousin made it difficult to obtain much privacy, but 'I go into the warehouse, stable or anywhere,' he wrote, 'to be alone with God. And some most precious seasons I have.' On another occasion he wrote,

I have a stronger desire than ever to go to China. That land is ever in my thoughts. Think of it – 360 million souls, without God or hope in the world! Think of more than twelve millions of our fellow creatures dying every year without any of the consolations of the Gospel. Barnsley including the Common has only 15,000 inhabitants. Imagine what it would be if all these were to die in twelve months! Yet in China year by year *hundreds* are dying, for every man, woman and child in Barnsley. Poor, neglected China! Scarcely anyone cares about it.

As the unstudied correspondence of a lad of only eighteen with a sister several years younger, the above quotations have a special interest. So also has the following letter bearing more directly upon the matter that was exercising his heart.

In your last note you suggest that it might be a good plan to write to the Chinese Association and ask whether they could send me out as a married man. I think that to do so would be effectually to prevent them. They would naturally conclude that I wanted to get married without means, and that I hoped they would insure me from the consequences of such conduct. It would not do to write to them at all at present.

I have not, as you know, the slightest idea how I shall go. But this I know, I shall go, either alone or married. I know God has called me to the work, and He will provide the means. But as you see I cannot send the information you desire. It is not reasonable to suppose that Miss V. would be willing to go and starve in a foreign land. I am sure I love her too well to wish her to do so. You well know I have nothing, and nothing (financially) to hope for. Consequently I can enter into no engagement under present circumstances. I cannot deny that these things make me very sad. But my Father knows what is best. 'No good thing will he withhold.' I must live by faith, hang on by faith, simple faith, and He will do all things well.

Think not I am cold or indifferent. But what *can* I do? I know I love her. To go without her would make the world a blank. But I cannot bring her to want. Oh, pray for me! It is enough to distract me.

You say you are sure I might win her if I could see my way to provide for her. But you see I cannot. And if I could, how do you know that I might have her? Do let me know, for I am so anxious about it. You say I should ensure this best by being sent out. Very true. But who is to send me? The Wesleyans have no station in China. The Established Church have one or two, but I am not a Churchman, and would not do for them. The Baptists and Independents have stations there, but I do not hold their views. The Chinese Association is very low in funds. So God and God alone is my hope, and I need no other.

With you I could wish, were it possible, that the matter should be decided at Christmas. But what reason have you for thinking it might if circumstances were favourable? Do you suppose she thinks or knows that I love her? Or does she, think you, care about me? Do answer these questions plainly.

A reply seems to have come from his sister that perplexed while it encouraged him.

'I wonder how often I have read and re-read your letters,' he wrote a fortnight later, 'especially the last. As I do so, my mind is filled with conflicting hopes and fears. But I am determined to trust in God.'

Thus winter passed slowly by, and with early spring came a first step toward China. He felt the time had come for more definite preparation for his life-work. Five years in his father's business had made him quite at home in dispensing medicines and even prescribing for ordinary ailments. He needed still to earn his own living, but felt that as assistant to a doctor in good practice he might at the same time make progress with his medical studies.

'I am determined not to waste time any more in writing letters as I have done,' he wrote to his sister, 'but to endeavour in all things to be about my Master's work. May He help me. It is my desire in all my ways to acknowledge Him: and He shall direct my path.

'Now that I have decided to leave home, I want you to ask that the Lord will guide me into a suitable situation, where I may get and do good and become fitted for China.'

Shortly after this he had occasion to write again to Mr. Pearse in London.

The letter is worth quoting, as illustrating his careful attention to detail, and sense of stewardship.

21 CHEAPSIDE, BARNSLEY,
March 31, 1851.

MR. GEORGE PEARSE.

DEAR SIR – You will almost think I have forgotten the Chinese Union and have not its interests at heart, on account of my long silence. Such, however, is not the case, although from pressure of business I have not been able to devote to it the attention it deserves. I have collected rather more than £2. Please send me word as to how I shall remit this sum to you. If I send a post office order it will cost sixpence; but I can get it placed to your credit at Glynn & Co. or any other London banker's for two or three pence. Meanwhile I will do all in my power to get a few more subscribers, as the interests of China lie very near my heart. May I be fitted to engage in this great work. Please excuse haste, and – Believe me, yours in our Risen Lord,

J. H. TAYLOR.

On receiving the necessary information, he wrote again:

. . . I have paid through our Bankers £2.5s. to your credit at Messrs. Jones, Lloyd & Co., Lothbury, according to your directions, and you will receive it on Monday. Please acknowledge the receipt of this sum, that I may be able to show the subscribers that it has been remitted. Have you a Report, or any other publication telling of the work done by your Society, and how the funds are applied? I enclose a list of the contributors. The amounts are small, but I have no doubt that when more is known about the Society and its operations I shall be able to collect more.

The field truly is great, and the means at present employed for its cultivation appear very inadequate. But it is 'not by might nor by power' but by the influence of the Holy Spirit alone that good can be accomplished, and God often makes the weak things of this world to confound the mighty. He and He only can raise up and qualify suitable labourers and own and bless those already on the field.

I have devoted myself to missionary work in China in obedience, I believe, to His call, and am at present studying medicine and surgery that I may have more opportunities of usefulness and perhaps be able to support myself when there. This, however, I leave in His hands believing that if I seek first the Kingdom of God and His righteousness all these things shall be 'added' according to His promise.

Any suggestions you may be able to give me as to means for promoting the cause or fitting myself for more extensive usefulness would be thankfully received by

Yours in our Risen Lord,

J. H. TAYLOR.

Mr. Pearse was evidently interested. He seems to have consulted his Committee and to have written intimating that the Society might be willing to help in the expense of a medical education if they considered young Hudson Taylor a suitable candidate for China.

Meanwhile an opening had occurred in Hull for an assistant to one of the busiest doctors there, Dr. Hardey, brother-in-law to one of Hudson Taylor's aunts. It was not London, but in many ways it seemed the very thing he needed, and from his point of view was none the less desirable for being within easy reach of Barton, where Amelia and the young music teacher were still in Mrs. Hodson's school.

It was on his nineteenth birthday that the new apprentice took up his duties and the day was naturally a busy one. Not till nearly midnight did he find time for the few lines to his sister that could not be omitted.

Then his thoughts carried him away from his new surroundings and across the Humber to the quiet, old-world township in which not only Amelia, but the attractive young music teacher lived. How near he was to her at last! His heart beat quick with hope as he realized that almost any day he might see her.

'I am to have an hour to myself at dinner and another at tea-time,' he wrote eagerly to Amelia. 'I almost think I shall be able to run over to Barton sometimes in the evening, by a little arrangement and being willing to stay overtime when needed.

'You cannot think how happy I feel in my Saviour's love. Oh, He has loved me, the chief of sinners! I love Him for it. He has hitherto granted all my prayers and He will grant me more before midsummer. "The crooked shall be made straight." You understand, Love. Farewell.'

CHAPTER 3

From Faith to Faith

(1851–1852)

Dr. Robert Hardey of 13 Charlotte Street was well known in the city of Hull as a busy medical man and a consistent Christian. Tall and vigorous in appearance, he was gentle and full of fun, so that in spite of themselves those under his care had to look on the bright side of things. His surgery was at the far end of the narrow strip of garden at the back of his house, and here Hudson Taylor soon found himself at home. He was quick and eager to learn, and his knowledge of book-keeping proved valuable to the busy doctor, who was glad to leave it to him. For a short time he lived in the doctor's home, then, when his room was needed for a member of the family, moved to his aunt's.

Though happy in outward circumstances, however, he was anything but free from anxiety and unrest. He had come to Hull eager to fit himself for medical work as a step towards China, but after attending lectures at the medical school his busy days with Dr. Hardey left little time for study. Constantly he pondered the problem of how to prepare and enter upon his life-work and he found it hard to wait in patience, on God alone. The quiet surgery witnessed many an hour of anxious thought as well as many an hour of prayer, and all through that summer and autumn there was a good deal of unnecessary exercise of heart. For there was another fire within consuming not a little of his spiritual strength.

He was out of harmony with God in the matter of his deepest affections, that inner citadel of being so often the last stronghold yielded to His control. Unconsciously, it may be, he was holding something back – something, the best thing in his manhood – not recognizing that in that realm also 'every thought' must be brought into subjection to 'the obedience of Christ'. He was giving far too much of himself to the one who had come as a bright, beautiful vision into his life a year and a half before. It was one thing, he discovered, to think of her in Barnsley where she was out of reach, and quite another in Hull, where any day they might meet. His love was growing too strong for him, quickened by hopeful indications of its being returned on her part.

And yet he had begun to feel instinctively that her life was not fully yielded to God. Though there was no engagement between them they understood one another without words, and he could not but be conscious that her influence was all against a future she was unwilling to face.

'Must you go to China?' she questioned at times, her tone clearly implying, 'How much nicer it would be to stay and serve the Lord at home!'

Fervently he prayed that she might come to feel as he did; for nothing, not even the loss of her love, could alter his call from God. But how could he go forward at such a cost? How face the anguish of losing her just when it seemed she might be won? Oh, the struggle of those autumn days when he could no longer escape the fear that their paths must lie apart! Older people may pass on, perhaps, with little perception of what such a situation means; but young hearts understand, and there is one infinite Heart that is always young, always touched with the feeling of our griefs. The Friend that sticketh closer than a brother did not fail Hudson Taylor.

It was no small mercy, for example, that led him during this sojourn in Hull into fellowship with a company of Christians exceptionally fitted to meet his need. Shortly before leaving home he had for conscientious reasons resigned his connection with the denomination in which he had been brought up. During the progress of a widespread Reform Movement he and his parents had felt obliged to side with the minority and join 'the Reformers', afterwards known as the Methodist Free Church. Hudson personally, however, had begun to feel himself something more than a Wesleyan, bound by more important ties to all who love the Lord Jesus Christ in sincerity and truth. While still in Barnsley he had enjoyed the meetings of the so-called Plymouth Brethren, and now in Hull was glad to renew associations that had already proved helpful.

He was hungry for the Word of God, and their preaching was for the most part a thoughtful exposition of its truths. He needed a fresh vision of eternal things, for he was facing a difficult future, and they set before him an example of faith in temporal as well as spiritual things that surpassed his utmost thought. For this meeting was in close touch with George Müller of Bristol, whose work was even then assuming remarkable proportions. He had already hundreds of orphan children under his care, and was looking to the Lord for means to support a thousand. But this did not exhaust his sympathies. With a deep conviction that these are the days in which the Gospel must be preached 'for a witness unto all nations', he sustained in whole or part many missionaries, and was engaged in circulating the Scriptures far and wide in Roman Catholic as well as heathen lands. All this extensive work, carried on by a penniless man through faith in God alone, with no appeals for help or guarantee of stated income, was a wonderful testimony to the power of 'effectual, fervent prayer'. As such it made a profound impression upon Hudson Taylor, and encouraged him more than anything else could have in the pathway he was about to enter.

'I think it is very difficult', he wrote, 'to set our affections wholly on things above. I try to be a "living epistle" of the Lord, but when I look within I wonder many a time He does not cast me off. I seek to subdue my will, to blend it with His, and say and feel in all things "Thy will be done". But even while I try, I can scarcely keep back the tears. For I seem to have an impression that I shall lose my dear one, and God only knows the struggle it is to say, "Nevertheless, not my will but thine be done".

'Do you think I should be justified in going to London shortly? If it were only for pleasure, I could decide at once; for much as I should like to go, my pleasures must not stand in the way of duty. But sometimes I think that Lobscheid might give me information worth going for. I shall be glad to hear from you and have your advice.'

That idea about going to London certainly came at the right time. The German missionary Lobscheid, to whom he referred, had recently returned from China and was one of the few people who could speak from experience of the practicability of missionary work away from the Treaty Ports. Possessing some medical knowledge, he had been enabled to travel repeatedly in what was then considered 'the interior', a populous district on the mainland, north of Hong Kong; and now that he was for a short time in England Hudson Taylor was anxious to profit from his advice.

His parents approving the idea, and Dr. Hardey giving him a week's holiday, he decided to take advantage of a special train running up to London, and (at his expense) it was arranged that his sister should accompany him, an artist uncle providing accommodation for them in his Soho lodgings. Never had they visited the great metropolis before, and he was just as eager to meet Mr. Pearse and the missionary from China as she was to explore the first International Exhibition at the Crystal Palace.

It was her sixteenth birthday, and together they went to the Exhibition and wandered among the ferns and flowers in which its fairy-like scenes were set. They lunched at a restaurant in proper style, investing in a pineapple, a rare luxury in those days. Then they traversed the gay, crowded city to the Bank of England, where a rendezvous had been arranged with Mr. Pearse.

A busy member of the Stock Exchange as well as Secretary of the Chinese Evangelization Society, Mr. Pearse had not much time for visitors in office hours. He was glad, however, to meet his correspondent from Barnsley, and as he talked with the earnest lad and his modest, charming little sister, interest soon deepened to a warmer feeling. Tottenham – yes, he must take them to Tottenham and the Brook Street meeting. There they would be sure to find a welcome and a real spirit of prayer on behalf of China. So to Tottenham they went with him the following Sunday.

In surroundings as nearly perfect as wealth and refinement could make them, a number of Christian families lived in the pleasant suburb, as it was in those days. Home-like rooms, beautifully furnished, opened on lawns shaded by spreading cedars. Friends from far and near gathered around the ample board, where quiet talk flowed freely on the deepest interests of the Kingdom of God. And best of all, the love of Christ possessed and permeated everything.

The friendships begun that day endured throughout a lifetime.

'I love Tottenham,' Hudson Taylor wrote from China a few years later. 'I love those I know there dearly. Of no other place can I say that my every recollection is sweet and profitable, marred by no painful thought or circumstance, save that I see it no more.'

And the Tottenham friends on their part, what did they think of him? They saw a simple, Yorkshire lad, quiet and unassuming. Introduced by Mr. Pearse as an intending missionary, he was observed more closely by some of the younger people than he might otherwise have been. He did not fit in exactly with their idea of a missionary, for he looked young and delicate and was evidently full of fun. But they liked him none the less for that, and felt his earnestness and absorbing interest in China. In a word, he won their confidence just as his little sister won their hearts.

The missionary he had come so far to see seems to have been less encouraging, however.

'Why, you would never do for China,' he exclaimed at length, drawing attention to his fair hair and grey-blue eyes. 'They call *me* "Red-haired Devil", and would run from you in terror! You could never get them to listen at all.'

'It is God who has called me,' replied Hudson Taylor quietly, 'and He knows all about the colour of my hair and eyes.'

It was shortly after his return to Hull that the nest began to be stirred up about him. He was again settled in the home of his relatives where every want was anticipated and where, as far as circumstances were concerned, nothing could have been more desirable. But this was not all God's love had planned for moulding this young life in view of China. Already, through discipline of heart, the lad was learning lessons of patience and submission to the will of God. But something more was needed, something even of outward trial to prepare him for the life-work that was to be. Away in an unfrequented suburb a little home was waiting – a single room in which he could be alone as never before, alone with God. The steps by which he was led to it were very simple, beginning, as he himself records, with a conscientious difficulty about remaining where he was. Recalling this experience, he wrote:

Before leaving Barnsley my attention was drawn to the subject of setting apart the first-fruits of all one's increase and a certain proportion of one's possessions for the service of the Lord. It seemed to me desirable to study the question, Bible in hand, and in this way I was led to the determination to set apart not less than one-tenth of whatever monies I might earn or become possessed of, for the Lord.

The salary I received as medical assistant in Hull would have allowed me to do this without difficulty, but in addition to the sum I had previously received, the exact amount was allowed me that I had to pay for board and lodging.

Now arose in my mind the reflection, 'Ought not this also to be tithed?' It was surely a part of my income, and had it been a question of government income tax would certainly not have been excluded. But to take a tithe from the whole would have left me insufficient for other purposes, and for a time I was embarrassed to know what to do.

After much thought and prayer, I was led to leave the comfortable home and pleasant circle in which I resided, and engage a little lodging in the suburbs, a sitting-room and bedroom in one, undertaking to board myself. I was thus enabled to tithe the whole of my income; and while one felt the change a good deal, it was attended with no small blessing. More time was given in my solitude to the study of the Word of God, to visiting the poor and to evangelistic work on Sunday evenings than would otherwise have been the case. Brought into contact in this way with many who were in distress, I soon saw the privilege of still further economizing, and found it possible to give away much more than I had at first intended.

It all reads so simply and naturally that one can hardly imagine any special sacrifice to have been involved. Let us hunt up this 'sitting-room and bed-room in one', however, and find out what were in actual fact the surroundings for which he had given up his home on Kingston Square. The change could scarcely have been more complete.

'Drainside', as the neighbourhood was termed, consisted of a double row of workmen's cottages facing each other across a narrow canal. The canal was nothing but a deep ditch into which Drainside people were in the habit of casting their rubbish, to be carried away in part whenever the tide rose high enough. It was separated from the town by desolate spaces of building-land, across which ran a few ill-lighted streets ending in makeshift wooden bridges. The cottages, like peas in a pod, were all the same size and shape down both sides of the long row. They followed the windings of the Drain for half a mile or more, each one having a door, and two windows one above the other. The door opened straight into the kitchen, and a steep stairway led to the room above. A very few were double cottages with a window to right and left of the door and two rooms overhead.

On the city side of the canal, one of these larger dwellings stood at a corner opposite The Founder's Arms, a public house whose lights were useful as a landmark on dark nights, shining across the mud and water of the Drain. The cottage, known as 30 Cottingham Terrace, was tenanted by the family of a seafaring man, whose visits home were few and far between. Mrs. Finch and her children occupied the kitchen and upper part of the house, and the downstairs room on the left as one entered was let at a rental of three shillings a week. It was too high a charge, seeing the whole house went for little more. But the lodger in whom we are interested did not grudge it, especially when he found how much it meant to the woman whose remittances from her husband came none too regularly.

Mrs. Finch was a true Christian and delighted to have 'the young doctor' under her roof. She did her best no doubt to make the little chamber clean and comfortable, polishing the fireplace opposite the window and making up the bed in the corner farthest from the door. A plain deal table and a chair or two completed the appointments. The whole room was less than twelve feet square and did not need much furniture. It was on a level with the ground and opened familiarly out of the kitchen. From the window one looked across the narrowest strip of 'garden' to the Drain beyond, whose mud banks afforded a playground for the children of the neighbourhood.

Whatever it may have been in summer, toward the close of November, when Hudson Taylor made it his home, Drainside must have seemed dreary enough, and the cottage far from attractive. To add to the discomforts of the situation, he was 'boarding himself', which meant that he lived upon next to nothing, bought his meagre supplies as he returned from the surgery, and rarely sat down to a proper meal. His walks were taken alone across the waste, unlighted region on the outskirts of the town; his evenings were solitary beside the little fire in his otherwise cheerless room; and his Sundays were spent by himself, but for the morning meeting and long hours of work in his district or among the crowds that frequented the Humber Dock.

More than this, he was at close quarters with poverty and suffering. Visiting in such neighbourhoods he had been accustomed to for a few hours at a time, but this was very different. He had cast in his lot with those who needed all the help and comfort he could bring. This gave new purpose to his life and taught him some of its most precious lessons.

> I soon found that I could live upon very much less than I had previously thought possible. Butter, milk and other luxuries I ceased to use, and found that by living mainly on oatmeal and rice, with occasional variations, a very small sum was sufficient for my needs. In this way I had more than two-thirds of my income available for other purposes, and my experience was that the less I spent on myself and the more I gave to others, the fuller of happiness and blessing did my soul become.

For the Lord is no man's debtor; and here in his solitude Hudson Taylor was learning something of what He can be to the soul that leaves all for Him. In these days of easy-going Christianity is it not well to remind ourselves that it really does cost – to be a man or woman God can use? One cannot obtain a Christlike character for nothing; one cannot do a Christlike work save at great price. And is there not a sense in which even Christ Himself is to be *won*? It is easy to pray a little, help a little, love a little; but the missionary apostle meant more than this when he said:

> I count all things but loss for the excellency of the knowledge of Christ Jesus my Lord: for whom I have suffered the loss of all things, and do count them but refuse, *that I may win Christ* (Phil. 3.8).

Much prayer had been going up for China, and countless hearts had been stirred more or less deeply for its evangelization. When disappointment came and unexpected failure, however, prayer meetings dwindled to nothing, would-be missionaries turned aside to other callings, contributions dropped off. Only here and there in His own training schools were those the Lord could count upon: and in a quiet lodging at Drainside was such a man. With all his youth and limitations, Hudson Taylor desired supremely a Christlike character and life. As test after test came that might have been avoided, he chose the pathway of self-emptying and the cross. He was in an attitude that did not hinder blessing.

Adversaries there certainly were to oppose his progress at this time. He was entering upon one of the most fruitful periods of his life, rich in blessing for himself and others. Is it any wonder that the Tempter was at hand? He was alone, hungry for love and sympathy, living a life of self-denial hard for a lad to bear. It was just the opportunity for the devil, and he was permitted for a while to do his worst, that even that might be overruled for good.

It was just at this juncture, when he had been a few weeks at Drainside and was feeling his position keenly, that the dreaded blow fell. Seeing that nothing could dissuade her friend from his missionary purpose, the young music teacher made it plain at last that she was not prepared to go to China. Her father would not hear of it, nor did she feel herself fitted for such a life. This could mean but one thing, and for him the two years' dream was over.

It was not only an overwhelming sorrow, it was a tremendous test of faith. The tempter did everything in his power to call in question the love and faithfulness of God. Only break down his trust, make him give up the struggle now, and the usefulness of his after-life would be marred.

Sunday morning came, December 14. It was cold and cheerless in the little room at Drainside. The lad was benumbed with sorrow, for instead of turning to the Lord for comfort he kept it to himself and nursed his grief. He did not want to pray. The trouble had come in between his soul and God. He could not, would not go as usual to the morning meeting. He was too full of bitter questionings and pain. Then came the insidious suggestion:

'Is it all worthwhile? Why should you go to China? Why toil and suffer all your life for an ideal of duty? Give it up now, while you can yet win her.

Earn a proper living like everybody else, and serve the Lord at home. For you can win her yet.' Writing to his sister, he said:

Satan seemed to come in as a flood, and I was forced to cry 'Save, Lord; I perish'. Still Satan suggested, 'You never used to be tried as you have been lately. You cannot be in the right path, or God would help and bless you more', and so on, until I felt inclined to give it all up. I felt no desire to go to the meeting.

But, thank God, the way of duty is the way of safety. I went to the meeting after all, as miserable as could be; but did not come away so. One hymn quite cut me to the heart. I was thankful that prayer followed, for I could not keep back my tears. But the load was lighter.

In the afternoon as I was sitting alone in the surgery I began to reflect on the love of God; His goodness and my return; the number of blessings He has granted me; and how small my trials are compared with those some are called to endure. He thoroughly softened and humbled me. His love melted my icy, frost-bound soul, and sincerely did I pray for pardon for my ungrateful conduct.

Yes, He has humbled me and shown me what I was, revealing Himself as a present, a very present help in time of trouble. And though He does not deprive me of feeling in my trial, He enables me to sing, 'Yet I will rejoice in the Lord, I will joy in the God of my salvation'. I can thank Him for *all*, even the most painful experiences of the past, and trust Him without fear for all that is to come.

A new tone was perceptible in his letters now. They were less introspective from this time onward and more full of missionary purpose. China came to the front again in all his thinking.

'I cannot tell, I cannot describe how I long to be a missionary, to carry the Glad Tidings to poor, perishing sinners,' he wrote to his mother. 'For this I could give up everything, every idol, however dear. *I feel as if I could not live if something is not done for China.*'

This was no mere emotion. It was not that he had taken up missionary work as a congenial branch of Christian activity, but that the need of the perishing in heathen lands, the need and longing of the heart of Christ – 'them also *I must bring*' – had gripped him and held him fast. He believed that the heathen are perishing, and that without a knowledge of the one and only Saviour they must be eternally lost. He believed that it was in view of *this* and because of His infinite love, that God had given 'His only begotten Son that whosoever believeth in him should *not* perish, but have everlasting life'. And these convictions pledged him to the only life possible in view of such stupendous facts – a life wholly given to making that great redemption known, especially to those who had never heard.

Yet much as he longed to go, and go at once, there were considerations that held him back.

'To me it was a very grave matter', he wrote of that winter, 'to contemplate going out to China, far from all human aid, there to depend upon the living God alone for protection, supplies, and help of every kind. I felt that one's spiritual muscles required strengthening for such an undertaking. There was no doubt that if faith did not fail, God would not fail. But what if one's faith should prove insufficient? I had not at that time learned that even "if we believe not, yet he abideth faithful, he cannot deny himself". It was consequently a very serious question to my mind, not whether He was faithful, but whether I had strong enough faith to warrant my embarking in the enterprise set before me.

' "When I get out to China," I thought to myself, "I shall have no claim on anyone for anything. My only claim will be on God. How important to learn, before leaving England, to move man through God by prayer alone".'

He knew that faith was the one power that could remove mountains, conquer every difficulty and accomplish the impossible. But had he the right kind of faith? Could he stand alone in China? Much as he longed to be a missionary, would such faith as he possessed be sufficient to carry him through all that must be faced?

He realized that the faith he longed for was a 'gift of God', and that it might 'grow exceedingly'. But for growth, exercise was needed, and exercise of faith was obviously impossible apart from trial. Then welcome trial, welcome anything that would increase and strengthen this precious gift, proving to his own heart at any rate that he had faith of the sort that would really stand and grow.

In taking this attitude before the Lord, Hudson Taylor was wholly earnest and sincere. He was bringing 'all the tithes into the storehouse', a most important consideration; living a life that made it possible for him to exercise faith to which God could respond in blessing. In a word, there was no hindrance in himself to the answer to his prayers; and experiences followed that have been made an encouragement to thousands the world over.

The story though well known will bear repetition, illustrating as it does the only principle of growth in spiritual things, 'From faith to faith'; the law reiterated by our Lord Himself, 'He that hath, to him shall be given'.

'To learn before leaving England to move man through God by prayer alone,' this and nothing less was the object Hudson Taylor had before him now, and it was not long before he came to see a simple, natural way of practising this lesson.

At Hull my kind employer, always busy, wished me to remind him whenever my salary became due. This I determined not to do directly, but to ask that God would bring the fact to his recollection, and thus encourage me by answering prayer.

At one time as the day drew near for the payment of a quarter's salary I was as usual much in prayer about it. The time arrived, but Dr. Hardey made no allusion to the matter. I continued praying. Days passed on and he did not remember, until at length on settling up my weekly accounts one Saturday night, I found myself possessed of only one remaining coin, a half-crown piece. Still, I had hitherto known no lack, and I continued praying.

That Sunday was a very happy one. As usual my heart was full and brimming over with blessing. After attending Divine Service in the morning, my afternoons and evenings were taken up with Gospel work in the various lodging-houses I was accustomed to visit in the lowest part of the town. At such times it almost seemed to me as if Heaven were begun below, and that all that could be looked for was an enlargement of one's capacity for joy, not a truer filling than I possessed.

After concluding my last service about ten o'clock that night, a poor man asked me to go and pray with his wife, saying that she was dying. I readily agreed, and on the way to his house asked him why he had not sent for the priest, as his accent told me he was an Irishman. He had done so, he said, but the priest refused to come without a payment of eighteen pence which the man did not possess, as the family was starving. Immediately it occurred to my mind that all the money I had in the world was the solitary half-crown, and that it was in one coin; moreover, that while the basin of water-gruel I usually took for supper was awaiting me, and there was sufficient in the house for breakfast in the morning, I certainly had nothing for dinner on the coming day.

Somehow or other there was at once a stoppage in the flow of joy in my heart. But instead of reproving myself I began to reprove the poor man, telling him that it was very wrong to have allowed matters to get into such a state as he described, and that he ought to have applied to the relieving officer. His answer was that he had done so, and was told to come at eleven o'clock the next morning, but that he feared his wife might not live through the night.

'Ah', thought I, 'if only I had two shillings and a sixpence instead of this half-crown, how gladly would I give these poor people a shilling!' But to part with the half-crown was far from my thoughts. I little dreamed that the truth of the matter simply was that I could trust God *plus* one-and-sixpence, but was not prepared to trust Him only, without any money at all in my pocket.

My conductor led me into a court, down which I followed him with some degree of nervousness. I had found myself there before, and at my last visit had been roughly handled. My tracts had been torn to pieces and such a warning given me not to come again that I felt more than a little concerned. Still, it was the path of duty and I followed on. Up a miserable flight of stairs into a wretched room he led me; and oh, what a sight there presented itself! Four or five children stood about, their sunken cheeks and temples all telling unmistakably the story of slow starvation, and lying on a wretched pallet was a poor, exhausted mother, with a tiny infant thirty-six hours old moaning rather than crying at her side, for it too seemed spent and failing.

'Ah!' thought I, 'if I had two shillings and a sixpence, instead of half-a-crown, how gladly should they have one-and-sixpence of it.' But still a wretched unbelief prevented me from obeying the impulse to relieve their distress at the cost of all I possessed.

It will scarcely seem strange that I was unable to say much to comfort these poor people. I needed comfort myself. I began to tell them, however, that they must not be cast down; that though their circumstances were very distressing there was a kind and loving Father in Heaven. But something within me cried, 'You hypocrite!

telling these unconverted people about a kind and loving Father in Heaven, and not prepared yourself to trust Him without a half-a-crown.'

I was nearly choked. How gladly would I have compromised with conscience, if I had had a florin and a sixpence! I would have given the florin thankfully and kept the rest. But I was not yet prepared to trust in God alone, without the sixpence.

To talk was impossible under these circumstances, yet strange to say I thought I should have no difficulty in praying. Prayer was a delightful occupation in those days. Time thus spent never seemed wearisome and I knew no lack of words. I seemed to think that all I should have to do would be to kneel down and pray, and that relief would come to them and to myself together.

'You asked me to come and pray with your wife,' I said to the man, 'let us pray.' And I knelt down.

But no sooner had I opened my lips with 'Our Father which art in heaven', than conscience said within, 'Dare you mock God? Dare you kneel down and call Him Father with that half-crown in your pocket?'

Such a time of conflict then came upon me as I have never experienced before or since. How I got through that form of prayer I know not, and whether the words uttered were connected or disconnected I cannot tell. But I arose from my knees in great distress of mind.

The poor father turned to me and said, 'You see what a terrible state we are in, sir. If you can help us, for God's sake do!'

At that moment the word flashed into my mind, 'Give to him that asketh thee.' And in the word of a King there is power.

I put my hand into my pocket and slowly drawing out the half-crown, gave it to the man, telling him that it might seem a small matter for me to relieve them, seeing that I was comparatively well off, but that in parting with that coin I was giving him my all; what I had been trying to tell them was indeed true – God really was a Father, and might be trusted. The joy all came back in full floodtide to my heart. I could say anything and feel it then, and the hindrance to blessing was gone – gone, I trust, for ever.

Not only was the poor woman's life saved; but my life, as I fully realized, had been saved too. It might have been a wreck – would have been, probably, as a Christian life – had not grace at that time conquered, and the striving of God's Spirit been obeyed.

I well remember how that night, as I went home to my lodgings, my heart was as light as my pocket. The dark, deserted streets resounded with a hymn of praise that I could not restrain. When I took my basin of gruel before retiring, I would not have exchanged it for a prince's feast. I reminded the Lord as I knelt at my bedside of His own Word, 'He that giveth to the poor lendeth to the Lord'; I asked Him not to let my loan be a long one, or I should have no dinner next day. And with peace within and peace without, I spent a happy restful night.

Next morning for breakfast my plate of porridge remained, and before it was finished the postman's knock was heard at the door. I was not in the habit of receiving letters on Monday, as my parents and most of my friends refrained from posting on Saturday, so that I was somewhat surprised when the landlady came in holding a letter or packet in her wet hand covered by her apron. I looked at the letter, but could not make out the handwriting. It was either a strange hand or a feigned one, and the postmark was blurred. Where it came from I could not tell. On opening the envelope I found nothing written within; but inside a sheet of blank paper was folded a pair of kid gloves, from which, as I opened them in astonishment, half-a-sovereign fell to the ground.

'Praise the Lord,' I exclaimed. '400 per cent for twelve hours' investment – that is good interest! How glad the merchants of Hull would be if they could lend their money at such a rate.' Then and there I determined that a bank that could not break should have my savings or earnings, as the case might be – a determination I have not yet learned to regret.

I cannot tell you how often my mind has recurred to this incident, or all the help it has been to me in circumstances of difficulty in after-life. If we are faithful to God in little things, we shall gain experience and strength that will be helpful to us in the more serious trials of life.

But this was not the end of the story, nor was it the only answer to prayer that was to confirm his faith at this time. For the chief difficulty still remained. Dr. Hardey had not remembered; and though prayer was unremitting, other matters appeared entirely to engross his attention. It would have been easy to remind him. But what then of the lesson upon the acquirement of which Hudson Taylor felt his future usefulness depended – 'to move man through God, by prayer alone'?

This remarkable and gracious deliverance was a great joy to me as well as a strong confirmation of faith. But of course ten shillings however economically used will not go very far, and it was none the less necessary to continue in prayer, asking that the larger supply which was still due might be remembered and paid. All my petitions, however, appeared to remain unanswered, and before a fortnight elapsed I found myself pretty much in the same position that I had occupied on the Sunday night already made so memorable. Meanwhile I continued pleading with God more and more earnestly that He would Himself remind Dr. Hardey that my salary was due.

Of course it was not the want of money that distressed me. That could have been had at any time for the asking. But the question uppermost in my mind was this: 'Can I go to China? or will my want of faith and power with God prove so serious an obstacle as to preclude my entering upon this much-prized service?'

As the week drew to a close I felt exceedingly embarrassed. There was not only myself to consider. On Saturday night a payment would be due to my Christian landlady, which I knew she could not well dispense with. Ought I not, for her sake, to speak about the matter of the salary? Yet to do so would be, to myself at any rate, the admission that I was not fitted to undertake a missionary enterprise. I gave nearly the whole of Thursday and Friday, all the time not occupied in my necessary employment, to earnest wrestling with God in prayer. But still on Saturday morning I was in the same position as before. And now my earnest cry was for guidance as to whether I should still continue to wait the Father's time. As far as I could judge I received the assurance that to wait His time was best, and that God in some way or other would interpose on my behalf. So I waited, my heart being now at rest and the burden gone.

About five o'clock that Saturday afternoon, when Dr. Hardey had finished writing his prescriptions, his last circuit for the day being taken, he threw himself back in his arm-chair, as he was wont, and began to speak of the things of God. He was a truly Christian man, and many seasons of happy fellowship we had together. I was busily watching, at the time, a pan in which a decoction was boiling that required a good deal of attention. It was indeed fortunate for me that it was so, for without any obvious connection with what had been going on, all at once he said:

'By the by, Taylor, is not your salary due again?'

My emotion may be imagined. I had to swallow two or three times before I could answer. With my eye fixed on the pan and my back to the doctor, I told him as quietly as I could that it was overdue some little time. How thankful I felt at that moment! God surely had heard my prayer and caused him in this time of my great need to remember the salary without any word or suggestion from me. He replied,

'Oh, I am so sorry you did not remind me! You know how busy I am. I wish I had thought of it a little sooner, for only this afternoon I sent all the money I had to the bank. Otherwise I would pay you at once.'

It is impossible to describe the revulsion of feeling caused by this unexpected statement. I knew not what to do. Fortunately for me the pan boiled up and I had a good reason for rushing with it from the room. Glad indeed I was to get away and keep out of sight until after Dr. Hardey had returned to his house, and most thankful that he had not perceived my emotion.

As soon as he was gone I had to seek my little sanctum and pour out my heart before the Lord for some time before calmness, and more than calmness, thankfulness and joy were restored. I felt that God had His own way, and was not going to fail me. I had sought to know His will early in the day, and as far as I could judge had received guidance to wait patiently. And now God was going to work for me in some other way.

That evening was spent, as my Saturday evenings usually were, in reading the Word and preparing the subject on which I expected to speak in the various lodging-houses on the morrow. I waited perhaps a little longer than usual. At last about ten o'clock, there being no interruption of any kind, I put on my overcoat and was preparing to leave for home, rather thankful to know that by that time I should have to let myself in with the latchkey, as my landlady retired early. There was certainly no help for that night. But perhaps God would interpose for me by Monday, and I might be able to pay my landlady early in the week the money I would have given her before had it been possible.

Just as I was about to turn down the gas, I heard the doctor's step in the garden that lay between the dwelling-house and surgery. He was laughing to himself very heartily, as though greatly amused. Entering the surgery he asked for the ledger, and told me that, strange to say, one of his richest patients had just come to pay his doctor's bill. Was it not an odd thing to do? It never struck me that it might have any bearing on my own case, or I might have felt embarrassed. But looking at it simply from the position of an uninterested spectator, I also was highly amused that a man rolling in wealth should come after ten o'clock at night to pay a bill which he could any day have met by a cheque with the greatest ease. It appeared that somehow or other he could not rest with this on his mind, and had been constrained to come at that unusual hour to discharge his liability.

The account was duly receipted in the ledger, and Dr. Hardey was about to leave, when suddenly he turned and handing me some of the banknotes just received, said to my surprise and thankfulness:

'By the way, Taylor, you might as well take these notes. I have no change, but can give you the balance next week.'

Again I was left, my feelings undiscovered, to go back to my little closet and praise the Lord with a joyful heart that after all *I might go to China*. To me this incident was not a trivial one; and to recall it sometimes, in circumstances of great difficulty, in China or elsewhere, has proved no small comfort and strength.

The importance of something higher far than money, in relation to the service of God, now began to impress Hudson Taylor. His quiet life at Drainside was working a change in his attitude toward many things. There were memorable hours that winter in which he saw from the Divine standpoint as never before. Now it was no longer a question of money. It was the far more important question of souls.

'If I stay here another two years,' he wrote to Amelia, 'and save £50 or £60 to pay my expenses to China, I shall land there no better off than if I go at once and work my passage out. And in two years there will die in that land at least twenty-four million people. In six or eight months I should be able to talk a little Chinese. And if I could instruct in the truths of the Gospel one poor sinner, and the Spirit accompanied the word with power to his soul and he were saved – to all eternity he would be happy, praising the Redeemer. Then what would the hardships of a four or five months' voyage weigh in comparison?'

To his mother also he wrote a characteristic letter about this thought of working his passage out to China. His idea was, failing a berth as assistant to a ship's surgeon, to go as a sailor before the mast, and he had fully informed himself as to all that would be involved. His landlady's seafaring husband had warned him of the hardships of a five months' voyage under the latter conditions, assuring him that he could never stand either the work or the companionship that must fall to his lot, but of this he said little to his mother.

'I am deeply thankful', he wrote, referring to one of her recent letters, 'that you do not wish to recall the offering you made of me to the Lord. Perhaps He means to try our sincerity in this respect sooner than either of us anticipated. If I do not know the intensity of a mother's love, I feel so much the strength of a son's love, a brother's love, of love to friends and brethren in the Lord, that the thought of leaving *all* seems like tearing away part of one's very self. But, praise God, I know something also of a Saviour's love, though but little as yet. He is to me a *satisfying* portion, and I can truly say,

I all on earth forsake,
Its wisdom, fame and power,
And (Thee) my only portion make,
My Shield and Tower.

But ready though he was for the sacrifice involved, Hudson Taylor was not to work his way out to China before the mast. 'He was not to be tried thus far,' wrote his mother, recalling with thankfulness the guidance given in answer to their prayers. It was well, no doubt, that it was in his heart to leave all and follow wherever the Master led. But was He leading just at that time to China? To his parents and friends it seemed not. He had been praying that if it were the Lord's will for him to go without delay, they might recognize it and bid him God-speed. Rather to his surprise, all advised against it.

It was hard to give up his carefully thought-out plans, but he was learning that there may be self-will even in what looks like devotion. He wrote to his mother:

As to my going to China – in accordance with the unanimous advice of those I have consulted here and with your own opinion, I intend, *D.V.*, to remain in Hull another year and wait upon the Lord for guidance. I was much pleased with your judgment, as I had prayed the Lord, to whom all hearts are open, to bring us definitely to one mind. If it be His will for me to go sooner, He can thrust me out or open the way unmistakably.

A week spent at home in the lovely month of April, while it brought untold refreshment, made the dreariness of Drainside on his return all the more apparent. But though 'rather unhinged at first', as he wrote to his sister, he soon settled down to hard work and solitude once more. As the days lengthened, he turned to good account the strip of waste land in front of the cottage for the benefit of Mrs. Finch and her family. His love of plants and nature generally was so great that even mustard and cress growing outside his window was better than nothing, and his efforts at gardening afforded him much satisfaction.

That was a precious summer. Time seemed all too short for the many duties crowded into it, but he was learning how much more can be accomplished in a day from which an hour is deliberately taken for prayer, than in the same time wholly given to one's ordinary occupations. He was deeply feeling at this time his need of wisdom, for his employer had put before him generous proposals regarding the completion of his medical studies. The plan he suggested, however, involved a contract for several years, and

Hudson Taylor eventually declined it. It was not easy to take this step, eager as he was to become a medical man, but he dared not bind himself by any such agreement, not knowing when or how the way might open to China.

Just about this time another test found him unprepared. His father at home in Barnsley, an active man of only forty-five, was feeling somewhat restless. Stirred by longings for a wider field, he wondered if the new world of Canada or the United States might present opportunities for carrying on his business in a more spiritually needy sphere than Barnsley. The mother was accordingly deputed to find out from Hudson what he would think of taking charge at home for the next two years.

Hudson was filled with surprise and almost consternation. Gladly would he have gone home for two years, or ten, to liberate his father for evangelistic work in China – indeed, he had at one time suggested it. But a business journey to America, even though combined with an evangelistic purpose, seemed to him a very different proposition. What he wrote in his first prompt reply is not recorded, but a second letter following hard on it gives some indication of its contents:

> Conscience has repeatedly troubled me about the answer I sent to your inquiry as to whether I was willing to come home for two years. Though I mentioned the sacrifices I should have to make in coming home, I said nothing about those you have so willingly made for me – the sleepless hours, the anxious thoughts, the expense to which you have been put, the education you have given me by which I am able to procure all the comforts I now enjoy. And this is the return I have made for all these kindnesses. I have written of the sacrifices I should have to make in undertaking to manage for a short time the business at which you have toiled for twenty years for my benefit. Father, I have been an ungrateful son . . . I am deeply sorry. Will you forgive me?
>
> I will earnestly endeavour, by the grace of God, to be more dutiful in future, and if you still wish me to come home for two years I will do so willingly.

But again in the providence of God the sacrifice he was ready to make was not required. For the father abandoned the idea of going abroad, and soon settled down as before to his useful, honoured life in Barnsley. Thus Hudson was free to reconsider his own movements and the question of going to London.

He was now twenty years of age, and London attracted him because of its advantages for medical study. He had not forgotten the help proffered by Mr. Pearse and the Chinese Evangelization Society, before he came to Hull. They had then been willing to bear the expense of his fees at the London Hospital if he could obtain employment that would leave him time for study, or otherwise provide his board and lodging. Did that offer still hold good, he wondered, and, if so, could he avail himself of it?

Gradually as he prayed over the matter it became clear to him that he ought not to remain in Hull much longer. He had learned all he could from Dr. Hardey under present conditions, and to stay on meant loss of time, as far as preparation for China was concerned. Yes, go he ought and must, in faithfulness to his future service. But how was it to be accomplished?

The clearer became his conviction of what the Lord would have him do, the greater seemed the difficulties in the way of carrying it out. He felt quite sure that the right thing was to give notice to Dr. Hardey without delay, and go forward to his medical studies in London. But all his efforts to find suitable employment proved unavailing. With no means to fall back upon, save the small sum laid by to provide an outfit for China; with few friends in the great city, and no home open to him there, he might well have been discouraged. But all through July and August he was delighting in the promises of the thirty-seventh Psalm.

Trust in the Lord, and do good; so shalt thou dwell in the land, and verily thou shalt be fed. Delight thyself also in the Lord, and he shall give thee the desires of thine heart. Commit thy way unto the Lord, trust also in him, and he shall bring it to pass . . .

As he thought upon these assurances, so full and so explicit, an unlooked-for change came over everything, and he began to see in the light that only shines from the Unseen. What was he really waiting for? Was it his duty to go forward? What though there seemed no solid ground to tread upon! Was his Master there upon the unknown sea before him? Was it His voice heard across the waters? Then he could leave the little boat without hesitation and go to Jesus. If it be Thou, Lord, 'if it be thou, bid me come'. And the answer was in tones he could not doubt. In a letter to his mother on August 27, he wrote,

With regard to London, I began prayerfully to consider *why* I desired to take the step contemplated; and I believe my only object is that I may be enabled to serve the Lord better and be more useful in the advancement of His Kingdom. This step I have every ground for thinking will be a valuable preparation for China. Then why do I not take it? Simply because I am in doubt about the wherewithal. If my earthly father had offered to send me five or ten pounds in case of need, I should have resigned my position here without hesitation. How much more should I go forward trusting in Him who says: 'Take no thought, saying, What shall we eat? or, What shall we drink? or, Wherewithal shall we be clothed? . . . Your heavenly Father knoweth that ye have need of all these things.' 'Trust in the Lord, and do good; so shalt thou dwell in the land, and verily thou shalt be fed.'

To go on depending on circumstances seems to me like doubting the Lord. Consequently I gave notice to Dr. Hardey on Saturday last, and shall go up to London whether I obtain a situation or not, trusting in the Lord. I have heard of one to-day and shall write about it, though I do not think it will suit me on account of distance from the hospital. As to getting a salary, that is quite out of the question. If I can find a position that will allow six or eight hours a day for lectures, that is all I can expect.

This decision arrived at, Hudson was not afraid to burn his bridges behind him. He wrote at once to his cousin who was still in Barnsley, suggesting that he should apply to Dr. Hardey for the post he was himself vacating.

Shortly after, the way began to clear before him. His uncle in London had already offered a temporary home; the Chinese Evangelization Society renewed their arrangement with regard to his hospital fees; and the Meeting he attended in Hull gave him introductions to a few Christian friends who would be accessible from his Soho quarters. Other offers of help reached him which, though not accepted, confirmed his assurance that he was being guided aright. Full of thankfulness he wrote to his sister in the middle of September:

Oh, the love of God, the goodness of my Father and your Father, my God and your God! How kind of Him to keep me in such perfect peace and full of joy and happiness when outwardly in the most difficult position. Had I left the question 'Shall I go or stay?' to be settled by circumstances, how uncertain I should have been. But as the Lord enabled me to take the step without hesitation, because it was for His glory, leaving everything in *His* hands, my mind has been just as peaceful as it would otherwise have been unsettled.

Praise the Lord for His goodness! He has provided, so far, all that is necessary. Now I have a home to go to, money to pay the fees of the Ophthalmic Hospital as well as the course at the London, and some Christian friends. Last autumn I was fretting and stewing, reckoning and puzzling about how to manage this and that – like a person in water who cannot swim, or a fish out of it. But it all came to nothing. Now, when the Lord opens the way, though everything seems adverse, He first removes one difficulty and then another, plainly saying 'Be still, and know that I am God'.

CHAPTER 4

The Lord will Provide

(1852–1853)

FOG-HORNS were sounding on every hand when a coasting-steamer plying between Hull and London made her way slowly up the Thames. It was Saturday evening, September 25, and Hudson Taylor amongst others was expecting to land that night. But the pall of mist only gathered more and more heavily over the great city, until there was nothing for it but to cast anchor and wait till morning. By noon it was possible to reach the Tower, and most of the passengers went ashore. A quiet Sunday followed for those who remained on board, for which Hudson Taylor was specially thankful in view of the new phase of life opening before him.

How new it was and how great his need of the strength that comes from God alone no one had any idea but himself. Not to his mother, nor even to the sister who spent the last days with him at Drainside had he spoken of the decision taken before leaving Hull that now filled his mind as he paced the deck.

Of that decision the following is his own account:

I felt that I could not go to China without having still further developed and tested my power to rest upon His faithfulness; and a marked opportunity for doing so was providentially afforded me.

My father had offered to bear all the expense of my stay in London. I knew, however, that, owing to recent losses, it would mean a considerable sacrifice for him to undertake this just when it seemed necessary for me to go forward. I had recently become acquainted with the Committee of the Chinese Evangelization Society, in connection with which I ultimately left for China. Not knowing of my father's proposition, the Committee also kindly offered to bear my expenses while in London. When these proposals were first made to me, I was not quite clear as to what I ought to do, and in writing to my father and the secretaries, told them that I would take a few days to pray about the matter before deciding any course of action. I mentioned to my father that I had had this offer from the Society, and told the secretaries also of his proffered aid.

Subsequently, while waiting upon God in prayer for guidance, it became clear to my mind that I could without difficulty decline both offers. The secretaries of the Society would not know that I had cast myself wholly on God for supplies, and my father would conclude that I had accepted the other offer. I therefore wrote declining both, and felt that without anyone having either care or anxiety on my account I was simply in the hands of God, and that He who knew my heart, if He wished to encourage me to go to China, would bless my effort to depend upon Him alone at home.

It was with a brave heart, therefore, that he presented himself at Mr. Ruffles's boarding-house near Soho Square, early on Monday morning. Here lived his uncle, Benjamin Hudson, and a cousin from Barton-on-Humber who was apprenticed to Mr. Ruffles, a builder and decorator by trade. The uncle, a bright, genial man, was not only a skilful portrait painter, he was something of a poet also, and a clever *raconteur* with a remarkable memory for 'good stories'. He was decidedly popular in the boarding-house and among a large circle of acquaintances, including more than one medical man to whom he was willing to introduce his nephew with a view to an apprenticeship. The cousin too was friendly, offering to share his attic room with the newcomer and so lessen expenses, if he decided to remain in Soho. This arrangement Hudson gladly availed himself of, for it was a comfort to belong to someone, and Tom Hodson seemed almost like a breath of home.

What a drop in the ocean he felt amid the tides of city life now surging around him! He was in anything but a religious circle, surrounded by people who moved in a world of which he knew next to nothing. Business, politics and pleasure-seeking absorbed their attention, and his uncle and cousin did their best to draw him into the same sort of life. They had quite approved his coming to London to study medicine, and were ready in their own way to give him a helping hand. But his point of view annoyed them.

'Talk about trusting God,' his cousin would exclaim, 'one must trust one's own exertions too!'

Then his unwillingness to bind himself by an ordinary apprenticeship on account of a call to missionary work in China was something they could not understand, especially when it seemed that the Society to which he was looking was more than indifferent about the matter. And this to Hudson Taylor was the most painful surprise of all.

For when he went to the office of the Chinese Evangelization Society he was told that nothing definite was arranged as yet. They were awaiting his arrival. Now that he was ready to begin work at the hospital the matter must be laid before the Committee. This would take time, of course. The best thing if there were any urgency would be to send in his application at once, so that it might not miss the next Committee meeting on October 7, for they only gathered once a fortnight.

October 7 – and it was not yet the end of September. If his case could not be dealt with at the first meeting, he would have to wait another two weeks, and perhaps another. Meanwhile he could take no position; his store of savings was diminishing; and what would they say at the boarding-house where his indefiniteness was a source of amusement already?

If he had known all this in Hull! And yet what difference did it really make? He had not come to London depending on his own resources or on the help of man. If the winds and waves were boisterous, was there not One beside him whose hand was as strong to uphold as His word to bring peace? He knew the end from the beginning; and since He had been Alpha would surely be Omega, and everything between.

The application was sent in, and while awaiting the issue Hudson Taylor settled down to study as well as he could in the room shared with his cousin. The latter's occupation allowed him to be frequently at home, and his criticisms, however good-natured, were not a help to quietness of mind.

And the uncertainty was not over when the Committee met. All the action taken was the passing of a resolution requesting him to procure an elaborate set of testimonials to be laid before them at their next meeting. It was Hudson Taylor's first experience of the working of a fully organized Society, and though he subsequently came to understand the need for a certain amount of 'red tape' in such affairs, it was an experience he never forgot in his own dealings with would-be missionaries.

'Now this is a very serious delay,' he wrote to his mother, 'and I intend to see Mr. Pearse today, if possible, and talk with him about it. The required testimonials I do not quite understand, and if they are all considered necessary I shall thank the Committee for their kindness and trouble them no further, as I do not see them consistent with my views. Thank God, I am quite as willing to lose as to gain their assistance. If I have time after seeing Mr. Pearse I will add a few lines, if not I will write by a later post.

' "Let not your heart be troubled", dear mother. He who has hitherto provided for, protected and guided me, still keeps my mind in perfect peace and will do all things well. How sweet it is to be enabled to trust in Him for *all*.'

He went over to Hackney in time to catch the busy Secretary before he left for the Stock Exchange, and as he explained his difficulties, Mr. Pearse seems to have understood. The result was that the testimonials were seen to be superfluous and only a letter or two required from those who knew him best.

'I am happy to say that things seem to be assuming a more settled appearance,' he wrote on October 24, 'and I expect all being well to commence work at the hospital tomorrow.'

This was not the only answer to his prayers, however, that filled his heart with thanksgiving. Studying as well as he could in that little attic-chamber, he was unconscious that the one who shared it with him was being drawn in spite of himself to the only source of abiding joy and peace. Yet so it was. Tom Hodson, keenly watching his cousin's experiences, found himself face to face with conclusions he could neither escape nor gainsay. Nothing else, perhaps, would ever have made him feel his own distance from God and need of something more real and satisfying than he had ever possessed. But this did. And before the close of the year Hudson had the joy of seeing him brought to 'like precious faith' in Christ, and openly taking his stand in the boarding-house as a Christian.

The hospital at last! It was now almost three years since that December day that had brought Hudson Taylor his definite call to China. Ever since that time he had had medical study in view as the best preparation he could make for future usefulness. With little help and in spite of many obstacles he had persevered, making considerable progress with the practical side of his work. But now the broad highway lay open before him – the lectures, the wards, and all the advantages of a city hospital.

But it is not so much with his outward experiences we are concerned, during this period in London, as with the development of his inward life – the growth of both faith and faithfulness.

Owing to heavy rains, the season was specially depressing. Much of the East End was flooded, with serious results for those who lived near the river or whose employment kept them in the damp, foggy streets. And Hudson Taylor, for a considerable part of every day, was among their number. Lodging at Soho for the sake of remaining with his cousin, he was fully four miles from the hospital in which most of his work was done. This meant a walk of at least two hours daily, from Oxford Street to Whitechapel, and back across the City to Oxford Street again. The only public conveyance was the old-fashioned omnibus with its three-penny fare each way, a price that was quite prohibitive. So there was nothing for it but to walk; for the young medical student was economizing very strictly, denying himself everything that could be done without, partly with a view to helping others.

> 'After various experiments,' he wrote, 'I found that the most economical way was to live almost exclusively on brown bread and water. Thus I was able to make the means that God gave me last as long as possible. Some of my expenses I could not diminish, but my board was largely in my own control. A large twopenny loaf of brown bread, purchased daily on my long walk from the hospital, furnished me with supper and breakfast; and on this diet with a few apples for lunch I managed to walk eight or nine miles a day, besides being a good deal on foot attending the practice of the hospital.'

Did the baker guess, who sold that large twopenny loaf of bread, why his customer always waited to have it cut in half? Only half could be taken that night for supper; the remainder had to suffice for the morrow, and experience had proved how very hard it was to make such a division impartially. When at first he tried it for himself, supper had so much the advantage of breakfast that the lad often went hungry the following day. The baker, however, was disinterested, and laid him under obligation by settling the question on the spot.

Brown bread, apples and water amid the stress and strain of London life proved a very inadequate diet. Hunger and weariness of body, however, were of little moment compared with the longing of his soul. It was the end in view that meant so much – China in its unutterable need, and what he could do to meet it; God's purpose, to be apprehended only by faith and prayer.

'No,' he wrote in reply to his mother's inquiries, 'my health does not suffer. On the contrary, everyone says how well I look, and some even that I am getting fat! Though this, I believe, can only be perceived by rather a brilliant imagination. The walks do not fatigue me as they did at first. But the profane conversation of some of the students is utterly sickening.'

The testing of this period was intensified by an unexpected drain on his already meagre income. Still in touch with his Drainside landlady, he was able to help her by going periodically to a shipping office near Cheapside to draw and forward to her the half-pay from her husband's salary as chief officer of a ship that sailed from London. On one occasion he was too occupied in working for an examination to take the time to go and collect the money, so sent it to her from his own pocket, intending to visit the shipping office later. When he eventually went, however, he was told that no payment could be made, as the officer in question had run away from his ship and gone to the gold diggings.

Very soon after this, possibly the same evening, while sewing together some sheets of paper on which to take notes of lectures, I accidentally pricked the first finger of my right hand, and in a few moments forgot all about it. The next day at the hospital I continued dissecting as before. The body was that of a person who had died of fever, and was more than usually disagreeable and dangerous. I need scarcely say that those of us who were at work upon it dissected with special care, knowing that the slightest scratch might cost our lives. Before the morning was far advanced I began to feel weary, and while going through the surgical wards at noon was obliged to run out, being suddenly very sick – a most unusual circumstance with me, as I took but little food and nothing that could disagree with me. After feeling faint for some time, a draught of cold water revived me and I was able to rejoin the students. I became more and more unwell, however, and during the afternoon lecture on surgery found it impossible to hold the pencil and continue taking notes.

By the time the next lecture was over my whole arm and right side were full of pain, and I was both looking and feeling very ill.

Finding that I could not resume work, I went into the dissecting-room to bind up the portion I was engaged upon and put away my apparatus, and said to the demonstrator, who was a skilful surgeon:

'I cannot think what has come over me,' describing the symptoms.

'Why,' said he, 'what has happened is clear enough. You must have cut yourself in dissecting, and this is a case of malignant fever.'

All at once it occurred to me that I had pricked my finger the night before, and I asked him if it were possible that a prick from a needle at that time could have been still unclosed. His opinion was that this was probably the cause of the trouble, and he advised me to get a hansom, drive home as fast as I could and arrange my affairs forthwith:

'For,' said he, 'you are a dead man.'

My first thought was one of sorrow that I could not go to China; but very soon came the feeling, 'Unless I am greatly mistaken, I have work to do in China and shall not die.' I was glad, however, to take the opportunity of speaking to my medical friend, who was a confirmed sceptic, of the joy that the prospect of soon being with my Master gave me, telling him at the same time that I did not think I should die, as unless I were much mistaken I had work to do in China, and if so, however severe the struggle, I must be brought through.

'That is all very well,' he answered, 'but get a hansom and drive home as fast as you can. You have no time to lose, for you will soon be incapable of winding up your affairs.'

I smiled a little at the idea of driving home in a hansom, for by this time my means were too exhausted to allow of such a proceeding, and I set out to walk the distance if possible. Before long, however, my strength gave way, and I felt it was no use to attempt to reach home by walking. Availing myself of an omnibus from Whitechapel Church to Farringdon Street, and another from Farringdon Street onwards, I reached, in great suffering, the neighbourhood of Soho Square, behind which I lived. On going into the house I got some hot water from the servant, and charging her very earnestly – literally as a dying man – to accept eternal life as the gift of God through Jesus Christ, I bathed my hand and lanced the finger, hoping to let out some of the poisoned blood. The pain was very severe. I fainted away, and was so long unconscious that when I came to myself I found I had been carried to bed.

My uncle sent for his own medical man, an assistant surgeon at the Westminster Hospital. When the surgeon came and learned all particulars, he said,

'Well, if you have been living moderately you may pull through, but if you have been going in for beer and that sort of thing there is no manner of chance for you.'

I thought that if sober living was to do anything, few could have a better chance! I told him I had lived abstemiously and found that it helped me to study.

'But now,' he said, 'you must keep up your strength, for it will be a pretty hard struggle.' And he ordered me a bottle of port wine every day and as many chops as I could consume.

I smiled inwardly, having no means for the purchase of such luxuries. This difficulty, however, was met by my kind uncle, who sent me at once all that was needed.

I was much concerned, notwithstanding the agony I suffered, that my parents should not be made acquainted with my state. Thought and prayer had satisfied me that I was not going to die, but that there was indeed a work for me to do in China. If my dear parents should come up and find me in that condition, I must lose the opportunity of seeing how God was going to work for me now that my money was almost come to an end. So, after prayer for guidance, I obtained a promise from my uncle and cousin not to write to my parents, but to leave me to communicate with them myself. I felt it a very distinct answer to prayer when they gave me this promise, and I took care to defer all communication with Barnsley until the worst was over. At home they knew that I was working hard for an examination and did not wonder at my silence.

Days and nights of suffering passed slowly by; but at length, after several weeks, I was sufficiently restored to leave my room; and then I learned that two men, though not from the London Hospital, who had had dissection wounds at the same time as myself, had both succumbed, while I was spared in answer to prayer to work for God in China.

Now he was faced with the necessity of getting back to his home in Yorkshire for convalescence. Still determined to prove to himself that God would send help in response to his prayer, he told no one of his need for money for the fare. 'What am I to do?' he prayed, and waited for the answer. To his surprise, he found his mind directed to the shipping office, to inquire about the wages he had previously been unable to draw.

I reminded the Lord that I could not afford to take a conveyance, and asked whether this impulse were not a mere clutching at a straw, some mental process of my own rather than His guidance. After prayer, however, and renewed waiting upon God, I was confirmed in my belief that He Himself was directing me to go to the office.

The office was at least two miles away, and he had needed help even in coming downstairs. But his weakness only provided another occasion to prove the efficacy of prayer.

I asked in the name of Christ that the strength might immediately be given: and sending the servant up to my room for my hat and stick, I set out not to *attempt* but to *walk* to Cheapside.

Never had he taken so much interest in shop windows as on that occasion! He paused every few yards to regain strength, and when eventually he reached his destination, had to sit on the stairs for a while before ascending to the first floor where the office was situated.

I felt my position to be a little peculiar, sitting there on the steps so evidently spent, and the gentlemen who rushed up and downstairs looked at me with an inquiring gaze. After a little rest, however, and a further season of prayer, I succeeded in climbing the staircase, and to my comfort found in the office the clerk with whom I had hitherto dealt in the matter. Seeing me looking pale and exhausted he kindly inquired as to my health, and I told him that I had had a serious illness and was ordered to the country, but thought it well to call first and make further inquiry, lest there should have been any mistake about the mate having run off to the gold diggings.

'Oh,' he said, 'I am so glad you have come, for it turns out that it was an able seaman of the same name that ran away. The mate is still on board; the ship has just reached Gravesend and will be up very soon. I shall be glad to give you the half-pay up to date, for doubtless it will reach his wife more safely through you. We all know what temptations beset the men when they arrive at home after a voyage.'

But before giving me the sum of money, he insisted on my coming inside and sharing his lunch. I felt it was the Lord indeed who was providing for me, and accepted his offer with thankfulness. When I was refreshed and rested, he gave me a sheet of paper to write a few lines to the wife, telling her of the circumstances. On my way back I procured in Cheapside a money order for the balance due to her, and posted it; and returning home again felt myself now quite justified in taking an omnibus as far as it would serve me.

Very much better the next morning, I made my way to the surgery of the doctor who had attended me, feeling that although my uncle was prepared to pay the bill it was right for me now that I had money in hand to ask for the account myself. The kind surgeon refused to allow me as a medical student to pay anything for his attendance, but he had supplied me with quinine which he allowed me to pay for to the extent of eight shillings. When that was settled, I saw that the sum left was just sufficient to take me home; and to my mind the whole thing seemed a wonderful interposition of God on my behalf.

I knew that the surgeon was sceptical, and told him that I should very much like to speak to him freely, if I might do so without offence; that I felt that under God I owed my life to his care, and wished very earnestly that he himself might become a partaker of the same precious faith that I possessed. So I told him my reason for being in London, and about my circumstances, and why I had declined the help of both my father and the officers of the Society in connection with which it was probable that I should go to China. I told him of the recent providential dealings of God with me, and how apparently hopeless my position had been the day before when he had ordered me to go to the country, unless I would reveal my need, which I had determined not to do. I described to him the mental exercises I had gone through; but when I added that I had actually got up from the sofa and walked to Cheapside, he looked at me incredulously and said,

'Impossible! Why, I left you lying there more like a ghost than a man.'

And I had to assure him again and again that, strengthened by faith, the walk had really been taken. I told him also what money was left to me and what payments there had been to make, and showed him that just sufficient remained to take me home to Yorkshire, providing for needful refreshment on the way and the omnibus journey at the end.

My kind friend was completely broken down, and said with tears in his eyes, 'I would give all the world for a faith like yours.'

Two days later he was back in his parents' home, and so full of joy at the Lord's help and provision that he could not keep it to himself. Before he returned to London his mother had discovered the way in which he had been living.

I need scarcely say that when I went up again to town I was not allowed to live, as indeed I was not fit to live, on the same economical lines as before my illness.

A change in his circumstances eased matters further, when after six months at Soho he obtained a position as assistant to a surgeon in the city.

Meanwhile, events were taking place in China that deepened his longing to go there. News was slowly filtering its way from the inland provinces that filled the Western world with astonishment. The Taiping Rebellion, first recognized in 1850, had attained remarkable proportions. Arising in southern China, it had swept over the central provinces and was now in possession of the larger part of the Yangtze valley, including the famous city of Nanking. There, in the former capital of the Empire, the new ruler had established his seat of government, and with a conquered country behind him had rallied his forces for the march upon Peking. But it was not only the success attending this movement that made it a matter of such extraordinary interest in Christian lands. There was about it a character such as no analogous events in history had ever before possessed.

Arising among a heathen people, entirely apart from foreign influence, this mighty upheaval, as far as it had developed, appeared to be a crusade upon distinctively Christian lines. The Ten Commandments formed the moral code of the new kingdom. Idolatry in all its phases was abolished with unsparing hand, and the worship of the true and living God substituted, in purpose at any rate. The Christian Sabbath was recognized as a day of rest and prayer, and all restrictions were removed from the preaching of the Gospel.

'I have promulgated the Ten Commandments,' wrote the Taiping leader to the only missionary of his acquaintance,[1] 'throughout the army and the rest of the

[1] This was the Rev. F. J. Roberts of the American Baptist Missionary Union. Hung Siu-ts'üen, founder and leader of the Taiping movement, first learned the Truth from a tract given him during a literary examination in Canton, by Liang A-fah, one of Morrison's converts. Subsequently he returned to Canton to hear more of the new doctrine, and spent two or three months in studying the Scriptures under the direction of Roberts. Though he did not remain long enough to be baptized and received into church fellowship, he had learned enough of the spirit and teaching of Christianity to make him a missionary to his own people on his return to Kwangsi, the province in which his fervent propaganda began. It was not until bitter persecution from the Chinese authorities had driven his followers to arms, that the movement took on a revolutionary character.

population, and have taught them all to pray, morning and evening. Still those who understand the Gospel are not many. Therefore I deem it right to send the messenger in person to wish you peace, and to request you, Elder Brother, if you are not disposed to abandon me, to (come and) bring with you many teachers to help in making known the Truth and to administer the ordinance of baptism.

'Hereafter, when my enterprise is successfully terminated, I will disseminate the Doctrine throughout the whole Empire, that all may return to the one Lord and worship the true God only. This is what my heart earnestly desires.'

Scarcely less surprising was their attitude toward Western nations. Opium-smoking was utterly prohibited, and the Taiping leader made no secret of his purpose to stop the importation from abroad. But for foreigners as such, their Christian 'brothers' from across the seas, they expressed a deep cordiality of feeling.

'The great God', they said, 'is the universal Father of all under Heaven. China is under His government and care. Foreign nations are equally so. There are many men under Heaven, but all are brethren. Many women are under Heaven, but all are sisters. Why should we continue the selfish practice of regarding a boundary here or a limit there? Why indulge the wish to devour and consume one another?'

No wonder Hudson Taylor with many others saw in all this the moving of God's providence. What kings and governments could never have accomplished, was not He in His own wonderful way rapidly bringing to pass? But how immense the responsibility thus imposed upon the Church, and how little prepared was she to meet it!

In view of all these happenings, though he was studying medicine Hudson Taylor felt no inclination to tie himself down to distinctively medical work. His desire was to use his knowledge rather as an aid to evangelization in districts that had never yet been reached. This was the work to which the Lord had called him; deep down in his own soul he knew it beyond a doubt. But whether the Chinese Evangelization Society would approve was quite another question.

To judge from their rules and regulations they would expect, at any rate, to maintain absolute control over the movements of their representatives. These were spoken of as Agents, and were expected to subscribe to by-laws that perplexed him with their detailed requirements; and over against all this was his growing conviction about the work to which he personally was called. The hand of God was upon him. So far as he was concerned, this was the great fact, the chief consideration. And if the rightful authority of the Committee in London had to be considered as well, how would the two fit in?

Eventually he wrote to the Society stating what appeared to him to be obstacles to his entering the College of Surgeons at their expense.

'Their rules are no doubt reasonable and essential for such an organization,' he explained to his mother. 'But to me, to be educated at their expense and of course subject to these regulations would be like removing myself from the direct and personal leading of God, because I should become the servant of the Society. Having no money I could not release myself honourably, and in any case, for nine months at least (the period required as notice) I should be unable to act. It is possible to pay too dearly even for great advantages, and this is more than my conscience allows me to do.'

But all this preoccupation with important matters was not allowed to interfere with daily duties, and he did not attempt to evade or to defer the supreme duty of leading men to Christ. The unsaved at home were just as much a burden on his heart as the unsaved in China. Always and everywhere he was a soul-winner.

One of his employer's patients had been a hard drinker, and now in middle life was suffering from senile gangrene. His condition was serious, and his hatred of everything to do with religion so intense that it seemed hopeless to try to influence him. Hudson Taylor wrote:

The disease commenced as usual insidiously, and the patient had little idea that he was a doomed man and probably had not long to live. I was not the first to attend him, but when the case was transferred to me I became very anxious about his soul. The family with whom he lived were Christians, and from them I learned that he was an avowed atheist and very antagonistic to anything religious. They had without asking his consent invited a Scripture Reader to visit him, but in great passion he had ordered him from the room. The vicar of the district had also called, hoping to help him, but he had spat in his face and refused to allow him to speak. His temper was described to me as very violent, and altogether the case seemed as hopeless as could well be imagined.

Upon first commencing to attend him I prayed much about it, but for two or three days said nothing of a religious nature. By special care in dressing his diseased limb I was able considerably to lessen his sufferings, and he soon began to manifest appreciation of my services. One day with a trembling heart I took advantage of his grateful acknowledgments to tell him what was the spring of my action, and to speak of his solemn position and need of God's mercy through Christ. It was evidently only a powerful effort of self-restraint that kept his lips closed. He turned over in bed with his back to me, and uttered no word.

I could not get the poor man out of my mind, and very often through each day I pleaded with God, by His Spirit, to save him ere He took him hence. After dressing the wound and relieving the pain, I never failed to say a few words to him which I hoped the Lord would bless. He always turned his back looking annoyed, but never made any reply.

After continuing this for some time my heart sank. It seemed to me that I was not only doing no good but perhaps really hardening him and increasing his guilt. One day after dressing his limb and washing my hands, instead of returning to the bedside I went to the door and stood hesitating a moment with the thought in my mind, 'Ephraim is joined to his idols, let him alone'. Looking at my patient I saw his surprise, as it was the first time since opening the subject that I had attempted to leave without saying a few words for my Master.

I could bear it no longer. Bursting into tears, I crossed the room and said: 'My friend, whether you will hear or whether you will forbear, I *must* deliver my soul,' and went on to speak very earnestly, telling him how much I wished that he would let me pray with him. To my unspeakable joy he did not turn away, but replied:

'If it will be a relief to you, do.'

I need scarcely say that falling upon my knees I poured out my soul to God on his behalf. Then and there, I believe, the Lord wrought a change in his soul. He was never afterwards unwilling to be spoken to and prayed with, and within a few days he definitely accepted Christ as his Saviour.

The now happy sufferer lived for some time after this change, and was never tired of bearing testimony to the grace of God. Though his condition was most distressing, the alteration in his character and behaviour made the previously painful duty of attending him one of real pleasure. I have often thought since in connection with this case and the work of God generally of the words, 'He that goeth forth and *weepeth*, bearing precious seed, shall doubtless come again with rejoicing, bringing his sheaves with him'. Perhaps if there were more of that intense distress for souls that leads to tears, we should more frequently see the results we desire. Sometimes it may be that while we are complaining of the hardness of the hearts of those we are seeking to benefit, the hardness of our own hearts and our own feeble apprehension of the solemn reality of eternal things may be the true cause of our want of success.

Very shortly after this the way cleared suddenly for Hudson Taylor. All had seemed uncertain before him, and especially since his letter to the Chinese Evangelization Society about discontinuing his studies he had scarcely been able to see a step ahead. Very earnestly had he been praying for guidance, longing with all his heart to know and do the will of God. And now the light shone suddenly, and in the way he had least expected: because the time had come, and there is behind events, as the old prophet tells us, 'a God . . . which worketh for him that waiteth for him' (Isa. 64. 4 *R.V.*).

Events had succeeded one another in China with startling rapidity. Since their conquest of Nanking in March, the Taipings had carried all before them, sweeping over the central and northern provinces until Peking itself was almost within their grasp.[1] This could mean but one thing: if Peking

[1] From the zenith of its triumphant advance on Peking commenced this summer of 1853, the Taiping Rebellion degenerated into a corrupt political movement, deluging the country with blood and sufferings untold during the eleven remaining years of its course. Even so the Imperial Government was powerless to bring it to an end until

surrendered, China would forthwith be thrown open to the Gospel. The very possibility, imminent as it was, proved a powerful stimulus to missionary effort. Christian hearts everywhere were aflame. Something must be done, and done at once to meet so great a crisis. And for a time, money poured into the treasuries.

In the light of these new developments the Committee of the C.E.S. had been reconsidering their position. The only representative they had in China was the German missionary Lobscheid, labouring near Canton. They had long wished to supply him with a fellow-worker, and now decided to send two men to Shanghai also, to be ready for pending developments. Money was not the difficulty, their income having considerably increased within the last few months, but suitable men would not be easy to find.

Thus it was that early in June a letter was written to Hudson Taylor.

17 Red Lion Square,
June 4, 1853.

My dear Sir – As you have fully made up your mind to go to China, and also not to qualify as a surgeon, I would affectionately suggest that you lose no time in preparing to start. At this time we want really devoted men, and I believe your heart is right before God and your motives pure, so that you need not hesitate in offering.

I think you will find a difficulty in carrying out your plan (of self-support), as even Mr. Lobscheid could not get a free passage. It is a very difficult thing to obtain. The expense for a single man is about £60. Might not the time you want to spend in acquiring a knowledge of Ophthalmics be spent more profitably in China?

If you think it right to offer yourself, I shall be most happy to lay your application before the Board. It is an important step, and much earnest prayer is needed. But guidance will be given. Do all with thy might, and speedily. – I am, my dear sir, very truly yours,

Charles Bird.

After that things moved rapidly. Only a few weeks later the following paragraph appeared in *The Gleaner:*

On Friday, the 9th of September, a meeting was held at the rooms of the Chinese Evangelization Society at 7 o'clock in the evening, for the purpose of commending to the protection and blessing of God, Mr. James Hudson Taylor, on going out as a missionary to China. Mr. J. H. Taylor embarked on the *Dumfries*, Captain A. Morris, for Shanghai. The vessel left Liverpool on the 19th of September.

Thus was Hudson Taylor launched on his life-work.

---

succoured by Western Powers. England, in the person of General Gordon, Chinese Gordon as he is still appreciatively called, delivered the empire at last from what had become an intolerable evil. Nanking fell before General Gordon in 1864.

CHAPTER 5

China at Last

(1853–1854)

MOORED at her landing in a Liverpool dock lay the double-masted sailing ship *Dumfries,* bound for China. A little vessel of barely 470 tons, she was carrying but one passenger, so there were few well-wishers to see her off. Repairs that had delayed her sailing had just been hurried to completion, and the crew were still busy getting the cargo on board. But in the stern cabin, amid the din and hubbub, Hudson Taylor knelt in prayer for the last time with his mother.

Hardly could they realize that it was indeed the last time for so long. Since the decision of the Committee there had been much to do and think of, and they had had little time to dwell upon the meaning of it all. After a visit to Barnsley, where he took leave of his sisters, and meetings at Tottenham and in London commending him to God, the outgoing missionary had come on to Liverpool, where he had been joined by his mother. His father, and Mr. Pearse representing the Chinese Evangelization Society, had also come to see him off, but on account of delays in the sailing of the ship had been obliged to return. So the mother and son were much alone as the time drew near, and now the parting had come. Here is her account of it:

Dear Hudson engaged in prayer. Only once was there a slight falter, while commending the objects of his love to the care of his heavenly Father – a momentary struggle, and all was calm again. Yet he did not forget that he was entering upon a course of trial, difficulty and danger; but looking forward to it all he exclaimed, 'None of these things move me, neither count I my life dear unto myself, so that I might finish my course with joy, and the ministry, which I have received of the Lord Jesus, to testify the gospel of the grace of God.' It was a time ever to be remembered.

Then came my moment of trial – the farewell blessing, the parting embrace. A kind hand was extended from the shore. I stepped off the vessel, scarce knowing what I did, and was seated on a piece of timber lying close at hand. A chill came over me and I trembled from head to foot.

As the vessel was receding we lost sight of him for a minute. He had run to his cabin, and hastily writing in pencil on the blank leaf of a pocket Bible, '*The love of God which passeth knowledge* – J.H.T.', came back and threw it to me on the pier.

Another 'Farewell, God bless you', and the deep waters of the Mersey became a separating gulf between us. While we still waved our handkerchiefs, watching the departing ship, he took his stand at its head and afterwards climbed into the rigging, waving his hat. Then his figure became less and less distinct, and in a few minutes passenger and ship were lost to sight.

His own recollections of that parting, recorded long after, show how deeply the son too shared its cost.

My beloved mother had come over to Liverpool to see me off. Never shall I forget that day, nor how she went with me into the cabin that was to be my home for nearly six long months. With a mother's loving hand she smoothed the little bed. She sat by my side and joined in the last hymn we should sing together before parting. We knelt down and she prayed – the last mother's prayer I was to hear before leaving for China. Then notice was given that we must separate, and we had to say good-bye, never expecting to meet on earth again.

For my sake she restrained her feelings as much as possible. We parted, and she went ashore giving me her blessing. I stood alone on deck, and she followed the ship as we moved toward the dock-gates. As we passed through the gates and the separation really commenced, never shall I forget the cry of anguish wrung from that mother's heart. It went through me like a knife. I never knew so fully, until then, what 'God *so* loved the world' meant. And I am quite sure my precious mother learned more of the love of God for the perishing in that one hour than in all her life before.

Oh, how it must grieve the heart of God when He sees His children indifferent to the needs of that wide world for which His beloved, His only Son suffered and died.

The voyage thus begun was long and tedious in some ways to the solitary passenger on board the *Dumfries*. Five and a half months passed during which they touched nowhere, and heard no tidings of the rest of the world. But it was a health-giving, enjoyable experience on the whole, after the first terrible days were over.

For never surely did vessel weather worse perils than this little sailing ship before she could reach the open sea. It almost seemed as though the great enemy, 'the prince of the power of the air', knowing something of the possibilities enfolded in one young life on board, was doing his utmost to send her to the bottom. For twelve long days they beat about the Channel, alternately sighting Ireland and the dangerous Welsh coast. During the first week they were almost continuously in the teeth of an equinoctial gale, until driven into Carnarvon Bay they were within two boats' length of being dashed to pieces on the rocks. That midnight scene amid the foaming breakers, and the way in which they were delivered when all hope seemed gone, made a profound impression upon Hudson Taylor. He wrote describing it:

It was a fearful time. The wind was blowing terrifically, and we were tearing along at a frightful rate – one moment high in the air and the next plunging head foremost into the trough of the sea as if about to go to the bottom. The windward side of the ship was fearfully elevated, the lee side being as much depressed; indeed the sea at times poured over her lee bulwarks.

Thus the sun set, and I watched it ardently.

'Tomorrow thou wilt rise as usual,' I thought, 'but unless the Lord works miraculously on our behalf a few broken timbers will be all that is left of us and our ship.'

The night was cold, the wind biting, and the seas we shipped continually, with foam and spray, wet us through and through.

As the sun went down a sense of loneliness and desolation began to come over him, so that for a time he was 'much tried and very anxious.' He thought of the sorrow involved to his loved ones should the *Dumfries* be lost; of the expense to the Society, his passage and outfit having cost little short of £100; of the unprepared state of the crew, as well as of 'the coldness of the water and the struggle of death'. About his eternal happiness he had not a moment's doubt. Death itself was not dreaded. But death in such circumstances! The journal continues:

I went below, read a hymn or two, some Psalms and John 13–15, and was comforted; so much so that I fell asleep and slept for an hour. We then looked at the barometer and found it rising, and I asked the Captain whether we could clear Holyhead or not.

'If we make no leeway,' he replied, 'we may just do it. But if we drift, God help us!'

And we did drift. Our position was now truly awful. The night was very light, the moon being unclouded, and we could just see land ahead. I went below. The barometer was improving, but the wind in no way abated. I took out my pocket-book and wrote in it my name and home address, in case my body should be found. I also tied a few things in a hamper which I thought would float and perhaps help me or someone else to land. Then commending my soul to God my Father, and my friends and *all* to His care, with one prayer that if it were possible this cup might pass from us, I went on deck.

I asked the Captain whether boats could live in such a sea. He answered, 'No'. Could we not lash the loose spars together and make some sort of raft? He said we should probably not have time.

The water was now becoming white. Land was just ahead.

'We must try to turn her and tack,' said the Captain, 'or all is over. The sea may sweep the deck in turning and wash everything overboard but we must try.'

This was a moment to make the stoutest heart tremble. He gave the word and we tried to turn outwardly, but in vain. This would have saved us room. He then tried the other way, and with God's blessing succeeded, clearing the rocks by not more than two ships' length. Just as we did so, the wind most providentially veered two points in our favour, and we were able to beat out of the Bay.

Had not the Lord thus helped us, all our efforts must have been in vain. Truly His mercy is unfailing. 'Oh that men would praise the Lord for his goodness and for his wonderful works to the children of men.'

Safe for the present, it was with unspeakable thankfulness they saw the sun rise on Monday morning and the storm gradually pass away.

Many years later, writing of this experience, Hudson Taylor lifted the veil on another aspect of it not recorded in his letters home.

One thing was a great trouble to me that night. I was a very young believer, and had not sufficient faith in God to see Him in and through the use of means. I had felt it a duty to comply with the earnest wish of my mother, and for her sake to procure a swimming-belt. But in my own soul I felt as if I could not simply trust in God while I had it, and my heart had no rest until on that night, after all hope of being saved was gone, I had given it away. Then I had perfect peace, and strange to say put several light things together, likely to float at the time we struck, without any thought of inconsistency!

After the storm was over, the question was settled for me through the prayerful study of the Scriptures. God gave me then to see my mistake; probably to deliver me from a great deal of trouble on similar questions. It is a mistake that is very common in these days, when erroneous teaching on faith healing does much harm, misleading some as to the purposes of God, shaking the faith of others and distressing the minds of many. When in medical or surgical charge of any case, I have never thought of neglecting to ask God's guidance and blessing in the use of appropriate means, nor yet of omitting to give thanks for answered prayer and restored health. It would now appear to me as presumptuous and wrong to neglect the use of those measures which He Himself has put within our reach, as to neglect to take daily food, and suppose that life and health might be maintained by prayer alone.

In the Bay of Biscay Hudson Taylor discovered that there was one more earnest Christian on board, the Swedish carpenter, and assured of his help, asked the Captain's permission to commence regular services among the crew.

Sixty times during the remainder of the voyage meetings were held, Hudson Taylor giving unwearied prayer and preparation to this ministry. It was a great help to him personally and did much to save him from the spiritual declension that so often accompanies life at sea, his only sorrow being that so little permanent change was found in the lives of the men. They were interested, and would come to him at times for private talk and prayer, but though some were very near the Kingdom, none of them came out fully on the side of Christ. This was a keen disappointment but no doubt in some ways the experience was useful, preparing him 'to sow beside all waters', even when for a long time no fruit appeared.

There were times in his solitude when home seemed far away and the longing for those he loved became intense.

How widely we are separated, who last year were so near. Praised be God, He is unchangeable; His mercy never fails.

Found in a book lent me by Captain Morris, *The Hebrew Mother*, and was much affected by it. Never shall I forget the last time I heard it. Mother was present: my dearest —— played it; and when we came to the lines:

I give thee to thy God,
The God that gave thee –

Mother broke down, and clasping me in her arms wept aloud at the thought of parting. May the Lord bless her and comfort her heart day by day.

Jesus *is* precious. His service is perfect freedom. His yoke is easy and His burden light. Joy and peace His people have indeed. Absent from home, friends, and country even, Jesus is with me. He is all, and more than all. Much as my heart yearns to see them, the love of Christ is stronger, more constraining.

This love of Christ in him was deepening, face to face with facts that had been only hearsay before. The lonely inhabitants of many an island, for example, between Java and the Philippines drew forth his compassion. They had already sighted land some weeks before, in rounding the Cape of Good Hope, but not until the nearest point to Australia was reached did they begin to enter the archipelago lying between the Indian and Pacific Oceans. For almost a month they were hardly ever out of sight of beautiful, fertile, populous islands, of which he wrote.

O what work for the missionary! Island after island, many almost unknown, some densely peopled, but no light, no Jesus, no hope full of bliss! My heart yearns over them. Can it be that Christian men and women will stay comfortably at home and leave these souls to perish?

But with all its interests the voyage seemed tedious toward the close, especially in the frequent calms of this Eastern Archipelago. Only for a single day during that month among the islands had they a steady wind, and more than once their log did not exceed seven miles in the twenty-four hours. Such experiences were not only tedious, they were accompanied with serious danger.

'Never', as Hudson Taylor put it, 'is one more helpless than in a sailing ship with a total absence of wind and the presence of a strong current setting toward a dangerous coast. In a storm the ship is to some extent manageable, but becalmed one can do nothing; the Lord must do all.'

One definite answer to prayer in such circumstances was a great encouragement to his faith. They had just come through the Dampier Strait but were not yet out of sight of the islands. Usually a breeze would spring up after sunset and last until dawn. The utmost use was made of it, but during the day they lay still with flapping sails, often drifting back and losing a good deal of the advantage gained at night.

This happened notably on one occasion when we were in dangerous proximity to the north of New Guinea. Saturday night had brought us to a point some thirty miles off the land, and during the Sunday morning service which was held on deck I could not fail to see that the Captain looked troubled and frequently went over to the side of the ship. When the service was ended I learnt from him the cause: a four-knot current was carrying us toward some sunken reefs, and we were already so near that it seemed improbable that we should get through the afternoon in safety. After dinner the long-boat was put out and all hands endeavoured, without success, to turn the ship's head from the shore.

After standing together on the deck for some time in silence, the Captain said to me: 'Well, we have done everything that can be done. We can only await the result.'

A thought occurred to me, and I replied:

'No, there is one thing we have not done yet.'

'What is that?' he queried.

'Four of us on board are Christians. Let us each retire to his own cabin, and in agreed prayer ask the Lord to give us immediately a breeze. He can as easily send it now as at sunset.'

The Captain complied with this proposal. I went and spoke to the other two men, and after prayer with the carpenter we all four retired to wait upon God. I had a good but very brief season in prayer, and then felt so satisfied that our request was granted that I could not continue asking, and very soon went up again on deck. The first officer, a godless man, was in charge. I went over and asked him to let down the clews or corners of the mainsail, which had been drawn up in order to lessen the useless flapping of the sail against the rigging.

'What would be the good of that?' he answered roughly.

I told him we had been asking a wind from God; that it was coming immediately; and we were so near the reef by this time that there was not a minute to lose.

With an oath and a look of contempt, he said he would rather see a wind than hear of it. But while he was speaking I watched his eye, following it up to the royal, and there sure enough the corner of the topmost sail was beginning to tremble in the breeze.

'Don't you see the wind is coming? Look at the royal!' I exclaimed.

'No, it is only a cat's paw,' he rejoined (a mere puff of wind).

'Cat's paw or not,' I cried, 'pray let down the mainsail and give us the benefit.'

This he was not slow to do. In another minute the heavy tread of the men on deck brought up the Captain from his cabin to see what was the matter. The breeze had indeed come! In a few minutes we were ploughing our way at six or seven knots through the water, and though the wind was sometimes unsteady we did not altogether lose it until after passing the Pelew Islands.

Thus God encouraged me ere landing on China's shores to bring every variety of need to Him in prayer, and to expect that He would honour the name of the Lord Jesus and give the help each emergency required.

It was on a foggy Sunday at the end of February that the last stage of the long journey was reached, and the yellow, turbid water surging around the *Dumfries* told that they were already in the estuary of a great river. Muffled in his heaviest wraps Hudson Taylor paced the deck, doing his best to keep warm and be patient. It was a strange Sunday, this last at sea. For days he had been packed and ready to leave the ship, and hindered by storm and cold from other occupations had given the more time to thought and prayer.

'What peculiar feelings', he wrote, 'arise at the prospect of soon landing in an unknown country, in the midst of strangers – a country now to be my home and sphere of labour. "Lo, I am with you alway." "I will never leave thee nor forsake thee." Sweet promises! I have nothing to fear, with Jesus on my side.

'Great changes probably have taken place since last we heard from China. And what news shall I receive from England? Where shall I go, and how shall I live at first? These and a thousand other questions engage the mind. But the most important question of all is, "Am I now living as near to God as possible?" '

As afternoon wore on, what were those boats in the distance – looming toward them through the mist? One beat its way up before long, eagerly watched from the *Dumfries*. Yes, there was no mistaking that picturesque sail and curiously painted hull, nor the faces of the men as they came into sight. There they were, twelve or fourteen of them, blue-garbed, dark-eyed, vociferating in an unknown tongue – the first Chinese Hudson Taylor had ever seen. And how his heart went out to them! Behind the strange exterior he saw the treasure he had come so far to seek – the souls for which Christ died.

'I did long', he wrote, 'to be able to tell them the Glad Tidings.'

A little later the English pilot came on board and received a hearty welcome. There was no hope of reaching Woosung that day, still less Shanghai, fifteen miles farther up the tidal river; but there was much he could tell them, while waiting for the fog to clear, of the long winter's doings since they had left England.

From him they learned, for example, of the troubles between Russia and Turkey that within a few weeks were to lead to the Crimean War. The allied fleets of England and France had already reached the scene of conflict and nothing, it was feared, could avert the serious issue. But startling though it was to hear of war-clouds hanging over Europe, it was scarcely as great a shock as the news from China itself, and especially from the port at which they were about to land. Not only was the Taiping Rebellion still devastating province after province in its progress toward Peking; Shanghai itself, both the native city and the foreign Settlement, was plunged in all the horrors of war. A local band of rebels known as the 'Red Turbans' had obtained possession of the city, around which was now encamped an Imperial army of forty to fifty thousand men, the latter proving a more serious menace to the European community than even the rebels themselves.

For the rest, bad as their passage had been they had arrived ahead of vessels that set out before them, but just too late for the February mail. They must be prepared, moreover, to find everything at famine prices, for the dollar had risen from four shillings, its ordinary value, to six or seven, and would soon be higher: a discouraging outlook for one with a small income in English money!

All this and more the pilot told them, and they had time to think over his communications. Monday was still so foggy that they could not proceed, and though they weighed anchor on Tuesday morning it was only to beat up against the wind a few miles nearer to Woosung. But that night the fog lifted, and the young missionary pacing the deck caught sight of a low-lying shore, running far to north and south, that was *no island*. How it arrested him! His prayers were answered; the dream of years come true. He was looking on China at last, under the evening sky.

Not until 5 p.m. next day however (Wednesday, March 1) was he able to land in Shanghai; and then it was quite alone, the *Dumfries* being still detained by adverse winds.

'My feelings on stepping ashore,' he wrote, 'I cannot attempt to describe. My heart felt as though it had not room and must burst its bonds, while tears of gratitude and thankfulness fell from my eyes.'

Then a deep sense of the loneliness of his position began to come over him; not a friend or acquaintance anywhere; no single hand held out to welcome him, or anyone who even knew his name.

Mingled with thankfulness for deliverance from many dangers and joy at finding myself at last on Chinese soil came a vivid realization of the great distance between me and those I loved, and that I was a stranger in a strange land.

I had three letters of introduction, however, and counted on advice and help from one especially, to whom I had been commended by mutual friends, whom I knew well and highly valued. Of course I inquired for him at once, only to learn that he had been buried a month or two previously, having died of fever while we were at sea.

Saddened by these tidings I asked the whereabouts of a missionary to whom another of my introductions was addressed, but only to meet with further disappointment. He had recently left for America. The third letter remained; but it had been given me by a comparative stranger, and I expected less from it than from the others. It proved, however, to be God's channel of help.

This letter then in hand, he left the British Consulate near the river to find the compound of the London Missionary Society at some distance across the Settlement. On every side strange sights, sounds and smells now greeted him, especially when the large houses of the wealthy gave place to smaller shops and squalid buildings. Here nothing but Chinese was to be heard, and few if any but Chinese were to be seen. The streets grew narrower and more crowded, and overhanging balconies above rows of swinging signboards almost hid the sky. How he found his way for a mile or more does not appear; but at length a mission chapel came in sight, and with an upward look for guidance Hudson Taylor turned in at the ever open gateway of *Ma-ka-k'üen*.[1]

Several buildings stood before him, including a hospital and dwelling-houses, at the first of which he enquired for Dr. Medhurst to whom his letter was addressed. Sensitive and reserved by nature, it was no small ordeal to Hudson Taylor to have to introduce himself to so important a person, the pioneer as well as founder (with Dr. Lockhart) of Protestant missionary effort in this part of China, and it was almost with relief he heard that Dr. Medhurst was no longer living on the compound. He too, it seemed, had gone away.

More than this Hudson Taylor was unable to make out, as the Chinese servants could not speak English, nor could he understand a word of their dialect. It was a perplexing situation until a European came in sight. His name was Edkins and he was one of the junior missionaries, he explained, as he welcomed the new arrival. Dr. and Mrs. Medhurst had moved to the British Consulate, he said, but Dr. Lockhart remained; and he went to find him.

It was quite an event in those days for an Englishman and especially a missionary to appear in Shanghai unannounced. Most people came by the regular mail-steamers once a month, whose arrival caused general excitement. None was expected then, and even the *Dumfries* was not yet in port; so that when another of the L.M.S. people came in, during the absence of Edkins, Hudson Taylor had to explain all over again who and what he was. But Alexander Wylie soon set him at ease, and entertained him until Edkins returned with Dr. Lockhart.

It did not take long for these new friends to understand the situation, and then there was nothing for it but to receive the young missionary into one of their own houses. They could not leave him without a home, and the Settlement was so crowded that lodgings were not to be had at any price. Dr. Lockhart was living alone, his wife having been obliged to return to England, and with genuine kindness he welcomed Hudson Taylor as his guest, permitting him to pay a moderate sum to cover board expenses.

[1] The three characters mean 'Medhurst Family Enclosure'. Dr. Medhurst was the author of *China*, the book Hudson Taylor had borrowed as a lad in Barnsley, which emphasized the value of medical missions and thus directed him in seeking medical training in preparation for missionary work.

This arrangement made, Edkins took him to see Mr. and Mrs. Muirhead, who completed the L.M.S. staff in Shanghai, and introduced him also to Mr. and Mrs. Burdon, of the Church Missionary Society, who had rented an unoccupied house on the same compound. The Burdons invited him to dinner that evening. They were young and newly married, having been only a year or two in China, and from the first were drawn to Hudson Taylor in a sympathy he warmly reciprocated.

'The fireside looked so homelike, their company was so pleasant and all the news they had to tell,' he wrote, 'so full of interest that it was most refreshing.'

Here then was an answer to many prayers, the solution of many ponderings.[1] For the moment he was provided for in favourable circumstances, and though he could not trespass upon the doctor's hospitality for long, it would afford him at any rate a little while in which to look about and make permanent arrangements. Thankfully he lay down to sleep for the first time in China.

He awoke next morning to the song of birds, a welcome change from the lapping of water on the side of the *Dumfries*, and looked with enjoyment at the budding plants out in the garden. It was good to sniff the perfumed air after so long at sea.

Breakfast over, he went to the Consulate, and though disappointed to find only one letter (on which he had to pay no less than two shillings postage), it was a letter from home, containing enclosures from both mother and sisters.

'Never did I pay two shillings more willingly in my life,' he assured them, 'than for that letter.'

Soon the *Dumfries* was reported, and with a Chinese helper he managed to get his things brought up to Dr. Lockhart's. It was a peculiar sensation to be marching at the head of a procession of coolies through the crowded streets, all his belongings swinging from bamboo poles across their shoulders, while at every step they sang or shouted 'Ou-ah Ou-ay' in varying tones.

[1] Among the honoured names on the long roll of L.M.S. missionaries few take a higher place than Medhurst, Lockhart, Wylie, Muirhead, Edkins, and Griffith John who joined them a few months later. It was through them that most of the large cities in Kiangsu and north Chekiang provinces first heard the Word of life. Dr. Lockhart was the first medical missionary from England to China. He landed in Canton four years after Dr. Peter Parker from America, and accompanied Dr. Medhurst when, in 1843, he commenced missionary operations in central China. The Rev. J. S. Burdon was the first representative of the Church Missionary Society to commence work in Peking, which became his headquarters for eleven years. A remarkable group of men, reinforced by a remarkable addition in the coming among them of Hudson Taylor.

They were not really in pain or distress, he realized, although it sounded like it; and by the time some of the copper cash he had received in exchange for a Mexican dollar had been distributed amongst them, he had had his first lesson in business dealings in the Orient.

Then came the daily service in the hospital, conducted on this occasion by Dr. Medhurst, and Hudson Taylor listened for the first time to Gospel preaching in the tongue with which he was to become so familiar. In conversation afterwards, Dr. Medhurst advised him to commence his studies with the Mandarin dialect, the most widely spoken in China, and undertook to procure a teacher. Evening brought the weekly prayer meeting, when Hudson Taylor was introduced to others of the missionary community, thus ending with united waiting upon God his first whole day in China.

Before the week closed he began to see another side of Shanghai life, however. The journal tells of guns firing all night, and the city wall not half a mile away covered with sentry lights; of sharp fighting seen from his windows, in which men were killed and wounded under his very eyes; of a patient search for rooms in the Chinese part of the Settlement, only emphasizing the fact that there were none to be had; of his first contact with heathenism; and of scenes of suffering in the native city which made an indelible impression of horror upon his mind.

Of some of these experiences he wrote to his sister ten days after his arrival:

On Saturday (March 4) I took a walk through the Market, and such a muddy, dirty place as Shanghai I never did see! The ground is all mud; dry in dry weather, but one hour's rain makes it like walking through a clay-field. It scarcely is walking, but wading! I found that there was no probability of getting a house or even apartments, and felt cast down in spirit.

The following day, Sunday, I attended two services at the L.M.S., and in the afternoon went into the city with Mr. Wylie. You have never seen a city in a state of siege, or been at the seat of war. God grant you never may! We walked some distance round the wall, and sad it was to see the wreck of rows upon rows of houses near the city. Burnt down, blown down, battered to pieces – in all stages of ruin they were! And the misery of those who once inhabited them, driven from house, home and everything, is terrible to think of.

At length we came upon a ladder let down from the wall, by which provisions were being conveyed into the city. We entered also. The soldiers on guard offered no opposition, and for a long time we wandered through the city, Mr. Wylie talking with people here and there, and giving them tracts. We went into some of the temples and the priests also received tracts from us. Everywhere we seemed welcome.

As we passed the West Gate, we saw hundreds of the Rebel soldiery assembled there, and we met many more going in that direction. They were about to make a sally upon the Imperialists, who would not be expecting it from that quarter.

We then proceeded to the L.M.S. chapel, and found it crammed with people.

Dr. Medhurst was preaching, after which six bags of rice were distributed among the poor creatures, many of whom must perish but for this assistance, rendered daily, as they can do nothing now to earn a living. Windows smashed in the chapel, and lamps broken by passing bullets tell of the deadly work that is going on.

By the time we came to the North Gate they were fighting fiercely outside the city. One man was brought in dead, another shot through the chest, and a third whose arm I examined seemed in dreadful agony. A ball had gone clean through the arm, breaking the bone in passing.

A little farther on we met some men bringing in a small cannon they had captured, and following them were others dragging along by their tails (queues) five wretched prisoners. The poor fellows cried piteously to us to save them, as they were hurried by, but alas, we could do nothing. They would probably be at once decapitated. It makes one's blood run cold to think of such a thing.

All this Hudson Taylor doubtless felt the more in that it was so unexpected. Trial and hardship he had looked for, of the kind usually associated with a missionary's lot, but everything was turning out differently from his anticipations. External hardships there were none, save the cold from which he suffered greatly; but distress of mind and heart seemed daily to increase. He could hardly look out of his window, much less take exercise in any direction, without witnessing misery such as he had never dreamed of before. The tortures inflicted by the soldiery of both armies upon unhappy prisoners from whom they hoped to extort money, and the ravages perpetrated as they pillaged the country for supplies, harrowed him unspeakably. Meanwhile his eagerness to get hold on the language made him devote every moment to study, even to the neglect of prayer and daily feeding upon the Scriptures. This reacted on his own spiritual life. The channels of outflow to others were sealed, and it was a little while before he realized that they must be kept all the more clear and open toward God. The great enemy took advantage of all this, as may be seen from early letters.

To Mr. Pearse he wrote:

I felt very much disappointed on finding no letter from you, but I hope to receive one by the next mail. Shanghai is in a very unsettled state, the Rebels and Imperialists fighting continually. This morning a cannon fired near us awoke me before daybreak, shaking the house and making the windows rattle violently.

There is not a house to be obtained here, or even part of one; those not occupied by Europeans are filled with Chinese merchants who have left the city. The pilot told me they will give for only three rooms as much as thirty dollars a month, and in some instances more. The missionaries who were living in the city have had to leave, and are residing with others here in the Settlement at present; so that had it not been for the kindness of Dr. Lockhart I should have been quite nonplussed. As it is I scarcely know what to do. How long the present state of things may last it is impossible to say. If I am to stay here, Dr. Lockhart says that the only plan will be to buy land and build a house. The land would probably cost from 100 to 150 dollars, and the house three or four hundred more. If peace was restored, Dr. Lockhart thinks I could rent a house in the city at from two to three hundred dollars per annum. So that in any case the expense of living here must be great. I do not know whether it would be less at Hong Kong or any other port?

Please excuse this hasty, disconnected letter with all its faults. It is so cold just now that I can scarcely feel pen or paper. Everything is very dear, and fuel costs at times an almost fabulous price. Coal is now at thirty dollars (nearly £10) a ton. Once more I must beg you to excuse this letter, and please reply with all possible expedition that I may know what to do.

May the Lord bless and prosper you. Continue to pray much for me, and may we all, sure of Jesus' love when everything else fails, seek to be more like Him. Soon we shall meet where sorrow and trial shall be no more. Till then may we be willing to bear the cross, and not only to do but to suffer His will.

'The cold was so great and other things so trying,' he continued to his parents a week later, 'that I scarcely knew what I was doing or saying at first. What it means to be so far from home, at the seat of war, and not able to understand or be understood by the people was fully realized. Their utter wretchedness and misery, and my inability to help them or even point them to Jesus, powerfully affected me.'

In another letter he wrote,

I would give anything for a friend with whom to consult freely. My position is so perplexing that if I had not definite promises of Divine guidance to count upon, I do not know what I should do. There is, I fear, no probability of my being able to keep within my salary under present circumstances. If I had quarters of my own I could live on rice (not bread, that would be too expensive) and drink tea without milk or sugar, which is cheap enough here. But that I cannot do now. Things are increasing in expense all the while and dollars are getting dearer. They were at 6s. 1d. when last I heard, and if we are involved in further hostilities may rise to double that price – and yet have no more purchasing value. Well, He will provide.

It may seem exaggerated, at first sight, to dwell much upon the trials of Hudson Taylor's position. True, he was at the seat of war, but as far as circumstances permitted he was living in safety and even comfort. He was so well off, apparently, that one wonders at the undertone of suffering in his letters, until a little consideration reveals another side of his experiences. The welcome assistance received from Dr. Medhurst and other L.M.S. missionaries yet gave rise to an embarrassing situation. If he had belonged to their Society and had been preparing to work with and for them, nothing could have been better. But as it was, he felt almost like an unfledged cuckoo – an intruder in another bird's nest. That his companionship at every meal in solitary *tête-à-tête* was somewhat wearisome to his generous host, he could not but feel. He received nothing but kindness from Dr. Lockhart and his associates, but he was not as they were, highly educated and connected with a great denomination and important work. The preparation providentially ordered for him had been along different lines, and his religious views made him singular, while his position as a missionary was isolated and open to criticism.

He had been sent out, hurried out almost, by his Society, before his medical course was finished, in the hope of reaching the Rebels at Nanking. Misled by optimistic reports about the Taiping Movement, the Secretaries of the C.E.S. had taken a position that to practical men on the field seemed wholly absurd. It was not long before Hudson Taylor discovered that the Chinese Evangelization Society, with its aims and methods, was the butt of no little ridicule in Shanghai. It was humiliating as *The Gleaner* came out month by month to hear it pulled to pieces in this spirit although he could not but acknowledge that many of the strictures were deserved.

He realized the weakness of the C.E.S., or was coming to, no less clearly than others did; but he knew and respected many members of the Committee, and to some (including the Secretaries) he was attached with grateful love. This put matters in a very different light. Fellowship with them in spiritual things, at Tottenham and elsewhere, could never be forgotten, and even when feeling their mistakes most keenly he longed for their atmosphere of prayer, their love of the Word of God and earnest zeal for souls.

The influence of the world was tremendously strong in Shanghai, even in missionary circles. It was the heyday of the Settlement, as regards financial and commercial opportunities. Many a fortune was to be made in Shanghai in those days, and lavish expenditure on luxury, with its attendant evils, was to be found on every hand.

Such a state of things was not without its effect on the missionary community. The great expense of living necessitated increased salaries; and it was unavoidable that there should be a good deal of intercourse with government officials, to whom the missionaries were useful as interpreters, and with officers from the gunboats stationed at Shanghai for the protection of the Settlement. A general spirit of sociability fell far short of Hudson Taylor's ideal of missionary life.

He himself, on the other hand, certainly did not fit in with the current conception of what a missionary should be. That he was good and earnest could easily be seen; but he was connected with no particular denomination, nor was he sent out by any special Church. He expected to do medical work, but he was not a doctor. He was accustomed, evidently, to preaching and pastoral care of others, and yet was not ordained. And strangest perhaps of all, though he belonged to a Society that seemed well supplied with funds, his salary was insufficient and his appearance shabby compared with those by whom he was surrounded.

That Hudson Taylor felt all this, and felt it increasingly as time went on, is not to be wondered at. He had come out with such different expectations! His one longing was to go inland and live among the people. He wanted to keep down expenses and continue the simple, self-denying life he had lived at home. To learn the language that he might win souls was his one ambition. He cared nothing at all about worldly estimates and social pleasures, though he did long for fellowship in the things of God. With a salary of £80 a year, he found himself unable to manage upon twice that sum. So he was really poor and in serious difficulty before long; and there was no one to impress the fact upon the Committee at home or make them understand the situation.

Then, too, he was unavoidably lonely. The missionaries with whom he lived were all a good deal older than himself, with the exception of the Burdons who were fully occupied with their work. He could not trespass on their kindness too frequently, and having no colleague of his own found it impossible to speak of many matters connected with the Society and future developments that were on his heart. Soon he learned to mention such affairs as little as possible.

Much as he felt his position, however, it was well for the young missionary that he could not hive off just then or attempt to live on rice and tea minus milk or sugar. He would have done it had he been his own master. He would have done anything along lines of self-sacrifice to make the money given for missionary purposes go as far as possible. But it would have been a dangerous experiment during the hot season in an unaccustomed climate. And more than this – were there not higher purposes in view in the providential limitations imposed upon him at this time? He longed to be free and independent, and the Lord saw fit to keep him in the very opposite position, letting him learn from experience what it is to be poor and weak and indebted to others even for the necessities of life. For His own, His well-beloved Son, there was no better way; and there are lessons still that can be learned only in this school.

But for such circumstances early in his missionary career, Hudson Taylor would never have been able to feel for others as it was necessary he should. By nature he was resourceful and independent to a fault, desiring freedom to follow the guidance of the Lord as it came to him personally, untrammelled by obligations even to the Society with which he was connected. And now at the very opening of his new life in China, he found himself cast upon the generosity of strangers.

As spring advanced, his journal gave evidence of more depression of spirits than could be attributed to the climate. His eyes, never strong, became inflamed through the sunshine and excessive dust, and he suffered also a great deal from headache. In spite of this he worked at Chinese on an average five hours every day, besides giving time to necessary correspondence. To Mr. Pearse he wrote as fully as possible, trying to supply information that would interest readers of *The Gleaner*, as well as detailed statements of the condition of things around him with a view to the future conduct of the work.

From these letters one sees how much he was beginning to feel the monotony of a young missionary's life, occupied mainly with study. There was little of interest to write about, and it is clear that he was passing through a stage of weariness and disillusionment in which it is so easy to lose spiritual usefulness and power.

Thanks to good judgment and sensible home-training, Hudson Taylor was in less danger than many young missionaries during those months of language study. From early childhood he had been encouraged to take an interest in 'nature study', his butterflies and insects being always housed with consideration though at some cost to his parents in their limited surroundings. This stood him in good stead, for now he not only knew the value of such recreation, but also how to take it up. The journal for April records,

April 25: Ordered a cabinet for insects, and worked at Chinese and photography.

April 28: Very warm again. Worked at Chinese five hours. Had a bad headache all day. Caught a few insects as a commencement of my collection.

April 29: At Chinese six hours. After dinner took a walk in search of nocturnal insects. Had some difficulty in getting into the Settlement again, the gates being closed.

'Today,' he wrote to his mother in May, 'I caught sight of a large black butterfly with swallow-tail wings, the largest living butterfly I have ever seen. At first I thought it must be a small bird, although it seemed to fly so strangely. But when it settled on a tree and I saw the splendid creature, it nearly took my breath away, it was so fine!

'I intend also to collect botanical specimens. There are some trees here that have a strange look to our eyes, being covered with blossoms before a single leaf appears. Among the wild plants I see many old friends – the violet, forget-me-not, buttercup, clover, chickweed, dandelion, hemlock, and several common herbs. There are also wild flowers that are new to me and very pretty.'

In addition to working hard at Chinese this summer he was diligently keeping up other studies, medicine and chemistry especially, that he might not lose the benefit of his hospital course. The classics he gave as much time to as possible, and he seems always to have had some useful book on hand dealing with history, biography, or natural science. The following is a typical entry in a journal-letter to his sister:

Before breakfast read Medicine, then Chinese nearly seven hours. After dinner, Greek and Latin exercises, each an hour. After poring over these things till one can scarcely see, it is a comfort to have a fine, clear, large-type Bible, such as Aunt Hardey gave me. It is quite a luxury. Well, all these studies are necessary. Some of them, the classical languages of Europe, ought to have been mastered long ago; so it is now or never with me. But the sweetest duties of the day are those that lead to Jesus – prayer, reading and meditation upon His precious Word.

All through this trying season Hudson Taylor kept up his studies, never falling below his average of five hours at Chinese every day. Once or twice he went into the country with his friend Burdon, and felt well rewarded by the welcome met with from the village people, who were only too glad to see them out again.

'I think I may say I have one friend now,' he added, telling of a happy evening with the Burdons after one such excursion. 'But I do not want to go over there too often, as I am only one of his circle and he has a wife for company. I feel the want of a companion very much. The day is spent with my teacher, but my evenings generally alone in writing or study.'

Much time was given during his first year in China to correspondence, and he looked eagerly for letters from home. When none arrived the disappointment was intense.

'When last mail came in,' he wrote to his mother in the middle of June, 'after walking a mile and a half to the Consulate on a broiling hot day and waiting nearly two hours, which lost me my "tiffin" or midday meal, I had the pleasure of bringing up letters and papers for everyone at the Mission except myself. When I found there really was nothing for me, I felt quite sick and faint and could scarcely manage to walk home, for it was reported that we should have no other mail for six or eight weeks.'

Another trial of those summer months, and one he felt still more keenly, was his financial position, overlooked apparently by the Society. The first quarter since his arrival in China was now at an end, and his balance in hand was so small that it would be necessary to draw again very soon, and he had already spent more than 130 dollars. At that rate his salary would be exhausted before half the year was over, and what would the Committee say and think?

With anxious care he explained to Mr. Pearse every item in these accounts, the first he ever sent home from China, revealing touching details as to needs he had not supplied because of his desire to save expense as far as possible.

'I feel quite oppressed when I think of what a cost I am to the Society,' he wrote, 'and yet how little good I am able to accomplish.'

And just then, to add to his perplexity, news reached him in a roundabout way that seemed a climax to his troubles. The Society was sending another missionary to Shanghai, and not a bachelor like himself, but a married man with a family. Dr. Parker, a Scot who had applied to the C.E.S. before Hudson Taylor left England, was already on his way to join him and might be expected in a few months. Glad as the young missionary would have been of such tidings in other circumstances, what arrangements could he make for a married couple with three children, when he himself was dependent on the generosity of others? He hardly dared mention it to those with whom he was living, and yet the news would soon be the talk of the Settlement whether he kept silence or not.

Anxiously he awaited letters from the Committee explaining the situation. Surely they would send him notice, in view of all he had written, of such an addition to their staff, and instruct him fully how to act. But mail after mail came in with no reference to Dr. Parker's coming. Repeated requests for directions as to how to arrange for himself had as yet received no answer, and before summer was over Hudson Taylor saw that he must act on his own initiative.

Meanwhile comments and questions were not wanting that made the position more trying. 'Is it true that a medical man is about to join you, with a wife and family? When did you hear it? Why did you not tell us? Have you bought land? Why do you not begin to build?' And so forth! To all of which no satisfactory replies were forthcoming.

The more he thought over the situation, the more he felt that there was nothing for it but to seek a native house in the Chinese part of the Settlement, in which to receive the travellers who were drawing nearer every day. So in spite of overpowering heat and his lack of a sedan-chair, he set about the weary search once more. It was four or five months now since he had hunted for quarters on his first arrival without finding even a room available, and if anything the conditions seemed worse than before. Hudson Taylor would have been almost in despair, had he not been learning precious lessons of his own helplessness – and of Almighty strength.

'As you know,' he wrote in July, 'I have been much tried since coming here, "pressed beyond measure" almost at times. But the goodness of God is never-failing; and the last few days I have enjoyed such a sweet sense of His love, and such a personal application of some of the promises as though they were written or spoken directly to me, that the oil of joy has indeed been given me for mourning. I feel sure that dear friends in England have been specially remembering me in prayer, and I am truly grateful.'

CHAPTER 6

Building in Troublous Times

(1854)

IT MUST have seemed almost too good to be true when only two days later Hudson Taylor heard of a house, and before the month was over found himself in possession of premises large enough to accommodate his expected colleagues. Though it was only a native house, built of wood and very ramshackle, it was right among the people, near the North Gate of the Chinese city.

It did not all come about, however, as easily as the statement is made. The house first heard of was not the one finally obtained, nor was the price first demanded one that he could or would give; and between the two lay much weary negotiation that had to be carried on through interpreters and deepened the debt he was already under to other missionaries. And even when the agreement was signed and sealed, much yet remained to be accomplished.

My house has twelve rooms, doors without end, passages innumerable, outhouses everywhere, and all covered with dust, filth, rubbish and refuse. What all the outhouses have been for I cannot imagine. There are no less than thirty-six of them, none of which I want or shall use. I have been getting a whole batch of doors fastened up, for however well it may suit a Chinese to have six or eight ways into his house, it does not please me at all just now. I see how to arrange it so that with one pair of gates I can shut off the dwelling itself from all the outhouses.

But he had had no experience so far of unsupervised workmen. One August day, in spite of overpowering heat, he got a few men to clear the place and remove rubbish. Early next morning he was on the scene again and discovered his men absorbed in watching the bricklayers, never dreaming of setting to work themselves. Having found them plenty to do, he went to inquire about a box expected from Hong Kong. Returning in an hour, what was his surprise to find one man writing, another smoking and the rest asleep. The third time he came it still seemed as though nothing had been done.

'So I have brought over my desk and a chair,' he wrote that afternoon, 'to remain on the premises; and even so they perpetually relapse into idleness. I say, for instance, "Now this must be thoroughly washed". For a while there is a noise of splashing, but soon all is still. I go to see, and the man looks quite astonished when I remark that only the outside has been cleaned. "Oh," he replies, "you want within-and-without washing." "Yes," I say, "I do," and return to my letter for a few minutes. Amusing though it may seem at first, this kind of thing becomes wearisome, especially when one can get nothing else.'

It was, however, the least serious part of the new life he was undertaking. The unavoidable outlay weighed on his mind far more.

'To save the expense of a sedan,' he wrote to his mother, 'I have tried staying indoors altogether during the great heat, or walking out only in the evening; but several attacks of illness as well as threatenings of ague have warned me to desist.

'These things sometimes make me cry with David, "My flesh and my heart faileth". But that is not his last word; and by grace I too can add, "God is the strength of my heart and my portion for ever." Though often cast down, I am where I would be and as I would be – save for more likeness to Christ and more familiarity with the language.'

Still more serious than the question of expense, however, was the danger involved in his intended move. Not only was he leaving the Settlement, to live entirely alone among the Chinese, he was going to a house very near the Imperial camp and within range of the guns of both parties. It was a position, as he well knew, of considerable danger, but no other residence had been procurable and the time had come when something must be done.

I am thankful that my way is hedged up on every side, so that no choice is left me. I am obliged to go forward, and if you hear of my being killed or injured, do not think it a pity that I came, but thank God I was permitted to distribute some Scriptures and tracts and to speak a few words in broken Chinese for Him who died for me.

On August 30 Hudson Taylor bade farewell to the kind host who for six months had afforded him a home, and, near the North Gate of the native city, set up housekeeping. In the solitude that was now his lot, the soul began to revive again and grow as the blessing of the far-away days at Drainside seemed to come back. He lived his own life as then, the simple self-denying life in which brighter spiritual experience seemed possible.

It was now September, almost a year from the time he had left home, and his joy in being able to do something for the people round him was very great. His new teacher was an earnest Christian, and able to conduct morning and evening worship to which all who came were made welcome. After this there were patients to see, visitors to entertain and housekeeping to attend to, in all of which Teacher Sï was indispensable. His pupil, too, was rapidly learning useful terms and polite phrases, as well as carefully chosen sentences in which to convey the Gospel. On Sundays they went out together to distribute tracts and preach in the crowded streets. The dispensary was making many friends, and when a day school was added both for boys and girls they had no lack of occupation. Before long, Sï had to give all his time to these operations, and another teacher was engaged for the language. And then, with everything in working order and his heart full of the blessing of the Lord, Hudson Taylor began to taste some of the real joys of missionary life.

To this period belongs a letter to his parents which shows the cheerful spirit in which he was working.

NORTH GATE, SHANGHAI,
September 20, 1854.

MY DEAR FATHER AND MOTHER – Whether you weary of my letters or not, I cannot but write them, and I will take it for granted that this one at any rate will be welcome, as it is to inform you that the experiment made in coming to this house has been so far successful, and that now though not doing much I am at any rate doing something. . . . I can assure you I do not spend much time in bed – as I never go till I can keep awake no longer.

The other day I had an interesting excursion to Woosung with Mr. Edkins and a young American missionary named Quaterman. We went by boat arriving there at noon, with a large supply of Scriptures and tracts. These we distributed on many junks going northward, receiving promises from not a few captains and others that they would read them and pass them on to friends in the ports to which they were travelling.

Returning home in the evening well pleased with our excursion, we were puzzled to know how we should pass the Imperial fleet in safety. They are somewhat random with their fire after dark, and might easily have taken us for Chinese, if not Rebel spies. Mr. Edkins came to the rescue, proposing that we should sing as we passed them, that they might know we were foreigners. The suggestion seemed good and the boatmen were pleased with the idea, the only objection being that as we had already been singing a good deal we had exhausted all the hymns and tunes we had in common and were more than ready for a rest.

Having perfected our arrangements, we approached some ships we took to be the fleet, and passed them singing lustily. But just as we were about to congratulate one another on our success, the boatmen shouted to us to recommence, as we had been mistaken in what we supposed to have been the fleet and were just coming within range of their guns.

So we had to tune up again without delay, and sang 'The spacious firmament on high', to that beautiful tune *Creation*. Unfortunately we concluded just opposite the largest ship of the fleet. It was now quite dusk.

'What next?' cried Mr. Edkins, as the alarm-gong struck on board the ship. 'There is not a moment to lose.'

He then commenced singing I know not what. Quaterman struck up a truly American tune to 'Blow ye the trumpet, blow!' while I at the same moment raised a third with all the voice I could command. The men on the warship were shouting loudly, our boat's crew outdoing them if possible, and the whole thing was so ludicrous that I could control myself no longer and burst into a fit of laughter most inappropriate to the occasion.

'Who goes there?' was shouted from the Imperial ship.

'*Peh-kuei*' (white devils), yelled our men, while we cried simultaneously, '*Ta Ing-kueh*' (Great English Nation) and '*Hua-chu-kueh*', which means Flowery Flag Country, or America.

After a little further explanation we were allowed to pass, upon which my companions began to lecture the boatmen for having called us "white devils". The poor men who had not yet received their day's pay were very penitent, and explained that they had been so frightened that they really did not know what they were saying and would be most careful to refrain from such expressions in future.

My eyes, the lamp and paper alike inform me that I must be drawing to a close. But I must not forget to tell you that the other day a Sungkiang man presented me with a couple of valuable crickets in a glass box. They require two freshly boiled grains of rice daily, and are kept on account of their song, which is quite different from the sound made by English crickets, and very pleasant.

And now Good-night, or rather Good-morning. – Ever my dear parents, your affectionate son,

J. HUDSON TAYLOR.

Mingled with joy in his new work, however, came difficulties, great and small – problems of household management, quarrels between his servants and the neighbours, anxiety about his cook who was laid up with typhus fever, disappointment with the second teacher who had to be dismissed, great discouragement about the language, and repeated attacks of illness that left him low-spirited and unfit to bear the strain of constant skirmishing so close at hand.

'There has been a great deal of fighting for several days,' he wrote in the middle of September, 'and the Rebels have been gathering at the bottom of this street. Several cannon balls have passed near these premises. It is easy to tell whether a gun is loaded or not, as the ball makes a *whizz* which once heard is not likely to be forgotten.'

Beside all this, he was increasingly burdened about money matters. Obliged to exceed his salary for the necessities of life, he had made use of a Letter of Credit provided against emergencies, but was still uncertain as to how far his bills would be honoured. This cost him many a wakeful night as well as many a prayer.

Thus September ended, and looking back upon it he could say:

Though in some ways I never passed a more anxious month in my life, I have never felt so conscious of God's presence with me. I begin to enjoy the sweet, peaceful rest in the Lord and in His promises experienced first in Hull. That was the brightest part of my spiritual life, and how poor at the best! Since then I have been in a declining state, but the Lord has brought me back; and as there is no standing still in these things, I trust to go on to apprehend heights and depths, lengths and breadths of love divine far exceeding anything I have yet entered into. May God grant it, for Jesus' sake.

One cannot but be impressed in reading the letters of this period with the sacred ambition of Hudson Taylor's prayers; a subject worth pondering, if it is true that prayer, not circumstances, moulds the life, and that as are our deepest desires before God so will the trend of our outward experiences be. Certainly nothing is more significant in the life before us than the longing for usefulness and likeness to the Lord he loved. Not honour or success, but usefulness, 'widespread usefulness', was his constant prayer.

His prayers were indeed to be answered beyond anything he asked or thought; but he must pray with yet fuller meaning, and go through with all the training needed at the Master's hands. The iron must be tempered to steel, and his heart made stronger and more tender than others, through having loved and suffered more, with God. He was pioneering a way in China, little as he or anyone else could imagine it, for hundreds who were to follow. Every burden must be his, every trial known as only experience can teach it. He who was to be used of God to dry so many tears, must himself weep. He who was to encourage thousands in a life of childlike trust, must learn in his own case deep lessons of a Father's loving care. So difficulties were permitted to gather about him, especially at first when every impression was vivid and lasting, difficulties attended by many a deliverance to encourage him.

As much of his usefulness later on was to consist in helping and providing for young missionaries, it is not to be wondered at that a large part of his preparation at this time had to do with financial matters and the unintentional mismanagement of the home Committee. He had to learn how to do and how not to do for those who on the human side would be dependent on him; a lesson of vital importance, lying at the very foundation of his future work. Hence all this trial about a small, settled income and large uncertain needs; about irregularity of mails and long-unanswered letters; about rapidly changing opportunities of service on the field, and the slow-moving ideas and inaccessibility of Committees at home. He did his best, and the inexperienced Secretaries in London did their best also. But something, somehow, was wanting; and just what it was Hudson Taylor had to discover, and later on to remedy. The iron was entering into his very soul; but from this long endurance was to spring heart's ease for many another.

NORTH GATE, SHANGHAI,
October 17, 1854.

MY DEAR PARENTS – You wish to know all about my pecuniary as well as other affairs, so I am enclosing a copy of a list of expenses I am just forwarding to Mr.

Pearse. As you will perceive, they so largely exceed the sum we were led to suppose would be sufficient (£80 per annum) that I am sending full details, so that the Secretaries can see for themselves. I shall have to draw again this year, probably next month. I am not sure that I can get credit, for my authorization from the Society does not exceed £40 a quarter, and if the agents here knew that I had just received a copy of the Committee's Resolution stating that they will not accept bills for more than that amount, of course it would be refused.

You will not wonder that anxiety about expenses and as to whether my bills will be honoured or not, added to the dangers of my present position, has proved rather much for me lately. I have been very poorly for a fortnight.

Everything is dear in Shanghai now, Chinese as well as foreign goods. Just to think that in seven months I have spent more than £100! Is it not frightful? £200 per annum will barely cover my expenses, unless the exchange falls, and other things too. The Church Missionary Society allows single men $700 (about £210 at the present rate of exchange) beside paying rent, medical expenses, and a sum sufficient for Chinese teacher and books.

Saturday, Oct. 21. It is very cold today. I am better than I was earlier in the week, but still far from well. Fortunately I have been able to buy a second-hand stove for ten dollars that will burn wood. A new one would have cost thirty. And now having had another month's expenses to settle, I have only twelve dollars left. What can I do? I must draw soon. And even if I can get a bill accepted here, I am in terror of its being refused by the Committee, which would put me in a pretty fix. I think and study night and day, and cannot tell what to do.

Last Wednesday night, a fire that seemed very near awoke me at three o'clock in the morning. Dressing hastily, I climbed on to the roof to ascertain if it were coming this way. Chinese houses like these, built only of wood, burn very quickly on a windy night. It was an anxious moment, for in the darkness I fancied the burning building was only four or five doors away. Just then, as I was praying earnestly for protection, it began to rain. The wind fell, for which I was most thankful, and gradually the fire smouldered down.

I have never passed, as you will well believe, such a trying time in my life. But it is all necessary, and I feel is being made a blessing to me. I may have to leave here suddenly. But whatever happens, I do not regret coming to this house, and would do it again under similar circumstances. Our Society must provide better, however, for its missionaries. This sort of thing will not do.

I must now conclude, trusting that the Lord, who is precious to me in my extremity, is proving Himself near also to you. – With love. Believe me, your ever affectionate son,

J. Hudson Taylor.

That Resolution of the Committee not to honour bills exceeding £40 a quarter hurt like a wound inflicted by one from whom he had expected sympathy. In a letter to Mr. Pearse of November 2, he expressed himself as follows:

And lastly, in reference to the Resolution of June 29, 1854: your Board ought to be very careful how they bind their Secretaries to such a course in present times. Your missionaries are sent into a country in a state of revolution, where it is literally true that they know not what a day or an hour may bring forth. They should be well provided against contingencies before you adopt such an *ultra* measure, a measure that would at once and for ever destroy their credit, if they have any, and compared with which their dismissal by the Society would not be severe. At any rate, if not accepted, such bills should not be positively refused before you hear the reasons which led to their being drawn. But more I need not say. Your hearts are in the work as well as mine, and I know you will excuse these remarks when you remember that half the world lies between us.

Crisp, sharp autumn weather had now set in, forecasting the bitter cold of winter. His Chinese house was not only unwarmed but unwarmable, draughts sweeping through it mercilessly, from unnumbered cracks and crevices. His blankets, only two in number, were fit for nothing but summer use, and all the clothing he had brought from home was now so shabby that he was ashamed to be seen amongst other foreigners. Yet he had far exceeded his allowance, and dared not spend a penny save for actual necessities. And to add to his perplexity he was driven to see that the house he had secured with so much difficulty in view of the arrival of the Parkers would not be a place they could come to even for a night.

Three weeks later he wrote again to the Secretaries:

There is a great deal of firing going on here now, so much so that I am seldom able to get half a night's sleep. What Dr. Parker and his family are to do, I do not know. Their coming here as things are now is out of the question. This constant anxiety for them as well as myself, together with another still more trying (the expense I am unable to avoid) is by no means a desirable addition to the difficulties of language and climate.

We have heard nothing of the *Swiftsure*, but she is hardly due as yet. I shall be thankful when Dr. Parker is here and we are able to consult together about the future.

Pray for me, for I am almost pressed beyond measure, and were it not that I find the Word of God increasingly precious and feel His presence with me, I do not know what I should do.

But the Lord knew, and He had not forgotten His tried servant. At that very moment, when the *Swiftsure* was nearing the end of her long and perilous voyage, the Lord had a home in view into which to receive the Parkers and their children. He was not shut up to the house on the North Gate Street, though Hudson Taylor was; and just in time, when lessons had been learned that He saw to be needed, the way was opened to a safer residence.

On the compound of the London Missionary Society, through the coming of a great sorrow, a little house stood empty that in comparison with Hudson Taylor's quarters offered a haven of security and peace. Shadowed as it was with the suffering of his dearest friends in China, the Burdons, he had not thought of it as other than their home. There he had found them in their early married life, rejoiced with them in the gift of a precious child, and shared the bereavement that only a few months later left the little girl motherless. Then he had helped Burdon to move with his infant daughter to the care of the Chaplain's household. The little house at *Ma-ka-k'üen* stood empty, and just as the situation of the native city was becoming desperate, word was sent to Hudson Taylor that if he wanted Burdon's house he could take it at once. Paying the rent out of his own meagre resources, he secured a home for the family so soon to arrive in the Settlement.

Then he was urged to sublet half the premises to another missionary in distress who, not knowing where to take his wife and children for safety, was thankful to pay half the rent. True, the house was very small for two families, but it was a relief to have his financial obligations lessened and a comfort to be able to help somebody else. So with many regrets at parting from his school-children and neighbours, Hudson Taylor left the scenes in which he had commenced his first direct missionary work, and on Saturday, November 25, returned to a house shared with others on the familiar compound of the London Missionary Society.

Two days later he was again at the North Gate to remove the last of his belongings, when he was recalled by a message from Dr. Lockhart. Hurrying back with many conjectures as to what the summons might mean, he found the doctor at lunch with a pleasant-looking stranger – none other than his own long-expected colleague, Dr. Parker. So they had come at last! And he was only just in time with arrangements for their accommodation.

At first in the joy of meeting and all the excitement of bringing up their belongings from the ship, Hudson Taylor had hardly time to realize how the narrowness of their quarters would strike his new-found friends. But when they were all in them, including the baby whose first appearance had been made at sea, the three rooms seemed even more crowded than he had feared they would be. Strong, sensible Scots people, the Parkers were quite prepared to put up with hardships, and accommodated themselves to the situation as well as could be expected. But to Hudson Taylor it was a painful experience to have to reveal the pitifulness of his preparations.

If the rooms had been suitably furnished it would have been another matter; but his Chinese bed, two or three square tables, and half a dozen chairs seem to have been all that he possessed. He had only just moved in on Saturday night, and had not had time to get into working order, and now the sudden advent of a family with all their paraphernalia made confusion worse confounded, and the despair of a thrifty housewife with three little children to provide for may be better imagined than described.

Oh, the trying, difficult days that followed, could they ever be forgotten! For to make matters worse, the Shanghai community began to call upon the new arrivals, and those with whom Hudson Taylor was acquainted were not sparing in their comments upon what seemed his negligence.

It was all very well for him to live in Chinese style if he liked, and put up with a hundred and one discomforts. But people who knew what was what could not be expected to fall in with such ways. Why had he not furnished their rooms properly, and provided warm carpets and curtains? Did he not know that children must be protected from the bitter cold of winter? Had he no stoves in readiness, no proper supply of fuel? Had he not written to tell them that they would need warm clothes and bedding on their arrival in November? And as to unpacking and getting settled, how could it be done without shelves or cupboards, chests of drawers or book-cases in which to stow their belongings?

All of which was true, no doubt, and unanswerable; for how could the young missionary let it be known that he had gone far beyond the limits of authorized expenditure in taking the house at all; that he had done it entirely on his own responsibility, and that after paying the first instalment of rent he had been left with only two or three dollars in hand, not enough to cover a week's expenses?

His hope was, of course, that Dr. Parker would be supplied with all that was necessary, and would be the bearer of instructions from the Society about Mission headquarters in Shanghai or elsewhere, as well as some more satisfactory arrangement for financial transactions in the future. The very reverse, however, was the case. Dr. Parker had nothing with him but a few dollars for immediate use. He was expecting a Letter of Credit to be awaiting him in Shanghai, understood to have been sent off before he left England. As to supplies, they had abundance of clothing for the tropics, but had not been at all prepared for cold weather, so that the children were in immediate need of winter outfits. And for the rest, nothing had been said about how they were to live and work in Shanghai, or in what way their salary was to reach them. All this they seem to have taken for granted that Hudson Taylor would be able to arrange.

No special anxiety was felt as yet, however. A large mail was waiting their arrival, and among the letters would doubtless be one containing the document on which so much depended. The Secretaries had assured Dr. Parker while he was still in London that his Letter of Credit, if not already on its way to Shanghai, would be there long before his own arrival. But on going through his mail he found no trace of it. The Letter of Credit had evidently been overlooked and forgotten.

Another mail was due within a day or two, however, and that no doubt would put matters right. In the meanwhile, they were thankful for the little preparation Hudson Taylor had been able to make, and with his few dollars and their own laid in a small supply of what was indispensable.

The mail came in. Yes, there were letters from the Secretaries dated September 15, more than three months after the Parkers had left London. There seemed to be no enclosures; but perhaps they had sent the Letter of Credit direct to their Shanghai agents, and would mention having done so. No, nothing was said about it. There was positively no allusion to the matter. What could be the meaning of such an omission? To Dr. Parker it seemed inexplicable. But Hudson Taylor, with more experience of the working of things, was not altogether surprised, and found it less easy to be hopeful, though he acceded to the only suggestion that could be made, that they should go at once to the agents and inquire. Dr. Parker was satisfied that this must bring a conclusion to their difficulties, so with a light heart as far as he was concerned they presented themselves at the office of Messrs. Gibb, Livingston and Co.

Hudson Taylor had had dealings before with the manager of this firm, and though he had found him a friend in need on more than one occasion, it was not possible to forget the sarcasm of some of his remarks, nor the emphasis with which he said, 'The management or rather mismanagement of your Society is very bad.' It was with some trepidation, therefore, he introduced Dr. Parker and asked if any advice had been received as to his Letter of Credit.

'No,' answered the manager promptly, 'none.'

'Is it possible,' queried Dr. Parker, 'that you have heard nothing from the Society as to the amount I am entitled to draw?'

'It is more than possible,' replied the manager, 'to judge by past experiences'; though when he saw how this information was received, he was inclined to be more sympathetic.

Humiliating as the position was in itself, it was rendered still more so by the necessity they were under of explaining matters to this comparative stranger, with his prompt, efficient, business-like ways, upon whom for the time being they were dependent. If he had not seen fit to advance them money upon such evidence of their genuineness as they could afford, they would have been reduced to sore straits indeed. But his friendliness, both then and after, was the Lord's way of answering their prayers, and providing for them in the absence of the Letter of Credit that for long months did not make its appearance.

Dr. Parker said little about all this, but he must have felt it keenly, and probably all the more so as he came to realize the tempting possibilities opened to him as a medical man in China. How easily he could have supported his family in comfort, had he been willing to turn aside from missionary work! But in spite of poverty and many privations, prolonged all through the winter, spring, and the following summer, he and his wife held on their way with quiet self-sacrifice that never wavered.

From the first Sunday after landing, he went out regularly with Hudson Taylor to evangelize in the city or surrounding villages, and frequently made longer excursions, giving away tracts and attending to simple ailments, while others more familiar with the language did the talking. And at home in their crowded quarters he devoted himself assiduously to study, although the only place to do it was in Hudson Taylor's room next to the nursery.

'No one who has not experienced it', Hudson Taylor wrote, 'can understand the effect of such incessant strain on mind and body. It makes one so nervous and irritable that we sorely need your prayers as well as our own to enable us at all times to manifest a proper spirit.

'How gracious of God thus to keep us from being deluded into supposing that we are free from the evils that belong to fallen nature, and to make us long the more earnestly for the time when we shall see our blessed Master and be perfected in His likeness. Thank the Lord, there *does* remain a rest for us. I am so apt to grow weary and selfishly wish I were there, instead of desiring only to do His will and wait His time; to follow the footsteps of Jesus and finish all that He will give me to do. Indeed, the work of grace seems only just begun in my heart. I have been an unfruitful branch, and need no small amount of pruning. May these present trials result only in blessing, preparing me for more extensive usefulness here and a crown of rejoicing hereafter.'

'The continued strain to which I have been subjected of late,' he wrote in another letter, 'has caused a degree of nervous irritability never before experienced, requiring the greatest watchfulness to prevent the manifestation of an unsuitable spirit before those by whom I am surrounded. What a solemn thing it is to be a *witness* for God, sent into the midst of heathen darkness to show forth in our lives all that by our words we teach. Pray for me that I may have more grace, humility and reliance on the power of God, that I may prove henceforth more efficient, by His blessing, in this holy service.'

Somewhat different in tone was the first letter addressed to Mr. Pearse after the arrival of Dr. Parker and his family. In addition to their own difficulties about which he had to write, Hudson Taylor was suffering from imprudent statements in *The Gleaner* calculated to give serious offence to the L.M.S. missionaries in Shanghai; 'men who,' as he put it, 'however much you may differ from them in judgment, are more thoughtful for the shelter and support of your missionaries than the Society that sends them out, if not more wishful.'

I trust you will not deem it unkind or disrespectful of me to write thus. For though

I feel these things and feel them keenly, were it not for the sake of others and the good of the Society I would pass over them in silence. To do this, however, would be unfaithfulness on my part. For not only is it morally wrong and thoughtless in the extreme to act as the Society has acted towards Dr. Parker, but you must surely see that men who can quadruple their salary by professional practice, or double it by taking a clerk's berth will not be likely, if they find themselves totally unprovided for, to continue in the service of the Society. I do not make these remarks with respect to Dr. Parker, who seems thoroughly devoted to the work and by his spirit has encouraged me not a little. But they are true none the less. And I may add that a vacant post at £200 a year, the whole duties of which would not occupy two hours in the evening, did look inviting to me at a time when I had been obliged to incur a responsibility of £120 for rent, and a Resolution upon my last letter to the Committee informed me that missionaries drawing more than was authorized would not have their bills honoured by the Society.

Dr. Parker arrived on Monday, a week ago today, calling forth true gratitude to God for deliverance from the many dangers that had beset their path. Of course he found our half of the house nearly empty, as my few things did not go far in furnishing. The missionaries, when they discovered this lack of preparation, blamed me very much. Could I tell them that having paid nearly £20 for rent I had only three dollars left, a sum not sufficient to purchase provisions for a week at the present high rate of prices?

Fortunately Dr. Parker had a few dollars, for which, however, we had to give twenty to thirty per cent discount to get them into cash. He was not a little surprised to find that Mr. Bird's communication contained no Letter of Credit nor allusion to one. And when I learned that he had none with him, I was no less astonished. And while we both cherish the warmest and most affectionate regard for many members of the Committee personally, and especially for its Secretaries, we cannot but feel that the Society has acted disgracefully.

Difficulties notwithstanding, they tackled their work bravely, and between long, busy Sundays among the people, settled down as well as they could to study. It was almost impossible to concentrate attention upon the language at this time, for the condition of the people around them was heart-rending. Hundreds were dying of cold and starvation, and there seemed no hope of relief until one side or other could win a decisive victory.

For still the Rebels would not yield, although the French in violation of their promised neutrality were taking sides more and more against them. A French frigate and steamer stationed opposite the native city deliberately cut off supplies that might have come to it by water, while on land the same end was served by a massive wall built and guarded by French forces. All this, it was becoming evident, was part of a Jesuit policy bent on supporting the reigning dynasty. For the Taipings and other insurgents were confessedly hostile not only to idolatry in all its forms, but to Roman priestcraft and image worship, and to the growing habit of opium smoking. If success crowned their long and desperate struggle, Romanism as well as opium and idolatry were bound to fall before them, and this was known at the Vatican as well as at the Court of St. James. First the French therefore and later on the English lent efficient aid to the Imperial cause, and the activity of the former in Shanghai at this time was the beginning of the foreign interference which ultimately led to the suppression of the Taiping movement.

Ever since the arrival of Dr. Parker, this open interference on the part of the French had been rousing the hatred of the Rebel soldiery. Their attitude was becoming menacing, and the Chinese who favoured their cause, both in and around the Settlement, were plotting revenge upon the whole European community. This made evangelistic work both difficult and dangerous, and might not unreasonably have formed an excuse for lessened activity for the time being. But as far as the missionaries on the L.M.S. compound were concerned it had no such effect. Dr. Medhurst and his colleagues still planned and carried out their excursions to the interior, as well as constant evangelization in the neighbourhood of Shanghai; and Dr. Parker made many visits in company with Hudson Taylor to towns and villages within a radius of ten or fifteen miles. Down the Hwangpu River they went, and up the creeks and canals where shipping congregated, everywhere searching out serious and intelligent persons with whom to leave Scriptures and tracts. In this way in the month of December alone they distributed many hundreds of New Testaments and Gospels, together with a still larger number of tracts explaining the way of life.

'These have been given with all possible care,' wrote Hudson Taylor to the Committee, 'and in most cases to men who we knew were able to read. A considerable number were taken on junks travelling to the northern provinces.'

But before the year closed an opportunity came for more aggressive efforts. An invitation came to him from Edkins to accompany him on a journey to Kashing-fu, a notable centre of wealth and industry inland. On Saturday, 16 December 1854, therefore, Hudson Taylor set out on his first inland evangelistic journey.

CHAPTER 7

First Evangelistic Journeys

(1854–1855)

EVERYTHING had an interest all its own that first night aboard the Chinese one-sail houseboat that was to be their home for a week. Anchored amid a fleet of other boats, they were out among the people at last, as Taylor had so often longed to be. Each boat had its family as well as crew, and cheerful was the clatter that went on while the evening meal was in preparation. Rising before daylight means retiring early, however, and soon the only sound the young missionary heard above the soft lapping of the water was the gong of the night-watchman along the shore. With the turn of the tide after midnight, a stir began on the boats. Anchors were drawn up, sails hoisted, and the junks got under way. But the two travellers slept on to find themselves, on awaking, some forty miles south of Shanghai, within sight of the Fu city[1] of Sungkiang.

It was here that Hudson Taylor saw, for the first time, a Buddhist recluse. Edkins and he had come to a temple courtyard where a great crowd gathered to gaze at the strange sight of religious teachers in the dress of western lands, and listen to their preaching. The foreigners were giving away books as well, and not until their supply was exhausted did they make a move to pass on. Some of the monks then pressed forward, inviting them to rest awhile in the monastery, and especially to visit the 'holy man'. Surrounded by the yellow-robed, shaven-headed priests, the missionaries were escorted to the cell where the poor devotee had been walled up for years. The only access was a small opening left when the wall was in process of building, through which a man could scarcely pass his hand. Edkins spoke to him, and very earnest were their prayers that the 'glad tidings of great joy', heard under these circumstances for the first time, might bring light and salvation to his soul.

In the same city a very different experience awaited them, and one that made them appreciate the eighty-nine stone bridges to be found within its walls. Followed by a noisy rabble as they were seeking their boat, the visitors turned down a side street leading to a landing-stage, which they took to be that of the public ferry. To their dismay it was a private wharf protected

[1] A *Fu* was the governing city of a prefecture (or group of counties), seven to fourteen of which went to make up a province. The word was also applied to the prefect or Mandarin.

by a pair of gates they had hardly noticed in passing. To return by the way they had come was impossible, for the narrow street was filled with an uproarious crowd, who, to prevent escape in that direction, swung to the gates and swarmed all over them, watching between the bars for the next move of the strangers. The position was far from pleasant in an unknown city, with the crowd growing larger and more noisy all the time, and no bridge in sight. But the missionaries quietly looked to the Lord in prayer, and kept their wits about them.

'There were plenty of boats at hand,' wrote Hudson Taylor, 'but none of them would take us. We called to several, to the great amusement of the crowd, but in vain. At length seeing that something must be done I took "French leave", jumped into a boat that was passing, and pulled it to the side for Mr. Edkins. Taken by surprise the men made no objection, and off we went to the chagrin of our tormentors who opened the gates and rushed to the waterside shouting tumultuously.'

Before leaving the city that night, a second or third supply of literature being all distributed, a turn in the road brought them suddenly on the base of the Square Pagoda. Grey and imposing the massive structure rose before them that for 900 years had been the glory of Sungkiang. The priest in charge consented to admit them, and soon the crowding of the streets gave place to the sombre quiet of the old pagoda and the view to be seen from a gallery near the top.

Long and silently they stood looking down upon the myriad homes outspread before them. Far reached the ancient wall enclosing its hundreds of thousands, and beyond it the tent-like roofs still stretched away toward the setting sun. And this was only one great centre. All about it lay the rich, level country, dotted as far as eye could see with villages and hamlets, while distant pagodas and temples told of other cities within easy reach.

It was the first time Hudson Taylor had looked out on such a scene, and the fact of China's immense population began to assume new meaning from that hour.

On returning to Shanghai he had to face, with Dr. Parker, extreme perplexity in money matters, for nothing had yet been heard of the missing Letter of Credit. Tidings that new missionaries of the L.M.S. were about to sail for China reminded them that even the premises they now occupied would have to be vacated before long. This it was that gave urgency and definiteness to their consultations, and resulted in several letters setting forth 'plans of usefulness', that for the next few months largely occupied their thoughts.

To begin with, a permanent centre was needed and must be obtained without delay. Of the five Treaty Ports open to the residence of foreigners, none was more suitable than Shanghai – within reach of many important cities, and holding a strategic position with regard to mid-China. In Shanghai, therefore, their headquarters should be located.

This again necessitated a certain adequacy of method and equipment, they felt, for other missions were there before them, and had established precedents that could not be ignored. Plan as simply as they might, they would at least require a doctor's house and a school building, in addition to hospital and dispensary. From this central station, their plan was to visit the surrounding country and establish branch-schools and dispensaries wherever possible. These would be regularly supervised by one or other of the missionaries, and would become in their turn centres of Christian effort.

It was all admirable no doubt, and the estimate of £1,000 for land and buildings was not immoderate. But it was based upon conclusions that in their case were misleading, and just because the good is often the enemy of the best, would have thwarted their real life-usefulness, foreordained in the purposes of God.

Meanwhile, little as he realized what it foreshadowed, Hudson Taylor found himself unable to disregard the appeal of the unreached. He was working hard at two dialects, and also carrying on a school, but the need of the unevangelized regions pressed heavily on him. The ice had been broken. He had been on one evangelistic tour already, and had seen how such work could be done. Perhaps it was this that drew him on? Perhaps it was something deeper, more significant.

At any rate, he set out again, this time without a companion, travelling in a boat he had bought for half its value. A few miles south of Shanghai a tributary stream was reached, leading to a district little known to foreigners. Lying between the Hwangpu river and the coast, the region was one infested with smugglers, and even its larger centres of population had rarely if ever been visited with the Gospel. Travelling on far into the night, however, he was conscious of a Presence that precluded fear, and robbed the unknown of its possible terrors.

Far from promising must have seemed the awakening, however, when they found themselves next morning frozen in between high, snow-covered banks, the water covered with a thick coating of ice, necessitating breaking a channel for the boat a foot at a time.

Slow progress was all that they could make. Accompanied by a servant to carry books, the undeterred young missionary went ashore and walked from hamlet to hamlet. His dress, speech and occupation everywhere aroused the intensest interest, and great was the eagerness to obtain his beautifully bound and printed books.

Two governing cities and a market town were visited on this journey, besides many villages. In reading the journal one is surprised at the thoroughness with which the work was done. Every street in Chwansha was visited, for example, and in each of the suburbs; all the reading men he could find being supplied with gospels and tracts. There was no companion to fall back upon, and unless he preached himself the people might never hear. So looking to the Lord for help, Hudson Taylor made the most of his few sentences, following up long days ashore with hours of medical work and private conversation on the boat at night.

Not until late on February 1 did he return to Shanghai, but once there he promptly gave attention to a matter that was specially on his heart.

A few weeks previously, three men of his acquaintance had been seized in the North Gate house, dragged out of bed in the middle of the night, and handed over as rebels to the local authorities. Upon hearing of it the young missionary had at once sought their release. But though assured that they would soon be at liberty, no charge having been proved against them, the poor fellows were only hurried from prison to prison, everywhere starved and tortured to make them confess alleged crimes. Again and again Hudson Taylor had appealed on their behalf, but as long as there was any chance of extorting money the case seemed hopeless. Now, returning encouraged from his journey, he went once more and to his great joy was successful. The men still lived, and before long he had the satisfaction of seeing them in such comfort as their homes could afford.

But how small a thing it seemed to relieve the sufferings of one group of people amid all the horrors that were going on! Shanghai was in a worse condition than ever, if that were possible. After more than a year of desultory fighting, the Imperial forces seemed roused at length to take the city. A large new camp quite near the Settlement had cut off the last hope of relief on the landward side, and it was only too evident that a wholesale massacre would be the end of the tragedy.

It happened shortly after Hudson Taylor, this time in company with older missionaries, had set out on another preaching tour. The little party had apparently travelled as far as Tsingpu when they saw from the top of a hill the smoke of an immense conflagration. So great a fire in that direction could mean but one thing. Shanghai was in flames! And what of their families in the foreign Settlement?

Setting out at once to return, their apprehensions were confirmed by Rebel soldiers who met them, seeking protection. This the defenceless missionaries were unable to afford; and shortly after the poor fellows were taken and beheaded before their eyes. Silently continuing their journey, they soon came upon abundant traces of the catastrophe that had taken place, and as they passed the native city had to turn away from sights of horror on every hand.

'Shanghai is now in peace,' Hudson Taylor wrote on March 4, 'but it is like the peace of death. 2,000 people at the very least have perished, and the tortures some of the victims have undergone cannot have been exceeded by the worst barbarities of the Inquisition. The city is little more than a mass of ruins. From the South to the North Gate, on one side only, sixty-six heads and several bodies are exposed by the sanguinary Imperialists, including those of old men with white hair, women and children.'

Thus ended in a holocaust of human lives the sufferings of the siege that had been in progress ever since Hudson Taylor's arrival in China twelve months previously. But the worst was over, and relieved from the strain of that terrible winter the missionaries looked forward to largely increasing their work. A new Shanghai would soon arise upon the ruins. As far as possible they must purchase land before it was taken up, enlarge their schools, open preaching halls, found hospitals; and take a front rank among the builders of the new time.

The hearts of Hudson Taylor and his colleagues, still anxiously waiting the reply of the Committee, were stirred. Three months had now elapsed since their plans had been laid before the Society, and communications that had crossed their own had not been encouraging. Meanwhile it was more and more difficult to wait on in uncertainty. The American missionary who shared their little house was building premises of his own, but Dr. Parker's Letter of Credit had not come, nor did the Society seem to remember that he had any financial needs.

Missionaries, even the most devoted, are only human after all. Some things were said that hardly seem in keeping with Hudson Taylor's simple faith in God, as may be seen from his letters. In March he wrote to his parents,

You *are* going to have a fine chapel in Barnsley! I wish some wealthy friend would send us £1,000 to put up our hospital, school, and other premises, for we are in a shocking position now, with only three rooms to live in. What we are to do when the hot weather comes, I cannot imagine.

We have written to the Society laying a definite plan before them, and if they do not take it up we mean to try and carry it through without their aid. If they oppose it, as contrary to their principle of not working in the Ports, we must try to have the principle modified. And if they will not alter and we cannot find other better means of working, it may become a question as to which we shall dispense with – the Society, or our plans of usefulness.

But our plans will be formed with prudence, in the fear of the Lord, and not without seeking His direction. But useful we must and will be, if the Lord bless us, at any cost.

Do you think a bazaar could be got up anywhere, to assist us in the purchase of ground and erection of suitable buildings? If you could get the ladies interested, it would be sure to succeed. The sum we want is really so trifling that a few good collections would soon raise either the whole or the greater part.

But though carried away for the time, he was not allowed to involve himself in responsibilities that would have hindered his life-work. Strangely the currents mingled at this time – one drawing him to the settled life of the Ports, the other carrying him far afield, to regions beyond any that had yet been reached. He could not even wait for the expected reply of the Committee, so eager was he to set out upon another evangelistic journey. The local rebellion was at an end, Dr. Parker needed change from study, their boat was lying in the Creek – was it not just the opportunity for a preaching tour which should include a good deal of medical work?

Leaving Shanghai by the Soochow Creek they travelled north and west to the county town of Kiating, where a novel experience awaited them. Accustomed as they were to large, excited crowds, they hardly knew what to make of it when grown-up people as well as children fled in terror, so that the streets were literally cleared at their approach. Yet this was what happened in Kiating. No one would venture near them, and it was strange to see people of all classes hurrying to the nearest buildings as if for protection from imminent danger.

So strong were these unreasoning fears, due to the fantastic stories in circulation about foreigners, that it is doubtful whether any entrance could have been gained for more favourable impressions but for the influence of the medical work.

Realizing that in all probability they were the first foreigners to visit the city, Dr. Parker and his companion made it known that they were physicians, 'able to prescribe for both external and internal complaints', and that on the morrow they would *k'an-ping*, or 'investigate diseases', providing each patient gratuitously with the appropriate remedy. This seemed to turn the tide of popular feeling, and as they went about the streets and made the circuit of the city wall they heard many remarks as to their being *shan-ren*, or 'doers of good deeds'.

'Long before breakfast', wrote Dr. Parker of the following morning, 'the banks of the river were crowded with persons desiring medical aid. We were welcomed in some of the very houses the doors of which had been shut against us the day before.'

What a turning of the tables in favour of the missionary! and all due to ointments, pills, and powders, prescribed with sympathy and prayer. After this there was nothing but friendliness as they walked through the city, and they had all they could do to supply books to those who came for them.

Throughout the remainder of their journey the value of the medicine chest as an aid to evangelization was still further proved in a variety of ways. At one important city the missionaries were kept busy all day long handing gospels and tracts from the boat to a steady stream of applicants.

In his report of this journey Hudson Taylor stated that with Dr. Parker's help he had distributed during the first three months of the year 3,000 New Testaments and Scripture portions and more than 7,000 other books and tracts.

> The excursion from which we have just returned was particularly interesting for the illustration it afforded of the scarcely to be exaggerated value of medical work as an aid to missionary labour.
>
> The crying need for a hospital was brought home to us afresh by cases in which life or limb could have been saved and chronic diseases relieved had we been able to care for the sufferers. I sincerely trust that funds for this purpose are on the way to us. The door is widely open and no man can shut it.

But though these accounts and others of later journeys aroused much interest at home, the £1,000 needed was not forthcoming. Trying as was this long waiting and uncertainty, it was brightened by tokens for good, two of which took the form of especially encouraging financial help.

Of these gifts in aid of the work, one was handed to Dr. Parker by a resident, and consisted of fifty dollars toward the purchase of land for a hospital. The other, received by Hudson Taylor himself, had a special interest as being the first that ever came to him apart from the Society for the cause so dear to his heart.

And when one records the name of the donor, W. T. Berger of Saint Hill, near London, what a vista is opened up into the providence of God! Mr. Berger, a frequent visitor at the Tottenham Meeting, had met the young missionary on one or more occasions before he sailed for China. His interest had been awakened, no doubt deepened later by Hudson Taylor's letters from Shanghai. The result was this gift of £10, thankfully appropriated toward the support of a child the missionaries were anxious to adopt; a first step, as they hoped, toward a permanent boarding-school.

But how much more was in the plan of the Great Giver! Could Hudson Taylor have foreseen how many hundreds, even thousands of pounds would come to him through the same channel, and the still more important gifts of counsel, sympathy, and brotherly love in the work he and Mr. Berger were to do together for the Lord, how amazed and overwhelmed he would have been! But all this and far more was being brought to pass by Him who even then was working out His own purposes in the life of His servant.

Meanwhile Burdon and Hudson Taylor were responding to a new call. In the estuary of the Yangtze distant only thirty miles from Shanghai lay the great island of Tsungming. Sixty miles long by fifteen or twenty broad, covered in springtime with blossoming peach orchards amid a sea of early wheat, it was the home of more than a million people. But though so near the foreign Settlement it was off the beaten track, and had never yet been visited by Protestant missionaries. Little wonder that it attracted them, about to set out on a longer itineration than any yet attempted.

Their plan on this occasion was to penetrate as far inland as possible, testing what could be done in a good many places rather than spending much time in any one. In Tsungming they found inquiries had been made about them from the *yamen*, so felt it wise to call upon the Mandarin. This official proved to be a grave though rather young man, who received them with courtesy. He accepted copies of the New Testament and other books, and listened attentively while they explained their contents, putting before him the way of salvation through faith in Christ. He made no objection to their visiting the island. This interview alone, they felt, would well have repaid their coming to Tsungming.

The temple of the city-god was a busy scene during the remainder of that day. Mud or no mud, the people came; and while Hudson Taylor did his best to attend to patients in one of the side rooms, Burdon occupied the crowd with books and preaching in the open courtyard. Only when his voice gave out was the medical work interrupted; for the greater part of his audience then surged over to the improvised dispensary, and no more doctoring was possible.

Before leaving Tsungming city the travellers spent one morning in looking up the principal schools, to leave Christian literature with both scholars and teachers. Thirteen schools and a college were visited, the pupils varying in number from nine to twenty-five. The teachers were in many cases intelligent men, able to give information as to the chief centres of population on the island.

After leaving Tsungming, a favourable wind and tide carried them far up the Yangtze, and when the sun rose in a cloudless sky they found themselves nearing the sacred mountains that command the north and south banks of the river, just where its estuary narrows away from the sea. It was a day of unusual beauty, and their voices being in need of rest they decided to make the ascent of the northern range, and learn all they could of the lie of the land around them. Directing the boatmen therefore to enter the nearest tributary stream and await their return in the latter part of the day, the young men set out full of expectancy. Describing it later Hudson Taylor wrote:

As we approached the hills the scene became beautiful beyond description. Of the five summits the central one was the highest, crowned by a fine pagoda. At the foot of this hill and running up its side was a Buddhist temple and monastery so extensive that at a little distance we mistook it for a village.

The day happened to be a festival, and thousands of persons of all classes were gathered to join in the ceremonies. Nothing could be more evident than that idolatry was here a *living* system, flourishing unmolested by soldiers of the Cross. Heavy fumes of incense filled the air; and the clinking of cash, as the passers-by threw their coins into baskets placed before the idols, mingled with strains of music, the buzz of conversation and tramp of passing feet. Upon reaching the summit we entered the halls connected with the pagoda – the hideous figures of the idols, seen through smoke and flames from burning paper,[1] making it seem like a place where Satan's seat is.

Turning sadly away we mounted the pagoda, and what a contrast was the scene outspread before our eyes! No words can describe the landscape, and the more one looked the more fresh beauties lay revealed. The country below, covered with early crops and tended like a garden, was of the brightest hue, owing to recent rains. Streams intersected it in every direction, bordered with drooping willows. Farm-houses with their fruit trees and neat willow fences, cemeteries here and there, cypress-shaded, and numerous villages and hamlets dotted the foreground. Beyond these lay the magnificent Yangtze, fifteen to twenty miles broad, its great northerly sweep looking calm as a lake and bearing many a boat and junk with graceful sails, some snowy white, some brown or black with age. Beyond again rose the 'sacred mountains' of the southern shore, crowned with their monasteries and temples, and other ranges of more distant hills.

The opposite side of the square pagoda presented an entirely different view. There to the north-west lay the great city of Tungchow surrounded by a populous plain; and several little lakes shining like molten silver put a finishing touch to the beauty of the scene.

With hearts greatly moved by this panorama, they stood looking out as Moses over the promised land. Yes, this was China, seen at last, away from the narrow limits of a Treaty Port. How great it was, how far-reaching! Shanghai and its surroundings began to dwindle in importance, in view of all this. So many lights seemed gathered there, as they thought of all the Missions. After the appeal of unreached Tsungming, this told. From this time onward Hudson Taylor swung free from influences that had held him, returning more and more in heart to his earlier position, his first sense of call to preach the Gospel 'not where Christ was named'.

The following day they set out to visit Tungchow, the city seen from the pagoda, whose unenviable reputation had already reached them. It might be months, years even, before other evangelists would reach it, and they could not bear the responsibility of leaving its vast population any longer in ignorance of the way of life. If nothing more were possible, they could at any rate distribute their remaining Scriptures within its walls.

Our Chinese teachers did their best to persuade us not to go, but we determined that by God's help nothing should hinder us. We directed them to remain in their boat,

[1] Offerings of money and other objects made in paper, expressly for burning before the idols.

and if we did not return to learn whatever they could respecting our fate, and make all possible haste to Shanghai with the information. We then put our books in two bags and, with a servant who always accompanied us on these occasions, set off for the city, distant about seven miles. We had not gone far before our servant requested permission to go back, as he was thoroughly frightened by reports concerning the local soldiery. Of course we at once consented, not wishing to involve another in trouble.

At this point a respectable-looking man came up and earnestly warned us against proceeding, saying that if we did so we should find to our sorrow what the Tungchow militia were like. We thanked him for his advice, but could not act upon it, as our hearts were fixed. Whether it were for bonds, imprisonment, and death, or whether to return in safety we knew not, but we were determined, by the grace of God, not to leave Tungchow any longer without the Gospel.

After this my wheelbarrow man would proceed no farther and I had to seek another, fortunately not difficult to find. As we went on, the ride was anything but agreeable in the mud and rain, and we could not help feeling the danger of our position – though wavering not for a moment. At intervals we encouraged one another with promises from Scripture and verses of hymns, which were very comforting.

Nearing the western suburb of the city, the prayer of the early Christians when persecution was commencing came to my mind, 'And now, Lord, behold their threatenings: and grant unto thy servants, that with all boldness they may speak thy word': a petition in which we most heartily united. Before entering the suburb we laid our plans so as to act in concert, and told our barrow-men where to await us, that they might not be involved in trouble on our account. Then, looking up to our heavenly Father, we committed ourselves to His keeping, took our books and set off for the city.

For some distance we walked along the principal street leading to the West Gate unmolested, but before long a tall, powerful man, half-drunk, seized Burdon by the shoulders. I turned to see what was the matter, and in almost no time we were surrounded by a dozen or more of his companions, and hurried on to the city at a fearful pace.

My bag now began to feel heavy. I was soon in a profuse perspiration and scarcely able to keep up with them. We demanded to be taken before the chief magistrate, but were told, with the most insulting epithets, that they knew where to take us and what to do. The man who first seized Burdon soon afterwards left him for me, and became my principal tormentor, for I was neither so tall nor so strong as my friend and was less able to resist him. He all but knocked me down again and again, seized me by the hair, took hold of my collar so as almost to choke me, and grasped my arms and shoulders, making them black and blue. Had this continued much longer I must have fainted. All but exhausted, how refreshing was the remembrance of a verse quoted by my dear mother in one of my last home letters:

We speak of the realms of the blest,
  That country so bright and so fair:
And oft are its glories confessed—
  But what will it be, to be there!

To be absent from the body, present with the Lord, free from sin. And this is the end of the worst that man's malice can ever bring upon us.

As we were being hurried along, Burdon tried to give away a few books that were under his arm, not knowing whether we might have another opportunity. But the fearful rage of the soldier, and the way he insisted on manacles being brought, which fortunately were not at hand, convinced us that in our present position it was useless to attempt such work. There was nothing to be done but quietly to submit and go along with our captors.

Once or twice a quarrel arose as to how we should be dealt with, the more mild of our conductors saying that we ought to be taken to the *yamen*, but others wishing to kill us at once without appeal to any authority. Our minds were kept in perfect peace, and when thrown together on one of these occasions we reminded each other that the Apostles rejoiced that they were counted *worthy* to suffer in the cause of Christ. Having succeeded in getting a hand into my pocket, I produced a Chinese card (if the large red paper bearing one's name may be so called) and after this was treated with more civility. I demanded that it should be given to the chief official of the place, and that we should be led to his office.

Oh, the long weary streets we were dragged through! I thought they would never end. And when we arrived at the *yamen* we passed through some great gates and came in sight of a large tablet with the inscription *Min-chï fu-mu* (the Father and Mother of the people).

Our cards were again sent in, and after a short delay we were ushered into the presence of Ch'en Ta Lao-ie (The Great Venerable Grandfather Ch'en) who, as it proved, had formerly been Tao-tai in Shanghai and knew the importance of treating foreigners with civility. This Mandarin who seemed to be the highest authority in Tungchow and wore an opaque blue button on his cap, came out to meet us with every possible token of respect. He took us to an inner apartment, a more private room, followed by a large number of writers, runners, and semi-officials. I explained the object of our visit and begged permission to give him copies of our books, for which he thanked me. I tried to say a little about them, and also to give him a brief summary of our teachings. He listened very attentively, as of course did all the others. He then ordered refreshments to be brought, which were very welcome, and himself partook of them with us.

After a long stay, we asked permission to see something of the city and to distribute the books we had with us before returning. To this he kindly consented. We then mentioned that we had been most disrespectfully treated as we came in, but did not attach much importance to the fact, being aware that the rough soldiery knew no better. Not desiring, however, to have such experiences repeated, we requested him to give orders that we were not to be further molested. This also he acceded to and accompanied us to the door of his *yamen*, sending several 'runners' to see that no trouble arose. We distributed our books well and quickly, and after visiting the Confucian temple left the city quite in state. It was amusing to see the use the 'runners' made of their queues. When the way was blocked by the crowd they turned them into whips and laid them about the people's shoulders to right and left!

Early in the evening we got back to the boats in safety, sincerely thankful to our heavenly Father for His gracious protection and aid.

Thus the vision was clenched with suffering, and Hudson Taylor's first sight of the great unreached interior was immediately followed by his first experience of danger to life itself at the hands of those he sought to help. What could be more calculated to deepen, while at the same time it tempered his life purpose?

CHAPTER 8

Emptied from Vessel to Vessel

(1855–1856)

THE joy of preaching Christ where He had never before been named had now laid hold of Hudson Taylor, weaning his heart at last from plans and hopes of settled work in Shanghai. For months that thought had occupied him, but now it began to take a secondary place.

No answer had yet been received from the Committee as to the plans laid before them, so it was all the more natural that Hudson Taylor should be drawn in the one direction that was providentially open, that of evangelistic journeys. His fitness for this work was becoming so evident that the British and Foreign Bible Society was willing not only to supply him with as many Scriptures as he could distribute, but also to meet the larger part of his travelling expenses.

Ten days at home and the young evangelist set out upon a longer absence than any he had previously undertaken, this time alone. He seems to have had in view the purpose with which he had been sent to China, of penetrating inland as far as Nanking, the headquarters of the Taiping Rebellion. Be that as it may, he steered his course up the Yangtze, exploring the southern shore, travelling a distance of over 400 miles.

Starting on May 8 he did not reach home again until June 1, having preached in fifty-eight cities, towns and larger villages, fifty-one of which had never before been visited by a Protestant missionary. It was a lonely journey and a courageous one. He was exceeding the most liberal interpretation of treaty rights, and could claim no protection either from his own Consul or from the local authorities. At any point he knew that he might be seized, tortured, and even put to death as a rebel or foreign spy.

'I have felt a degree of nervousness since we were so roughly treated in Tungchow which is quite a new experience, a feeling that is not lessened by being quite alone,' he wrote in his diary on the third day out. 'I could not help feeling sad and downcast.'

Nevertheless, his diary for the twenty-five days gives a record of almost unremitting labour, continuing until early June when he returned to Shanghai. Here a warm welcome awaited him in more ways than one. In a letter to his mother he reported:

The Chinese authorities have had me up before the Consul for violating the treaty with England by travelling in the interior. He said very little, not more than he was obliged to, but told me that if I continued to exceed treaty rights his position admitted of no respect of persons; he must punish me as he would a merchant.

Hudson Taylor was to hear more of this later. Meanwhile, he embarked on another itineration of a slightly different nature, little realizing all it was to bring into his life.

He, Burdon and Dr. Parker set out on a preaching tour that was to include a visit to Ningpo for partial rest and change. Missionaries of several societies were at work in that important city, and the blessing of God was manifestly resting upon their labours. Hudson Taylor and his colleague looked forward to much help from this visit. Twilight was falling when after several days' travel they made their way through the multitudinous craft that lined the chief approaches to the city, and following Burdon through the darkness of the narrow streets it was good to be welcomed into a hospitable mission compound. During the next few days they were introduced to a peculiarly united community in which they were received with great kindness.

Eleven foreigners in all represented several British and American societies. In addition there was a school carried on by an Englishwoman, Miss Aldersey, who six years before China was opened to the residence of foreigners had settled in Java to work among Chinese women there. After the Treaty of Nanking in 1842 she sailed for China, and coming to Ningpo in 1843 was one of the pioneer missionaries to settle in that city, where she opened the first school for girls on Chinese soil.

She had as her assistants the orphan daughters of one of the earliest members of the London Missionary Society. Born under the tropical sun of the Straits Settlements, and brought up in a missionary home, Burella and Maria Dyer at eighteen and twenty years of age were already fluent in the Ningpo vernacular, efficient and well loved in the work to which they were devoting themselves. Not surprisingly the presence of these girls enhanced the attraction of the foreign community in Ningpo.

Only one thing seemed lacking to the all-round development of the missions in the area. There was no hospital. The missionaries felt this drawback keenly, and as they came to know something of Dr. Parker a new hope sprang up. It was not until after he and his companions had returned to Shanghai, however, that a unanimous invitation was given to him to come and join them. When he and Hudson Taylor settled in again in the little house in *Ma-ka-k'üen*, it was as crowded as ever, and there seemed no prospect of relief. Gradually it was becoming evident that the Chinese Evangelization Society was not prepared to endorse their suggestion with regard to mission headquarters in any of the Treaty Ports. 'Our professed intentions are not to work in the five Ports, but in the interior,' they wrote. 'We do not wish our representatives to spend money in Shanghai.' It was a matter of principle with the Committee not to put money into bricks and mortar, even though it seemed that their representatives could be housed in no other way.

It is easy enough now for us to realize that the Shanghai idea, as far as Hudson Taylor and Dr. Parker were concerned, was a mistaken one, but it was anything but easy for them. The Scottish physician had not yet received the invitation to Ningpo, and Hudson Taylor, eager though he was to go inland, knew all too well the need for a good home base.

'It is hard to be ever on the move,' he wrote to his sister, 'and to have no settled dwelling. I have some thought of buying a set of Chinese garments soon, and seeing how I could get on with them. If I could get a little place somewhere in the interior, perhaps I might settle down and be useful. As things are at present, we cannot hope to see much fruit – for we have no station, no chapel, no hospital, no house even of our own. Pray for me, for I am very weak and unworthy, and have been a good deal tried of late.'

It was August 6 when Hudson Taylor and his colleague received the long-expected notice that the house they were occupying must be vacated by the end of September. Two new missionaries were on the way from England and would require the premises. Just then further letters from their own Committee put a final veto upon their plans for Shanghai as a permanent centre. No, they were not to build, though permission was given Dr. Parker to rent rooms for a dispensary. How or where they were to live was left a matter of uncertainty, the Committee apparently having no suggestion to make.

The Lord, however, was caring for His workers as well as His work. Another letter, also received early in August, gave full proof of this. Several weeks previously the unanimous invitation of the missionaries in Ningpo had reached Dr. Parker, earnestly requesting that he would go and settle among them. He had replied that he could not feel justified in doing so unless assured that in connection with such a position he could support a hospital for the Chinese, the expense of which would be at least 800 dollars per annum. And now, after eight months in China, the opening came that was to determine his life-work.

'You will be glad, I am sure, to learn', he wrote to his Committee on August 22, 'that the friends in Ningpo have become surety for the amount required, and rejoice in the prospect of a missionary hospital there – the only Treaty Port without one.

'This, of course, shuts me up to taking the step, unless I set at nought the plain indications of Providence. And as I believe it to be God's will, I have resolved to go, and to do so at once.'

While this cleared the way for Dr. Parker and his family, it only left Hudson Taylor the more cast upon God. Now he would be lonely indeed, bereft of companionship as well as home. Feeling, as he did, that his work in Shanghai was not yet finished, he at once set about seeking quarters to which he might remove his belongings. But, as before, the search proved useless.

'They all want heavy deposits that I am not able to pay,' he wrote to his sister. 'It is wearisome work, and if I do not succeed soon I shall adopt Chinese dress and seek a place in the country. These changes are not easy. Do pray for me.'

Chinese dress and a home somewhere in the country – the thought was becoming familiar. But it was an expedient almost unheard of in those days. Sometimes on inland journeys a missionary would wear Chinese dress as a precautionary measure, and Dr. Medhurst himself had suggested it to Hudson Taylor. But it was invariably discarded on the traveller's return, and he would have been careless of public opinion indeed who would have ventured to wear it always, and in the Settlement.

Nevetheless it was nothing less than this that the young missionary was meditating, driven to it by his longing to identify himself with the people, and by the force of outward circumstances.

Another week went by in almost incessant house-hunting, and the time drew near when Dr. Parker was to leave for Ningpo. Hudson Taylor had promised to escort him as far as Hangchow Bay, to see him through the more difficult part of the journey. They were to start on Friday morning the 24th, and up to Thursday afternoon the search for premises had been in vain.

Yes, it was growing clearer. For him, probably, the right thing was a closer identification with the people, including chopsticks, Chinese cooking and Chinese dress at all times – even to the queue. How much it would simplify travelling in the interior! Already he had purchased an outfit of Chinese clothing. If, after all the prayer there had been about it, he really could not get accommodation in Shanghai, it must be that the Lord had other purposes. He would send his few things down to Ningpo with Dr. Parker, who had offered to store them, and living on boats would give himself to evangelistic work until his way opened up somewhere in the interior.

Thursday night came, and Dr. Parker was to leave the following morning. It was useless to seek premises any longer, so Hudson Taylor went down to engage the junk that was to take them to Hangchow Bay with their belongings. His Chinese dress was ready for the following morning when he expected to begin a pilgrim life indeed.

This, apparently, was the point to which it had been necessary to lead him. On these new lines could now be given the answer to weeks and months of prayer. Even as he was on his way, a man met him. Did he want a house in the Chinese city? Would a small one do, with only five rooms? Because near the South Gate there was such a house, only it was not quite finished building. The owner had run short of money and hardly knew how to complete the work. If it suited the foreign teacher, no deposit would be asked: it could be had in all probability for an advance of six months' rent.

Feeling as though in a dream, Hudson Taylor followed his guide to the southern quarter of the city, and there found a small, compact house, perfectly new and clean, with two rooms upstairs and two down, and a fifth across the courtyard for the servants – just the very thing he needed, in the locality that suited him best, and all for the moderate sum of £10 to cover a half-year's rent.

What it must have been to him to pay the money over that night, and secure the premises, is more easily imagined than described. The Lord had indeed worked on his behalf. Prayer was being answered. He had not missed or mistaken the guidance for which he had waited so long. It almost seemed as if the Lord had broken silence, to confirm and encourage His servant at this critical time. And best of all was the wondering consciousness that He Himself had done it when, humanly speaking, it seemed impossible: 'I being in the way, the Lord led me'.

That night he took the final step in transforming himself into a Chinese. He described the experience a few days later in a letter to his sister:

> . . . I had better tell you at once that on Thursday last at 11 p.m. I resigned my locks to the barber, dyed my hair a good black, and in the morning had a proper *queue* plaited in with my own, and a quantity of heavy silk to lengthen it out according to Chinese custom. Then, in Chinese dress, I set out with Dr. Parker, accompanying him about 100 miles on his way to Ningpo. This journey we made an occasion for evangelistic work, and now that I am returning alone I hope to have even better facilities for book distribution and preaching.
>
> But I have not commenced the recital of my tribulations, and the sooner I begin the better. First then, it is a very sore thing to have one's head shaved for the first time, especially if the skin is irritable with prickly heat. And I can assure you that the subsequent application of hair-dye for five or six hours (litharge 1 part; quick lime, freshly slaked, 3 parts; water enough to make a cream) does not do much to soothe the irritation. But when it comes to combing out the remaining hair which has been allowed to grow longer than usual, the climax is reached! But there are no gains without pains, and certainly if suffering for a thing makes it dearer, I shall regard my *queue* when I attain one with no small amount of pride and affection.
>
> Secondly, when you proceed to your toilet, you no longer wonder that many Chinese in the employ of Europeans wear foreign shoes and stockings as soon as they can get them. For Chinese socks are made of calico and of course are not elastic, and average toes decidedly object to be squeezed out of shape, nor do one's heels

appreciate their low position in perfectly flat-soled shoes. Next come the breeches – but oh, what unheard-of garments! Mine are two feet too wide for me round the waist, which amplitude is laid in a fold in front, and kept in place by a strong girdle. The legs are short, not coming much below the knee, and wide in proportion with the waist measurement. Tucked into the long, white socks, they have a bloomer-like fullness capable, as Dr. Parker remarked, of storing a fortnight's provisions! No shirt is worn. But a white, washing-jacket, with sleeves as wide as ladies affected twenty years ago, supplies its place. And over all goes a heavy silk gown of some rich or delicate colour, with sleeves equally wide and reaching twelve or fifteen inches beyond the tips of one's fingers – folded back, of course, when the hands are in use.

While still with Dr. Parker on the way to Hangchow Bay I was frequently recognized as a foreigner, because of having to speak to him in English, but today in going about Haiyen City no one even guessed that such a being was near. It was not until I began to distribute books and see patients that I became known. Medical work is evidently to be one's chief help for the interior. Women and children, it seems to me, manifest more readiness to come for medical aid now than they did before, and in this way too, I think the Chinese costume will be of service.

Thus he returned to Shanghai as summer merged into autumn, to take up in the old surroundings a very different life. For the change he had made after so much prayer was soon found to affect more than his outward appearance. The Chinese felt it, Europeans felt it, and above all he felt it himself – putting an intangible barrier between him and foreign associations, and throwing him back as never before upon the people of his adoption.

The covert sneer or undisguised contempt of the European community he found less difficult to bear than the disapproval of fellow-missionaries. But this also had to be faced, for he was practically alone in his convictions, and certainly the only one to carry them into effect. The more he suffered for them, however, the more they deepened, and the more he gave himself to the Chinese in consequence.

It was Monday, September 17, when he resumed upon moving into his new quarters a solitary life. Within the walls of the native city his living arrangements were of the simplest, but only three weeks later he wrote to tell his mother of the sweetest joy he had ever known.

This morning my heart was gladdened by the request of Kuei-hua (my adopted pupil's brother) to be baptized. I cannot tell you the joy this has brought me. Were my work ended here, I feel I could say with Simeon, 'Lord, now lettest thou thy servant depart in peace . . . for mine eyes have seen thy salvation'. If one soul is worth worlds, mother, am I not abundantly repaid? And are not you too?

Kuei-hua was the first convert he baptized in China. But this was not the only encouragement of which he had to tell before the month was over. For that October mail brought another letter from W. T. Berger. Satisfied with the use made of his first gift of £10, this kind friend now repeated it, undertaking to do so every half year, and thus provide entirely for Han-pan's education. But more than this, he wrote 'a very affectionate letter', urging the young missionary to expect great things from God, and enclosing a further sum of £40 to be used as he thought best in the interests of the work.

It seems to have been with an almost solemnized sense of the goodness of God that Hudson Taylor pondered all this in the light of the past, and in its relation to the future. How long he had looked forward to the joy of winning his first convert among the heathen! How keenly he had felt lack of means properly to develop the work! Now souls were being given, not Kuei-hua only, but one or two other promising inquirers; and this generous friend in England was being drawn more and more into sympathy with the line of things to which he felt himself called.

Already the Lord was more than making up for all the trials undergone. And straight to his heart came the message of Mr. Berger's letter:

> 'Open thy mouth wide, and I will fill it.' O yes! God is not straightened. If we expect much from Him, He surely will not disappoint us.

It was during that autumn that Taylor obtained a home of his own in the interior. It must have seemed like a dream to him, to be quietly living among the people, in Sin-k'ai-ho a day's journey from the nearest Treaty Port.

It all came about in answer to prayer no doubt, but the Chinese dress he was wearing had had a great deal to do with it. As soon as he could leave the South Gate house in charge of Teacher Sï he had set out on another evangelistic journey, which was to include a second visit to the island of Tsungming. But he had got no further than this first place at which he landed, for there the people simply would not hear of his leaving.

What made them want so much to have him does not appear. Perhaps it was the medicine chest. Perhaps it was the preaching. At any rate there was nothing in his outward appearance to frighten them away, and the difference between this experience and anything he had met with on previous journeys taught him afresh the value of Chinese dress.

The second day of his stay there a house had been discovered with some sort of an upper storey whose owner was quite willing to receive the missionary. Indeed he could rent the entire premises, if they pleased him, for a moderate sum. Before Monday was half over the agreement was concluded that gave him possession of his first home in 'inland China'.

Busy indeed were the days that followed – one of the hardest worked and happiest times the young missionary had ever known in his life. His servant Kuei-hua and an earnest inquirer from the South Gate named Ts'ien were invaluable in helping him to preach the Gospel, morning, noon and night. But even so he finished up the week with an attack of ague, due to over-weariness and the change to autumn weather.

After that things settled down to a regular routine. Patients were seen and daily meetings held, and a few inquirers began to gather. One of these was a blacksmith named Chang, and another an assistant in a grocery store. Ts'ien was invaluable in helping these beginners and in receiving guests, and both he and Kuei-hua were so eager to learn more themselves that they made the most of the little while Taylor could give them at night when outsiders had all gone home.

And all about them stretched the populous island – a parish of a million, every one of whom he longed to reach. The town itself contained only twenty to thirty thousand, but villages were numerous in every direction, and the medical work was making friends. Wherever Taylor and his helpers went they found somebody ready to welcome them, and as frequently as possible they spent a day in the country preaching the Gospel.

> 'It is almost too much to expect', he wrote at the beginning of this work, 'that I shall be allowed to remain on without molestation, so I must use every effort to sow the good seed of the Kingdom while I may, and be earnest in prayer for blessing. Should it please the Lord to establish me in this place and raise up a band of believers, it seems to me that by making a circuit somewhat on the Wesleyan plan we should be enabled to do the greatest amount of good.
>
> 'Pray for me. I sometimes feel a sense of responsibility that is quite oppressive – the only light-bearer among so many. But this is wrong. It is Jesus who is to shine in me. I am not left to my own resources. The two Christians are a great comfort. May I be enabled to help them by life as well as teaching.'

After three weeks supplies began to run short and Taylor had to return to Shanghai for money and medicines. Not anticipating a long absence, he arranged for the meetings to go on without him, and leaving Ts'ien in charge, sailed for the mainland.

He was absent little more than a week from the island, but much may happen in that time. A storm was brewing at Sin-k'ai-ho. Ts'ien had come over hurriedly, and finding no one at the South Gate had returned to his post leaving letters to explain the situation. Amid many exciting rumours one clear fact emerged: a proclamation had been issued to the effect that the foreigner who had unwarrantably taken up his abode on Tsungming was to be sent back to Shanghai at once where he would suffer the severest penalty, and that all persons who had aided his presumptuous action would also be punished after the strictest letter of the law. A fortnight later he wrote to his parents,

It seems that the two doctors and four druggists of this town have begun to find me rather a serious rival. Bad legs of many years' standing have been cured in a few days. Eye medicine exceeding theirs in potency can be obtained for nothing. A whole host of itch cases, regular customers for plasters (!) have in some way disappeared. Ague patients are saying that the doctors are without talent, and asthmatics are loud in praise of foreign cough-powders. What was to be the end of it all? That was the question.

So the fraternity met together, took tea, tobacco and counsel, and sent twelve dollars to the Mandarin to have the intruder expelled.

On my return I felt a little anxious, not for my own sake but on account of those who would be implicated if trouble were to arise. But I continued to see patients as before, going every alternate day to preach in neighbouring towns and villages till Monday, November 26th, which with yesterday have been days of intense anxiety.

On Monday morning while we were at breakfast the Mandarin from Tsungming city passed by, his attendants making it known that he had come for the double purpose of seizing some pirates at a town below and of examining into our affairs. Ts'ien and Kuei-hua were to be dragged before him, the landlord also, and an old man of over seventy who had acted as go-between; and unless their replies were 'satisfactory' they would be beaten from 300 to 1,000 blows each. We had morning worship, specially praying for protection, and then preached and saw patients as usual. Toward the close of the afternoon we were told that the Mandarin had gone to seize the pirates first, and would deal with our matters on his return journey.

Next day I kept all who were concerned in the house, that none might be taken without my knowledge. We saw patients, some having come many miles, and preached as usual. In the afternoon, as I was operating on the eye of a woman, who should pass but the Mandarin with all his followers. It was well that the operation was over, or I should have found it difficult to complete it, for I was trembling with excitement. It was not until two hours later that we definitely learned that he had gone on to the capital without stopping. Then our prayers were turned into praise indeed! It may be that he is not even aware of my presence, and that the whole story was an attempt to extort money on the part of his underlings.

Now that the storm had blown over, the young missionary was more than ever earnest in making the most of his opportunities. To see the inquirers growing in grace and in the knowledge of the Lord was a joy no words could express. The blacksmith, Chang, now closed his shop on Sundays, and both he and Sung openly declared themselves Christians. The change that had come over them awakened interest among their fellow-townsmen, several of whom were attending the services regularly. So that the blow when it fell was all the more painful for being unexpected – and it came from an unforeseen quarter.

It was December 1, and Hudson Taylor had gone over to Shanghai to obtain money and send off letters. To his surprise an important looking document was awaiting him at the South Gate, which read as follows:

BRITISH CONSULATE, SHANGHAI,
November 23, 1855.

British Consul to Mr. J. H. Taylor.

SIR – I am directed by Her Majesty's Consul to inform you that information has been lodged at this office by His Excellency the Intendant of Circuit, to the effect that you have rented a house from a Chinese named Si Sung-an, at a place called Sin-k'ai-ho in the island of Tsungming, and opened this house as a physician's establishment in charge of one of your servants named Lew Yang-tsuen, you yourself visiting it occasionally. His Excellency refers to a former complaint lodged against you for visiting Ts'ingkiang, upon which subject you appeared before Her Majesty's Consul.

Her Majesty's Consul has therefore to call upon you to appear at this office without delay, in order that he may investigate the matter above referred to. – I am, Sir, your most obedient servant,

FREDERICK HARVEY (*Vice-Consul*).

Of course he went at once and explained the true facts of the case, but his plea to be allowed to remain on at Sin-k'ai-ho where all now seemed peaceful and friendly was in vain. The Consul reminded him that the British Treaty only provided for residence in the five ports, and that if he attempted to settle elsewhere he rendered himself liable to a fine of 500 dollars. The young missionary well knew that there was a supplementary treaty in which it was stipulated that all immunities and privileges granted to other nations should apply to British subjects also. Roman Catholic priests, Frenchmen, were living on the island supported by the authority of their Government, and why should he be forbidden the same consideration?

Yes, replied the Consul, that was undoubtedly a point, and if he wished to appeal for a higher decision, Her Majesty's representative (Sir John Bowring) would be arriving in Shanghai before long. As far as his own jurisdiction went, the matter was at an end. Mr. Taylor must return to Tsungming at once, give up his house, remove his belongings to Shanghai, and understand that he was liable to a fine of 500 dollars if he again attempted residence in the interior.

'I shall probably appeal against the Consular decision, 'Hudson Taylor wrote to Mr. Pearse a few days later. 'I feel the importance of this case in many respects. It will test the footing on which Protestant missionaries really stand. . . .'

Sir John Bowring, however, was unaccountably delayed just then. He did not arrive by the mail steamer on which he was expected, nor by the next: and meanwhile the young missionary was brought into contact with the one God had prepared to help him at this stage in his life.

The name of William Burns was in the best sense a household word in Scotland, for where in town or country was there a Christian family that did not recall the Revival of 1839? The young evangelist of those days, moving in Pentecostal power from place to place, everywhere accompanied by marvellous tokens of the divine presence and blessing, had become the toil-worn missionary – his hair already tinged with grey, his spirit more mellow though no less fervent, his sympathies enlarged through experience and deeper fellowship with the sufferings of Christ.

Just returned to China after his first and only furlough, Burns had not resumed, as might have been expected, his former successful work in Amoy. He felt strongly drawn to the Yangtze Valley, for Nanking was on his heart, and the unknown leaders of the Taiping movement in whose hands the future of China still seemed to lie. But as events had already proved, this was not the purpose for which he had been brought to central China.

Unsuccessful in his attempt to reach Nanking, he had returned to Shanghai by the southern reaches of the Grand Canal, much impressed with the need and accessibility of that part of the country. With the concurrence of the local missionaries, all too few to meet the overwhelming needs, he had devoted himself for several months to its evangelization – living on boats in very simple style, and travelling up and down the endless waterways spread like a network over the vast alluvial plain. Thus it was that he was still in that locality when Hudson Taylor returned from Tsungming, and engaged in the very work so dear to the younger missionary's heart.

Where and how they met does not appear, but one can readily believe that they were drawn together by sympathies of no ordinary kind. The grave, keen-eyed Scotsman soon detected in the English missionary a kindred spirit, and one sorely in need of help that he might give. The attraction was mutual. Each was without a companion, and before long they had arranged to join forces in the work.

In a little house at the South Gate or on Burns's boat almost the first subject they would discuss would be the difficulty about Tsungming with its bearing on the future, and it was not long before the spiritual point of view of the older man seemed to change the whole situation. It was not a question really of standing on one's rights, or claiming what it might be justifiable to claim. Why deal with second causes? Nothing would have been easier for the Master to whom 'all power' is given than to have established His servant permanently on the island, had He so desired it. And of what use was it, if He had other plans, to attempt to carry the thing through on the strength of Government help? No, 'the servant of the Lord must not strive', but must be willing to be led by just such indications of the Divine will, relying not on the help of man to accomplish a work of his own choosing, but on the unfailing guidance, resources and purposes of God.

And so, very thankfully, Hudson Taylor came to realize that perhaps he had felt unduly discouraged. Nothing the Lord permitted could permanently hinder His own work. All the while had He not been preparing for His servant this unexpected blessing, by far the most helpful companionship he had ever known?

It was the middle of December when Hudson Taylor left Shanghai once more, setting out on his tenth evangelistic journey, the first with William Burns. Residence on Tsungming had been forbidden, but he saw no reason why he should not accompany another missionary to whose itinerations no objection had been raised. Travelling in two boats, each with their Chinese helpers and a good supply of literature, they were at the same time independent and a comfort to one another. Practical and methodical in all his ways, Burns had a line of his own in such work that his companion was glad to follow.

Choosing an important centre, in this case the town of Nanzin, just south of the Great Lake, in Chekiang, they remained there eighteen days, including Christmas and the New Year. Every morning they set out early with a definite plan, sometimes working together and sometimes separating to visit different parts of the town. Burns believed in beginning quietly on the outskirts of a place in which foreigners had rarely if ever been seen, and working his way by degrees to the more crowded quarters. Accordingly they gave some days to the suburban streets, preaching whenever a number of people collected and giving away gospels and tracts. This was repeated in all the quieter parts of the town, gradually approaching its centre, until at length they could pass along the busiest streets without endangering the shopkeepers' tempers as well as their wares.

Then they visited temples, schools and tea-shops, returning regularly to the most suitable places for preaching. Announcing after each meeting when they would come again, they had the satisfaction of seeing the same faces frequently.

But everywhere, Burns noticed, his young companion had the more attentive hearers and was occasionally asked into private houses, he himself being requested to wait outside. The riff-raff of the crowd always seemed to gather round the preacher in foreign dress, while those who wished to hear what was being said followed his less noticeable friend. The result was a conclusion come to, and communicated to his mother a few weeks later:

TWENTY-FIVE MILES FROM SHANGHAI,
January 26, 1856.

Taking advantage of a rainy day which confines me to my boat, I pen a few lines in addition to a letter to Dundee containing particulars which I need not repeat.

It is now forty-one days since I left Shanghai on this last occasion. An excellent young English missionary, Mr. Taylor of the Chinese Evangelization Society, has been my companion, he in his boat and I in mine, and we have experienced much mercy, and on some occasions considerable assistance in our work.

I must once more tell the story I have had to tell more than once already, how four weeks ago, on the 29th December, I put on Chinese dress, which I am now wearing. Mr. Taylor had made this change a few months before, and I found that he was in consequence so much less incommoded in preaching, etc., by the crowd, that I concluded that it was my duty to follow his example.

This change into Chinese dress was found to have so many advantages that Burns never again resumed European clothing. Of the comfort of the dress there could be no doubt.

'It is real winter now,' wrote Hudson Taylor on New Year's eve, 'and the north wind is very cutting, but I am, thanks to the Chinese costume, as warm as toast.

'Indeed, we have many mercies to be thankful for. A good boat, costing about two shillings a day, gives me a nice little room to myself, with an oyster-shell window that gives light while it prevents people from peeping in, a table at which I write and take meals, a locker on which my bed is spread at night and a seat round the remaining space, so that two visitors, or even three, can be accommodated.

'How very differently our Master was lodged! Nowhere to lay His head. Oh, may I be enabled to glorify *Him* with my whole spirit, soul and body, which are His.'

Deep as his longing had ever been for likeness to and fellowship with the Lord, Hudson Taylor was increasingly conscious of this heart-hunger in companionship with William Burns. He too had found how sadly possible it is to be professedly a witness for Christ amid the darkness of a heathen land, 'and yet breathe little of the love of God or the grace of the Gospel.' Nothing was more real to him than the fact that a low-level missionary life can, and too often does, make even 'the cross of Christ of none effect'.

'I was preaching last Sabbath day', Burns wrote on one occasion, 'from Matthew 24.12, "because iniquity shall abound, the love of many shall wax cold"; and alas! I felt it was solemnly applicable to my own state of heart. Unless the Lord the Spirit continually uphold and quicken, oh how benumbing is daily contact with heathenism! But the Lord is faithful, and has promised to be "as rivers of water in a dry place, and as the shadow of a great rock in a weary land".'

Upon such promises he counted, and he had not found them fail. The presence of the Lord was the one thing real to him in China as it had been at home. 'He did not consider that he had a warrant to proceed in any sacred duty,' his biographer tells us, 'without a consciousness of that Divine presence. Without it, he could not speak even to a handful of little children in a Sunday School; with it he could stand unabashed before the mightiest and wisest in the land.'

Ruled by such a master principle, it was no wonder there was something about his life that impressed and attracted others. Prayer was as natural to him as breathing, and the Word of God as necessary as daily food. He was always cheerful, always happy, witnessing to the truth of his own memorable words:

I think I can say, through grace, that God's presence or absence alone distinguishes places to me.

Simplicity in living was his great delight. 'He enjoyed quietness and the luxury of having few things to take care of', and thought the happiest state on earth for a Christian was 'that he should have few wants'.

'If a man have Christ in his heart,' he used to say, 'Heaven before his eyes, and only as much of temporal blessing as is just needful to carry him safely through life, then pain and sorrow have little to shoot at.'

Cultured, genial and overflowing with mother-wit, he was a delightful companion. A wonderful fund of varied anecdotes gave charm to his society, and he was generous in recalling his experiences for the benefit of others. Many a time his life had been in danger in Ireland and elsewhere at the hands of a violent mob, and the stories he had to tell could not but encourage faith and zeal, although at times they might provoke a smile.

'*The devil's dead,*' shouted one Irish voice above the uproar of a crowd determined to put an end to his street-preaching. But the quick-witted reply, touched with sarcasm, '*Ah then, you are a poor fatherless bairn!*' not only won the day, but carried home a deeply solemn lesson.

Sacred music was his delight, greatly to the satisfaction of his young companion. Many were the hymns they sang together both in English and Chinese. The fact that they did not belong to the same missionary society, the same denomination, the same country even, made no difference in their relations. Burns was far too large-hearted to be narrowed by circumstances or creeds.

Yet his faithfulness to conviction was unflinching, and his testimony against wrong-doing never withheld. His denunciations of sin could be terrible, strong men cowering before them, pale and trembling, under an overwhelming sense of the Divine presence. He did not hesitate, for example, on this very journey, to mount the stage of a Chinese theatre in the presence of thousands of people and stop an immoral play in full swing, calling upon the audience gathered under the open heavens to repent of their iniquities and turn to the living God.

But it was toward himself he was most of all severe, in the true apostolic spirit, 'We suffer all things, *lest we should hinder* the gospel of Christ'. There are glimpses in his journal of many a day or night spent in prayer – 'seeking personal holiness, the fundamental requisite for a successful ministry'. Yet he felt himself wholly unworthy to represent the Lord he loved. 'Oh, that I had a martyr's heart,' he wrote, 'if not a martyr's death and a martyr's crown.'

The friendship of this man was the gift of God to Hudson Taylor at this particular juncture. Week after week, month after month they lived and travelled together, the exigencies of their work bringing out resources of mind and heart that otherwise might have remained hidden. Such a friendship is one of the crowning blessings of life. It comes as love unsought, and only to the equal soul. Young and immature as he was, Hudson Taylor had the capacity to appreciate, after long years of loneliness, the preciousness of this gift. Under its influence he grew and expanded, and came to an understanding of himself and his providential position that left its impress on all after-life. William Burns was better to him than a college course with all its advantages, because he lived out before him right there in China the reality of all he most needed to be and know.

CHAPTER 9

Who Shutteth and No Man Openeth

(1856)

IT WAS the middle of February 1856, and William Burns and Hudson Taylor were in Shanghai again. They had been on two evangelistic trips together, and were glad to be once more at the weekly prayer meeting at Dr. Medhurst's which was a rendezvous for all in the great port who were concerned for the work of God.

On this occasion a Christian captain was present whose vessel had just arrived from Swatow. His heart was burdened with the condition of things in that southern port to which he carried cargo and passengers from time to time. An important and growing centre of commerce, it was the resort of increasing numbers of people greedy of gain and wholly unscrupulous in their ways of obtaining it. The opium trade and the equally iniquitous 'coolie traffic' were carried on with shameless activity. Piracy flourished to such an extent that even Chinese merchants had taken to shipping their goods in foreign vessels that they might obtain the protection of British and other flags. Thus, although Swatow was not an open port and foreigners had no business to be there as far as treaty rights were concerned, quite a European settlement had sprung up, connived at by the local authorities. On Double Island, five miles out of Swatow, captains of opium ships and other foreigners had bought land and built houses just as they might at Hong Kong, their presence, sad to say, only increasing the vices of this notoriously wicked place. And neither there nor in Swatow itself was there any witness for Christ or any influence that made for righteousness. No missionary or minister was to be found nearer than Amoy, 150 miles away; and in the absence of family life, as well as the restraints of law and order, the condition of things was as bad as it could be.

From this place Captain Bowers had just come, and in the meeting he urged the importance of Swatow as a centre for missionary operations. If merchants and traders could live there, of all nationalities, why should not ministers of the Gospel? But the missionary who would pioneer his way amid such darkness must not be afraid, he said, to cast in his lot with 'the offscourings of Chinese society, congregated there from all the southern ports'.

Silently that evening the friends returned to their boats, thinking of what they had heard. To Hudson Taylor, at any rate, the call of God had come while Captain Bowers was speaking, and he was struggling against rebellion of heart in view of the sacrifice involved.

'Never had I such a spiritual father as Mr. Burns,' he wrote long after; 'never had I known such holy, happy intercourse; and I said to myself that it could not be God's will that we should separate.'

Thus several days passed by, and he could not escape the conviction that Swatow was where the Lord would have him.

In great unrest of soul, I went with Mr. Burns one evening to visit some friends of the American Presbyterian Mission near the South Gate of Shanghai. After tea, Mrs. Lowrie played over to us 'The Missionary Call'. I had never heard it before, and it greatly affected me. My heart was almost broken before it was finished, and I said to the Lord in the words that had been sung:

And I will go.
I may no longer doubt to give up friends and idle hopes,
And every tie that binds the heart . . .
Henceforth then it matters not if storm or sunshine be my
earthly lot, bitter or sweet my cup;
I only pray, God make me holy, and my spirit nerve for the stern
hour of strife.

Upon leaving, I asked Mr. Burns to come to the little house that was still my headquarters, and there with many tears I told him how the Lord had been leading me, and how rebellious I had been, and unwilling to leave him for this new sphere. He listened with a strange look of surprise and pleasure rather than of pain, and replied that he had determined that very night to tell me that he had heard the Lord's call to Swatow, and that his one regret had been the severance of our happy fellowship.

Thus the Lord not only gave, but gave back, the companionship that meant so much in the life of Hudson Taylor. Together they went next morning to Captain Bowers and told him that the way seemed clear for them both to go to Swatow. So overjoyed was the captain to hear it that he offered them forthwith a free passage on his ship which was returning in a few days. This was gratefully accepted, and on March 6, two years from Hudson Taylor's first arrival in Shanghai, they sailed for their new field of labour.

Anchored in a fog that night off Gutzlaff Island, everything must have recalled to Hudson Taylor the February Sunday when he first reached that spot. Then he had never seen the shores of China nor looked into the face of anyone belonging to that land. Now how familiar it had grown. He was at home in two dialects, one of which was the language of four-fifths of China, and was about to learn a third as an incident of his service. Seasoned as a good soldier of the Cross by many a trial and hardship, he was ready to stand alone in a peculiarly difficult sphere. War, with all its horrors, prolonged distress through insufficient supplies, the discipline of indebtedness to others, even for a home, and then of loneliness in his own quarters, sickness, change, uncertainty, and great discomfort as to material surroundings – all these had schooled his heart to patience, and brought a deeper dependence upon God. Evangelistic journeys, alone or with other missionaries, had greatly widened his outlook. Eleven such itinerations lay behind him within these first two years. How much each one had meant, with its necessary exercise of mind and heart, its strain upon endurance, dangers by land and water, 'perils in the city . . . perils of robbers . . . labour and travail', and all its secret springs of faith and prayer.

And now encouragement had come and a friendship richer and deeper than any he had given up or ever hoped to know. Freedom also as to funds was a new and welcome experience.

'I understand that the funds of the Chinese Evangelization Society were much reduced a short time ago,' he wrote in April of this year. 'It does not affect me, however, as I have not needed to draw on my Society for the last two quarters, and have now in hand enough for six months to come. Only by last mail a valued friend and devoted servant of Christ, who has sent me £100 since last October, wrote urging me to tell him of any additional way in which he could forward the work by supplying the means. So as you truly say, if we are in the will of God, difficulty or trial as to circumstances cannot hinder us. Nothing can by any means harm us or frustrate His designs.'

In one thing only the years since he came to China seemed to have made no advance: he had still no home, no permanent work, no settled plans ahead. Where or how he was ultimately to labour was no more clear than it had been at the beginning. But the way of faith was clearer, and he had learned to leave the future in the hands of God. One who knew the end from the beginning was guiding and would guide. So a great rest had come about it all, and he was not concerned to make everything fit in. How this visit to Swatow would eventuate for him personally, how it would affect his life-work he could not tell. He only knew the Lord had set before him this open door, and he was increasingly content to walk a step at a time.

'As to Swatow,' he wrote just before leaving, 'we go looking to the Lord for guidance and blessing. As we are led, we shall return sooner or later or not at all. Having no plans, we have none to tell. May the Lord be with us, bless us abundantly, and glorify His own great name. Pray for us.'

Thus in prayer and faith they drew near the great province of Kwangtung, and on March 12 anchored off Double Island a few miles from their destination. It would have been quite possible to settle here among other Europeans, and from comfortable headquarters to visit the mainland for their missionary operations. But such a plan had no attractions for either William Burns or Hudson Taylor. Avoiding even proximity to the vice and luxury of the Settlement, they went on to Swatow itself, to seek a footing among the people they had come to reach. In this their Chinese dress was of great assistance; and though at first it seemed that not a corner could be found, prayer was again answered and their faith strengthened by one of those 'chance providences' so often prepared for the children of God.

Situated on the delta of the Han between two of its principal channels, Swatow had little room to extend save by banking out its water-frontage, an operation in which hundreds of workmen were engaged. Houses were running up as rapidly as possible, for the supply was altogether unequal to the demand; and meanwhile the missionaries almost despaired of finding quarters.

After two days' fruitless search during which they were thankful for Captain Bowers's continued hospitality, they 'happened' to meet a Cantonese merchant whom Burns addressed in his mother tongue. Delighted at hearing excellent Cantonese from a foreigner, and a foreigner wearing Chinese dress, this gentleman interested himself on their behalf, and through a relative who 'happened' to be the highest official in the town succeeded in securing them a lodging. It was not much of a place, it is true, just a single room over an incense-shop in a crowded quarter, but how glad they were to take possession before Captain Bowers had to sail for Singapore.

That it did not meet with Captain Bowers's approval is hardly to be wondered at. Great was his love and admiration for Burns, and he could not bear to leave him in such surroundings. Of his visit to the incense-shop he wrote to a mutual friend:

'Seeking out his wretched lodging in Swatow amongst the degraded of every class, I remarked, "Surely, Mr. Burns, you might find a better place to live in." He laughingly told me that he was more content in the midst of this people than he would be at home surrounded with every comfort. He said his expenses amounted to ten dollars a month. "Mr. Burns," I exclaimed, "that would not keep me in cigars!" He said it was sufficient for him.'

But to the missionaries themselves, ten dollars a month and a single room, into which they had to climb through an opening in the floor, did not seem so bad. It was in touch with the people, that was the chief thing, and they were very conscious that the Lord was with them. The single room they divided as well as they could into three tiny apartments – two running east to west, and one north and south, which included the hole in the floor.

'My bedroom is on the south,' Taylor wrote two weeks later. 'Mr. Burns takes the north side, and the strip on the west we use as our study. The partitions are made of sheets and a few boards. We have only just obtained exclusive possession, a passage having been needed for the landlord's family until alterations were made in the house. We are promised a trap-door next week, and then shall have more privacy.

'Our beds are a few deal boards, and our table the lid of a box supported on two bags of books. We may get a better some day, but nothing of that sort is to be bought ready-made in Swatow. So for the present, at an outlay of 230 cash (1s. 1d.), we have completely furnished the house – with two bamboo stools and a bamboo easy-chair.'

Here, then, amongst the worst and lowest, the little seed was planted that was to result in an abundant harvest. Years before, a solitary missionary of the Basel Missionary Society had laboured there in face of overwhelming odds. Driven from place to place he had itinerated widely in the surrounding country, living a life of Christlike patience and love. But since 1852, when he had been driven back to Hong Kong, no one had taken his place, and Swatow had remained without testimony to the Gospel.

William Burns's knowledge of Cantonese enabled him to make himself understood from the first, but for his companion this was a much more serious matter. As the only way to usefulness was to be able to talk freely with the people, Hudson Taylor set himself once more to study.

'There is plenty of work to be done,' he wrote to his mother soon after their arrival, 'but I cannot do it. It is a great trial after being able to speak freely to begin again in a place where one cannot understand a single sentence. But if only we are used here, what a privilege is ours. Pray for me, and do not be uneasy about me. The Lord will undertake.'

If his mother and friends could have realized the conditions under which he was living, they would have felt more concern at this time than probably they did. For Swatow was a dangerous as well as difficult field. Two great evils already mentioned flourished under the protection of foreigners, and made the very sight of a European odious to the people. The same letter states:

About 200 boxes of opium are imported monthly; each box contains forty balls of about 4 lbs. weight. Thus not less than 32,000 lbs. of opium enter China every month at this port alone, the cost of which is about a quarter of a million sterling. After this you will not be surprised to learn that the people are wretchedly poor, ignorant and vicious.

A cruel slave trade also is carried on under the name of the 'coolie traffic'. The men are engaged (nominally) for a certain term of years, but few live to return. A bounty is paid them, and they are told that they are going to make their fortunes, or they are entrapped by worse means. Once on the ship the agent receives so much a head for the poor fellows, who soon find themselves in captivity of the most horrible kind. Some jump overboard in their efforts to escape, but they are generally retaken and flogged. Some ships carry 1,000 and others three or four hundred, and very many die before reaching their destination – Cuba, Havanna and Callao. Of one ship with several hundreds on board, I heard the surgeon say that not more than two-thirds would survive the voyage.

It was little wonder under such circumstances, and with many of the traders living on Double Island, that the missionaries endeavouring to obtain a foothold in Swatow should be regarded with hatred, suspicion and scorn. The usual term 'Foreign Devil' was here reinforced by more offensive epithets, 'Foreign Dog', 'Foreign Pig' and worse, hissed out with bitterest scorn. It was a humiliating experience, and as new to William Burns as to Hudson Taylor.

In towns and villages at a little distance a more friendly spirit was manifested, but the same poverty and degradation prevailed, and the people were so turbulent that those who went amongst them had to face constant danger. In their visits to the country the missionaries were liable to be seized at any moment and held to ransom, and they frequently heard the saying that the whole district was 'without Emperor, without rulers and without law'. One small town in which they were preaching had recently captured a wealthy man belonging to a neighbouring clan. Refusing to pay the exorbitant sum demanded for his release, he had been subjected to cruel tortures, his ankle-bones finally being smashed with a club, after which his tormentors succeeded in obtaining all they desired.

'There was nothing but the protection of God', wrote Hudson Taylor, 'between us and the same sort of treatment. The towns were all walled, many of them containing ten or twelve thousand people who might be and frequently were at war with a neighbouring town. To be kindly received in one place was often a source of danger in the next. But amid such circumstances the preserving care of our God was the more manifest.'

Trusting in His unfailing presence, the missionaries were enabled to go on steadfastly through all, embracing many opportunities for bringing light into the darkness. Burns frequently visited Double Island, holding services in English that were well attended. Taylor, whenever he could spare a day from study, joined him in expeditions to the surrounding country which, in spite of attendant danger, were refreshing, especially as the heat of the summer came on. Even in May it was intensely hot. Sitting quietly at study Taylor had to keep a towel by him to wipe the perspiration streaming from face and hands. Burns, already acclimatized to a southern summer, was able to be out at all hours without danger, but his companion suffered seriously. Still, right on into June, he worked with unremitting diligence, eating hardly anything till evening came, when, in the coolness of a breeze that usually sprang up, they made their evening meal.

But more distressing than the heat, harder to bear than sleepless nights and all the weariness their work involved, was the sin and suffering that surged around them.

Sin does indeed reign here, and, as always, those most to be pitied and whose case seems most hopeless are the women. Looked upon as hardly having any soul, girls are sold here for wives or slaves, and are left entirely without education. Married women and families are not numerous in proportion to the population, but the number of unfortunate women is very great. I say unfortunate advisedly, for they are bought and brought up for this very purpose. They are the absolute property of their owners, and have no escape from that which many of them abhor. Only a few nights ago I was distressed by heart-rending screams from two female voices and, on inquiring, was told that they were most likely newly bought women in a house nearby, who were being tortured into submission. 'And that,' added my informant, 'is very common here.' The cries went on for about two hours. Poor things! poor things!

This is hardly a fit subject to write to you about, but, unless you know, how can you pity and pray for them? English women little realize all they owe to the Gospel. And how few have love enough for Christ to come out here and seek to save the perishing. It does mean sacrifice; but low as they would have to stoop, Jesus stooped lower.

Here, then, amid such surroundings, he quietly endured week after week, month after month, drawing his strength from God. Frequently separated from Burns for the work's sake he was much alone. Keenly the people watched him coming and going from the incense-shop, and inquired into every detail of his life and doings. It was an open life, lived within sight of his neighbours all day long – a life whose love and purity told far more than he had any idea. Three years later in London, at the annual meeting of the Chinese Evangelization Society, Dr. De la Porte[1] from Double Island was one of the speakers.

He had had the pleasure and honour, he said, of an intimate acquaintance with one of the agents of the Society, labouring at the time in Swatow – a Mr. Hudson Taylor, to whose zeal and devotion he could bear the most cordial testimony.

He had seen that young man come home at the close of the day footsore and weary, his face covered with blisters from the heat of the sun, and throw himself down to rest in a state of utter exhaustion, only to rise again in a few hours to the toil and hardship of another day. It had been very evident that he enjoyed the highest

---

[1] A Christian man, who subsequently joined William Burns as a medical missionary in Swatow.

respect from the Chinese, and was doing a great amount of good among them, his influence diffusing the sweetness of true Christianity around him.

Six months of intercourse with William Burns had now gone by, and little as either of them expected it they were nearing the close of their congenial fellowship. To them it seemed that their work together was only just beginning. The needs around them were so great and the help they were to one another so evident that they were looking forward to doing something really adequate together. But Swatow was only one needy field out of the vast whole of unreached China. For that wider work to be done the Lord was making preparation, as well as for widespread blessing in the region He had specially laid upon their hearts. William Burns for Swatow and other strategic points in the great seaboard provinces, and Hudson Taylor, by and by, for far-reaching inland China – such was the purpose of Him who sees the end from the beginning. So the days of their pilgrimage together drew to a close.

It was in the middle of June that Burns returned from the neighbouring town of Ampo, where he had been living for ten days. He had had an encouraging stay in this busy, important place. Not only was there a constant stream of visitors coming for books and conversation, but several interested neighbours were regularly attending morning and evening worship. The change back to Swatow was not a little irksome, especially as continued rain prevented outside work. But it gave a welcome opportunity for prayer and conference over many problems connected with their position.

By the close of the week Taylor was evidently unwell. The close confinement to their narrow quarters was telling upon him, especially when – with their servants and two Chinese helpers – they were 'so thick on the ground' as he expressed it.

When brighter days came and Burns was able to return to Ampo with his Chinese helpers, he knew he must bid farewell to his English companion for a time. The greatest heat of summer was still before them, and Taylor was in no condition to meet it under existing circumstances. There were indications also that for the good of the work he ought to pay a visit to Shanghai.

They had been disappointed in efforts to open a preaching chapel, for the people of Swatow were far too suspicious of foreigners to let them have a room for nothing but preaching, but premises for medical work would be quite another matter. The foreign doctor was always *persona grata*, and if he must tell more or less about his religion – well, his medicines were so good that the preaching could be tolerated.

This being so even in Swatow, the two friends had almost decided to begin hospital work, or at any rate to open a dispensary. They were still praying about it, wondering whether Taylor should take the long journey to Shanghai to fetch his instruments and medicines, when the chief Mandarin of the place was taken ill and the local doctors were unable to relieve him. Hearing from a friend that one of the foreigners in Chinese dress was a skilful physician, he sent for Hudson Taylor and put the case into his hands. The treatment proved beneficial, and no sooner was he well himself than he strongly advised the missionaries to commence medical work in Swatow for the assistance of other sufferers.

As though the shadow of a longer parting lay upon his heart, Hudson Taylor was very reluctant, even then, to leave his friend. But when just at this juncture a free passage was offered him all the way to Shanghai by an English captain, the matter seemed taken out of his hands. It really seemed as though all they needed was the medical outfit waiting in Shanghai to enable them to enter upon fruitful labours.

And so early in July the parting came; and full of thankfulness for the past and hope for greater blessing in the days to come they committed one another to the care and keeping of God.

'Those happy months were an unspeakable joy and comfort to me,' wrote Hudson Taylor long after, looking back upon the companionship thus ended with William Burns. 'His constant communings with God made fellowship with him satisfying to the deep cravings of my heart. His accounts of revival work and of persecutions in Canada, Dublin, and southern China were most instructive as well as interesting; for with true spiritual insight he often pointed out God's purposes in trial in a way that made all life assume quite a new aspect and value. His views especially about evangelism as the great work of the Church, and the order of lay-evangelists as a lost order that Scripture required to be restored, were seed thoughts which were to prove fruitful in the subsequent organization of the China Inland Mission.'

They never met again. All unexpectedly Hudson Taylor found his path diverging from that of his friend. Dark clouds were gathering over southern China, soon to lead to war. On a boat near Swatow William Burns was taken prisoner and sent under escort, by river and canal, a journey of thirty-one days to Canton and the nearest British authorities. Returning to Swatow some months later he was enabled to take advantage of the growing feeling in his favour to establish a permanent work. Known as 'The Man of the Book', he was allowed to go in and out freely, the trusted friend of the people, when all other Europeans were confined to their houses and in considerable danger on account of the iniquities of the coolie traffic; and the Swatow Mission of the English Presbyterian Church later flourished as an outcome of those early labours.

Passing on to other fields when initial difficulties were conquered, Burns was led to Peking at length, and there spent four years in literary and evangelistic work. And then, true to the commanding vision of his life, the veteran missionary turned his face once more to the 'regions beyond'. North of the Great Wall and stretching far away – an almost unknown world – lay the plains of Manchuria. Alone with a single Chinese helper, he set out for Newchwang, his life and teachings so impressing the captain of the junk on which they travelled that he would take no fare from the man whose very presence seemed a blessing.

Then came the closing days, setting the seal of God's own benediction upon this life of singular devotion. Four months of earnest, pioneering work – preaching in English on Sundays to the handful of fellow-countrymen in the Treaty Port, and in Chinese all through the week in the native quarter in which he lived – and after that an illness, the result as it seemed of chill, brought the quiet, unexpected end.[1]

Alone among the Chinese to the last, planting with his dying hand the standard of the Cross far afield amid the darkness, what could be more after the pattern of his whole life, more in keeping with his heart's desire?

A brief absence was all that Hudson Taylor anticipated when he parted from Burns in Swatow. On reaching Shanghai, however, he learned that the premises of the London Missionary Society had been visited by fire and that his medical outfit left there for safety had been destroyed. As everything in Swatow seemed to depend upon the medical work they were now in a position to undertake, there was little use in his returning without medicines – but where was a new supply to come from? He could not purchase in Shanghai, on account of the extravagantly high prices of imported articles, and six or eight months might be required before they would reach him from home. It was a position in which the young missionary, as he tells us, was more disposed to say with Jacob, 'All these things are against me', than to recognize with cheerful faith that 'All things work together for good to them that love God'.

I had not then learned to think of God as the one great Circumstance in whom we live and move and have our being, and of all lesser circumstances as necessarily the kindest, wisest, best, because either ordered or permitted by Him. Hence my disappointment and trial were very great.

The only thing was to go to Ningpo and see what Dr. Parker could do

[1] The Rev. Wm. C. Burns passed away on April 4, 1868, nearly three years after the formation of the China Inland Mission which he had watched with the warmest interest.

To the far-away homeland he sent as his last message an appeal to take up the work he was thus laying down; an appeal nobly responded to by the arrival of the first representative of the Irish Presbyterian Mission in the following year, and of the sister Church of Scotland three years later.

to help. If he could spare a small supply of medicine to go on with, they might still be able to begin work. So in the hope of retrieving his losses Hudson Taylor set out for the neighbouring city.

A set of new difficulties began forthwith. On the way to Ningpo his servant gave him the slip, made off with his baggage, and left him stranded. Not realizing that this had happened, and thinking they had merely missed each other, Hudson Taylor spent some time searching for Yoh-hsi, spending one night in a very uncomfortable inn and the next, having tried in vain to find a lodging, on the steps of a temple. It was between one and two in the morning, when, footsore and exhausted, he lay down there

. . . and putting my money under my head for a pillow should soon have been asleep, had I not perceived a person coming stealthily towards me. As he approached I saw he was one of the beggars so common in China, and had no doubt his intention was to rob me of my money. I did not stir, but watched his movements, and looked to my Father not to leave me in this hour of trial. The man came up, looked at me for some time to assure himself that I was asleep (it was so dark that he could not see my eyes fixed on him), and then began to feel about me gently. I said to him in the quietest tone, but so as to convince him that I was not nor had been sleeping,

'What do you want?'

He made no answer, but went away.

I was thankful to see him go, and when he was out of sight put as much of my cash as would not go into my pocket safely up my sleeve, and made my pillow of a stone projection of the wall. It was not long ere I began to doze, but I was aroused by all but noiseless footsteps of two persons approaching; my nervous system was rendered so sensitive by exhaustion that the slightest sound startled me. Again I sought protection from Him who alone was my stay, and lay still as before, till one of them came up and began to feel under my head for the cash. I spoke again, and they sat down at my feet. I asked them what they were doing. They replied that, like me, they were going to pass the night outside the temple. I then requested them to take the opposite side as there was plenty of room, and leave this side to me. But they would not move from my feet. So I raised myself up and set my back against the wall.

'You had better lie down and sleep,' said one of them, 'otherwise you will be unable to work tomorrow. Do not be afraid; we shall not leave you, and will see that no one does you harm.'

'Listen to me,' I replied. 'I do not want your protection. I do not need it. I do not worship your vain idols. I worship God. He is my Father, and I trust in Him. I know well what your intentions are, and shall keep my eye on you and not sleep.'

Upon this one of them went away, only to return with a third companion. I felt very uneasy but looked to God for help. Once or twice one of them came over to see if I was asleep.

'Do not be mistaken,' I said, 'I am not sleeping.'

Occasionally my head dropped and this was a signal for one of them to rise. But I at once roused myself and made some remark. As the night slowly wore on, I felt very weary, and to keep myself awake as well as to cheer my mind, I sang several hymns, repeated aloud some portions of Scripture, and engaged in prayer, to the annoyance of my companions, who seemed as if they would have given anything to get me to desist. After that they troubled me no more, and when shortly before dawn of day they left me, I got a little sleep.

He was awakened by a young man who threateningly demanded money.

This aroused me, and in an unguarded moment, and with very improper feeling, I seized his arm with a grasp he little expected and dared him to lay a finger on me again. This quite changed his manner!

Further enquiries for his servant and his belongings having convinced him that as far as he was concerned, both were lost, there remained nothing for it but to return to Shanghai. He set out to walk to Shih-mun-wan, where he hoped to find a passenger boat to take him to his destination. On arrival, however, to his dismay he found that no boats were leaving. The river bed was too dry.

His money was almost spent by this time, and his only remaining hope was in obtaining passage on a private boat going in his direction. His search for one, however, proved in vain until suddenly he saw, at a turn in the canal, a letter-boat.

This I concluded must be one of the Kashing boats that had been detained, and I set off after it as fast as hope and the necessities of the case would carry me. For the time being weariness and sore feet were alike forgotten, and after a chase of about a mile, I overtook it.

'Are you going to Kashing-fu?' I called out.

'No', was the only answer.

'Are you going in that direction?'

'No.'

'Will you give me a passage as far as you do go that way?'

Still 'No', and nothing further.

Completely discouraged and exhausted, I sank down on the grass and fainted away.

It was at this point that the tide of events began to turn for him. As he was regaining consciousness voices reached his ears, and he realized that people in a junk on the opposite side of the canal were speaking about him. 'He speaks pure Shanghai dialect,' he heard someone say, and from their speech he knew that they themselves were Shanghai people. He was taken on board and his story, when he told it, evoked considerable sympathy. Eventually a boat was found going to Shanghai, and the captain of the junk arranged for him to travel on it.

'This gentleman is a foreigner from Shanghai who has been robbed,' he said. 'If you will take him with you as far as you go, and then engage a sedan chair to carry him the rest of the way, he will pay you in Shanghai. I will stand surety, and if this gentleman does not pay you when you get to Shanghai, I will do so on your return.'

And so, three weeks after he set out for Ningpo, he found himself back where he had started. His record for Saturday, August 9, 1856, reads as follows:

About 8 a.m. reached Shanghai and the hospitable abode of Mr. Wylie of the London Mission, completing a journey full of mercies though not unmixed with trial. Never since I have been in China have I had such opportunities for preaching the Gospel, and though the termination was far from what I desired it has been greatly blessed to me, and I trust the Word preached and distributed may bear fruit to the glory of God.

That, in the midst of such disturbing experiences, he should have been enabled to preach the Word at all was due, surely, to something which happened in the secret places of his own heart, where the Lord Himself met afresh with His servant. It was as he was trudging back along the road to Shih-mun-wan, after spending the night on the temple steps. After a meal in a tea-shop, followed by a rest and sleep for several hours,

I set off, much refreshed, to return to the city at the South Gate of which I had parted with my servant and coolies two days before. On the way I was led to reflect on the goodness of God, and recollected that I had not made it a matter of prayer that I might be provided with lodgings last night. I felt condemned too that I should have been so anxious for my few things, while the many precious souls around me had caused so little concern. I came as a sinner and pleaded the blood of Jesus, realizing that I was accepted in Him – pardoned, cleansed, sanctified – and oh the love of Jesus, how great I felt it to be! I knew something more than I had ever known of what it was to be despised and rejected and have nowhere to lay one's head, and felt more than ever I had before the greatness of the love that induced Him to leave His home in glory and suffer thus for me – nay, to lay down His very life upon the Cross. I thought of Him as 'despised and rejected of men, a man of sorrows and acquainted with grief'. I thought of Him at Jacob's well, weary, hungry and thirsty, yet finding it His meat and drink to do His Father's will, and contrasted this with my littleness of love. I looked to Him for pardon for the past and for grace and strength to do His will in the future, to tread more closely in His footsteps and to be more than ever wholly His.

And now the question arose as to what was to be done about his servant. The case was one of deliberate robbery, Yoh-hsi's own letters brought final proof of that. It would not have been difficult to institute legal proceedings for the recovery of the property, and Taylor was strongly urged to secure the punishment of the thief; but the more he thought about it, the more he shrank from anything of the sort.

Yoh-hsi was one whose salvation he had earnestly sought, and to hand him over to cruel, rapacious underlings who would only be too glad to throw him into prison that he might be squeezed of the last farthing would not have been in keeping, he felt, with the spirit of the Gospel. Finally, concluding that his soul was worth more than the £40 worth of things he had stolen, Taylor decided to pursue a very different course. In the middle of August he wrote,

I have sent him a plain, faithful letter to the effect that we know his guilt, and what its consequences might be to himself; that at first I had considered handing over the matter to the *yamen*, but remembering Christ's command to return good for evil I had not done so, and did not wish to injure a hair of his head.

I told him that he was the real loser, not I; that I freely forgave him, and besought him more earnestly than ever to flee from the wrath to come. I also added that though it was not likely he would give up such of my possessions as were serviceable to a Chinese, there were among them foreign books and papers that could be of no use to him but were valuable to me, and that those at least he ought to send back.

If only his conscience might be moved and his soul saved, how infinitely more important that would be than the recovery of all I have lost. Do pray for him.[1]

This matter settled, it only remained to set out once more to obtain from Dr. Parker the supplies needed for the medical work at Swatow. This time the journey was accomplished in safety; and just before setting out Taylor was encouraged by an unexpected letter that relieved him of what might have been financial embarrassment. The sale of furniture left at the South Gate had brought in something, and then – just as he was starting came this letter that had been eight or ten weeks on the way:

'Please accept the enclosed,' it said, 'as a token of love from myself and my dear wife.' And the enclosed was a cheque for no less than £40 from Mr. and Mrs. Berger.

Posted long before Hudson Taylor had left Swatow, it arrived by the very first mail after the robbery.

Arriving at Ningpo (the 'City of the Peaceful Wave' as the Chinese characters imply) on August 22, Taylor remained for seven weeks with Dr. Parker, throwing himself heartily into all that was going on. The experiences of another year in China had prepared him more fully to appreciate both the missionaries and their work. Never before had he realized the

[1] In course of time, and far away in England, this letter came into hands for which it had never been intended. Mr. George Müller of Bristol, founder of the well-known Orphan Homes, read it, and from that time Hudson Taylor had an interest in his prayers. Furthermore, as soon as the incident became known to him, he sent straight out to China a sum sufficient to cover Taylor's loss, continuing thereafter to take a practical share in his work, until in a time of special need he was used of God as the principal channel of support to the China Inland Mission.

comfort and advantage of labouring among comparatively friendly people, not embittered against the missionary simply on account of his being a foreigner. Although there was of course the usual ignorance and superstition in Ningpo, and at times much anti-foreign feeling, there was also a large element of interest and even inquiry about the Gospel. And then the missionaries themselves – how delightful to be in the midst of so united and efficient a community!

Welcomed by them in a most generous spirit, Dr. Parker had been successful in building up a practice among the foreign residents, the proceeds of which he devoted entirely to his Medical Mission. Rapidly acquiring the local dialect, in spite of every hindrance to study, he had made the spiritual care of the patients his first work. In this he was assisted by both English and American missionaries, who took it in turn to preach in the dispensary (in which 9,000 patients received treatment within the first twelve months) and to visit the temporary hospital. Converts were free to join any of the churches, Dr. Parker declining to influence them and making it very clear that his sympathies were with all.

With money contributed in Ningpo he had purchased a site on the city side of the river, on the brink of the great waterway and close to the Salt Gate with its constant stream of traffic. A better position could hardly have been found for the permanent hospital, and already the energetic doctor was having the ground levelled for building operations. Hudson Taylor, who was expecting to return to such very different scenes in Swatow, wrote early in September:

> I am now enjoying a season of rest with the friends here, but it must be of short duration. To me it would be very pleasant to remain on here or at Shanghai, among more civilized and friendly people than we have in Swatow. But my call is to a more arduous post; and in my brother Mr. Burns I have an inestimable companion whom I shall rejoice to meet again.
>
> I sometimes wonder whether I shall ever be settled, and long for permanent work and a partner to share all my joys and sorrows. I think in His own time I shall be so circumstanced. The Lord knows. But while one longs for quiet, even now after a week of it I am eager to be at work again, telling of His surpassing love, His glorious redemption.

And work he did with all his usual energy in spite of summer heat. Careful attention to the peculiarities of local speech soon enabled him to make himself understood even by Ningpo people, and there were so many strangers settled there from other places that he found all the dialects he knew of service. A little later he wrote,

> The weather is very warm, nevertheless I have been twice in the country, once with Mr. Jones to Tseki and once with Mr. Quaterman to Chinhai Hsien. Today

I have been to a small village a mile or two away with Mr. Jones. He took some Portuguese Testaments and found three men able to read them, a Singapore man also who could read English and to whom he gave a Bible; while I had an attentive audience to whom I told of pardon, peace and Heaven through the once-offered sacrifice of Jesus, leaving with them a number of Chinese tracts and Scriptures.

Oh, what an abundant harvest may soon be reaped here! The fields are white and so extensive round us, but the labourers are few! I do thank God that He has given me such opportunities. I have met with a good many even from Formosa with whom I have been able to speak of Jesus Christ and Him crucified. I sometimes wish I had twenty bodies, that in twenty places at once I might publish the saving Name of Jesus.

The place where the need was greatest, however, had for him the strongest claim, and before the month was over he was ready to return to William Burns at Swatow. Dr. Parker had fitted him out with medicines and Taylor was just setting out for Shanghai when a delay arose. Mr. and Mrs. Way of the Presbyterian Mission had to take the journey too, and said that if Taylor could wait a day or two, they would hurry their preparations for the sake of joining his party. He was already escorting Jones and his little son, newly arrived members of his own Mission, and it would mean a great deal to the Ways to travel in their company.

Regretting the delay but having no reason against it, Hudson Taylor waited, and almost a week went by before the final start could be made. When they did get away the winds were against them, Jones developed a painful malady, and not until early in October did they reach Shanghai. Having discharged his commissions at last, it now only remained for Hudson Taylor to put his things on board the vessel that was to take him to Swatow.

Providentially as it seemed Captain Bowers was again in Shanghai, on the eve of sailing, and cordially welcomed the young missionary as his passenger. So with as little delay as possible Hudson Taylor sent his belongings on board the *Geelong* and prepared to leave Shanghai, it might be permanently.

And then the unexpected happened. A letter from the south coming to one of the members of the London Missionary Society made him go hurriedly in search of Hudson Taylor.

'If he has not started,' wrote Burns, 'please inform him at once of this communication.'

It was to the effect that all they had looked forward to in Swatow was at an end for the time being, William Burns having been arrested in the interior and sent to Canton. What could be the meaning of these tidings? Burns imprisoned and sent to Canton? The Chinese helpers still in confinement and in danger of their lives? The British authorities unwilling that he should return?

Almost dazed, it all came over him. First one check and then another; medicines destroyed, robbery and all it had entailed, visit to Ningpo, delay in getting away, tedious return journey, and now at the last moment nothing but a closed door – and a sick brother waiting to be taken back to the city from which they had come.

Yes, there was no question but to go back to Ningpo.

'Thine ears shall hear a word behind thee saying, This is the way, walk ye in it.' But for the moment the path that had seemed so clear was lost in strange uncertainty.

CHAPTER 10

Ebenezer and Jehovah Jireh

(1856–1858)

LIFE turns at times on a small pivot. 'It is interesting to notice,' wrote Hudson Taylor years later, 'the various events which united in the providence of God in preventing my return to Swatow and ultimately led to my settling in Ningpo.' How could he know that the upset of all his plans and the severance of a partnership in service more precious than any he had ever known was to prove the crowning blessing of his life on the human side, bringing him into association and at last union with the one of all others most suited both to him and his work?

Yet so it proved. God's hand was on the helm. The closed door was as much His providence as the open, and equally for the good of His servant, and the accomplishment of His own great ends.

Maria Dyer's was a deep and tender nature. Lonely from childhood, she had grown up longing for a real heart-friend. Her father she could hardly remember, and from the mother whom she devotedly loved she was parted by death at ten years of age, just as she and her brother and sister were leaving Penang to complete their education. After this the doubly-orphaned children had been brought up under the care of an uncle in London, most of their time being spent at school.

Then came the call to China, through Miss Aldersey's need of a helper in the Ningpo school. In offering for this post, the sisters were influenced not so much by a desire to take up missionary work as by the knowledge that it was what their parents would have desired. Young as they were they had had some training as teachers, and as they were self-supporting and did not wish to be separated Miss Aldersey invited both to join her instead of only one.

To the younger sister the voyage to China was memorable as the time of her definite entrance into peace with God. Previously she had striven to be a Christian in her own strength, feeling all the while that she lacked the 'one thing needful' and seeking vainly to obtain it. Now her thoughts were turned to Christ and His atoning work as the only ground of pardon and acceptance; the all-sufficient ground to which our prayers and efforts can add nothing at all. Gradually it dawned upon her that she *was* redeemed, pardoned, cleansed from sin, because He had suffered in her stead. God had accepted Christ as her substitute and saviour, and she could do no less. Simply and trustfully as a little child she turned away from everything and everyone else, content to take God at His word. 'There is therefore now no condemnation to them which are in Christ Jesus', and to prove that 'The Spirit himself beareth witness with our spirit that we are' here and now 'the children of God'.

This true conversion with all that flowed from it made her entrance upon missionary work very different from what it would otherwise have been. No longer a philanthropic undertaking to which she devoted herself out of regard for her parents' wishes, it had become the natural and even necessary expression of her great and growing love to Him who was her Saviour, Lord and King. He had changed everything for her, for time and for eternity, and the least she could do was to give herself entirely to His service. So with a peace and joy unknown before she took up her busy and often difficult life in Miss Aldersey's school.

'It was a model institution,' wrote Dr. W. A. P. Martin, who later became the first President of the Peking University. 'For three years at Miss Aldersey's request I ministered to the church in her house, and I cherish a vivid impression of the energy displayed by that excellent woman, notwithstanding a feeble frame and frequent ailments. The impression she made on the Chinese, whether Christian or pagan, was profound, the latter firmly believing that as England was ruled by a woman so Miss Aldersey had been delegated to be the head of our foreign community. The British Consul, they said, invariably obeyed her commands.

'Several shocks of earthquake having alarmed the people, they imputed the disturbance to Miss Aldersey's magic power, alleging that they had seen her mount the city wall before dawn of day, and open a bottle in which she kept confined certain strong spirits which proceeded to shake the pillars of the earth.

'No wonder they thought so! Her strange habits could not but suggest something uncanny. The year round she was accustomed to walk on the city wall at five o'clock in the morning, and with such undeviating punctuality that in winter she was preceded by a man bearing a lantern. A bottle she carried in her hand did really contain "strong spirits", spirits of hartshorn, which she constantly used to relieve headache and as an antidote for ill odours. In summer, unwilling to leave her school for the seaside, she would climb to the ninth storey of a lofty pagoda and sit there through the long hours of the afternoon, sniffing the wind that came from the sea. At such times she was always accompanied by some of her pupils, so that her work was not for a moment suspended. So parsimonious was she of time that she even had them read to her while she was taking her meals.

'I can truly say that in the long list of devoted women who have laboured in and for China, I know no nobler name than hers.'

But it was an exacting post for a girl in her teens, and especially one of so loving a spirit as Maria Dyer. Her sister's companionship she had, certainly, and the missionary circle in Ningpo gave her several friends. But her heart had never found its mate in the things that mattered most.

And then he came – the young missionary who impressed her from the first as having the same longings after holiness, usefulness, nearness to God. He was different from everybody else; there was a something about him that made her feel at rest and understood. He seemed to live in such a real world, and to have such a real, great God. Though she saw little of him, it was a comfort to know that he was near, and she was startled to find how much she missed him when after only seven weeks he went away.

Very real was her joy, therefore, as well as surprise, when from Shanghai he had to turn back again. Perhaps it was this that opened her eyes to the feeling with which she was beginning to regard him. At any rate, she soon knew, and with her sweet, true nature did not try to hide it from her own heart and God. There was no one else to whom she cared to speak about him; for others did not see in him, always, just what she saw. They disliked his wearing Chinese dress, and did not approve his making himself so entirely one with the people. So she prayed much though she showed little. The love of her life had come to her, and nobody knew but God.

Meanwhile, a little missionary family had come to live in Ningpo, in the southern part of the city where Miss Aldersey's school was situated. Mr. and Mrs. Jones had come out under the Chinese Evangelization Society some months previously, but had been detained at Hong Kong by serious illness, and by the death of their eldest child. They had already suffered much for the land to which their lives were given, and when they reached Ningpo, in June 1857, Maria Dyer laid herself out to be useful to the busy mother. As often as possible they went visiting together, for young as she was, and much occupied with her school classes, the young missionary could not be satisfied with anything less than soul-winning.

'That was what drew out my interest,' said Hudson Taylor long after. 'She was spiritually minded, as her work proved. Even then she was a true missionary.'

For it could not but be that the young Englishman should meet Maria Dyer from time to time at the house of his friends, and it could not but be also that he should be attracted. She was so frank and natural that they were soon on terms of good acquaintance, and then she proved so like-minded in all important ways that, unconsciously almost to himself, she began to fill a place in his heart never filled before.

Vainly he strove against the longing to see more of her, and did his utmost to banish her image from his mind. He was deeply conscious of his call to labour in the interior, and felt that for such work he should be free from claims of wife and home. Besides, all was uncertain before him. In a few weeks or months the way might open for his return to Swatow. Was he not waiting daily upon the Lord for guidance, with the needs of that region still in view? And if it were not to be southern China, it was his hope and purpose to undertake pioneering work nearer at hand, work that might at any time cost his life. No, it was not for him to cherish thoughts such as would rise unbidden as he looked into the face he loved.

What *right* had he to think of marriage, without a home, income, or prospect of any that he could ask her to share? Accredited agent of the C.E.S. though he was, it did not at all follow that they were to be depended upon for financial supplies. For months he had not drawn upon his Letter of Credit, knowing the Society to be in debt. Chiefly through the ministry of Mr. Berger, the Lord had supplied his needs. But this might not continue. It could not at any rate be counted on. And what would she say, and those responsible for her, to a life of faith in China, faith even for daily bread?

Yes, it was perfectly clear: he was in no position to think of marriage, and must subdue the heart-hunger that threatened at times to overwhelm him. And to a certain extent he was helped in turning his thoughts to other matters by events transpiring in the south.

For fourteen uneasy years England had been pressing China, by every argument that could be devised, to legalize the importation of opium. In spite of the refusal of the Emperor Tao-kwang to admit at any price 'the flowing poison', the smuggling trade had gone on growing in defiance of treaty rights. Since the conclusion of England's first war with China, justly called 'The Opium War', there had long been an inclination in certain quarters to bring on a second, and now a tiny spark had been fanned into a blaze. Notwithstanding the condemning voice of a large majority in the British Parliament, the two countries were at war, with British guns thundering at the gates of Canton.

In the middle of November news began to reach the northern ports, and in Ningpo, with its large proportion of Cantonese, feeling ran high. Early in January a plot was hatched for the destruction of all the foreigners in the city and neighbourhood. The plot was discovered in time, but

> 'The peril that threatened us', wrote Dr. Parker, 'was so great that the merchants of the Settlement prepared for flight by keeping at single anchor the vessel on which their valuables had been stored. They and some others had their houses guarded by armed men; and after much prayer several missionaries, including Mr. Jones and myself, were led to send our wives and children to Shanghai.'

Thus it was that Hudson Taylor, three months after settling in Ningpo, found himself called to move again. No one else seemed so free to escort the party, and his knowledge of the Shanghai dialect made it easy for him to do so. He could be just as useful in Shanghai as in Ningpo, an important consideration when the stay might be a long one.

Personally he would have given a good deal to have remained in Ningpo just then, if only to watch over the safety of Maria, for Miss Aldersey would not leave, and her young helpers decided to stay with her. She was just handing over her school, from the superintendence of which she felt it wise to retire, to the American Presbyterian Mission. Mrs. Bausum, a relative of the Dyer sisters, had come over from Penang, and into her hands the sixty girls with all the school affairs had to be committed. It was no time for unnecessary changes; and, taking what precautions she could for her own safety and that of her charges, Miss Aldersey stayed to complete her work.

But to leave them then was no easy matter to Hudson Taylor. The elder of the sisters had recently become engaged to his friend Burdon, and seemed in consequence to have a special protector; but the younger was left all the more lonely, and claimed for that very reason a deeper love and sympathy from his heart. Of course, he dared not show it. He had no reason to think that it would be any comfort to her, and – was he not trying to forget? So he suffered keenly as he left his little home on Bridge Street in Ningpo, not knowing if he would ever see it or her again.

Four and a half months followed, in which the young missionary was engrossed in work in his old surroundings. One of the chapels of the London Missionary Society placed at his disposal gave him important opportunities for preaching, besides which he daily addressed large and changing audiences in the temple of the City God. Returning regularly to these places he and Jones came to be known and expected, and many were the conversations held with interested inquirers.

'When I first heard you preach,' said a young incense-maker, 'I found what I was longing for. If you had instructed me to be immersed in fire instead of in water, I should have desired it with all my heart.'

Nevertheless their way was anything but easy at this time. During the whole period of their stay in Shanghai they were surrounded by suffering and distress of the most painful kind. Famine refugees from Nanking had poured into the city until there were thousands of destitute and starving persons added to the ranks of beggary. This meant that one never could go out without seeing heart-rending scenes, which the conditions of life around them made it almost impossible to relieve.

Furthermore, a debt of over £1,000 burdened the Society to which they belonged, and burdened still more the consciences of Hudson Taylor and his companions. For some time he had been corresponding with the secretaries on the subject, feeling that, unless a change could be made in the home-management, he would be obliged to withdraw from the service of the Society. This he was most reluctant to do, although the term of years agreed upon in his engagement had expired. He had even suggested that remittances should only be sent when there was money in hand, as he would far rather look to the Lord directly for supplies than draw upon borrowed money. But it seemed as though the Committee could not see anything wrong in their position, and for this reason especially he was much exercised about continuing his connection with them.

Neither then nor at any time did he wish to be 'a free lance', independent of the support and control of others, but it was hard to see in what connection he could labour, seeing he was unordained and without a medical degree.

> 'I am not sanguine as to any other Society taking me,' he wrote to his mother early in the spring: 'but, as always, the Lord will provide.'

It was in even more personal matters, however, that the young missionary was specially cast upon God, through his deep and growing love for Maria Dyer. He had thought, he had in a sense hoped, that absence would enable him to forget; that his love for her would be more under control when she was out of sight. And now quite the reverse was the case. Silently but steadily it gained a stronger hold upon his inmost being. He had loved before in a more or less boyish way; but this was different. Everything he thought, felt and did seemed permeated with the sense of that other life, so much a part of his own. He could not separate himself in thought from her; and when most consciously near to God he felt the communion of her spirit, the longing for her presence most.

In everything she satisfied his mind and heart; not only embodying his ideal of womanliness, but being herself devoted to the work to which his life was given. As one who having put his hand to the plough dared not look back, he could rest in the assurance that she would help and not hinder him in his special service. And yet the old question remained: how could he marry – with such prospects, such a future?

Of her thoughts and feelings about him, if she had any, he knew nothing. She had always been kind and pleasant, but that she was to everyone, with a sweetness of spirit that was unfailing. Apparently she did not wish to marry. Far more eligible men than he had failed to win her! What chance then could there be for one so poor and insignificant?

If anyone had known, if there had been anyone with whom he could have shared the hopes and fears within him, those first months in Shanghai would have been easier to bear; but it was not until the end of March, and through most unexpected circumstances, that the friends with whom he was living began to perceive the trouble of his heart. They had loved him from the first, and had been drawn very closely to him through their Shanghai experiences, but it was not until Mrs. Jones contracted smallpox among the people she was seeking to relieve, and had to hand over the care of household and children to their young fellow-worker, that they fully realized what he was. Devoted in his care of the little ones, he earned the parents' deepest gratitude, and in the weeks of convalescence that followed they were so united in prayer and sympathy that – how he could not tell – the love he had meant to hide was a secret no longer from his nearest friends.

He was even more surprised at the satisfaction they expressed. Far from discouraging him, they were full of thankfulness to God. Never had they seen two people more suited to each other. As to the outcome – his duty was perfectly clear: the rest must be left with Him to whom both their lives were given.

So the question was committed to writing that had been burning in his heart for months; and then Hudson Taylor could only wait. A week, ten days, two weeks, how long it seemed until the answer came!

He was little prepared, in spite of all the prayer there had been about it, for the tone and purport of his communication. It was her writing surely; the clear, pretty hand he knew so well. But could it be her spirit? Brief and unsympathetic, the note simply said that what he desired was wholly impossible, and requested him if he had any gentlemanly feeling to refrain from ever troubling the writer again upon the subject.

Could he have known the anguish with which those words had been penned, his own trouble would have been considerably lessened. But the one he loved was far away. He could not see her, dared not write again after such a request, and had no clue to the painful situation. Then it was that the tender, unspoken sympathy of his friends, the Joneses, became so great a solace. He could hardly have borne it without them, and yet the sight of their mutual happiness reminded him constantly of the blessing he had lost.

Meanwhile, far away in Ningpo, that other heart was even more desolate and perplexed. With what joy she had received that letter! When she could break away from her first glad thanksgiving she went to find her sister, who was most sympathetic. The next thing was to tell Miss Aldersey, hoping she would approve this engagement as she had Burella's. But great was the indignation with which she heard the story.

'Mr. Taylor! that young, poor, unconnected nobody. How dare he presume to think of such a thing? Of course the proposal must be refused at once, and that finally.'

In vain Maria tried to explain how much he was to her. That only made matters worse. She must be saved without delay from such folly. And her kind friend proceeded, with the best intentions, to take the matter entirely into her own hands. The result was a letter written almost at Miss Aldersey's dictation, not only closing the whole affair but requesting most decidedly that it might be never reopened.

Bewildered and heartbroken, the poor girl had no choice. She was too young and inexperienced, and far too shy in such matters, to withstand the decision of Miss Aldersey, strongly reinforced by the friends with whom she was staying. Stung to the quick with grief and shame, she could only leave it in the hands of her Heavenly Father. He knew; He understood. And in the long, lonely days that followed, when even her sister was won over to Miss Aldersey's position, she took refuge in the certainty that nothing, *nothing* was too hard for the Lord.

To Hudson Taylor in his sorrow, sympathizing hearts were open, but for her there was none. And she did not know that he would ever cross her path again. After such a refusal he would surely stay away from Ningpo, especially in view of the recommencement of work at Swatow which she knew he longed to share. Nothing was more probable now than that he would return to his friend William Burns. And this, no doubt, he would have done had he been acting on impulse and not holding steadfastly to the guidance of God. As it was, though he knew nothing of her feelings and had little if any hope of a more favourable issue, he was winning in the depths of his sorrow just the blessing it was meant to bring. He wrote to his sister in May,

> We have need of patience, and our faithful God brings us into experiences which, improved by His blessing, may cultivate in us this grace. Though we seem to be tried at times almost beyond endurance, we never find Him unable or unwilling to help and sustain us; and were our hearts *entirely* submissive to His will, desiring it and it only to be done, how much fewer and lighter would our afflictions seem.
>
> I have been in much sorrow of late; but the principal cause I find to be want of willing submission to, and trustful repose in God, my Strength. Oh, to desire His will to be done with my whole heart, to seek His glory with a single eye!

It is perhaps not surprising that one book in the Bible, that had never meant much to him before, should have opened up at this time in undreamed-of beauty. His deep understanding of the Song of Solomon seems to have begun in these days, when the love that welled up so irresistibly within him could only be given to God. Never had he understood before what the Lord can be to His people, and what He longs to find in His people toward Himself. It was a wonderful discovery, and one that only grew with all the glad fruition that lay beyond this pain. To those who knew Hudson Taylor best in later years, nothing was more characteristic than his love for the Song of Solomon and the way in which it expressed his personal relationship to the Lord.[1] Here is the beginning of it all, culled from letters to his mother and sister in that sad spring of 1857.

[1] Hudson Taylor's Bible readings on the Song of Solomon are published under the title *Union and Communion.*

My dear Amelia, it is very late, but I cannot retire without penning a few lines to you. All below is transitory; we know not what a day or an hour may bring forth. One thing only changes not – the love of God. Our precious Jesus is the same and ever will be, and soon He will come and take us to Himself.

Have you thought much about the Song of Solomon? It is a rich garden to delight in, and so is the forty-fifth Psalm. To think that even the sweetest, dearest of earthly ties but faintly shadows forth the love of Jesus to His redeemed, to me, is it not wonderful? Oh, how can we love our precious Jesus enough, how do enough for Him! Soon will He call us to a wedding feast, the marriage supper of the Lamb. Not as guests, but as *the bride* shall we take our place with joy, arrayed in the spotless robe of His righteousness. The time is short. May we live as those who wait for their Lord, and be ready with joy to meet Him.

With the first hot days of summer came a change in the conditions that had detained Hudson Taylor and his colleagues in Shanghai. The famine refugees began to disappear, as spring harvests drew them back to country villages all over the plain. Furthermore, a lull in the war with England made aggressive work in Ningpo and the neighbourhood possible; Hudson Taylor and Jones both realized the importance of labouring in some one, settled spot until by the blessing of God a local church could be raised up with pastors and evangelists for the wider opportunity of coming days. With this hope in view, they turned their faces to Ningpo again. This move was not made, however, before they had taken a step of great importance in its bearing on the future. For it was in the month of May, three years and three months after his arrival in China, that Hudson Taylor felt the time had come to resign his connection with the Chinese Evangelization Society. It was not all the difficulties under which he had laboured which led him to this step, but because the Society took a very different position from his own in the matter of debt. Recalling the circumstances, he wrote:

Personally I had always avoided debt and kept within my salary, though at times only with very careful economy. But the Society itself was in debt. The quarterly bills which I and others were instructed to draw were often met with borrowed money, and a correspondence commenced which terminated in the following year by my resigning from conscientious motives. To me it seemed that the teaching of God's Word was unmistakably clear, 'Owe no man anything'. To borrow money implied, to my mind, a contradiction of Scripture – a confession that God had withheld some good thing, and a determination to get for ourselves what He had not given. I could not think that God was poor, that He was short of resources, or unwilling to supply any want of whatever work was really His. It seemed to me that if there were lack of funds to carry on work, then to that degree, in that special development, or at that time, it could not be the work of God. To satisfy my conscience I was therefore compelled to resign my connection with the Society.

It was a great satisfaction to me that my friend and colleague, Mr. Jones, was led to take the same step, and we were both profoundly thankful that the separation took place without the least breach of friendly feeling on either side. Indeed, we had the joy of knowing that the step we took commended itself to several members of the Committee, although the Society as a whole could not come to our position. Depending on God alone for supplies, we were enabled to continue a measure of connection with our former supporters, sending home journals, etc., for publication as before, so long as the Society continued to exist.

The step we had taken was not a little trying to faith. But oh! I was learning to know Him. I would not even then have missed the trial. He became so near, so real, so intimate. The occasional difficulty about funds never came from an insufficient supply for personal needs, but in consequence of ministering to the wants of scores of the hungry and dying around us. And trials far more searching in other ways quite eclipsed these difficulties, and being deeper brought forth in consequence richer fruits. How glad one is now not only to know, with Miss Havergal, that

They who trust Him wholly
Find Him wholly true,

but also that when we fail to trust fully He still remains unchangingly faithful. He *is* wholly true whether we trust or not. 'If we believe not, he abideth faithful: he cannot deny himself.' But oh, how we dishonour our Lord whenever we fail to trust Him, and what peace, blessing and triumph we lose in thus sinning against the Faithful One. May we never again presume in anything to doubt Him.

What the more searching trials were that brought forth richer blessing it is not difficult at this point to divine. Twice daily in his walks to and from Bridge Street, Hudson Taylor had to pass very near Miss Aldersey's school. Carried on now by Mrs. Bausum and her young relatives it was still the home of the being dearest to him on earth. He had seen her again since returning to Ningpo in June, but a barrier had been raised between them that was hard to pass. Kind and gentle as she still was, he could not forget that she had charged him never to trouble her upon a certain subject; and Miss Aldersey had so spoken her mind to the friends with whom he lived that the position was doubly trying.

It was soon after their return from Shanghai that Mrs. Jones had invited Maria Dyer to go out visiting with her as before. Apart from the fact that there was no one else to whom she could look for such help, it was the best way in which the two young people could see more of each other. To the girl herself she said nothing, nor did Maria allude to the matter of which their hearts were full. But Miss Aldersey knew no such reticence, and seeking Mrs. Jones after the Ladies' Prayer Meeting, in another part of the city, poured out the vials of her wrath. She had good reason, she felt, to be indignant. Miss Dyer belonged to a different social circle from that of Mr. Taylor, and had a small but reliable income of her own. She was educated, gifted, attractive, and had no lack of suitors far more eligible in

Miss Aldersey's eyes. It was unpardonable that this person should presume upon her youth and inexperience, and still more so that he should return to Ningpo after its having been made plain that he was not wanted.

His position as an independent worker, upon the uncertain basis of 'faith', was severely criticized; and he was represented as 'called by no one, connected with no one, and recognized by no one as a minister of the Gospel'. Had this been all it would have been bad enough, but other insinuations followed. He was 'fanatical, undependable, diseased in body and mind', and in a word 'totally worthless'.

In the course of such a conversation many things come out, and before it ended Mrs. Jones could see pretty clearly how the land lay. Miss Aldersey's object was to obtain from her a promise that she would do nothing to forward Hudson Taylor's suit, and that the latter would never see or speak to Maria in their house. While not committing herself as far as this, Mrs. Jones felt it desirable to state that she would refrain from throwing the young people together, and that Taylor would not take advantage of Maria's visits to attempt to see her alone.

After this, of course, Hudson Taylor felt himself bound by Mrs. Jones's promise. He could not write to Maria or seek an interview in the house of his friends. Having learned that Miss Aldersey was not even related to the Dyers, however, he determined to ask whether he might write to their uncle in London for permission to cultivate a closer acquaintance.

Although he had no means of getting in touch with the one he loved, he believed the Lord could bring them together. And so it proved. He who can use ravens, if need be, or angels to do His bidding was answering His children's prayers, and on this occasion He seems to have employed a waterspout!

It was a sultry afternoon in July, when in regular rotation the Ladies' Prayer Meeting came to be held in the Jones's home at *Kuen-kiao-teo*. The usual number gathered, representing all the Societies, but as the sequel proved it was easier to come to the meeting that day than to get away. With scarcely any warning a waterspout, sweeping up the tidal river, broke over Ningpo in a perfect deluge, followed by torrents of rain. Jones and Taylor were over at Bridge Street as usual, and on account of the flooded streets were late in reaching home. Most of the ladies had left before they returned, but a servant from the school was there who said that Mrs. Bausum and Miss Maria Dyer were still waiting for sedan chairs.

'Go into my study,' said Jones to his companion, 'and I will see if an interview can be arranged.'

It was not long before he returned saying that the ladies were alone with his wife and that they would be glad of a little conversation.

Hardly knowing what he did Hudson Taylor went upstairs, and found himself in the presence of the one being he supremely loved. True, others were there too, but he hardly saw them, hardly saw anything but her face, as he told much more than he would have ever thought possible – in public. He had only meant to ask if he might write to her guardian for permission . . . But now it all came out; he could not help it. And she? Well, there was no one present but those who loved them and understood, and it might be so long before they could meet again! Yes, she consented, and did much more than that. With her true woman's heart she relieved all his fears, as far as they could be relieved by knowing that he was just as dear to her as she to him. And if the others heard, were there not angels too? And presently Hudson Taylor relieved the situation by saying, 'Let us take it all to the Lord in prayer.'

So the letter was written about the middle of July upon which so much depended, and they had to look forward to four months of prayer and patience before the answer could be received. In the circumstances they did not feel free to see one another or even communicate in writing, for they had as far as possible to mitigate Miss Aldersey's displeasure. Maria informed her that Hudson Taylor had written to her uncle asking permission for a definite engagement, and the older woman said she would at once communicate with Mr. Tarn himself, when he would of course see the impropriety of the request. There the matter had to rest until the slow mails returned.

It was about this time that a pair of scrolls made their appearance in the sitting-room at *Kuen-kiao-teo* that were as new as they were perplexing to the little company of Christians and inquirers gathered there on Sunday morning for worship. Beautifully written in Chinese each character in itself was intelligible, but what could be the meaning of the strange combination, *I-pien-i-seh-er*; *Je-ho-hua I-la*?

The young missionary who had been ill and confined to his room for a month could have explained. For it was there in quiet communion with God those inspired words had come to him in such fullness of meaning as to make them for ever memorable. *Ebenezer* and *Jehovah Jireh*: 'Hitherto hath the Lord helped us', and for all coming need 'The Lord will provide' – how he rejoiced as strength came back to unfold to his Chinese friends their precious message, leading them on to a deeper knowledge of the infinite God they too were learning to trust.

That little inner circle, small though it was in numbers, was the joy and rejoicing of Hudson Taylor's heart, and the illness that laid him aside during the whole of September was made the most of for prayer on their behalf. Taken out of the busy round of preaching and medical work he was able to give more time to individual inquirers, amongst whom Mr. Nyi, a business man in the city, was perhaps the most encouraging.

Passing the open door of the mission-house one evening soon after Jones and his colleague had settled there, he observed that something was going on. A big bell was ringing, and a number of people were passing in as if for a meeting. Hearing that it was a 'Jesus Hall', or place where foreign teachers discoursed upon religious matters, he too turned in; for as a devout Buddhist there was nothing about which he felt more concern than the pains and penalties due to sin, and the transmigration of the soul on its long journey he knew not whither.

A young foreigner in Chinese dress was preaching from his Sacred Classics, and this was the passage he read:

> As Moses lifted up the serpent in the wilderness, even so must the Son of man be lifted up: That whosoever believeth in him should not perish, but have eternal life.
> For God so loved the world, that he gave his only begotten Son, that whosoever believeth in him should not perish, but have everlasting life. For God sent not his Son into the world to condemn the world; but that the world through him might be saved.

Nyi came into the hall that evening one of the vast, the incredibly vast multitude who 'through fear of death are all their lifetime subject to bondage'; and as he sat there listening, hope dawned in his heart, old things for ever passed away and he was conscious of the sunrise that makes all things new.

The meeting was drawing to a close; the 'foreign teacher' had ceased speaking. Looking round upon the audience with the instinct of one accustomed to lead in such matters, Nyi rose in his place and said with simple directness:

'I have long sought the Truth, as did my father before me, but without finding it. I have travelled far and near, but have never searched it out. In Confucianism, Buddhism, Taoism, I have found no rest; but I do find rest in what we have heard tonight. Henceforward I am a believer in Jesus.'

The effect of this declaration was profound, for Nyi was well known and respected. But no one present was more moved than the young missionary to whom he specially addressed himself. Many interviews followed, and Hudson Taylor experienced the joy no words can express as he saw the Lord working with him and claiming this soul for His own.

Shortly after his conversion, a meeting was held of the society over which Nyi had formerly presided, and though he had resigned from its membership he obtained permission to be present and to explain the reasons for his change of faith. Taylor, who accompanied him, was deeply impressed by the clearness and power with which he set forth the Gospel. One of his former co-religionists was led to Christ through his instrumentality, and with Nyi himself became a valuable worker of the *Kuen-kiao-teo* church. Nyi, a dealer in cotton, frequently had time at his disposal, which he now devoted to helping his missionary friends. With Jones he went out almost daily, taking no payment for his services, and everywhere winning an entrance for the message he was so keen to bring.

He it was who, talking with Hudson Taylor, unexpectedly raised a question the pain of which was not easily forgotten.

'How long have you had the Glad Tidings in England?' he asked all unsuspectingly.

The young missionary was ashamed to tell him, and vaguely replied that it was several hundreds of years.

'What,' exclaimed Nyi in astonishment, 'several hundreds of years! Is it possible that you have known about Jesus so long, and only now have come to tell us?

'My father sought the truth for more than twenty years,' he continued sadly, 'and died without finding it. *Oh, why did you not come sooner?*'

Hardly had Hudson Taylor recovered from his illness and resumed his former activities when a call came to very different service.

Over on the compound of the Presbyterian Mission his friend Quaterman was taken seriously ill. A devoted pioneer evangelist, he had remained unmarried during the ten years of his life in China, finding a congenial home with his sister, Mrs. Way. His brother-in-law, one of the Presbyterian missionaries, was absent on a journey, when Mrs. Way discovered that her brother was suffering from smallpox. The patient had to be isolated, and with little children to care for Mrs. Way could not undertake the nursing.

To Hudson Taylor the circumstances were a clear call to go to the help of his friends. Night and day he tended the dying man, doing duty as doctor and nurse in one, that others might be spared the risk of infection.

'He has been taken home to be with Jesus,' he wrote a week later, 'and great was my privilege in being permitted to minister to the Lord in his person, and to see the power of sustaining grace.'

But he did not say how cast upon God he had been all through those terrible nights and days, nor how he felt the strain now that it was over. For the moment, indeed, more pressing considerations occupied him, and he was reminded in a practical way of the scrolls at *Kuen-kiao-tee* with their precious message.

For hardly had he performed the last offices for his friend before he found himself in an unforeseen dilemma. In his attendance night and day upon the patient he had been obliged to change his clothing frequently, and now all the garments used in the sick room had to be discarded for fear of spreading the infection. A Chinese tailor could soon have provided others, but as it happened the young missionary could not afford a fresh supply. It was not that he had been suffering from shortness of funds. On the contrary, ever since leaving the C.E.S. he had received from other sources more than he personally required. But he was sharing all that came to him with the Jones family, and recently had sent £37 to a brother missionary in need. Thus he had nothing laid by to fall back upon, and now the infected garments had to be destroyed he would have been in serious difficulty, but for the resource of prayer.

And just then, a long-lost box arrived containing among other belongings all the clothing he had left in Swatow fifteen months previously. For God is a real Father, and still knows His children's needs before they ask Him.

A little incident? Yes, but one that added meaning to the motto of the Mission that was yet to grow out of the growth of his soul:

'Hitherto hath the Lord helped us.
The Lord will provide.'

His attendance upon Quaterman proved too much for him at this time, however, and for some days he ran a high fever. Toward the close he had an experience which brought him untold comfort.

It was before day-dawn on October 20 when some noise in the street awoke Taylor with a sudden start. He could not sleep again, and though outwardly quiet, was distressed by palpitation due to his exhausted condition. Then, with the fatal ease of disordered nerves, one misgiving led to another, until he was overwhelmed with painful apprehensions. All the suspense and anguish of the long months of his love for the one who might never be his seemed to come back like a flood, gathering itself up in a great fear of what was yet to come. They had suffered so much; their love for one another was so intense, and the opposition it awakened so persistent that it seemed more than he could bear. Unreasoning anxiety laid hold upon him. But One whose comprehension is infinite was watching over His suffering child; and in the way of all others most sure to help, relief was given. He wrote to his sister later in the day,

All at once I became conscious of dear Maria's presence. She came in silently as a breath of air, and I felt such a tranquillity steal over me – I knew she must be there. I felt spellbound for a short time, but at length without opening my eyes, I put out my hand, and she took it in a warm, soft grasp. She motioned me not to speak, and put her other hand on my forehead, and I felt the headache and the fever retire under its touch and sink as through the pillow. She whispered to me not to be uneasy, that she was mine and I was hers, and that I must keep quiet and try to sleep. And so I did, awaking some hours later well of the fever though very weak.

A sweet dream, I would call it; only I was as wide awake as I am now, and saw and felt her touch as plainly as I do now pencil and paper. All my fear in the fever had been that our love would come to nothing, so you may guess how it soothed me.

With returning strength he was more than ever busy in the city. The preaching-station work he and Jones were doing was full of encouragement and they had added to it 'free breakfasts' for the very poor that were a special source of satisfaction to Hudson Taylor.

Feeding sixty to eighty people every day was a considerable tax on their resources, and more than once they had actually come to the last penny before fresh supplies were received. One instance of the care and faithfulness of God he could not but share with his home-circle.

'On Saturday morning', he wrote, 'we paid all expenses and provided for the morrow, after which we had not a single dollar left. How the Lord would care for us on Monday we knew not, but over our mantelpiece hung two scrolls in Chinese character – *Ebenezer* and *Jehovah Jireh* – and He kept us from doubting for a moment.

'That very day the mail came in a week before it was due, and Mr. Jones received a remittance for 214 dollars. So once again we thanked God and took courage.'

Very soon after this, Taylor found that the Lord had been working for him in other ways also. After careful inquiry in London Mr. Tarn had satisfied himself that Hudson Taylor was a young missionary of unusual promise. The Secretaries of the Chinese Evangelization Society had nothing but good to say of him, and from other sources also he had the highest references. Taking therefore any disquieting rumours he may have heard for no more than they were worth, he cordially consented to his niece's engagement.

And now, how distractingly difficult it was to arrange an interview between the two young people! For Hudson Taylor to cross the river forthwith and present himself at Mrs. Bausum's would have outraged the proprieties. Anywhere on the compound where Maria lived, indeed, they could not have met under any circumstances; his own home was still more out of the question. News of this sort flies fast, however, and in some way Mrs. Knowlton of the American Baptist Mission heard of the situation. She was in favour of the engagement, and lived in a quiet place outside the city wall and close to the river. She would send a note to the school. Maria Dyer could come to see her at any time; and if somebody else was there – well, such things will happen, even in China.

So it was in Mrs. Knowlton's drawing-room he waited while the messenger went slowly, slowly across the river and seemed as if he never would return. Let us hope that the windows overlooked the ferry, and that Hudson Taylor had not to keep up the form of conversaton. At last, at last! The slender figure, quick step, bright young voice in the passage – and then the door opened, and for the first time they were together alone.

More than forty years later the joy of that moment had not left him: 'We sat side by side on the sofa,' he said, 'her hand clasped in mine. It never cooled – my love for her. It has not cooled now.'

After this they were openly engaged, and it is good to know that in a life so serious as regards its outward surroundings there were still times when they could be young and gay. One refreshing glimpse into this side of things is afforded by an intimate friend of those days:

'To those who only knew Mr. Taylor in later life,' wrote Mrs. Nevius, 'it may be a surprise to learn that when he "fell in love" it was a headlong plunge, and by no means a slight or evanescent passion. And his fiancée with her strong, emotional nature was in this respect not unlike him. My husband was rather a special friend of both, and he sometimes indulged his propensities for good-natured teasing at their expense.

'One evening the young people were seated round a table playing a game that required their hands to be hidden beneath it. To his surprise Mr. Nevius received an unexpected squeeze. Guessing at once that it was a case of mistaken identity, and enjoying the situation, he returned the pressure with interest. In a moment Maria, his next neighbour, discovered her mistake, but when she would have withdrawn her hand it was held fast by its captor's strong fingers. Not until flushed cheeks and almost tearful eyes warned him that the joke had gone far enough did he release her. Those were days when to laugh was easy, and not such very funny things were sufficient to evoke much merriment.'

The wedding day, January 20, 1858, was perfect, setting a crown on all that had gone before.

In brilliant sunshine Hudson Taylor crossed the river and made his way to the old temple, near the Presbyterian compound, that did duty as a Consulate. The Rev. F. F. Gough was there already in his office as Chaplain, with friends from all the different Missions, officers from the British gunboat and a few other foreigners.

Very sweet and fair Maria looked in more than Hudson Taylor's eyes that day, in her simple grey silk gown and wedding veil. He was wearing ordinary Chinese dress, and to some the contrast between them must have seemed remarkable. But to those who could see below the surface the noteworthy thing about this wedding was the way in which bride and bridegroom were already 'perfect in one'.

The reception afterwards in the hospitable home of Mr. and Mrs. Way, the speeches and all the kind congratulations passed like a dream; but it began to seem more real when early sunset found them alone together among the Western Hills. And the days that followed were better far than any dream.

From the guest-room of the Nioh-wang monastery Hudson Taylor wrote a week later:

Jan. 28. We are so happy! The Lord Himself has turned our sorrow into joy, giving us 'the garment of praise for the spirit of heaviness'.

Jan. 29. He has answered all our prayers; overruled the opposition of those who would have separated us; justified the confidence He enabled us to place in Him, and made us very, very happy indeed.

And from Ningpo, when six weeks had gone by:

Oh, to be married to the one you *do* love, and love most tenderly and devotedly, that is bliss beyond the power of words to express or imagination conceive. There is no disappointment *there*. And every day as it shows more of the mind of your beloved, when you have such a treasure as mine, makes you only more proud, more happy, more humbly thankful to the Giver of all good for this best of earthly gifts.

Yet the first place in his heart was truly given to Him 'whose love exceeds all human affection', as he wrote in another letter, 'and who can fill the soul with gladness to which all other joy is unworthy to be compared'.

Now I know what it is to have my name written on His heart, and *why* He never ceases to intercede for me. His love is so great that He *cannot*. It is overwhelming, is it not? Such depths of love, and for me!

CHAPTER 11

Hidden Years

(1858–1865)

IT WAS over the chapel in Bridge Street, across the river from the Settlement, in the little rooms that were to form the cradle of the China Inland Mission, that the young missionaries began settled work. Downstairs everything remained as before, but a few rooms were fashioned above with inexpensive partitions. Missionary life was now no longer a one-sided bachelor affair for Hudson Taylor but rounded out and complete in all its relations. He began to feel in touch with the people in a new way and the days were very full. Preaching, teaching, prescribing and dispensing medicines, as well as entertaining visitors by the hour, Taylor had to manage single-handed, in addition to business affairs, correspondence, and evangelistic excursions with Jones.

It would have been possible, of course, to employ a heathen teacher in the school to which Maria gave six or seven hours daily; and they might also have taken on some of the inquirers with a view to training them for positions of usefulness. But either of these courses would have been a hindrance, they considered, rather than a help. To pay young converts, however sincere, for making known the Gospel must inevitably weaken their influence if not their Christian character. In their spiritual infancy they should be left to grow naturally in the circumstances in which God had placed them, strengthened by the very trials with which they found themselves surrounded.

Meanwhile special faith and devotion were needed to enable the missionaries to do so much themselves, and in their insufficiency God worked. He brought them in contact with hearts ready to receive the Gospel, and gave them as their children in the faith men and women who became *soul-winners*.

One of the first of these after their marriage was the basket-maker, Fang Neng-kuei. Introduced at Bridge Street by his friend Nyi, there was a something about the Christians that greatly attracted him. Long had he been seeking peace of heart, but neither in the ceremonies of Buddhism nor the philosophy of Confucius had he found any help. He had even attended for a time the services of the Roman Catholics, but not until he joined the little circle at Bridge Street did he begin to understand the rest of faith. Then nothing would satisfy him but to be there every night as soon as his work permitted, following eagerly all that was said and done.

It was about this time that Hudson Taylor, finding his audiences diminishing, bethought him of a plan to arouse fresh interest. He had at hand a set of coloured pictures illustrating the Gospel stories, and put up a notice to the effect that these would be on view at the evening services, when they would also be fully explained. The result was all he had hoped, and with a crowded room before him and eager faces peering in from the street, the young missionary preached one night on the Prodigal Son with more than ordinary freedom. The thought of God as such a Father was strangely new to most of his hearers, and when at the close Taylor invited any who wished to hear more to stay behind for conversation, almost the whole audience remained. Among the most interested were Neng-kuei and two friends whom he had brought to the meeting. Others drifted out by degrees, but these three stayed on, and seemed much in earnest when they said they wished to become followers of Jesus.

Hudson Taylor had recently started a night school in which inquirers might learn to read the New Testament by means of Roman letters. This exactly suited Neng-kuei and his friends, and for some time they were regular in their attendance. Then it began to be rumoured abroad that the basket-makers were becoming Christians, and they had a good deal of persecution to put up with. This of course tested the reality of their faith, and to the sorrow of the missionaries first one and then another ceased to come. Would Neng-kuei too drift away? But in his case the work proved deep and real. Persecution only brought him out more boldly as a 'good soldier of Jesus Christ', and ridicule taught him to defend his new-found faith in such a way that he became a most effective preacher of the Gospel.

Neng-kuei's earnestness in making known the truth as it is in Jesus was due to something deeper than external opposition. He was a man called of God to a special service, and placed by Divine providence in a special school. In spite of more than one fall like Peter's, whom he closely resembled in character, Neng-kuei was to be widely used in winning souls to Christ. Wherever he went in later years, he was enabled to raise up little churches that continued to thrive and grow under the care of others. Neng-kuei was not one who could long minister to them himself; but he realized this, and was always ready to pass on to new fields when his special work was done. And the zeal and devotion that characterized him must be attributed, under God, to the influences by which his Christian life was formed and nurtured.

Few though they were in number, Hudson Taylor gave himself to the young converts at this time, as if the evangelization of China depended upon their future efforts. In addition to all his other work he devoted several hours daily to their instruction.

Sunday with its special meetings in the Jones's home, morning, afternoon and evening, was made the very most of for the inner circle. It cost the Christians a great deal to leave their regular employments, sacrificing the practical possibilities of one day in seven. It was perhaps the hardest thing their Christian faith required of them. Neng-kuei, for example, found that it cost him a full third of his weekly wages to attend the meetings on Sunday. He was a skilled workman, and his master was quite willing that he should get through all there was to be done in six days, provided he went without pay on the seventh. If it gave him satisfaction to waste four days in every month he was at liberty to do so, only he must of course provide his food on those occasions and draw wages only for the time in which work was done. It was a clever arrangement as far as the master was concerned, but one that told heavily on the poor basket-maker. Twopence a day and his food had been little enough before, but now out of only twelve pence a week (instead of fourteen) he had to spend two or three on provisions for Sunday, which meant a total lessening of his hard-earned income by a third. Nevertheless he was quite willing for this, if only he could have the Lord's Day for worship.

He proved to be one whom the Lord could use. Indeed, of the little group of converts who gathered about the Taylors this winter no less than six were to come to their help in later years as fellow-workers in the China Inland Mission. But it was reserved for Neng-kuei to win a soul destined to become especially useful in winning others. A man named Wang was living in Ningpo at the time who was to be numbered among the Bridge Street Christians, and to exceed them all in the fruitfulness of his labours. But as yet he knew nothing of the Master he was to love and serve.

A busy workman, employed from morning till night in painting and decorating houses, how was he to come under the influence of the Gospel? He had no time to listen to preaching, though he seems to have been religiously inclined, and was no frequenter of tea-shops, his own home being at hand with the attractions of wife and infant child. So the Lord, who had chosen him for His service, sent across his pathway one whom He could trust to be faithful in little things, and who 'in season and out of season' would deliver His message.

It was a beautiful house young Wang was in that day, decorating one of the guest-halls. Presently a stir began – servants came hurrying from the inner apartments, a man with a load of baskets was ushered in, and several ladies, richly dressed, came out to give their orders. Of all this the painter on his scaffolding took little notice, but when the ladies began to speak in tones of some annoyance he pricked up his ears to listen.

'What! Not make baskets for holding incense? Refuse an order for anything to be used in the service of the gods?'

'Do not be angry, ladies,' replied the simple basket-maker. 'I am sorry not to comply with your wishes, but I cannot make or sell anything for the worship of idols.'

'And pray, why not?' was the astonished question.

'I am a believer in the Lord Jesus,' Neng-kuei answered respectfully; 'a worshipper of the true and living God.' And he went on to put before these ladies, who might never hear again, the way of pardon and peace through a dying, risen Saviour.

'What was that you were saying?'

The ladies had grown tired of listening, and had tottered away on their tiny feet, but Neng-kuei's attention was arrested, as he was about to leave, by a man in working clothes, who went on earnestly:

'You did not see me. I am painting up there,' indicating his ladder. 'What was it you were saying? I heard, but tell me again.'

That conversation we are left to imagine. We only know that Wang Lae-djün took the first step that day in a lifetime of devoted service to the Master.

Over in the home of the Taylors, in a darkened room, the husband knelt by the bedside of his dying wife. It was February 9 and only a few weeks had elapsed since the New Year dawned upon their perfect happiness, and now – was she to be taken from him, and his life shadowed with irreparable loss? Internal inflammation, the result apparently of chill, had brought her so low that life seemed ebbing fast away, and every remedy the physicians could suggest had proved unavailing.

Elsewhere in the city the united prayer meeting was going on, and the knowledge that others were praying with him upheld the lonely watcher as nothing else could have done. Noting with anguish the hollow temples, sunken eyes and pinched features, all indicating the near approach of death, Taylor was indeed 'shipwrecked upon God'. Faith was the only spar he had to cling to; faith in the Will that even then was perfect wisdom, perfect love.

Kneeling there in the silence – how was it that new hope began to possess his heart? A remedy! They had not tried it. He must consult Dr. Parker as quickly as possible. But would she, could she hold out until he came back again?

It was nearly two miles to Dr. Parker's, and every moment appeared long. On my way thither, while wrestling mightily with God in prayer, the precious words were brought with power to my soul, 'Call upon me in the day of trouble: I will deliver thee, and thou shalt glorify me'. I was enabled at once to plead them in faith, and the result was deep, deep unspeakable peace and joy.

All consciousness of distance was gone. Dr. Parker approved the use of the means suggested; but upon arriving at home I saw at a glance that the desired change had taken place in the absence of this or any other remedy. The drawn aspect of the countenance had given place to the calmness of tranquil slumber, and not one unfavourable symptom remained to retard recovery.

The Great Physician had been there. His Presence had rebuked the approach of death. His touch had once again brought healing.

This experience of what the Lord could and would do for His people in answer to believing prayer was one of the most wonderful Taylor ever had, and strengthened him for many an emergency, including those of the summer near at hand. Never could he forget those days and hours in which it seemed as though the Lord were saying: 'Son of man, behold, I take away from thee the desire of thine eyes with a stroke.' When, therefore, on July 31 a little daughter was born to them, they could find for her no more appropriate name than Grace.

Spared thus the loss of his own loved one, Hudson Taylor felt the more deeply for Dr. Parker when the angel of death visited his home. With scarcely any warning, on August 26, Mrs. Parker was stricken with dangerous illness, and passed away at midnight leaving four little ones motherless. The young missionaries at Bridge Street did what they could to come to the help of their friend, and others were ready with practical sympathy, but the shock proved too much for the bereaved husband. One of the children was seriously ill, and amid the difficulties of his changed position the doctor began to realize how much his own health was impaired by five years spent in China. He had neither heart nor strength for added burdens and decided before long to take his family home to the care of relatives in Scotland.

But what about the medical mission, outcome of so much prayer and labour? The hospital was full of patients, and the dispensary crowded day by day with a constant stream of people, all of whom needed help. No other doctor was free to take his place, and yet to stop the work seemed out of the question with the winter coming on. How would it be, in default of better arrangements, to ask his former colleague, Hudson Taylor, to continue the dispensary at any rate? He was quite competent for this, and with the hospital closed would not have much financial responsibility.

The suggestion sent the Taylors to their knees in earnest prayer. All they wanted was to know the Lord's will in the matter, and as they waited upon Him guidance was clearly given, in a direction they little anticipated.

I felt constrained to undertake not only the dispensary but the hospital as well, relying solely on the faithfulness of a prayer-hearing God to furnish means for its support.

At times there were no fewer than fifty in-patients, besides a large number who daily attended the dispensary. Thirty beds were ordinarily allotted to free patients and their attendants, and about as many more to opium-smokers who paid for their board while being cured of the habit. As all the wants of the sick in the wards were supplied gratuitously, as well as the medical appliances needed for the out-patient department, the daily expenses were considerable. A number of Chinese attendants also were required, involving their support.

The funds for the maintenance of all this had hitherto been supplied by the proceeds of the doctor's foreign practice, and with his departure this source of income ceased. But had not God said that whatever we ask in the name of the Lord Jesus shall be done? And are we not told to seek first the kingdom of God – not means to advance it – and that 'all these things' shall be added to us? Such promises were surely sufficient.

Had he been depending upon man for help, he would have waited until the need could be made known before assuming such heavy responsibilities. But it had come about so suddenly that no one at any distance was aware of the position or could be more prepared than he himself.

'Eight days before entering upon the care of the Ningpo hospital,' wrote Taylor, 'I had not the remotest idea of ever doing so; still less could friends at home have foreseen the need.'

The Lord had anticipated it, though, and already His provision was on the way.

The first step taken by the young missionary upon assuming independent charge of the hospital was to call together the assistants and explain the real state of affairs. Dr. Parker, as he told them, had left funds in hand for the expenses of the current month, but little more. After this provision was used up they must look to the Lord directly for supplies; and it would not be possible to guarantee stated salaries, because whatever happened he could not go into debt. In these circumstances, any who wished to do so were at liberty to seek other employment, though he would be glad of their continued service if they were prepared to trust the simple promises of God.

This condition of things, as Taylor had expected, led all who were not decided Christians to withdraw and opened the way for other workers. It was a change Dr. Parker had long desired to make, only he had not known how to obtain helpers of a different sort. Taylor, however, did; and with a greatly lightened heart he turned to the little circle that at this critical juncture did not fail him. To the Bridge Street Christians it seemed quite as natural to trust the Lord for temporal as for spiritual blessings. Was He not, as their 'Teachers' so often reminded them, a real Father, who never could forget His children's needs?

To the hospital, therefore, they came; some worked in one way and some in another; some giving freely what time they could spare, and others giving their whole time without promise of wages, though receiving their support. And all took the hospital and its concerns upon their hearts in prayer.

As for Maria, she was one of the most important elements in his success at this time. Thoroughly competent to undertake the direction of their enlarged establishment, she relieved him of account-keeping, correspondence, and all household cares, managing the servants and to a certain extent the staff, so that his strength was conserved for the medical and spiritual part of the work. She even found time to do a good deal among the women patients, both in the wards and in the dispensary.

> 'She was accustomed to take real comfort from a heartfelt belief in the overruling providence of God in small as well as great matters. She was accustomed, too, to seek His counsel in all things, and would not write a note, pay a call, or make a purchase without raising her heart to God.'

No wonder a new atmosphere began to permeate dispensary and wards. Account for it the patients could not – at any rate at first – but they enjoyed none the less the happy, homelike feeling, and the zest with which everything was carried on. The days were full of a new interest. For these attendants – Wang the grass-cutter and Wang the painter, Nyi, Neng-kuei and others – seemed to possess the secret of perpetual happiness, and had so much to impart. Not only were they kind and considerate in the work of the wards, but all their spare time was given to telling of One who had transformed life for them, and who they said was ready to receive all who came to Him for rest. Then there were books, pictures and singing. Everything indeed seemed set to song!

There are few secrets in China, and the financial basis upon which the hospital was now run was not one of them. Soon the patients knew all about it, and were watching eagerly for the outcome. This too was something to think and talk about; and as the money left by Dr. Parker was used up and Hudson Taylor's own supplies ran low, many were the conjectures as to what would happen next. Needless to say, alone and with his little band of helpers Taylor was much in prayer at this time. It was perhaps a more open and, in that sense, crucial test than any that had come to him, and he realized that the faith of not a few was at stake as well as the continuance of the hospital work. But day after day went by without bringing the expected answer.

At length one morning Kuei-hua the cook appeared with serious news for his master. The very last bag of rice had been opened, and was disappearing rapidly.

'Then,' replied Hudson Taylor, 'the Lord's time for helping us must be close at hand.'

So it proved to be. Before that bag of rice was finished a letter reached the young missionary that was among the most remarkable he ever received.

It was from Mr. Berger and contained a cheque for £50, like others that had come before. Only in this case the letter went on to say that a heavy burden had come upon the writer, the burden of wealth to use for God.

Mr. Berger's father had recently passed away, leaving him a considerable increase of fortune. The son did not wish to enlarge his personal expenditure. He had had enough before, and was now praying to be guided as to the Lord's purpose in what had taken place. Could his friends in China help him? The remittance enclosed was for immediate needs, and would they write fully, after praying over the matter, if there were ways in which they could profitably use more?

£50! There it lay on the table; and his far-off friend, knowing nothing about that last bag of rice or the many needs of the hospital, actually asked if he might send them more. No wonder Hudson Taylor was overwhelmed with thankfulness and awe. Suppose he had held back from taking charge of the hospital on account of lack of means, or lack of faith rather? Lack of faith – with such promises and such a God.

There was no Salvation Army in those days, but the praise-meeting held in the chapel fairly anticipated it in its songs and shouts of joy, and as the patients in the wards listened, 'Where is the idol that can do anything like that?' was the question upon many lips and hearts. 'Have they ever delivered us in our troubles, or answered prayer after this sort?'

Nothing is more contagious than spiritual joy, when it is the real thing, and of this there was abundance in the Ningpo hospital that winter. Answers to prayer were many. There were critical cases of illness in which life was given back when every hope seemed gone; there were operations successfully performed under unfavourable conditions, and patients restored from long and hopeless suffering: best of all there were dead souls brought to life in Christ Jesus, so that within nine months sixteen patients had been baptized and more than thirty others were enrolled as candidates for admission to one or other of the Ningpo churches.

It all told, however. 'Nothing without the cross' is true above all in spiritual things, and for Hudson Taylor the price that had to be paid was that of health. Six years in China had left their mark; and now, he was conscious only of two things – great and growing opportunities on the one hand, and rapidly failing health on the other; so that while longing to multiply himself into 100 missionaries, he was increasingly unequal to the work of one.

It is deeply interesting to notice, at this juncture, the means the Lord was using to bring about purposes of His own in connection with this little Ningpo Mission of which those most interested in it never dreamed. Poor, uninfluential and without what would ordinarily be regarded as training or talent for leadership, how unlikely that Hudson Taylor should ever become the founder and director of a world-wide organization embracing missionaries from all evangelical denominations!

Yet a beginning was to be made even now along the lines of that future development. All unconscious of what lay beyond the step to which he felt himself led, but constrained by the need for fellow-workers, Hudson Taylor wrote home early in the New Year:

Do you know any earnest, devoted young men desirous of serving God in China, who not wishing for more than their actual support would be willing to come out and labour here? Oh, for four or five such helpers! They would probably begin to preach in Chinese in six months' time; and in answer to prayer the necessary means would be found for their support.

Had he gone on living quietly at Bridge Street it might have been long before the young missionary would have been driven to such a step. There he and Jones were able to overtake the work, but removed suddenly from that position and entrusted with larger, more fruitful labours, Hudson Taylor was impressed as never before by the need.

So the appeal went home, and often was the matter remembered in prayer in the old home on the Market Place in Barnsley. It was over a good old-fashioned Yorkshire tea that a Class Leader learned one day that spiritual qualifications were needed rather than high educational attainments. This turned his thoughts to the young mechanic who was his right-hand helper in open air meetings and wherever a soul was to be won.

'James,' he said one day, 'I have a job for you. Will you undertake it?'

'What is it, sir?'

'Go to China,' was the unexpected reply. Then the Class Leader proceeded to tell James Meadows all he knew of the opening, ending up with the words,

'Will you go?'

'I will,' replied Meadows, 'if God is calling me. But I must have time to pray over it.'

The purposes of God were ripening slowly but imperceptibly. It was a time of wonderful blessing in the homelands, and the rising tide of revival was sweeping many into the kingdom of God. Prayer and sympathy were steadily on the increase for missionary work.

'Surely this is a day calling for no ordinary activity,' wrote Mrs. Berger, and in the envelope was £50. 'People are beginning to wake up. You doubtless see *The Revival* and other papers. Stirring meetings have been held all over London and in many parts of England to plead for the mighty working of the Holy Spirit in the Church and in the world.' While Mr. Pearse, in a letter written about the same time, reported,

'A kind friend has been raised up who sends £100 each to Brother Jones and yourself. You will be glad to hear that the revival has reached London and hundreds are being converted.'

In Ningpo, however, month after month went by without any prospect of helpers being forthcoming, and Hudson Taylor's strength was failing. A letter written to his parents on March 25 made mention that he had reason to suppose his lungs were affected with tuberculosis trouble. In May he wrote:

> What I desire to know is how I may best serve China. If I am too ill to labour here and by returning home might re-establish health, if only for a time, or if I might rouse others to take up the work I can no longer continue, I think I ought to try.

Into the prepared soil at home a little seed was to fall that would take root and grow all the more surely because the time was so opportune. Hudson Taylor's life, past, present and to come, was needed in the providence of God to foster that little seed. He must be taken home, and that before long. So the trial of failing health continued until it was evident that a voyage to England was the only hope of saving his life.

Closing the hospital with great reluctance the Taylors set out for England toward the end of June. And they did not go alone. The young painter Wang Lae-djün, who saw that the missionaries were unfit to travel alone, offered to go with them. Immense as was the distance between China and England in those days, Lae-djün was willing to leave his wife and child in his father's home and go to the ends of the earth with those to whom he owed so much.

Hudson Taylor's one consolation in leaving the converts in Ningpo was that he could serve them in England. A hymn-book and other simple works in their local dialect were greatly needed, and above all a more correct translation of the New Testament with marginal references. Immediately on landing from the four months' voyage, the young missionary threw himself into the task of getting the Bible Society and the Religious Tract Society to undertake these publications. So engrossed was he with meetings, interviews and correspondence that almost three weeks elapsed before he could even visit his parents in Barnsley.

Then came the question as to where to settle. He had decided to complete his medical studies in addition to the Ningpo Testament, and as the doors of his old Alma Mater, the London Hospital, were open to him, it was to a rented house in a side street in Whitechapel that he took his family. Here, among the toilers of London's East End, he made his home, that no time might be lost in going to and fro to attend lectures, etc. Thus began the discipline that was to lengthen out for four years, until he was ready for the wider vision that was yet to dawn upon him.

Well was it that the young missionaries could not foresee all that lay before them. At twenty-nine and twenty-four, long patience is not easy. They were in correspondence with candidates for the Ningpo Mission, and as health improved their hope brightened that a couple of years might set them free to return to China – medical degrees obtained and romanized publications in hand.

A glimpse into the daily life of that little home in Beaumont Street, so different from the sordid scenes about it, is afforded by the recollections of James Meadows, the Barnsley candidate who came up during the first year the Taylors were in London.

It was with immense interest that the young north countryman made his way to the address given. He was scarcely surprised to find himself in a poor neighbourhood. Hudson Taylor, he knew, was studying medicine at the London Hospital, and it was natural he should live near at hand. But the poverty of the little house itself did somewhat take him aback, when he got over the surprise of being welcomed by a Chinese in native gown and *queue*. The cottage he had left in Barnsley possessed more of comfort, as he soon discovered, than the scantily furnished rooms which contented the missionaries. They and their Chinese helper seemed to have little time for housekeeping, so keen were they on the chief work in hand, the revision of the New Testament. In a study devoid of all but actual necessities, he found Taylor engrossed with Mr. Gough[1] over a knotty point of translation, and it was some time before they could do more than give him a cordial welcome. So interested was he, however, in all that was going on that he forgot the bareness of the room, the low fire in the grate, though the day was bitterly cold, and the well-worn dress of the man whose spirit seemed in such contrast with his surroundings.

At table it was the same. Lae-djün was both cook and laundryman, and the table linen no less than the provisions told of the secondary place given to such details. But the conversation made him oblivious of the cooking, and he was surprised to find himself unruffled by things that would have upset his peace of mind at home. The 'gentle, earnest piety' of the missionaries deeply impressed him, as did their absorbing devotion to the work they had left, which was never far from their thoughts. The appalling fact of a million precious souls, month by month, perishing in China for lack of the Gospel was *real* to them, and found some adequate, corresponding reality in their daily life. Poor as they were – and it was not long before he discovered that they had no means in hand, or even in prospect, with which to send him to China – he was glad to accept such leadership, and to go out simply as a 'Scripture-reader' when before long funds were provided.[2]

And Hudson Taylor's care of his one missionary was not unworthy of

[1] The Rev. F. F. Gough of the Church Missionary Society, also on furlough from Ningpo, had joined Hudson Taylor in the revision. Mr. Gough's knowledge of Greek as well as Chinese enabled him to translate from the original.

[2] James Meadows and his bride sailed for China in January 1862, first of the five workers prayed for to reinforce the Joneses in the Ningpo Mission. Mr. Jones's health broke down not long after, and he died on the journey home.

this confidence. He had known what it was to be alone, in need, and apparently forgotten during his first years in China, and nothing that could be done by correspondence and attention to business details should be omitted to further the efficiency and well-being of his fellow-workers. Careful though he was of every penny, he invested in a good account book and a file for letters, and the clear entries in his own handwriting testify to the faithfulness with which he discharged these responsibilities. Mr. Meadows's only complaint, indeed, in his early correspondence illustrates the regularity with which he was cared for.

'James Meadows speaks of being well and regularly supplied with money,' Taylor wrote to his mother a year after the young couple had gone out. 'His only dissatisfaction is that his friends, knowing him to be looking to God only, would be anxious, while he is receiving remittances as regularly as though he had a salary. He seems distressed, in fact, at their being so regular and sufficient, as though such a state of things were incompatible with leaning upon God alone. I have explained in my reply that this is not the case, and that as neither he nor I have any promise of another farthing from anyone, we need to look to the Lord constantly to supply us as He sees fit.'

By this time Taylor's medical studies were completed and his diplomas taken. Of these hidden years of work and waiting, little would have been known in detail but for the preservation of a number of brief journals. Beginning soon after Taylor's medical degrees were taken, they cover a period of three years. Daily entries in his small clear writing fill the pages, which breathe a spirit words are poor to express.

Scarcely a day is recorded in which he did not have correspondence, visitors, meetings, medical visits to pay to friends or suffering neighbours, attendance at committees, or other public or private engagements *in addition* to the revision of the Ningpo Testament. That the latter was his chief occupation, and one to which he devoted himself with characteristic thoroughness, is evident from the journals. Every day he noted the number of hours spent in this work alone, and one frequently comes across such entries as the following:

April 26, Sunday: Morning, heard Rev. T. Kennedy on 'Do thyself no harm'. (Appropriate surely!) Afternoon, lay down, having headache and neuralgia. Evening, with Lae-djün[1] on Heb. 11, first part. Mr. Gough promised to begin tomorrow not

[1] The only Chinese Christian within reach, Lae-djün was not neglected spiritually. Regularly, as the journals testify, Taylor spent hours with him on Sunday, tired though they must often have been: hours of prayer and Bible study, that had not a little to do with Lae-djün's subsequent usefulness as the first and for thirty years one of the most devoted Chinese pastors working with the China Inland Mission.

later than 10.30. May God prosper us in our work this week, and in all other matters be our help and guide.

April 27: Revision seven hours (evening at Exeter Hall).
,, 28: ,, nine and a half hours.
,, 29: ,, eleven hours.
,, 30: ,, five and a half hours (B.M.S. meetings).
May 1: ,, eight and a half hours (visitors till 10 p.m.).
,, 2: ,, thirteen hours.
,, 3, Sunday, at Bayswater[1]: In the morning heard Mr. Lewis, from John 3.33; took the Communion there in the afternoon. Evening, stayed at home and engaged in prayer about our Chinese work.
May 4: Revision four hours (correspondence and visitors).
,, 5: ,, eleven and a half hours.
,, 6: ,, seven hours (important interviews).
,, 7: ,, nine and a half hours.
,, 8: ,, ten and a half hours.
,, 9: ,, thirteen hours.
,, 10, Sunday: Morning, with Lae-djün on Heb. 11, first part – a happy session. Wrote to James Meadows. Afternoon, prayer with Maria about leaving this house, about Meadows, Truelove, revision, etc. Evening, heard Mr. Kennedy on Matt. 27.42: 'He saved others, himself he cannot save'. Oh, to be more like the meek, forbearing, loving Jesus. Lord, make me more like Thee.

But it was not work only, it was faith and endurance in searching trial that made these years so fruitful in their after-results. The testing permitted was chiefly along two lines, those of the Ningpo Testament and the supply of personal needs. Taylor never at any time received financial help from the funds of the Ningpo Mission. Even in these early days he felt it important to be entirely independent, in this sense, of the work. He had long been looking to the Lord in temporal matters as in spiritual, proving in many wonderful ways the truth of the promise 'No good thing will he withhold from them that walk uprightly'. These years, however, in East London were marked by very special exercise of mind in this connection, and some periods of extremity never afterwards repeated. Such, for example, were the autumn days in 1863, of which we read as follows:

October 5, Monday: Our money nearly spent. Paid in faith, however, what was owing to tradesmen and servants. Found a very sweet promise for us in our revision work, I Chron. 28.20. Revision seven hours.

October 9: Our money all but gone. O Lord, our hope is in Thee! Revision six and a half hours. Mrs. Jones, Mrs. Lord, May Jones and Baby came from Bristol. (So they were responsible for quite a party.)

---

[1] Bayswater was the home at this time of Mr. and Mrs. B. Broomhall, the beloved sister Amelia who for many years was Taylor's chief correspondent.

October 10: Revision nine and a half hours. Went with Mrs. Jones to see Mr. Jonathan Hutchinson, who kindly refused to take any fee. Only 2s. 5½d. left, with the greatest management.

I must have all things and abound,
While God is God to me.

October 11, Sunday: Morning, with Lae-djün. Afternoon, engaged in prayer. Evening, went to hear Mr. Kennedy. We gave 2s. today to the collections, in faith and as due to the Lord.

It is not surprising to find, as the week wore on, special evidences of the Lord's watchful care. He was permitting their faith to be tested for sufficient reasons, but He was not unmindful of them in the trial. Early in the week Mrs. Jones's sister came up from the country, bringing 'a goose, a duck, and a fowl', with other good things, for the household; and a day or two later a relative called with more than £30 for their personal use.

Once, and once only, was there a liability that could not be met, for they sedulously obeyed the injunction, 'Owe no man anything, save to love one another'. It was the summer of 1864, the close sultry season so trying in East London. Ever since the beginning of August supplies had been running low, and on the 12th a brief entry closed with the words:

The tax-gatherer called, and I was obliged to defer him. Help us, O Lord, for Thy Name's sake.

Next day was Saturday, and there was little or nothing in hand. Seven and a half hours were given to revision just as usual, though the children's nurse had to be told the situation in case she might wish to leave.

Sought to realize that it is in weakness and need the strength of Jesus is perfected

is the entry that shows how deeply their hearts were exercised.

That night, though late, a friend who had left the house returned, and putting £7 into Taylor's hand begged him to accept it. £5 reached him by post on Monday, and £35 during the course of the week. Thus he was confirmed in the confidence that, for them at any rate, to give all their time and strength to the Lord's work and quietly wait His supplies was the right way.

Meanwhile, what of the bright hopes with which Taylor had entered upon the work entrusted to him by the Bible Society? To obtain a correct version of the New Testament – not in Chinese character but in Roman letters, representing the sounds of the local dialect, and thus comparatively easy both to read and understand – was an object worthy of considerable sacrifice. With the help of Mr. Gough, Wang Lae-djün and Maria (who was as much at home in the Ningpo dialect as in English), he hoped to accomplish it in reasonable time. Progress was not hindered by lack of diligence, but the task itself proved far more laborious than they had anticipated, extended as it was to include the preparation of marginal references.

Moreover it met with the strongest opposition from some at the Bible House, whose position gave weight to their criticisms. Once and again, it seemed as if it must be abandoned, and this not at the beginning, but after months and years of toil. For two or three months the situation was painful in the extreme.

'Humanly speaking there is little hope of the continued aid of either the C.M.S. or the Bible Society,' Taylor wrote to his mother on October 7. 'For *this* I care but little, as the Lord can easily provide the funds we need. But the help of Mr. Gough in the remainder of the work is very desirable, and under these circumstances it is improbable that we should have it. I would ask special prayer then.'

Barely two weeks later, the Bible Society reached a decision which came as a definite answer to prayer:

'There is no intention of taking it out of your hands,' wrote his friend Mr. Pearse, forestalling the letter of the Committee. 'They are evidently satisfied with what you are doing, and the way you are doing it.'

It meant that he was pledged more than ever to his part of the work – and the years were passing on. With returning strength the longing grew upon him to be back in China, especially when the death of Jones left the Bridge Street converts almost without pastoral care. Meadows, who had been bereaved of wife and child, was in sore need of companionship, and the local Christians of spiritual help. Everything pointed, humanly speaking, to Taylor's return, and increased his longing to be in direct missionary work once more. Important as the revision was, he was young and craved activity and the joy of winning souls to Christ. Yet did not the very answers to prayer that had been so marked bind him to continue the work that was detaining him, and carry it to completion?

But all the while another longing was taking possession of his soul, looming large and ever larger with strange persistence. Do what he would, he could not escape the call of inland China, the appeal of those Christless millions for whom no man seemed to care. On his study wall hung the map of the whole vast empire; on the table before him lay the ever-open Bible; and between the two how close and heart-searching the connection! Feeding, feasting, upon the Word of God, his eye would fall upon the map – and oh, the thought of those for whom nothing was prepared!

While on the field, the pressure of claims immediately around me was so great that I could not think much of the still greater need farther inland, and could do nothing to meet it. But detained for some years in England, daily viewing the whole country on the large map in my study, I was as near the vast regions of the interior as the smaller districts in which I had personally laboured – and prayer was the only resource by which the burdened heart could obtain any relief.

Laying aside their work, for Mr. Gough in measure shared this experience, they would call Maria and Lae-djün, and unitedly pour out their hearts in prayer that God would send the Gospel to every part of China. And they did more than pray. Alone, or together, they visited the representatives of the larger missionary societies, pleading the cause of those unevangelized millions. Everywhere they were met with sympathy, for the facts were their own argument; but everywhere also it was evident that nothing could or rather would be done. The objections raised were twofold: in the first place, financially, any aggressive effort was impossible. Neither the men nor the means were forthcoming. And were it otherwise, those remote provinces were practically inaccessible to foreigners. True, the treaty of 1860 provided for journeys and even residence inland, but that was merely on paper, and everywhere the conclusion was the same: 'We must wait until God's providence opens the door; at present we can do nothing.'

These objections, however, did not lessen the need or bring any lightening of the burden. Returning to the East End and his quiet study, Hudson Taylor found himself still challenged by the open Bible, the ever-accusing map. The Master had said nothing about politics or finance in His great commission. 'Go ye . . . Lo, I am with you.' 'All the world . . . all the days' so read command and promise. Was He not worthy of trust and utmost allegiance?

And there were others who thought as he did, friends who gathered weekly for prayer at Beaumont Street. Ever since the outgoing of the Meadows this meeting had been held on Saturday afternoons. None among those who attended was more interested in the Ningpo Mission than Mr. and Mrs. Berger, who came up from their beautiful home, a mansion near East Grinstead, to attend the meetings. As time went on and Hudson Taylor became increasingly burdened about the need and claims of China, Mr. Berger shared with him much of the exercise of heart involved, while in his gentle wife Maria found almost a mother's sympathy. How little any of them can have anticipated the developments for which provision through this friendship was thus being made. It was in the growing sense of responsibility that the chief bond of union lay. Accompanying Taylor to a farewell meeting for a young worker about to go out to China, Mr. Berger was surprised to find a small poor church, without a single influential member, undertaking the whole of his support. The joy with which they were making sacrifices brought to Mr. Berger a new sense of the privilege of giving and suffering for Jesus' sake, and the earnestness of Hudson Taylor's address moved him to a definite resolve. Rising at the close of the meeting he said that what he had seen and heard overwhelmed him with shame because he had done so little, comparatively, for the cause of Christ. It filled him with joy also; and he had determined that night to do ten times more, yes, by the help of God, a hundred times more than he had hitherto attempted. It is interesting that this experience took place on March 13, 1865, little more than three months before Taylor himself met the crisis of his life on the sands at Brighton.

Meanwhile Taylor had been drawn into a new undertaking, which was absorbing time and thought. Early in the year the pastor of the church to which he belonged (who was editor also of the *Baptist Magazine*) had asked for a series of articles on China with a view to awakening interest in the Ningpo Mission. These Taylor had begun to prepare, and one had even been published, when the editor returned the manuscript of the next. The articles, he felt, were weighty, and should have a wider circulation than his paper could afford.

'Add to them,' he said earnestly, 'let them cover the whole field and be published as an appeal for inland China.'

This seemed incompatible with Taylor's many engagements. The revision of the Ningpo Testament was still the main task, and in addition there was preparation to be made for returning at last to China, accompanied by several new missionaries. Just as all seemed ready for advance, however, the current of events changed. Free passages for a couple of missionaries were unexpectedly offered on a ship shortly to sail, and two accepted candidates took advantage of them, while the fiancée of one followed a fortnight later. Of the remainder, one decided he wanted more time for preparation, a second was unable to free himself from home claims, and a third had not fully made up his mind about going. His own departure thus delayed, Hudson Taylor saw the opportunity afforded by the publication of an appeal for China. Even before his party had been broken up, the study necessary for these papers was bringing to a crisis the exercise of mind through which he had been passing. Compiling facts as to the size and population of every province in China, and making diagrams to show their neglected condition, stirred him to a desperate sense of the sin and shame of allowing such a state of things to continue. Yet what was to be done? The number of Protestant missionaries, as he had discovered, was diminishing rather than increasing. Despite the fact that half the heathen population of the world was to be found in China, the missionaries engaged in its evangelization had actually been reduced, during the previous winter, from 115 to only ninety-one. This had come to light through his study of the latest statistics and, naturally, added fuel to the fire that was consuming him. But he had done all that was possible. No one would move in the matter. He must leave it now, until the Lord . . . But somehow that was not the final word.

Leave it, when he knew that he, small, weak, and nothing as he was, might pray in faith for labourers and *they would be given?* Leave it, when there stood plainly in his Bible that solemn word, 'When I say unto the wicked, Thou shalt surely die; and thou givest him not warning, nor speakest to warn the wicked from his wicked way, to save his life; the same wicked man shall die in his iniquity, but *his blood will I require at thy hand*'! Of this critical time he said,

I knew God was speaking. I knew that in answer to prayer evangelists would be given and their support secured, because the Name of Jesus is worthy. But there unbelief came in.

Suppose the workers are given and go to China; trials will come; their faith may fail; would they not reproach *you* for bringing them into such a plight? Have you ability to cope with so painful a situation?

And the answer was, of course, a decided negative.

It was just a bringing in of *self*, through unbelief; the devil getting one to feel that while prayer and faith would bring one into the fix, one would have to get out of it as best one might. And I did not see that the Power that would give the men and the means would be sufficient to keep them also, even in the far interior of China.

Meanwhile, *a million a month* were dying in that land, dying without God. This was burned into my very soul. For two or three months the conflict was intense. I scarcely slept night or day more than an hour at a time, and feared I should lose my reason. Yet I did not give in. To no one could I speak freely, not even to my wife. She saw, doubtless, that something was going on; but I felt I must refrain as long as possible from laying upon her a burden so crushing – these souls, and what eternity must mean for every one of them, and what the Gospel might do, would do, for all who believed, if we would take it to them.

The break in the journal at this point is surely significant. Faithfully the record had gone on for two and a quarter years; but now – silence. For seven weeks from the middle of April, lovely weeks of spring, there was no entry. First and only blank in those revealing pages, how much the very silence has to tell us! Yes, he was face to face with the purpose of God at last. Accept it, he dare not; escape it, he could not. And so, as long ago, 'there wrestled a man with him until the breaking of the day'.

It was Sunday, June 25, a quiet summer morning by the sea. Worn out and really ill, Hudson Taylor had gone to friends at Brighton and, unable to bear the sight of rejoicing multitudes in the house of God, had wandered out alone upon the sands left by the receding tide. It was a peaceful scene about him, but inwardly he was in agony of spirit. A decision had to be made and he knew it, for the conflict could no longer be endured.

> 'Well,' the thought came at last, 'if God gives us a band of men for inland China, and they go, and all die of starvation even, they will only be taken straight to Heaven; and if one heathen soul is saved, would it not be well worth while?'

It was a strange way round to faith – that if the worst came to the worst it would still be worth while. But something in the service of that morning seems to have come to mind. God-consciousness began to take the place of unbelief, and a new thought possessed him as dawn displaces night:

> Why, if we are obeying the Lord, the responsibility rests *with Him*, not with us!

This, brought home to his heart in the power of the Spirit, wrought the change once and for all.

> '*Thou*, Lord,' he cried with relief that was unutterable, '*Thou* shalt have all the burden! At Thy bidding, as Thy servant I go forward, leaving results with Thee.'

For some time the conviction had been growing that he ought to ask for at any rate two evangelists for each of the eleven unoccupied provinces, and two for Chinese Tartary and Tibet. Pencil in hand he now opened his Bible, and with the boundless ocean breaking at his feet wrote the simple memorable words: 'Prayed for twenty-four willing skilful labourers at Brighton, June 25, 1865.'

> 'How restfully I turned away from the sands,' he said, recalling the deliverance of that hour. 'The conflict ended, all was joy and peace. I felt as if I could fly up the hill to Mr. Pearse's house. And how I did sleep that night! My wife thought Brighton had done wonders for me, and so it had.'

New life, evidently, had come to Hudson Taylor with the decision taken that June Sunday on the sands at Brighton, for he was up with the lark next morning and off to London at 6.30 a.m. No record remains of that day, save that Maria was cheered to see him better, and that he went to have special prayer with one who was wishing to join the Ningpo Mission, whose way was beset with difficulties; but on the day following we read:

> *June* 27: Went with Mr. Pearse to the London & County Bank, and opened an account for the *China Inland Mission*. Paid in £10.

It was the first appearance of the name that was to become so familiar – China Inland Mission.

CHAPTER 12

The Mission that Had to Be

(1865–1866)

It was an anxious moment for the young missionary – fraught with possibilities of which he was keenly conscious. From an early hour that morning he had been alone with God, pleading for abiding results from this meeting. Now the great hall with its sea of faces lay before him; but how weak he felt, how inadequate to the opportunity! And no one was expecting his message. A stranger at Perth and indeed in Scotland, it had only been with difficulty he had persuaded the leaders of the Conference to give him a few minutes in which to speak on China – that vast empire with its four hundred millions, a fourth of the entire human race, about which his heart was burdened.

'My dear sir,' the Convener had exclaimed, scanning the introductions of this unknown Hudson Taylor, 'surely you mistake the character of the Conference! These meetings are for *spiritual edification*.'

But the missionary was not to be denied, nor could he see that obedience to the last great command of the risen Saviour was out of keeping with spiritual edification. To him it seemed rather to lie at the root of all true blessing, and to be the surest way to a deepened experience of fellowship with God. It was at no little cost, however, that he ventured to urge this point of view; for those were not days when foreign missions occupied a place of much importance, and his dread of public speaking was only less than his sensitiveness about putting himself forward. In the train between Aberdeen and Perth, Taylor had written to his wife,

> Through God's goodness I have got some letters of introduction to Perth. May the Lord help and guide and use me there. My hope is in Him. I do desire not to please myself, but to lay myself open for China's sake. I much need to add to faith courage: may God give it to me.

The facts, the great unseen realities, burned as a fire within him. He could not be at the Perth Conference and see those multitudes of Christian people, intelligent, influential, and caring deeply about spiritual things, without longing that they should see and feel needs incomparably greater than their own.

And now the moment had come. Trembling from head to foot as he rose, Hudson Taylor could only grasp the rail of the platform and command voice enough to ask his hearers to unite with him in prayer to God. To *Him* it was easy to speak; and unusual as this beginning was, even for a missionary address, it arrested attention and opened the way to many a heart. For there was about that prayer a peculiar reality and power. More simple it could not have been, and yet it revealed a sacred intimacy that awakened longing for just such confidence in and certainty of God. A strange hush came over the people before the prayer ended, and then all else was forgotten in scenes to which they found themselves transported.

For the missionary came at once to the heart of his message. Back again in thought in the land of his adoption, he was travelling by native junk from Shanghai to Ningpo. Among his fellow-passengers, one Chinese, who had spent some years in England and went by the name of Peter, was much upon his heart, for, though not unacquainted with the Gospel, he knew nothing of its saving power. Simply he told the story of this man's friendliness and of his own efforts to win him to Christ. Nearing the city of Sungkiang, they were preparing to go ashore together, when Taylor in his cabin was startled by a sudden splash and cry that told of a man overboard. Springing at once on deck he looked round and missed Peter.

'Yes,' exclaimed the boatmen unconcernedly, 'it was over there he went down!'

To drop the sail and jump into the water was the work of a moment; but the tide was running out, and the low, shrubless shore afforded little landmark. Searching everywhere in an agony of suspense, Taylor caught sight of some fishermen with a drag-net – just the thing needed.

'Come,' he cried as hope revived, 'come and drag over this spot. A man is drowning!'

'*Veh bin*,' was the amazing reply: 'It is not convenient.'

'Don't talk of convenience! Quickly come, or it will be too late.'

'We are busy fishing.'

'Never mind your fishing! Come – only come *at once*! I will pay you well.'

'How much will you give us?'

'Five dollars! only don't stand talking. Save life without delay!'

'Too little!' they shouted across the water. 'We will not come for less than thirty dollars.'

'But I have not so much with me! I will give you all I've got.'

'And how much may that be?'

'Oh, I don't know. About fourteen dollars.'

Upon this they came, and the first time they passed the net through the water brought up the missing man. But all Taylor's efforts to restore respiration were in vain. It was only too plain that life had fled, sacrificed to the callous indifference of those who might easily have saved it.

A burning sense of indignation swept over the great audience. Could it be that anywhere on earth people were to be found so utterly callous and selfish! But as the earnest voice went on, conviction struck home all the more deeply that it was unexpected:

> Is the body, then, of so much more value than the soul? We condemn those heathen fishermen. We say they were guilty of the man's death – because they could easily have saved him, and did not do it. But what of the millions whom we leave to perish, and that eternally? What of the plain command 'Go ye into all the world and preach the gospel to every creature', and the searching question inspired by God Himself, 'If thou forbear to deliver them that are drawn unto death, and those that are ready to be slain; if thou sayest, Behold, we knew it not; doth not he that pondereth the heart consider it? and he that keepeth thy soul, doth not he know it? and shall he not render to every man according to his works?'

China might be far off and little known; we might silence conscience by saying that its vast population was largely inaccessible; but every one of those men, women and children was a soul for whose salvation an infinite price had been paid; every one of them had a right to know that they had been ransomed by the precious blood of Christ, and to have the offer of eternal life in His Name. While we were busy about other things, quite profitably occupied it may be, they were living, dying without God and without hope – a million every month in that one land passing beyond our reach.

Rapidly, then, Hudson Taylor arrayed before his hearers facts that recent prayer and study had burned afresh upon his soul. Not the coast-board provinces only, to which the little band of Protestant missionaries was confined, but the great unreached interior, every part indeed of the mighty empire passed in review. To most if not all present it was a revelation. Millions upon millions of their fellow-creatures, unknown, unthought-of, were brought out of the dim mists of forgetfulness, and put before them in such fashion that their claim upon Christian hearts could never again be disregarded. Missionary addresses were not wont to be of that order. It was not speaking, so much, about these startling facts as letting the light of God fall upon them – making those present see as the speaker saw, hear as the speaker heard, God's view, God's verdict upon the matter.

And what a verdict that was!

In Scotland, with its population of four millions, several thousand ministers were needed to care for the spiritual interests of people already flooded with Gospel light. China, with a hundred times as many precious, immortal souls, had not even one Protestant missionary, on an average, to every *four millions*. Moreover, its ninety-one missionaries of all societies were not by any means evenly distributed. They were gathered in a few, a very few, centres near the coast. Confined to the treaty ports, they were in touch with a mere fringe of the population of the provinces in which they were found; while beyond lay the vast interior, inhabited by 200 millions of our fellow-creatures, amongst whom no voice was raised to tell of salvation, full and free, through the finished work of Christ. Yet we believe that 'the wicked shall be turned into hell, and all the nations that forget God'. Amazing inconsistency, appalling indifference to the revealed will of Him whom we call Master and Lord, and to the deepest needs of the human soul!

It was for these inland provinces and dependencies the speaker pleaded – populous regions as large as all the countries of Europe put together, in which no Protestant missionary was yet to be found.

'Do you believe that each unit of these millions has an immortal soul,' he questioned searchingly, 'and that there is "none other name under heaven given among men" save the precious name of Jesus "whereby we must be saved"? Do you believe that He and He alone is "the way, the truth, and the life", and that "no man cometh unto the Father" but by Him? If so, think of the condition of these unsaved souls, and examine yourself in the sight of God to see whether you are doing your utmost to make Him known to them or not.

'It will not do to say that you have no special call to go to China. With these facts before you, you need rather to ascertain whether you have a special call to stay at home. If in the sight of God you cannot say you are sure that you have a special call to stay at home, why are you disobeying the Saviour's plain command to go? Why are you refusing to come to the help of the Lord against the mighty? If, however, it is perfectly clear that duty – not inclination, not pleasure, not business – detains you at home, are you labouring in prayer for these needy ones as you might? Is your influence used to advance the cause of God among them? Are your means as largely employed as they should be in helping forward their salvation?'

Recalling a Ningpo experience, Taylor went on to tell how Nyi, full of joy in his new-found faith, had inquired:

'How long have you known this Good News in your country?'

'We have known it a long time,' was the reluctant answer; 'hundreds of years.'

'Hundreds of years,' exclaimed the ex-Buddhist leader, 'and you never came to tell us! My father sought the Truth,' he added sadly, 'sought it long, and died without finding it. Oh, why did you not come sooner?'

Shall we say that the way was not open? At any rate it is open now. Before the next Perth Conference twelve millions more, in China, will have passed for ever beyond our reach. What are we doing to bring them the tidings of Redeeming Love? It is no use singing as we often do:

'*Waft, waft ye winds the story.*'

The winds will never waft the story; but they may waft *us*.

The Lord Jesus commands us, commands us each one individually – 'Go,' He says, 'Go . . . into all the world and preach the gospel to every creature.' Will you say to *Him*, 'It is not convenient'? Will you tell Him that you are busy fishing – have bought a piece of land, purchased five yoke of oxen, married a wife, or for other reasons cannot obey? Will He accept such excuses? Have we forgotten that 'we must all appear before the judgment seat of Christ', that everyone may receive the things done in the body? Oh, remember, pray for, labour for the unevangelized millions of China, or you will sin against your own soul! Consider again whose Word it is that says:

'If thou forbear to deliver them that are drawn unto death, and those that are ready to be slain; if thou sayest, Behold, we knew it not; doth not he that pondereth the heart consider it? and he that keepeth thy soul, doth not he know it? and shall not he render to every man according to his works?'

So deep was the impression that the meeting broke up almost in silence. Many sought the speaker afterwards, to inquire about the work in which he was engaged and to offer such help as they could give. Far and wide reports were carried, both of the address and that Hudson Taylor was about to return to China. With no denomination at his back, no committee even or promise of supplies, he was taking with him a party of fellow-workers to attempt nothing less than the evangelization of the inland provinces of that great empire. And he was so calm about it, so sure that God had called them to this seemingly impossible task and would open the way before them! Amazed at his faith and vision, men felt almost as if a prophet had risen up among them, and one of the larger churches was filled with an audience eager to hear more of the projected Mission.

Further openings resulted, adding to those that had been providentially provided as the outcome of something that happened only a week after his visit to Brighton. He had gone to spend Sunday with his sister Amelia and her husband, Benjamin Broomhall. As the hour for public worship drew near, instead of going as usual to the chapel of which he was a member, Taylor sought definite guidance as to where he should worship that morning. Passing down Welbeck Street, it came to him to join the little company of 'Open Brethren' who had a meeting there. This he did.

It so happened that among the requests for prayer read out toward the close of the meeting was one that seemed in danger of being forgotten. Nobody took it up, and Taylor feared the service might close without united remembrance of this special need. The circumstances were quite ordinary – a case of illness, involving long-continued suffering – but, stranger though he was, he could not let the appeal for spiritual help pass unnoticed.

'Who was that?' inquired the Dowager Lady Radstock afterwards, deeply impressed by the simplicity of his prayer.

On learning that the visitor was Hudson Taylor, a missionary from China, she desired to see more of him. The outcome was an invitation to breakfast at Portland Place the following morning, and the commencement of a friendship with several members of the Waldegrave family that became fruitful in blessing for China.

All through the summer and autumn he had a succession of engagements that brought him in touch with influential circles. At first it rather took his breath away to speak at luncheons with titled people, or at drawing-room meetings at which everybody appeared in evening dress. It had come about entirely apart from his seeking, however, and in such a way as to leave no doubt that the One who had led him to settle in East London was opening to him also the drawing-rooms of the West.

Those early days were by no means only talk and meetings, either. He was preparing for the outgoing of J. W. Stevenson who for some months had been with him in London, and of a newer candidate from Scotland, George Stott. The branches were spreading out and the roots were striking deep in quiet hours of thought and prayer. With Mr. Berger especially, many were the consultations held upon practical questions, and as responsibilities increased it was an untold comfort to have his help in bearing them.

'When I decided to go forward,' said Taylor of this summer, 'Mr. Berger undertook to represent us at home. The thing grew up gradually. We were much drawn together. The Mission received its name in his drawing-room. Neither of us asked or appointed the other: it just *was so*.'

And what shall be said of the still more intimate help of the life nearest of all to his own – the tender love, the spiritual inspiration and practical wisdom of the one who shared his every experience? To Maria, necessarily, the new departure meant more than to any other; for, young as she was, not yet thirty, she had to mother the Mission as well as care for a growing family. To take four little children out to China was no light matter, and when the object in view is remembered – nothing less than to plant messengers of the Gospel in every one of the unopened provinces – a mother's heart alone can realize what hers must often have felt. It was not her husband's faith, however, upon which she leaned, great as were her joy and confidence in him. From girlhood, orphaned of both parents, she had put to the test for herself the Heavenly Father's faithfulness. Family burdens and the pressure of need might come, and this immense responsibility be super-added, but her resources did not fail, for she drew moment by moment upon 'all the fulness of God'.

The chief work that claimed Hudson Taylor and Maria after the decision at Brighton was that of completing the manuscript returned by the *Baptist Magazine* editor. It may have been easy to say, 'Add to it, let it cover the whole field and be published as an appeal for inland China', but to carry out the suggestion was another matter. Little information was to be had about that great closed land, and to make its needs real and appealing needed a touch other than they could give. The writing meant much study, thought, and prayer. Too busy during the week to obtain quiet, they gave what time they could on Sunday, without neglecting public worship, to this important task. Together in the little sitting-room at 30 Coborn Street (to which they had now moved), they prayed and wrote, wrote and prayed. *China's Spiritual Need and Claims* was the outcome.

'Every sentence was steeped in prayer,' Taylor recalled. 'It grew up while we were writing – I walking up and down the room and Maria seated at the table.'

Turning the pages thoughtfully, one feels again the power that touched and moved readers of that book for more than a generation. There is evidence in every paragraph not only of painstaking study, but of the spirit of prayer in which it was written. It is skilfully adapted to its purpose and, what is more, one stands from first to last in the light of God. *His* word it is that comes to one, His point of view from which there is no escaping. There is no self about it, no turning of the thought to man. The writer scarcely appears in the whole book. Mr. Berger is referred to by name, and so are the members of the Mission already in China or on the way thither, but Hudson Taylor is absent to a remarkable degree.

The overwhelming greatness of the task before the Mission is felt rather than dwelt upon, for yet another Reality shines out from these pages, preoccupying mind and heart. Than the greatness of the need, one thing only is greater – the fact of God: His resources, purposes, faithfulness, His commands and promises. 'All power is given unto me . . . go ye *therefore.*' That is enough; that alone could be enough.

Hence it follows that the principles of the new Mission are simply an adjustment of these two considerations – the need to be met and God. The writer has no other resources, absolutely none, and he desires no other. Every problem resolves itself into a fresh appeal to God, for there can be no need unmet in Him.

Feeling, on the one hand, the solemn responsibility that rests upon us, and on the other the gracious encouragements that everywhere meet us in the Word of God, we do not hesitate to ask the great Lord of the Harvest to call forth, to *thrust* forth twenty-four European and twenty-four Chinese evangelists, to plant the standard of the Cross in the eleven unevangelized provinces of China proper and in Chinese

Tartary. To those who have never been called to prove the faithfulness of the covenant-keeping God in supplying, in answer to prayer alone, the every need of His servants, it might seem a hazardous experience to send twenty-four European evangelists to a distant heathen land, 'with *only God to look to*'; but in one whose privilege it has been through many years to put that God to the test in varied circumstances, at home and abroad, by land and sea, in sickness and health, in dangers, in necessities and at the gates of death, such apprehensions would be wholly inexcusable.

Instance after instance is given from Hudson Taylor's experience of direct, unmistakable answers to prayer, and the deduction drawn is that with such a God it is safe and wise to go forward in the pathway of obedience – is indeed the only safe and wise thing to do.

Hudson Taylor said of this period,

We also had to consider whether it would not be possible for members of various denominations to work together on simple, evangelistic lines, without friction as to conscientious differences of opinion. Prayerfully concluding that it would, we decided to invite the co-operation of fellow-believers irrespective of denominational views, who fully held the inspiration of God's Word, and were willing to prove their faith by going to inland China with only the guarantee they carried within the covers of their pocket Bibles.

That Word had said, 'Seek first the kingdom of God and his righteousness, and all these things (food and raiment) shall be added unto you.' If anyone did not believe that God spoke the truth, it would be better for him not to go to China to propagate the faith. If he did believe it, surely the promise sufficed. Again, 'No good thing will he withhold from them that walk uprightly.' If anyone did not mean to walk uprightly, he had better stay at home; if he did mean to walk uprightly, he had all he needed in the shape of a guarantee fund. God owns all the gold and silver in the world, and the cattle on a thousand hills. We need not be vegetarians.

We might indeed have had a guarantee fund if we had wished it; but we felt it was unneeded and would do harm. Money wrongly placed and money given from wrong motives are both to be greatly dreaded. We can afford to have as little as the Lord chooses to give, but we cannot afford to have unconsecrated money, or to have money placed in the wrong position. Far better have no money at all, even to buy food with; for there are plenty of ravens in China, and the Lord could send them again with bread and flesh.

Our Father is a very experienced one. He knows very well that His children wake up with a good appetite every morning, and He always provides breakfast for them, and does not send them supperless to bed at night. 'Thy bread shall be given thee, and thy water shall be sure.' He sustained three million Israelites in the wilderness for forty years. We do not expect He will send three million missionaries to China; but if He did, He would have ample means to sustain them all. Let us see that we keep God before our eyes; that we walk in His ways and seek to please and glorify Him in everything, great and small. Depend upon it, God's work done in God's way will never lack God's supplies.

It was men and women of faith, therefore, who were needed for the China Inland Mission, prepared to depend on God alone, satisfied with poverty should He deem it best, and confident that His Word cannot be broken.

Much else comes out in these earnest pages, and much that is *not* said is significant by its absence. There is no mention even of a committee, no reliance upon organization or great names. The entire direction of the Mission was to be in the hands of its founder, himself the most experienced of its members, who like a general on active service would be with his forces in the field. So natural does this arrangement seem that one hardly recognizes the greatness of the innovation, or that in this as in other new departures Hudson Taylor was making a contribution of exceeding value to the high politics of missions. He had simply learned from painful experience how much a missionary may have to suffer, and the work be hampered, if not imperilled, by being under the control of those who, however well intentioned, have no first-hand knowledge of its conditions and are, moreover, at the other side of the world.

Another striking absence is that of any pleading for financial help. It is mentioned that an annual expenditure of £5,000 was anticipated and that gifts might be sent to Mr. Berger, Hudson Taylor's representative in England. And for the rest, the quiet words express a sense of *wealth* rather than need, 'although the wants are large, they will not exhaust the resources of our Father.'

Finally, there is not a word about government protection or dependence upon treaty rights. Many instances are given of *Divine* protection in the dangers inseparable from pioneering work such as the Mission looked forward to. Unarmed, in Chinese dress, and claiming no aid from consular authorities, the writer had found times of peril to be always times of proving the watchful care of One who is a refuge better than foreign flag or gunboat. It is God who looms large, not man.

'He can raise up, He will raise up "willing, skilful men" for every department of our service', was the quiet conclusion. 'All we are now proposing to do is to lay hold on His faithfulness who has called us into this service, and in obedience to *His* call and reliance on *His* power to enlarge the sphere of our operations, for the glory of His name who alone doeth wondrous things. It is upon past Ebenezers we build our Jehovah-Jireh. "They that know thy name will put their trust in thee." '

The manuscript was finished by the middle of October. Mr. Berger undertook to meet the expense of publication, and the pamphlet was distributed among the many hundreds who attended the Mildmay Conference ten days later.

Many were the letters that reached Hudson Taylor during the weeks that followed, showing that the book was doing its quiet work, and that in widely differing circles the China Inland Mission was hailed with thankfulness as a Mission that had to be. Offers of service came from the students' hall, the business counter, and the mechanics' shop. Invitations for meetings were numerous, and so great was the demand for literature that *China's Spiritual Need and Claims* had to be reprinted within three weeks.

Meanwhile preparations for a party of ten or twelve were going forward, and in the midst of other engagements proved almost more than Taylor could manage. The house in Coborn Street was now wholly inadequate, and the next-door premises falling vacant, they were glad to rent them also, thus doubling their accommodation.

'The revision is now going on,' he wrote to his mother in November. 'We have reprinted the pamphlet, and have missionary boxes on the way. I am preparing a magazine for the Mission, furnishing a house completely, setting up two founts of type for China, teaching four pupils Chinese, receiving applications from candidates and lecturing or attending meetings continually – one night only excepted for the last month. I am also preparing a New Year's address on China, for use in Sunday Schools, and a missionary map of the whole country. Join us in praying for funds and for the right kind of labourers, also that others may be kept back or not accepted, for many are offering.'

Was there a need just then for a reminder that work cannot take the place of prayer? Overwhelmingly busy, it certainly would not have been surprising if that little circle had been tempted to curtail quiet times of waiting upon God. It was in love, in any case, that the closing year was shadowed by an anxiety so acute as to bring them to their knees as never before. In one of the houses, strangely quiet now, Maria lay in a critical condition. Serious illness had so reduced her strength that when an operation became necessary there was little hope that she could live through it.

'It is very solemn to feel that all our married happiness may be so near its close,' Taylor wrote to his parents in Barnsley. 'She is resting happily in Jesus. Ask grace for me to mean and say, "Thy will be done".'

Three weeks later, his loved one spared to him, he was reviewing the progress made since that memorable Sunday at Brighton with all that it had brought. Besides the eight fellow-workers already in China, twenty or thirty others were desiring to join the Mission.

'How much we need guidance both for them and for ourselves', he wrote to the wider circle of his prayer-helpers. 'We have undertaken to work in the interior of China, looking to the Lord for help of all kinds. This we can only do in His strength. And if we are to be much used of Him, we must live very near to Him.'

The last day of December was set apart, therefore, as a day of fasting and prayer at Coborn Street, fitly closing the year that had witnessed the inauguration of a Mission so completely dependent upon God.

To understand aright the fruitfulness of this period it should be borne in mind that Hudson Taylor, among others, was reaping the aftermath of the great Revival of 1859. That wonderful spiritual awakening had not only swept thousands into the Church of Christ; it had prepared the way for new departures in the development of lay agency, and a striking fulfilment might be seen in many directions of the prophecy of Joel: 'Also upon the servants and the handmaids in those days will I pour out my spirit'.

The Salvation Army, Young Men's Christian Association, and other well-known organizations had their beginnings in that formative time. But as yet no opening had been found for the employment of a lay agency on the foreign field.

'When travelling in England, Scotland, and the north of Ireland in 1859 and '60,' wrote a Christian leader from the Continent, 'I repeatedly asked myself, "Where is the channel through which simple-hearted believers brought to Christ through these remarkable Revivals, wishing to devote themselves to missionary work in foreign lands, may reach their object?" But I found no such channel. All the colleges for missionary training require a preliminary education which one would seek in vain in youths of this sort. To raise a missionary agency of a humbler kind seems to be a special design of our Lord at this juncture, for the carrying out of which He has prepared His instruments in different countries, independently of each other.'

Into this prepared soil the seed-thought of the China Inland Mission was providentially cast. Young people in workshop and office heard of it and were encouraged. Perhaps in such a Mission, place might be found for faith and love even without much learning of the schools? So thought Rudland, for example, at his forge in a Cambridgeshire village, when a printed report of Taylor's address at Perth came to him as a call from God. The pamphlet, *China's Spiritual Need and Claims,* enclosed in a letter from a Christian woman inviting him to join her the following Saturday in going to a prayer meeting at Coborn Street, drew him there as a magnet. That prayer meeting – could he ever forget it? The crowded room, the map on the wall, the freedom of spirit, the unceasing flow of prayer and praise to God, all deeply impressed him. But it was the manifest presence of God and earnestness of all concerned that drew to the Mission that day one of its most successful labourers.

Hudson Taylor had now many openings. He was a man with a message, and a message Christian people wanted to hear irrespective of the denomination he or they might represent. The Mission drew its friends and workers from church and chapel alike, and the proposed sphere of its operations was so vast as to call forth unusual interest. It might have been, as Taylor felt from the first, quite possible to rob Peter to pay Paul, or in other words to deflect interest and gifts from previously existing channels. Every effort on behalf of China and other heathen lands was more than needed, and he longed that the new work should, by the blessing of God, be helpful to all and a hindrance to none. But how to avoid trespassing, in this sense, on the preserves of others was a problem not easy of solution.

To cut at the root of the difficulty, he and Mr. Berger, his chief adviser, saw that the faith principles of the Mission must be carried to the point of making no appeals for money and not even taking a collection. If the Mission could be sustained by the faithful care of God in answer to prayer and prayer alone, without subscription lists or solicitation of any kind for funds, then it might grow up among the older societies without the danger of diverting gifts from their accustomed channels. It might even be helpful to other agencies by directing attention to the Great Worker, and affording a practical illustration of its underlying principle that 'God Himself, God alone, is sufficient for God's own work'.

Was money after all the chief thing, or was it really true that a walk that pleases God and ensures spiritual blessing is of more importance in His service? But for the quiet years in Beaumont Street in which, like Paul in Arabia or Moses at the backside of the desert, Hudson Taylor had been shut in with God, he might have given a different answer to this and many other questions.

'In my short-sightedness,' he wrote of that period largely occupied with work on the Ningpo Testament, 'I had seen nothing beyond the use that the book with its marginal references would be to the Christians. But I have often realized since that without those months of feeding and feasting on the Word of God I should have been quite unprepared to form, on its present basis, a Mission like the China Inland Mission. In the study of that Divine Word I learned that to obtain successful labourers, not elaborate appeals for help, but first, earnest prayer to God "To thrust forth labourers", and second the deepening of the spiritual life of the Church, so that men should be unable to stay at home, were what was needed. I saw that the Apostolic plan was not to raise ways and means, but to go and do the work trusting in His promise who has said, "Seek ye first the kingdom of God and his righteousness, and all these things shall be added unto you".'

The chief need as he saw it was faith in God for such an increase of spiritual life among His people as to produce the missionary spirit. Not money, not the collection, was to him the object of a meeting, but to get people under the power of the Word and into fellowship with God.

'If our hearts are right,' he often said, 'we may count upon the Holy Spirit's working through us to bring others into deeper fellowship with God – the way the work began at Pentecost. We do not need to say much about the C.I.M. Let people see God working, let God be glorified, let believers be made holier, happier, brought nearer to Him, and they will not need to be asked to help.'

They were content with little to begin with in the way of organization. Essential, spiritual principles were talked over with the candidates, and clearly understood as the basis of the Mission. A few simple arrangements were agreed to in Mr. Berger's presence, that was all.

'We came out as children of God at God's command,' was Taylor's summing up of the matter, 'to do God's work, depending on Him for supplies; to wear Chinese dress and go inland. I was to be the leader in China, and my direction implicitly followed. There was no question as to who was to determine points at issue.'

In the same way Mr. Berger was responsible at home. He would correspond with candidates, receive and forward contributions, publish an *Occasional Paper* with audited accounts, send out suitable workers as funds permitted, and keep clear of debt. This last was a cardinal principle with all concerned. As Taylor pointed out:

It is just as easy for God to give *beforehand*; and He much prefers to do so. He is too wise to allow His purposes to be frustrated for lack of a little money; but money wrongly placed or obtained in unspiritual ways is sure to hinder blessing.

And what does going into debt really mean? It means that God has not supplied your need. You trusted Him, but He has not given you the money; so you supply yourself, and borrow. If we can only wait *right up to the time*, God cannot lie, God cannot forget: He is *pledged* to supply all our need.

Meanwhile it was hoped that Taylor and his party would sail in May, and much had to be got through in the way of preparation. In answer to all inquiries as to how many would be going with him, the leader of the Mission could only reply:

If the Lord sends money for three or four, three or four will go; but if He provides for sixteen, we shall take it as His indication that sixteen are to sail at this time.

Not that this meant uncertainty in his own mind. He had little doubt that the larger number would be provided for, and though no solicitation was made for money, the matter was not left to drift. He believed that to deal with God is at least as real as to deal with man; that when we get to prayer we get to work, and work of the most practical kind. £2,000, as nearly as he could tell, would be needed if the whole party were to be sent out; and in preparing the first *Occasional Paper* of the Mission early in the new year (1866), Taylor mentioned this sum. The MS went to press on the 6th

February, and that very day a noon prayer meeting was begun at Coborn Street for funds. Faith did not mean inaction. From twelve to one the households gathered for daily united waiting upon God, the would-be missionaries realizing that their first work was to obtain – from Him who was so ready to give – whatever would be necessary for as many of their number as He was sending forth.

Hudson Taylor himself was not able to be present on many of these occasions. Invitations for meetings were so pressing that he was giving as much time as possible to deputation work. Day by day he was with the little group at Coborn Street, however, in spirit, and they rejoiced to hear how their prayers for him were being answered.

For in the midst of many responsibilities he was kept wonderfully free from anxiety, and ready to take advantage of every opportunity for deepening interest in China. With little experience in such matters, he was scarcely conscious, perhaps, of the way in which he was gaining the confidence of spiritually minded people wherever he went. He only knew that in answer to prayer many were moved to help; that one opening led to another, and that the Lord seemed to have prepared hearts in all the churches, upon which He was laying the burden of China's perishing millions.

For example, meeting the young evangelist H. Grattan Guinness in Liverpool, Taylor accepted his invitation to Dublin to address the members of a theological class. Going ahead to make preparations, Guinness had much to tell about the new Mission, and especially its leader who, in faith, was attempting no less a task than the evangelization of inland China. Needless to say, the young men assembled at the hour of Taylor's arrival were on the tip-toe of expectation. John McCarthy was there, and Charles Fishe and his brother, little thinking they were that night to hear the call of God to their life-work. Tom Barnardo was there also, a bright lad of twenty whose interest in China, dating from that evening, was to bring him to his own among the waifs and strays of East London.[1]

What a shock of surprise, not to say disappointment, the members of the class experienced when the door opened and their visitor arrived! Or, had he not come after all? What – that young slender fair-haired man, so small in contrast with their teacher's familiar figure! Surely there must be some mistake? But no, their leader was undoubtedly introducing Hudson Taylor: and taking it all in in a flash, Barnardo – who was less in stature, even, than the stranger – whispered to McCarthy, 'Good, there's a chance for me!' and was all attention.

[1] T. J. Barnardo, coming to Coborn Street as a candidate for the China Inland Mission, was advised by Hudson Taylor to study medicine, and introduced accordingly to the London Hospital. Long after the work for waifs and strays began which has attained such wonderful proportions, he fully intended leaving it to others and going out himself to China.

Oh, the riveted interest, the burning hearts of that hour, as the young men listened to all the missionary had to tell!

> 'I think I see him now,' wrote John McCarthy after nearly forty years in China, 'So quiet, so unassuming in manner and address, but so full of the power of God! I found that night not only the answer to many prayers as to my sphere of service, but the God-given leader in the work to which the Lord had called me.' Ten or more promising candidates for the Mission resulted from that Irish visit.

Long after, impressions made were still fresh in the minds of many with whom Taylor came in contact at that time. A man deeply burdened, a man God-conscious had moved from place to place, everywhere awakening longing for the same God-consciousness. It made no difference whether meetings were large or small, influential or apparently otherwise; he gave the best he had to give and so earnestly that other hearts could not but come to share the burden. At Birmingham, for example, the night was so stormy that it seemed as if there could be no meeting at all. Taylor was tired, and the fireside looked specially attractive as the rain poured in torrents. No one could get to the Severn Street Schoolroom, his kind hostess assured him, and it would be taken for granted that the meeting would not be held.

'But it was announced for tonight, was it not?' asked Taylor quietly. 'Then I must go, even if there is no one but the doorkeeper.'

And there, in that almost empty schoolroom, the presence of the Lord was so real that both speaker and hearers felt it to be one of the best meetings they ever attended. Half the little audience of eight or ten, as Taylor often mentioned, either became missionaries themselves or gave one or more of their children to the foreign field, while the remaining half were from that day earnest and prayerful supporters of the C.I.M.

On his return to London, Taylor took the opportunity of going over the Mission cash-book to see how far the daily prayer for funds had been answered. In the first five weeks of the year, up to the 6th February when the noon meeting was begun, £170 had been received. Another five weeks had now elapsed, and eagerly he made the reckoning necessary to compare the periods. What was the surprise and thankfulness with which he discovered that the contribution of that second period of five weeks amounted to almost £2,000! It was manifest also that all the praying band were to go forward without delay to China.

And so it came about that the first issue of the *Occasional Paper* which was to represent the Mission had to have an inset slipped into each number saying that the whole sum needed for passages and outfits was already in hand – 'the response of a prayer-hearing God through His believing people'.

One more series of meetings was fitted in after this, in response to urgent invitations from the western counties. Hudson Taylor was specially glad to be going in that direction, as it gave the opportunity of paying a farewell visit to Bristol. In spite of many responsible and pressing occupations in caring for a family of over eleven hundred orphans, George Müller followed with keen interest the development of the China Inland Mission. He gave time whenever Taylor visited him to careful consideration of matters connected with the work.

How much his prayers meant the missionary leader could not but realize when he went over the Orphan Houses and saw those hundreds of children, sheltered and provided for without a penny of endowment, without an appeal of any kind for help, or even making their wants known. From the very commencement of his Christian life Taylor had been profoundly influenced by this quiet consistent testimony to the faithfulness of God; and now that he was himself being led out along similar lines, he valued more than ever George Müller's prayers and sympathy.

Back again in London Taylor found himself plunged in a very vortex of business and farewell meetings. It was the end of April, and in May the party was to sail for China. Apart from Maria, who was slowly convalescing from her recent illness, no one had any experience of the conditions to which they were going, and everything had to pass through his hands;

> 'Whatever needed doing, he seemed to know just how to do it,' wrote John McCarthy. 'Questions as to printing (lithographic or common), engraving, purchase of materials for outfits or supplies, and the thousand-and-one things that come up in connection with a large party setting out for a foreign land, all were found to have light thrown upon them by a reference to the leader who was supposed to know everything and who really did seem to have learned something about any and every matter however remotely connected with the work.'

But all this time, they had no ship in view to take them to China. Avoiding the expensive 'overland' route, via Suez, Taylor wished to travel round the Cape, and was seeking a sailing vessel of which they might engage the entire accommodation. As the party was to consist of eighteen adults and four children, the cabin space of an ordinary three-master would be none too much, and there were decided advantages for so long a voyage in being the only passengers. But here was already the beginning of May and a suitable ship had not been found. Daily at the Coborn Street noon prayer meeting the matter was remembered, the outgoing missionaries not only asking for a Christian captain, but for a crew every one of whom might find blessing through the voyage. Taylor was not anxious; he was sure the Lord would meet the need in good time, though he would have been glad to have it settled.

Just then, on the 2nd May, he was due in Hertfordshire for an important meeting, Colonel Puget, brother of the Dowager Lady Radstock, being his host and chairman. To this new friend it seemed a peculiar arrangement to have a missionary meeting without a collection, but understanding it to be the speaker's wish the announcement was made accordingly. When the time came, however, and the speaker proved unusually interesting, Colonel Puget realized that people would give generously if only they had the opportunity.

Rising therefore at the close of the address, he said that interpreting the feelings of the audience by his own he took it upon himself to alter the decision about the collection. Many present were moved by the condition of things Mr. Taylor had represented, and would go away burdened unless they could express practical sympathy. Contrary therefore to previous announcements an opportunity would now be given – but at that point Taylor interposed, asking to be allowed to add a few words.

It was his earnest desire, he said, that his hearers *should* go away burdened. Money was not the chief thing in the Lord's work, especially money easily given, under the influence of emotion. Much as he appreciated their kind intention, he would far rather have each one go home to ask the Lord very definitely what He would have them do. If it were to give of their substance, they could send a contribution to some missionary society. But in view of the appalling facts of heathenism, it might be much more costly gifts the Lord was seeking; perhaps a son or daughter or one's own life-service. No amount of money could save a single soul. What was wanted was that men and women filled with the Holy Spirit should give themselves to the work in China and to the work of prayer at home. For the support of God-sent missionaries funds would never be lacking.

'You made a great mistake, if I may say so,' remarked his host at supper. 'The people were really interested. We might have had a good collection.'

In vain Taylor explained the financial basis of the Mission and his desire to avoid even the appearance of conflicting with other societies. Colonel Puget was unconvinced.

Next morning, however, he appeared somewhat late at breakfast, explaining that he had not had a good night. In the study, after handing his guest several contributions given for the Mission, he went on to say:

'I felt last evening that you were wrong about the collection, but now I see things differently. Lying awake in the night, as I thought of that stream of souls in China, a thousand every hour going out into the dark, I could only cry, "Lord, what wilt thou have me to do?" I think I have His answer.

Then he handed Taylor a cheque for £500.

'If there had been a collection I should have given a five-pound note,' he added. 'This cheque is the result of no small part of the night spent in prayer.'

It was Thursday morning the 3rd May, and at the breakfast table a letter had reached Taylor from his shipping agents offering the entire accommodation of the *Lammermuir*, about to sail for China. Bidding farewell to his now deeply interested host, he returned to London, went straight to the docks, and finding the ship in every way suitable, paid over the cheque just received on account. This done, with what joy he hastened to Coborn Street with the tidings!

So the time came at length for the quiet, unostentatious start. Among packing-cases and bundles the Saturday prayer meetings were held, friends from far and near crowding the room, sitting up the staircase and on anything that came to hand. Upon the wall still hung the great map; on the table lay the open Bible; and all else was lost sight of.

'Our great desire and aim', Hudson Taylor had written in his pamphlet, 'are to plant the standard of the Cross in the eleven provinces of China hitherto unoccupied, and in Chinese Tartary.'

'A foolhardy business!' said those who saw only the difficulties.

'A superhuman task!' sighed others who wished them well.

'You will be forgotten,' was the chief concern of some. 'With no committee to represent you at home you will be lost sight of in that distant land.'

'I am taking my children with me', was Taylor's reply, 'and I notice that it is not difficult for me to remember that the little ones need breakfast in the morning, dinner at midday, and something before they go to bed at night. Indeed, I could not forget it. And I find it impossible to suppose that our Heavenly Father is less tender or mindful than I.'

Little wonder that the quietness and simplicity of it all, combined with such aims, such faith, drew out the sympathy of many hearts.

Sailing from London on the 26th May, it was the end of September before they reached Shanghai; and very determined were the onslaughts of the enemy, first to wreck the unity and spiritual power of the missionary party, and then to wreck the ship on which they travelled, sending them all to the bottom. But from the hour of parting, when they were commended to God in the stern-cabin of the *Lammermuir*, they were sustained by the prayers of Mr. and Mrs. Berger, who kept up the noon half-hour daily, no matter what guests or occupations they might have. The Saturday prayer meeting was continued by Mr. and Mrs. Gough (widow of Mr. J. Jones of Ningpo) and there were praying groups in Scotland, Ireland and the provinces in which the needs of the Mission were constantly remembered,

CHAPTER 13

My Presence shall Go with Thee

(1866)

THE sailors on the *Lammermuir* had looked forward to the voyage with anything but satisfaction. One missionary would have been bad enough, but a whole ship's load of them! 'A pretty go,' the first mate told his wife, 'I wish we were out of it!' After a few days, however, the men's attitude changed. The missionaries, after all, were not such a bad lot! When a difficult piece of forging had to be done, Nicol the Scottish blacksmith was better at it than any of themselves. Jackson and Williamson, the carpenters, were always ready to lend a hand; and in the absence of a ship's doctor Hudson Taylor's surgical skill was invaluable. He gave excellent lectures, too, talks on the eye, the circulation of the blood, first aid to the injured, etc., which helped to pass the time.

There was more than that, however. Seen at close quarters, these people were downright happy. It was inexplicable. What could there be in the life they had chosen to make them want to sing? Yet morning, noon, and night, in the stern-cabin with their harmonium or out on deck, whether two or three alone or the whole company together, they never seemed to tire. True, it was only hymns they sang, but what could touch deeper chords?

'Jesu, Lover of my soul.'

To them it all seemed so real! Yes, it was plain enough. Religion meant something to these people. And little by little not a few on board, instead of wishing themselves out of it, began to wish they were in it in a real sense.

The conversion of the second officer, twenty-five days out from Plymouth was a most encouraging answer to prayer, and was quickly followed by that of two of the midshipmen. This was the beginning of an awakening among the crew which continued for some time. Concern about spiritual things began to lay hold of them, and there was great joy among the missionaries as one after another came out into the light.

High-water mark was reached early in August, when the first mate, who had been a savage bully among the men, experienced a real change of heart. For a month or more his wretchedness had been pitiable; but though under deep conviction of sin, it was not without a desperate struggle he was able to break with the old life and enter into peace in believing.

'Had a special prayer meeting for the conversion of Mr. Brunton,' is the entry in Taylor's journal for August 3.

And the following morning:

> Could not retire without seeing Mr. Brunton. Read to him at 12.30 when he came from his midnight watch, part of Mackintosh on Exodus 12 (the Passover). After much conversation and prayer, the Lord brought him into liberty. First, told Maria and Miss Blatchley, then Mr. Williamson, who rose and joined me in praise and thanksgiving to God. Then I went to awake Mr. Sell, though it was 2.30 a.m. Oh, how glad our hearts were!

The news was quickly known all over the ship, and deep was the impression next day when this officer called out his watch and told them personally what God had done for his soul. One young midshipman to whom he spoke gave his heart to the Lord, and several of the crew who had been halting between two opinions were brought to decision.

Gladly would one leave the record at this point, telling only of the wonderful deliverance from shipwreck in the China Sea with which it ended. But to do so would be untrue to facts, and untrue moreover to universal experience. Where God is working the devil is sure to be busy; and the nearer one seeks to live to the Lord Himself, the more painful are the consequences of grieving Him. They were only little things that had come in between one and another of the party. Big temptations would have defeated their own end; but little criticisms, little coldnesses, little jealousies had brought in disunion that led to serious results. Prayer was hindered; and to the grief of all concerned, the work of the Holy Spirit was so checked, that for one whole month no souls were saved, and some who had been anxious remained sin-burdened and undecided. It was a startling experience, and deeply searching: a whole month without conversions, at a time when already many of the men had come over the line and others seemed ready to do so! And in their troubled hearts the missionaries themselves knew what was hindering.

Yet it was so hard to get right, and to keep right with one another! It was painful light on the inspired words, 'Behold, how good and how pleasant it is for brethren to dwell together in unity . . . for there the Lord commanded the blessing, even life for evermore'. The fact that most of them were living in true fellowship with God made the grief of failure the more distressing. It made it also the more necessary for the Lord to let that grief be felt. Evidences of the self-life in those who had not come so near to Him might be less disastrous in their results; but 'whom the Lord loveth he chasteneth'. It is the fruitful branch He purges, that it may bring forth more fruit.

To Hudson Taylor, needless to say, these developments caused great concern. Could he by more watchfulness have safeguarded his fellow-workers and prevented misunderstandings? Could he now, prevailing first with God, bring them to a better mind and restore 'the unity of the Spirit in the bond of peace'?

'This morning,' runs a little note in his journal early in July, 'had some conversation with Nicol about the present state of matters. Sell joined us and afterwards Williamson, and we decided on holding a special meeting for confession and prayer for the increase of love and unity. Spoke to most of them privately, and affectionately urged the need of a better spirit. We met in the evening, and the Lord was with us indeed. I trust He gave to all present a real desire to be united in love.'

But the danger was a recurring one, and a couple of months later a spirit of discord again crept in. It was on different grounds this time and with other members of the party, but the outcome was the same – criticism, discontent, loss of power and blessing.

'Almost all of the party deploring the want of more unity and love', is the record for September 8. 'The Lord make bare His arm on our behalf.'

The notable thing is that they did deplore it; that they saw and felt the danger; could not go on in such a condition, even on board ship, and gave themselves to heart-searching before the Lord. Prayer and fasting again turned the tide: for to those who humble themselves before Him it is still true, 'When the enemy shall come in like a flood, the Spirit of the Lord shall lift up a standard against him.'

Then the adversary changed his tactics. Unsuccessful in wrecking the spiritual usefulness of the party, it seemed as though 'the prince of the power of the air' let loose his fiercest legions, determined on the destruction in one way or other of the infant Mission. For fifteen days and nights the stress of storm and tempest lay upon them. Caught in one typhoon after another, they beat up the China Sea all but a wreck – sails gone, masts gone, everything gone but their steadfast hope in God.

'All through the storm,' said Rudland, 'Mr. Taylor was perfectly calm. When almost at its height the men refused to work any longer. The Captain had advised all to put on life-belts. "She can scarcely hold together two hours" was his verdict. At this juncture he was going to the forecastle, where the men were taking refuge, revolver in hand. Mr. Taylor went up to him. "Don't use force," he said, "till everything else has been tried." He went in quickly and talked to the men, telling them he believed God would bring us through, but that everything depended upon the greatest care in navigating the ship, in other words upon the men themselves. "We will all help," he added; "our lives are in jeopardy as much as yours." The men were completely reassured by his quiet demeanour and friendly reasoning, and with officers, midshipmen, and the rest of us went to work in earnest at the wreckage, and before long got in the great iron spars that were ramming the side of the ship.'

It was a bright September Sunday, five days after the storm passed away, when the *Lammermuir* at length came to anchor off the foreign settlement of Shanghai. Her broken, dismantled condition made her an object of general curiosity among the gaily painted junks and foreign shipping; but when it became known that she carried only missionaries, albeit the largest party that had yet come to China, interest soon subsided, and beyond a few facetious remarks in the papers little notice was taken of the new arrivals.

As for themselves, their hearts were full of thankfulness for recent deliverances – more wonderful, even, than they realized at the time. A vessel coming in soon after their own proved to have lost sixteen out of a ship's company of twenty-two, while on the *Lammermuir* none were missing or seriously injured; and no sooner had they reached a place of safety than terrific gales again swept the coast, which in their disabled condition they could not possibly have weathered.

'God grant that having been brought so near to eternity and then spared for awhile,' wrote one of the party, 'our lives may be more entirely devoted to Him and to the work before us. Through all I never felt the least regret, or anything but joy in the thought that I had come.'

The voyage over, Taylor had to face new difficulties. Looking out on that familiar scene – the crowded river, the European houses along the Bund, and the wall of the Chinese city beyond – he realized in a very practical way the responsibilities that had come to him. Where was he to find accommodation for so large a party that would afford the facilities required? Foreign hotels were very few and very costly; Chinese inns were out of the question for such a party; and the Chinese boats to which they might have been transferred would not have met the case, with boxes, drugs, printing presses, etc., soaked in sea water needing to be dried and stored. The missionary community in Shanghai at the time consisted of only nine married and three single men; and who among them would be able, however willing, to receive so many visitors? However, both from the *Lammermuir* and from friends at home, prayer had been going up for months past that the Lord would Himself provide, and He did.

A friend of Ningpo days had moved up to Shanghai, bringing with him the printing press of the American Presbyterian Mission. In a semi-foreign house he was living near the Chinese city, and with a view to future needs had purchased a disused building intended for a theatre, which formed a convenient warehouse or 'go-down' connected with his premises. Large and empty, this building immediately suggested itself when the *Lammermuir* appeared in the river and he learned that it carried Hudson Taylor's party. How they must need the cheer of a friendly welcome, and some place in which to dispose their belongings! If nothing better offered, his home was open to them, such as it was, with the 'go-down' in addition. So, taking a *sampan* that very afternoon, William Gamble sought out his friends to put at their disposal a bachelor's hospitality.

'So He gently clears our way,' wrote Maria the following Sunday. 'All our goods, with the exception of a few boxes not yet brought out of the hold, are safe in Mr. Gamble's "go-down", where Hudson and I and four of the young men sleep. The others are in Mr. Gamble's house, where we all take our meals; and he has kindly promised, though somewhat reluctantly I believe, to allow us to remunerate him for our board.'

In the midst of many occupations Taylor had little thought to give to the criticisms that buzzed about the foreign community. That English women should be brought out to wear Chinese dress and live in the interior roused indignation in certain quarters. It was freely hinted that Hudson Taylor must be a madman or worse, and that Bedlam would have been a safer destination for himself and his companions than Shanghai. 'But he went quietly on,' as Rudland remembered, 'saying little or nothing about it; always letting discourtesies drop out of sight so graciously, without affecting his own friendliness.'

One of the few letters Taylor did manage to write from Shanghai was to his mother.

The Lord is with us, and we are all, I trust, enjoying fellowship with Jesus. We have and may expect to have some trials:

But with humble faith to see
Love inscribed upon them all,
This is happiness to me.

Our Father not only *knows*, but sends them all in love.

To take so large a party inland at all was a step of faith, especially as it included little children, besides seven unmarried women. In the whole of China, at that time, there was not *one* unmarried woman missionary to be found away from the treaty ports.

For their protection as well as to lessen difficulties he considered the wearing of native dress essential, with a large measure of conformity to Chinese manners and customs. In a letter to help Mr. Berger in putting the matter before intending candidates, Taylor wrote:

In my judgment, the adoption of the Chinese costume would be desirable even were we residing in the treaty ports; but for work in the interior such as we contemplate I am satisfied that it is an absolute prerequisite.

I am not alone in the opinion that the foreign dress and carriage of missionaries (to a certain extent affected by some of their pupils and converts), the foreign appearance of chapels, and indeed the foreign air imparted to everything connected with their work has seriously hindered the rapid dissemination of the Truth among the Chinese. And why should such a foreign aspect be given to Christianity? The Word of God does not require it; nor, I conceive, could sound reason justify it. It is not the denationalization but the Christianization of this people that we seek. We wish to see Chinese Christians raised up – men and women truly Christian, but withal truly Chinese in every sense of the word. We wish to see churches of such believers presided over by pastors and officers of their own countrymen, worshipping God in the land of their fathers, in their own tongue, and in edifices of a thoroughly native style of architecture. 'It is enough that the disciple be as *his master*.' If we really wish to see the Chinese such as we have described, let us as far as possible set before them a true example. Let us in everything not sinful become Chinese, that we may by all means 'save some'.

This cannot but involve, of course, a certain measure of inconvenience, such as the sacrifice of some accustomed articles of diet, etc. . . .

But we give you credit, dear friends, for being prepared to give up not these little things only, but a thousand times more for Christ's sake. Let there be no reservation. Give yourself up wholly and fully to Him whose you are and whom you wish to serve in this work, and there can be no disappointment. But once let the question arise, 'Are we called to give up this or that?'; once admit the thought, 'I did not expect such and such inconvenience or privation', and your service will cease to be that free and happy one which is most conducive to efficiency and success. 'God loveth a cheerful giver.'

The *Lammermuir* party's change into Chinese dress was effected as soon as possible. The men submitted to the somewhat trying process of shaving the front part of the head and donning the *queue* and loose-fitting garb of the country, and Maria appeared in Chinese costume at Mr. Gamble's table. To her it meant no little sacrifice. She had not worn it during her previous residence in China, and experience enabled her to realize something of the restrictions it must involve.

'Things which are tolerated in us as foreigners, wearing foreign dress,' she wrote to Mrs. Berger, 'could not be allowed for a moment in Chinese ladies. The nearer we come to the Chinese in outward appearance, the more severely will any breach of propriety according to their standards be criticized. Henceforth I must never be guilty, for example, of taking my husband's arm out of doors! And in fifty or a hundred other ways we may, without great watchfulness, shock the Chinese by what would seem to them grossly immodest and unfeminine conduct. Pray much for us in respect to this matter.'

By this time William Gamble's interest had deepened into the warmest friendship, and he was reluctant to part from his adopted family, many though their claims had been upon his time and resources. Accompanying them to the river on Saturday evening, October 20th, he quietly laid a package on the seat of the *sampan*, stepped ashore, and was gone amid the shadows. It was the roll of dollars he had reluctantly accepted in payment for their board, and on a slip of paper he had written, 'For the good of the Mission'.

Dropping down-stream in the moonlight the travellers were soon alongside the dear old *Lammermuir*. The sailors saw them coming and were all on deck to meet them. In the forecastle a last, brief service was held. 'Yes, we part, but not for ever' was sung on the well-remembered deck. Then with a last look at their cabins, hallowed by sacred memories, and with many a farewell, the missionaries left for their boats. 'Whither, pilgrims, are you going?' was struck up by the ship's company.

> 'As we pushed off,' Emily Blatchley wrote, 'they stood along the bulwarks and, raising their caps, gave us three hearty English cheers. In the moonlight and stillness we glided round the stern – sailors and midshipmen following on to the poop, where they repeated the cheers and stood looking after us till we passed out of sight.'

Four weeks later it was a company thoroughly Chinese as to outward appearances that drew near the famous city of Hangchow. They did not know where they could stay, but here, too, the Lord had gone before. Just as in Shanghai, a home was ready, waiting!

Knowing that a friend of Ningpo days, belonging to the same Mission as William Gamble, had recently moved to Hangchow, Taylor called on him first of all to tell him of their arrival.

'We have been expecting you,' was the kindly welcome he received, 'and I have a message for you.'

A young American missionary, it appeared, had just left the city to bring his wife and child from Ningpo to the home he had prepared for them. His house, furnished and ready, would be empty for a week at least, and he had bethought him of Hudson Taylor's party.

'Tell them,' he said, 'to go straight to my place when they come. It is at their disposal for the time being.'

CHAPTER 14

And Enlarge My Coast

(1866–1868)

A WEEK later, early in the morning of the very day on which the American missionary was due to return, the *Lammermuir* party made their way through the silent streets of Hangchow and entered upon a home of their own. Large and well-built, though very dilapidated now, it had once been a Mandarin's residence, and was a regular rabbit warren of a place, occupied by a number of families, five of whom had not yet moved out. However, it was conveniently situated in a quiet corner near the city wall and busy streets, and would provide ample accommodation for the whole party, and for guest-halls, dispensary, chapel, printing press, servants' quarters, etc. It was the very first house to which Taylor had been directed in his urgent search for property.

After hearing the rent demanded he had made an offer which was not accepted, the landlord hoping to drive a better bargain. Sunday, however, had intervened, putting a stop as far as the missionaries were concerned to business transactions – though not to prayer! The landlord, seeing nothing of his would-be tenants on that day, had been fearful of losing them altogether, and on Monday had come to terms with surprising alacrity. Here, then, Hudson Taylor decided his party should remain for a time, quietly studying the language.

'By the time any of us are ready for work among the people,' wrote Emily Blatchley, who acted as his secretary, 'it will be known that a number of foreigners are living in the city, and we shall gain access to them, *D.V.*, exciting less suspicion than could otherwise have been the case. We trust also to find an advantage from coming direct to the capital of the province, as a footing gained here will pave our way, to some extent, to less important places.'

The thought of extension was already occupying Taylor's mind, and the very first Sunday in their Hangchow home found him not there at all but away in the neighbouring city of Siaoshan. Meadows and Crombie had come over from Ningpo to see if they could be of service, and he was glad to avail himself of their help in an evangelistic effort. Two days spent in the neighbouring city, where they had excellent opportunities for preaching the Gospel, so convinced them of its importance as a centre for missionary work that they were thankful to be enabled to rent a small house before leaving, with a view to settling out some of the new arrivals as soon as possible.

Meanwhile there was no lack of work immediately around them. From the first, one and another began to drop in to Chinese prayers attracted by the singing, and before the new arrivals had been a week in the house one woman was openly interested in the Gospel. Thus the work began, and before Christmas there were attentive audiences of fifty or sixty at the Sunday services.

With the Chinese New Year, early in February (1867), came golden opportunities. A dispensary had by that time been opened, precursor of all the medical work for which Hangchow has become famous. With much else upon his hands, it was not easy for Taylor to attend to scores of patients daily, but there was no other doctor nearer than Ningpo or Shanghai, and his heart went out to the people in their sufferings. From far and near the patients came with every variety of complaint both of body and soul; and when holiday-makers were added at the New Year season, the doctor and his helpers were overwhelmed with guests.

When reinforcements arrived from England (February 23), the first sent out after the sailing of the *Lammermuir*, Taylor was too busy to see anything of them until some hours later. He was standing on a table at the time, preaching to a crowd of patients in the courtyard, and could only call out a hearty welcome as the party entered, escorted by Meadows. It was not long before John McCarthy was at Taylor's side, soon to become his principal helper in the medical work. Those were days in which, amid external hardships, his fellow-workers had at any rate the privilege of close and constant association with the leader who embodied to so remarkable a degree their ideals of missionary service.

> 'If only Mr. Taylor could be in three or four places at the same time it would be a decided advantage,' Jennie Faulding wrote in May. 'He is wanting to visit the governing cities of this province, to look out the most eligible places for stations: he and Mr. Duncan have been on the point of starting several times. Then there is Ningpo where he is needed, and here he is overwhelmed with work. He wants to go to Shaohing too (Mr. Stevenson's station) that he may give further help with the colloquial dialect – there is hardly any knowing what his movements may be; yet he goes on so quietly and calmly always – just leaning upon God and living for others – that it is a blessing merely to witness his life.'

That within six months of their arrival the *Lammermuir* party should not only be settled in the interior, but that they should be cheered with so much of blessing in their rapidly growing work, was a wonderful answer to the prayers that had been going up on their behalf at home. No less strenuous than their own was the life the Bergers were living in the service of the

Mission. It was not easy for them to turn their quiet home into a Mission centre, using as offices both dining-room and study; to encumber the billiard room with packing-cases; to receive at their table candidates for China and friends of the missionaries; to direct wrappers, and send out with their own hands the *Occasional Paper*; to attend to a large correspondence, keep accounts, transmit money, arrange for the outgoing of new workers, see them off from any port at any hour of the day or night, and correspond with those already on the field. Yet all this they did with the loving interest of a father's and mother's heart. When it became necessary they went further, and adapted a cottage on their grounds for the young men candidates and another for a tutor who gave secretarial help.

How he could find time amid the claims of business as well as these self-imposed tasks to write regularly and freely to Taylor as he did is a marvel. He seems never to have missed a mail. Penned in joy and sorrow, as the tidings from China were cheering or otherwise, these letters breathed a faith and love that were unchanging, and formed a veritable storehouse of wisdom and encouragement.

Inevitably, there were hours of painful exercise of mind at Saint Hill as well as in Hangchow. Even on the voyage out, Taylor had become apprehensive about the spirit of certain members of the party, and as time went on their presence became an increasing difficulty. Among the letters, most of which brought only joy to the home-circle, were others of a very different nature. Complaints and criticism awakened Mr. Berger's concern, and plainly revealed an attitude on the part of some that threatened the harmony and indeed the very existence of the Mission. It was only one or two at first, who were not prepared to go all lengths in wearing Chinese dress and adapting themselves to their surroundings in accordance with the principles of the Mission. But their disaffection went as far as to permit of their carrying exaggerated reports to outsiders, one of whom, with the best intentions, took them up seriously and considered them sufficient ground for strenuous opposition to the work. So prejudiced was he, indeed, by what he heard against Taylor, that he would not inquire from him, or the members of the Mission who felt with him, as to the charges made. Without letting them even know of the course he was taking, this influential missionary wrote the strongest accusations to Mr. Berger and others, attacking not only the methods of the C.I.M. but Taylor's fitness for the position he occupied.

Having heard nothing of the other side, these painful letters came as a bolt out of the blue to the friends at Saint Hill. Never suspecting that the disaffected members of the Mission were writing home in a bitter spirit, far less that they had stirred up a comparative stranger to do so, the Taylors were saying nothing to the disparagement of any fellow-worker. They were endeavouring by prayer and patience to remove difficulties and conquer opposition, determined that none should be prejudiced in Mr. Berger's eyes by any word from them, as long as there was the least hope of improvement. The restraint was costing them dear.

In defiance of Taylor's wishes the missionaries in question, now stationed in Siaoshan, had gone back to English dress, to the serious detriment of their interests in that inland city. The Mandarin, who had left them in peace before, then determined upon their ejection. With his soldiers and underlings he had come upon them suddenly on the evening of January 28th, and had ordered them to leave the city before morning. To put them in fear he seized the evangelist, Tsiu, whom at great sacrifice Taylor had spared from Hangchow, and had him cruelly beaten. Sorely bruised and shaken, there was nothing for it but for Tsiu to make his way as best he could to the capital; and he was quickly followed by the rest of the party, who had to be accommodated in Hangchow while the matter was being adjusted.

Those were months of extreme trial to all the household at Hangchow. Taylor was overwhelmingly busy with medical work and the throngs of holiday-makers brought by the New Year season. In a reasonable and patient spirit he sought to draw the ejected missionaries into all that was going on, and to conquer causes of difficulty. But another influence, was at work; and instead of responding to his efforts they kept apart, openly wearing English dress, refusing to come to the meetings, and seeking to foment opposition to Taylor's authority and arrangements. In this, unhappily, they were encouraged by the afore-mentioned missionary, who was just leaving for furlough. Believing their reports to be true, he felt it his duty not only to write as we have seen, but personally to discredit the new methods of the C.I.M. among its supporters.

When one remembers the circumstances, it is easy to see that there may have been, in the practical working of the Mission, some cause for complaint. At thirty-four years of age there still remains much to learn, and Taylor's fellow-workers were all younger than himself. If only the older missionary could have used his experience to safeguard where he apprehended danger, how different the result might have been! As it was, he came very near accomplishing his avowed object, which was nothing less than to put a stop to the entire work.

Taking the course of true friendship, Mr. Berger wrote freely to Taylor, sending him copies of the correspondence.

'My earnest prayer to God', he said with the first detailed accusations, 'is that you may not be further moved by the letter than the Lord would have you be; and may He give the right spirit and the wisdom that will enable us both to do that which will please Him.

'The difficulties at home are neither few nor slight, but yours are truly mountainous

You need our every sympathy and prayer; and be sure, my dear Brother, whatever Mr. —— may have penned, you hold the same place in our hearts as before. That God will supply you and me with increasing wisdom and ability for the work to which He has called us, we need neither fear nor doubt. All that is required on our part is to lay aside everything we discover to be either faulty or erroneous, and constantly to be adding to our stock of both wisdom and love. O yes! we will commit this matter to the Lord who knows that we did our best. He is very pitiful, and will never leave nor forsake us in this our time of trial.'

How serious the trial was to be, and how long continued, the writer could not realize at the time. In spite of all that he himself was going through, he was steadfastly encouraging.

May 19: That you may be enabled to cast upon God the terrible trial resulting from Mr. ——'s conduct, and from those acting with him, I earnestly pray. Let us not fear, dear Brother, anything but our own failings; and these may we ever be discovering, confessing, and putting away. I quite expect God will appear for us in the right time.

Occasional Paper number eight will contain the cash account for twelve months, and judging from the contributions in the year (£2,800, of which I have contributed little more than £100) I think we ought to give unfeigned thanks, take courage, and go forward, though with great caution and prayerfulness of spirit.

It seems to me we must enlarge our field of vision in regard to this work; that you must not undertake so much of the detail, but a more enlarged oversight; that you must not have so many immediately depending upon you. Oh, what need for wisdom in every step of this work!

June 7: As regards your headship in China, I consider it is beyond being questioned, and that you must not allow the thought of appealing to me on the part of any. I think you will see that I must act in the same way in England, respecting candidates for China.

I am exceedingly rejoiced to notice that with the exception of —— none have sympathy with Mr. —— and his doings. The Lord will bring all these things to a calm in due time, I quite think. He will teach you the best method to adopt, and us at home. May we only be careful to be found in a teachable spirit.

August 24: It is not our mistakes but our refusing to correct them when discovered that will prove baneful.

The spirit in which the Taylors met these trials may be judged from letters written by Maria to Mrs. Berger, many of which remain. From the quiet of her room early in February she wrote – a little daughter five days old lying beside her:

I have been listening to my beloved husband and others playing and singing in the chapel some of our favourite hymns. One in particular, 'Oh, for the robes of whiteness, Oh, for the tearless eye', seemed to take me away in thought to happy

Saint Hill, and I was almost tempted to wish myself back in that home of rest and love. But it is not for the soldier on the battlefield, however sorely pressed or wounded, to wish himself back in safety and ease.

'Do pray for us very much,' she continued a few weeks later, 'for we do so need God's *preserving* grace at the present time. We have come to fight Satan in his very strongholds, and he will not let us alone. What folly were ours, were we here in our own strength! But our God will not fail nor forsake us. I should be very sorry to see discord sown among the sisters of our party, and this is one of the evils I am fearing now.

'What turn Mr. ——'s matters will take I cannot think. One is almost tempted to ask, "Why was —— permitted to come out?" Perhaps it was that our Mission might be thoroughly established on right bases early in its history.'

And all the while souls were being saved, and the prayer answered with which the *Lammermuir* party had entered the New Year: 'O that thou wouldest bless me indeed, and enlarge my coast, that thine hand might be with me, that thou wouldest keep me from evil, that it may not grieve me!'

In May came the first baptisms, amid the joy of which Maria wrote to the friends at Saint Hill:

Perhaps our dear Lord sees that we need sorrows to keep us from being elated at the rich blessing He is giving in our work.

Sorrows there were, for the discontented spirit of the Siaoshan party persisted. Having gone back from the first principles of the Mission, they were now unhappy in association with it. The Taylors did everything in their power to help this particular married couple, and what they endured from discourtesy, disloyalty and untrustworthiness is better left untold. Not the least part of it was to see the harmful influence exerted on others, especially three of the unmarried women missionaries.[1] All this greatly hindered Taylor in taking the pioneering journeys necessary if younger workers were to be planted out. All around them, even in that coast-board province, were millions upon millions to whom 'no tidings came' of the one, the only Saviour. To these in their sin and need His heart went out, moving those other hearts of the little missionary community with His own constraining love. No fewer than *sixty cities* in that one province were still without preachers of the Gospel, Chinese or foreign, nine of these being capitals of prefectures, or *Fu* cities from which the rest were governed. To open stations of the Mission in these centres was a purpose Taylor was prayerfully con-

[1] When, after two years, Taylor eventually had to dismiss the man for conduct 'utterly inconsistent with the position of a Christian missionary', he realized he might be opening the door for the retirement of these three also. So it proved – to the relief of all who had been associated with them, and who had marvelled at Taylor's patience for so long.

sidering. In a journey round the Ningpo district he had taken counsel with his more experienced fellow-workers, finding Meadows and Stott ready to move on to places as yet unreached. Two important *Fu* cities in the east and south – Taichow and Wenchow – were now allocated to them, Jackson of the *Lammermuir* party volunteering to accompany Meadows. This left the north and west more particularly to the Hangchow workers, several of whom were anxious to get out alone among the people, so as to make more progress with the language.

Freeing himself, therefore, with no little difficulty from headquarters, Taylor turned his face northward at the end of April, with Duncan, the stalwart Highlander, as a companion. Years before he had had some memorable experiences in the region of the Great Lake, when evangelizing with William Burns. Little or no progress had been made in that turbulent district since then, and it was with thankfulness the travellers found, even in the *Fu* city of Huchow, an open door for the Gospel. Taylor was not able to remain long, but so much was he impressed with the importance of this centre that he almost decided, a few months later, to make it his own headquarters. Meanwhile it was visited from time to time by his fellow-workers, one earnest convert giving them great joy, and becoming on his own account a real soul-winner.

'More than a year has elapsed', Taylor wrote to Mr. Berger (May 30), 'since we parted on the deck of the *Lammermuir*, but both you and I can still say – of the past, "Ebenezer", of the present, "Jehovah-nissi", and of the future, "Jehovah-jireh", thanks be to His grace! Burdens such as I never before sustained, responsibilities such as I had not hitherto incurred, and sorrows compared with which all my past sorrows were light have been part of my experience. But I trust I have, in some feeble measure, learned more of the blessed truth that

Sufficient is His arm alone,
And our defence is sure.

'I have long felt that our Mission has a baptism to be baptized with. It may not be past yet. It may be heavier than we can foresee. But if, by grace, we are kept faithful, in the end all will be well.'

Little reference has hitherto been made to an element that entered largely into Taylor's experience; he was the tenderest of fathers. His children meant more to him than is usually the case with a very busy man, and it had cost him much to bring them to China. Journeys that involved an absence from home of weeks at a time, with no means of communication save by special messenger, were a real test both to him and to those left behind.

'It is an easy thing to sing, "I all on earth forsake",' he wrote to his mother on the first of these occasions (January, 1867). 'It is not very difficult to think, and honestly though ignorantly say, "I give up all to Thee and for Thee". But God sometimes teaches one that that little word "all" is terribly comprehensive.'

A tiny sheet of pink notepaper with a flower painted in one corner followed him on this journey. The single word 'Papa' in large round hand on the envelope showed from whom it came, and inside were the loving words:

> Dear Papa, I hope God has helped you to do what you wanted, and that you will soon come back. I have a nice bead mat for you when you come home.

Carried in her father's pocket-book for many a long year, Gracie's little letter, probably the first she ever wrote, tells of the hard life he led no less than of his tender love for her. She was the eldest of his flock, the precious link with early years when he had first met, loved, and married her mother in Ningpo. Three sons had been given them in England, followed by the baby sister, whose arrival brought special joy to Gracie's heart. But though all were equally dear to their parents, there was about the little maiden of eight years old a peculiar charm. On the *Lammermuir* the wonderful change in some of the sailors when they came to know and love the Lord Jesus had so impressed her, that she too gave her heart to the Saviour as never before. Her deeply spiritual nature had developed like a flower in the sunshine, under the consciousness of His love, so that toward the end of this first summer in Hangchow her father could write to the grandparents:

> I do wish you had seen her lately. Since her conversion she had become quite another child. Her look was more soft, more sweet, more happy.

That first summer was intensely hot, and when the thermometer stood at 103° indoors it seemed time to seek relief. The children were all suffering, and Maria was so ill that it was with difficulty she could be got out of the city. A boat trip of six miles brought them to the hills, where amid the ruins of a once famous temple, accommodation had been found. Here the Hangchow party established themselves. The hills were lovely, though the glory of azaleas, wistaria, and other spring flowers had passed away. Pines, oaks, and elms afforded welcome shade, while mountain streams made music, and as far as eye could see there was one unbroken sweep of higher or lower ranges, canals, and rivers, with the Hangchow Bay and the open sea beyond. It would have been a paradise as compared with the city, but for the illness of several of the party, and the sorrowful sights and sounds of idol worship close at hand.

A week later, his heart overwhelmed within him, Taylor sat writing to Mr. Berger:

Beloved brother, I know not how to write or how to refrain. I seem to be writing, almost, from the inner chamber of the King of kings. Surely this is holy ground. I am trying to pen a few lines by the couch on which my darling little Gracie lies dying. Her complaint is hydrocephalus. Dear brother, our flesh and our heart fail, but God is the strength of our heart and our portion for ever.

It was no vain nor unintelligent act when, knowing this land, its people and climate, I laid my wife and children, with myself, on the altar for this service. And He whom so unworthily, with much of weakness and failure, yet in simplicity and godly sincerity, we are and have been seeking to serve, and not without some measure of success – He has not left us now.

'He makes no mistakes' was the unshaken conviction of these hearts. But the loss was so great, so overwhelming!

'Except when diverted from it by the duties and necessities of our position,' Taylor wrote to his mother in September, 'our torn hearts will revert to the one subject, and I know not how to write to you of any other. Our dear little Gracie! How we miss her! As I take the walks I used to take with her tripping at my side, the thought comes anew like a throb of agony, "Is it possible that I shall never more feel the pressure of that little hand, never more hear the sweet prattle of those dear lips, never more see the sparkle of those bright eyes?" And yet she is not *lost*. I would not have her back again. She is far holier, far happier than she could ever have been here.'

As their bereavement became known, they saw with thankfulness the chastening effect it was having upon others besides themselves. Tidings of it were no little cheer to Mr. and Mrs. Berger amid their difficulties at home.

'He is keeping Satan altogether under just now,' Emily Blatchley was able to write in October. 'How devoutly grateful we ought to feel for the state of things in the Mission now as compared with a few months ago – when our lute seemed too full of rifts for harmony ever to come back again.'

Meanwhile the great, waiting land, in all its need and darkness, was not forgotten. At the bedside of the dying child in the temple, Duncan, the steadfast Highlander, Taylor's chief companion on pioneering journeys, had been keeping watch. Nanking was upon his heart – the famous city twice capital of China, with its ancient wall twenty miles in circumference, and its large population still without any witness for Christ. Duncan was not specially gifted or cultured, but he possessed grit and perseverance and a great love for souls. He it was who had toiled at Chinese with the man at the wash-tub while waiting for a better teacher, sitting beside him for hours, repeating sentences as he said them or verses that he read from the Gospels, and winning him to Christ at length by his very earnestness in seeking to make the Saviour known. It was something of a risk, no doubt, to let

Duncan go forward in such an undertaking. But he could be spared; he was a man who, his resolution once formed, never wavered; and the burden of those souls was on his heart.

The early autumn, therefore, saw this solitary pioneer arrive at Nanking. He received no welcome there. Up and down its long streets he and his Chinese helper searched in vain for any lodging that would take them in. Immediately on hearing of a foreigner's arrival, word had been sent from the Prefect to every hostelry that they were on no account to receive him. Apparently, however, the priest in charge of the Drum Tower had not been included among possible hosts, and when the weary strangers sought his aid at nightfall he was not unwilling to render it. He had no proper room, he said, for visitors, but if they liked to sleep in the Drum Tower at night and be out all day, so as not to frighten people who came to worship, he would share with them his accommodation.

It was a miserable place! Very few would have thought it possible to live there at all, but,

'We gladly accepted it,' wrote Duncan, 'and managed very nicely, though we have rather more rats than I like. At night they want to devour everything!'

Between the depredations of these marauders and the solemn sound of the drum, beaten at intervals, it was not possible to get much sleep, and at day-dawn they had to roll up their bedding and turn out on the streets of the city. The tall figure of the missionary soon became familiar in the tea-shops and frequented thoroughfares, and the neighbourhood of the Drum Tower must have known him well before he succeeded in finding another residence. A carpenter at last had courage to receive him, dividing off a strip of his single upstairs room for the use of the foreigner. On the other side of the matting lived the Chinese family, while below was the shop and kitchen, so that the new arrivals had every opportunity for picking up colloquial conversation. After a time Duncan persuaded his landlord to share with him the lower room as well. A slight partition was put up, giving the missionary a long but very narrow street chapel, the first ever opened in Nanking; and there he sat, like Judson in his *zayat*, receiving and conversing with all who would turn in.

'I am not able to talk much,' he wrote, 'but God helping me, I will say what I can, and T'ien-fuh (the Chinese evangelist) makes them understand. Oh, to make everything conduce to the gathering in of precious souls and the glory of our Master!'

Thus was commenced permanent missionary work in the great city that later became one of the strongest centres of the Christian Church in China. Duncan may not have been able to do much; but he held the fort with quiet courage, and one soul at any rate was saved in that first street chapel.

In Hangchow, too, the Lord was working, and the sorrowful days of summer were giving place to the joy of harvest. The little church inaugurated in July with nineteen members was growing rapidly with Wang Lae-djün as its pastor. Of the October baptisms Maria wrote:

When I went down to the afternoon service I saw such a sight as would have rejoiced the hearts of dear friends at home. Our courtyard in front of the main part of the house is a large one, and it was more than filled with a quiet, attentive audience. 160 persons were seated. Dear Lae-djün baptized three men and three women, and the service was held there as being more convenient than the chapel.

This brings us to one of the important discoveries Taylor was making along the lines of women's work. The new departure of women missionaries dressed in Chinese clothes visiting in Chinese homes, was justified by results.

'I think if you could see how the people love and trust us you would rejoice,' Jennie Faulding wrote that autumn. 'It does so please them to see us liking to be like themselves in outward things. They express the greatest satisfaction, and are delighted especially that our shoes and style of hair-dressing should be the same as theirs. Instead of having difficulty in getting access to the people, they come here day after day saying,

'"*Fuh Ku-niang*,[1] we want you to come to our house and teach us about the religion."

'I should think when I go out I often speak to more than 200 persons. Yet I am never treated in any way rudely, but with all kindness.'

Rich and poor alike welcomed her, and the more she became known the more was she invited into homes of all sorts. It was largely due to such visiting that new faces were always to be seen in the chapel at Hangchow. The medical work had done much to attract; but Taylor as he watched it all could not but be profoundly impressed with this new line of things, new at any rate in China.

'In its actual influence on the people at large,' he wrote, 'I am strongly inclined to consider it the most powerful agency at our disposal.'

Fuller experience only justified the conclusion. Nevertheless of all the innovations connected with the Mission none met with stronger opposition. The presence of unmarried women missionaries in the interior at all was, with many, a sufficient ground for condemning the whole work, and

[1] *Fuh*, the character chosen as the nearest in sound to the surname Faulding, means happiness. *Ku-niang*, the title given to an unmarried woman.

determined efforts were made to secure their recall to the coast. It was strongly stated in letters home that to send unmarried women to inland stations was a waste of life and energy, as there was no opening for their labours. This moved Maria deeply, and she wrote to Mrs. Berger:

Mr. ——'s assertion about there being very little opening, etc., stirs me to hope and pray that God will show his mistake by pouring out a large blessing upon this instrumentality, feeble though it be in itself. Had we the right people and suitable accommodation, I believe that ten Miss Fauldings and ten Miss Bowyers could easily find work in Hangchow tomorrow. The Lord ever keep them as simple and true-hearted as they are!

I have always found that the great difficulty in the way of female agency has been location. So few married couples (and I do not wonder at it, or blame any for it) are prepared to give up the retirement and privacy which are so pleasant, and to receive comparative strangers into their family. My husband and I have at times discussed the feasibility of establishing some of the single women in a house by themselves, and perhaps after a time this might be done. May *the Lord* direct. It is His work we are doing, and He can and will raise up helpers.

Thus they were grappling with big problems, and obtaining, even then, glimpses of developments to which God was leading in His own way. And in the process He was developing *them*, preparing one and another for the special work that lay before them. How little anyone in those early days could have foreseen the work for which Rudland was being fitted. Of all the Hangchow party he was the one who seemed, at any rate to himself, least likely to do much in China. He could not get hold of the language; and the more he tried to study the worse became the headaches, that left him utterly discouraged. Taylor, however, who was developing as a leader no less than his fellow-workers along other lines, prayed for wisdom to meet the difficulty, then said to him one day,

'I am troubled about the printing-press. The workmen seem to get through so little when left to themselves, and I really have not time to look after them. You managed so well in putting the press together; do you think you could superintend it for me now?'

So Rudland, though protesting that he knew nothing about printing, left his books for the cheerful activity of the printing-room. The workmen were glad to have his company and proud to display their superior knowledge. Listening to their conversation by the hour together, he found himself picking up words and phrases more quickly than he could discover their English equivalents. The headaches were soon conquered, and the lines laid down for a life service, that was to include the translation and printing of almost the entire Scriptures in a dialect spoken by millions to whom the Word of God was thus made accessible.

Resourcefulness was one of the characteristics Taylor was developing to the advantage of those associated with him. None who were in Hangchow at the time ever forgot his arrival one night long after the city gates were shut and they had given up hope of seeing him. In his absence no medical help was available, and one of the party was seriously ill. A messenger was sent after him, and he turned back from a journey only to find himself too late to enter the city. Darkness had fallen, and the gates were closed and barred. There seemed nothing for it but to spend the night on the river, while a precious life might be at stake.

But who was this coming up behind him who seemed confident of getting in? A Government messenger with despatches! then the gate would be opened surely? But no; a basket, he saw, was being let down over the wall, in which the messenger was to be drawn up. It was no use asking for a passage in that uncertain craft, but Taylor's quick eye caught means of steadying it. Hanging from the basket was a rope, which it was the work of a moment to seize as it was ascending. It required pluck and determination, however, to hold on and face the angry guards at the top.

'I gave them two hundred good reasons,' said Taylor on reaching home, 'why they should allow me to proceed.'

'Two hundred! how had you time?'

'They came out of my cash-bag', was the smiling reply, 'so it did not take very long.'

Among all the mercies that crowned the year 1867 – the first complete year for the *Lammermuir* party in China – none was greater than the answer to the prayer with which it had opened, 'O that thou wouldest bless me indeed, and enlarge my coast'. The stations occupied by the Mission had doubled in number in that short period. At its commencement, the distance between the most widely separated had been only four days' journey; but at its close, Duncan in Nanking was as much as twenty-four days, by ordinary means of travel, from Stott in Wenchow – a considerably enlarged sphere of labour when one remembers that, with the exception of Hangchow, no Protestant missionaries save those of the C.I.M. were settled anywhere away from the coast or the treaty ports.

For the great land around them, as well as for their own spiritual needs, the last day of the year was again set apart for prayer and fasting. From eleven in the morning till 3 p.m. one meeting lasted,

'... without weariness,' Emily Blatchley wrote, 'God's Holy Spirit wrapping us round in renewed dedication and truly baptizing us: "He shall baptize you with the Holy Ghost and with fire". At 8.30 we again met for united prayer, and still that *power* gathered and increased. Mr. Taylor read the 90th Psalm. We continued in prayer and singing till the year ended, and at twelve partook of the Lord's Supper. A holier time I have never known.'

And there was need for such inward strengthening. In spite of success – *because*, indeed, of the footing gained in some places, there was great and increasing opposition in others. From his sick-bed, only a few weeks earlier, Taylor had been carried to the Governor's *yamen* to report in person the ill-usage of McCarthy's helpers, who had been set upon and almost beaten to death in Huchow. As soon as he could travel, he had gone direct to the scene of the riot, and giving two weeks of careful, patient effort to smoothing matters over, only to find that for the time being foreigners must retire. No sooner had the new year dawned than Williamson was driven out of Kin-hwa-fu, through attacks on those who had befriended him.

'I went to see the poor fellow in prison,' Williamson wrote. 'His back and legs were severely swollen and bruised. He was shut up in a den with a number of criminals, confined like so many wild beasts in a cage. The weather was very cold, and there seemed every probability of the poor fellow losing his life from the treatment he had received. Next morning the landlord was sent for to the *yamen*, while the mother and wife of the imprisoned man were threatening to commit suicide, blaming us for bringing all this trouble upon them. The same day, in order to save these poor people from further ill-usage, we left the house, returning to Hangchow.'

It was proving harder even than had been anticipated, this pioneering work – yet Taylor's heart still went out to the Christless multitudes around.

'Are there no servants of our common Lord rusting away at home,' he wrote to Mr. Berger, 'or at least doing work that others would do if they left it, who might be out here among these numberless towns and villages?'

Very easily might the whole Mission have become absorbed in that one coast-board province, small though it was among all the provinces of China. But, providentially, door after door was closed. Riots, disturbances, sickness, and other troubles hindered developments.

Meanwhile, Mr. Berger wrote,

If you will not smile at my planning in our dining-room, I will tell you my musings concerning your future movements. I fancy you will some day transfer your head-quarters to some desirable city or town very near the Yangtze River, perhaps within easy reach of Hangchow. Thus you would, I suppose, have access to a Consul, and facilities for going to Shanghai and up the river, so as to reach many provinces. The Lord guide you in all things: 'He that believeth shall not make haste'.

It was not easy after sixteen months in Hangchow to face the thought of leaving the work that had become so dear to them for 'some desirable city near the Yangtze' in which to begin all over again. Fifty baptized believers were gathered already in the little church under Pastor Wang's care, and there were many inquirers. John McCarthy and his wife with Jennie Faulding would remain in charge of the station, however, and Duncan at Nanking was sorely needing relief.

'It really was building the wall in troublous times,' Judd wrote of those days: 'one never knew what friends who were away might be suffering. Scarcely any station was opened without a riot. The noon meetings were solemn hours – often prolonged, because there was so much to pray about. One feels the thrill of them still.'

CHAPTER 15

The Exchanged Life

(1868–1869)

THE missionary and his Consul were being worsted. It was widely known that the deeds for the property in the Yangtze treaty port of Chinkiang had been signed, and the deposit paid. The Governor, however, was withholding the proclamation without which the landlord could not be kept to his bargain, and the whole affair was the laugh of tea-house and restaurant.

Hudson Taylor was carrying on these negotiations from the neighbouring city of Yangchow, where his wife and family and Emily Blatchley were settled in big rambling premises. The place was besieged with visitors at first, and Maria had her hands full. Exaggerated reports about the situation in Chinkiang, however, had suggested to the *literati* that the missionaries might be treated with as scant courtesy in Yangchow. Why allow them to make friends and settle down, when by carrying things with a high hand they could be ejected? A meeting was held and a decision arrived at to stir up trouble. This was done by means of anonymous hand-bills, attributing the most revolting and unnatural crimes to foreigners, especially those whose business it was to propagate 'the religion of Jesus'.

Early in August, the missionaries began to realize the change that was coming over the attitude of the people. Friendly visitors had given place to crowds of the lowest rabble about the door, and a fresh set of posters, quite unfit for translation, was as fuel to the fire.

> 'On Saturday the 15th,' wrote Reid who, with Rudland, had arrived from Nanking, 'Mr. Taylor received an anonymous letter, advising him to use all possible precautions, as on the following day there was to be a riot. The people assembled at an early hour, and began knocking and battering upon our door until we thought it best to go out and try to pacify them.'

The trouble went on, and on the 18th Emily Blatchley wrote:

> For the last few days we have been almost in a state of siege. Mr. Taylor, just up from a sick-bed and weak as he is, has hardly dared to leave the gate, Messrs. Reid and Rudland with him, and on Saturday night Mr. Duncan opportunely arrived. Today (Tuesday) was placarded as the day for attacking our house and setting it on fire, regardless of native or foreign occupants. Once or twice the mob has seemed inclined to break in by force, but the disturbance is less than on Sunday. God is with

us, we do not fear. As I write He is sending thunder and the threatening of rain, which will do more for us, Mr. Taylor was saying, than an army of soldiers. The Chinese shun rain; the most important matters they will postpone on account of it.

After this, it looked as though the worst was over. In spite of all that had been said against them, the quiet, friendly demeanour of the missionaries was winning its way, and the storm seemed to have spent itself without disaster. From Wednesday to Saturday the wearied household had a little respite, but before the close of the week an opportunity occurred for reviving the agitation. A couple of foreigners from Chinkiang came up to visit Yangchow, and were seen in various parts of the city. This was too good a chance to be lost, and no sooner had they left, with the impression that all was quiet, than reports began to be circulated that children were missing in all directions, entrapped by the 'foreign devils'. The weather was intensely hot, which always predisposes to excitable foregatherings. Children *had* disappeared, so the people believed – twenty-four at least had fallen a prey to the dreaded foreigners. And on their premises, as was well known, vast stores of treasures were accumulated! Boat-loads of goods had been brought in only a few days previously. Courage! Avenge our wrongs! Attack – destroy! Much plunder shall be ours.

Forty-eight hours later, in a boat nearing Chinkiang, Emily Blatchley's letter was bravely finished:

We have had to flee from Yangchow. I cannot stop now to describe the last few days, if indeed they are describable. The rioters sacked every room excepting mine, in which were all our most important papers and the bulk of our money – a considerable sum, $300, having reached us from Chinkiang only an hour before the breaking into the house.

Poor Mr. Reid is the most severely hurt of all; a brick-bat struck his eye while he was standing ready to catch Mrs. Taylor and me – as we had to escape for our lives by jumping from the verandah roof over the front of the reception hall. Mrs. Taylor hurt her leg very much. I, whose fall was not broken (as Mr. Reid was wounded, and so disabled from helping me), came down on my back on the stones, and it is only by God's great loving-kindness that I have not a broken spine or skull. I have only a wound on my arm, and that the left arm. It is getting very painful, but there is so much to be thankful for that this seems as nothing.

Murder, though intended, had been averted again and again. Both Taylor, exposed to all the fury of the populace on his way to seek help of the authorities, and those he had to leave in the besieged dwelling, were alike protected by the wonder-working hand of God.

'But for the protection afforded us by the darkness,' Taylor wrote of that desperate effort to summon aid, 'we should scarcely have reached the *yamen* alive. Alarmed by the yells of the people the gate-keepers were just closing the gates as we approached, but the momentary delay gave time for the crowd to close in upon us; the as yet unbarred gates gave way to the pressure, and we were precipitated into the entrance hall. Had the gates been barred, I am convinced that they would not have been opened for us, and we should have been torn to pieces by the enraged mob.

'Once in the *yamen*, we rushed into the judgment hall, crying "*Kiu-ming! Kiu-ming!*" (save life! save life!), a cry the Chinese Mandarin is bound to attend to at any hour of the day or night.

'We were taken to the room of the Chief Secretary, and kept waiting three-quarters of an hour before we had an audience with the Prefect, all the time hearing the yells of the mob a mile or more off, destroying, for aught we knew, not only the property, but possibly the lives of those so dear to us. And at last when we did get an audience, it was almost more than we could bear with composure to be asked as to what we really did with the babies; whether it was true we had bought them, and how many; what was the cause of all this rioting? etc., etc.

'At last I told His Excellency that the real cause of all the trouble was his own neglect in not taking measures when the matter was small and manageable; that I must now request him first to take steps to repress the riot and save any of our friends who might still be alive, and afterwards make such inquiries as he might wish, or I would not answer for the result.

' "Ah," said he, "very true, very true! First quiet the people and then inquire. Sit still, and I will go to see what can be done."

'He went out telling us to remain, as the only chance of his effecting anything depended on our keeping out of sight; for by this time the number of rioters amounted to eight or ten thousand.

'We were kept in this torture of suspense for two hours, when the Prefect returned with the Governor of the military forces of the city, and told us that all was quiet; that the Governor himself, the captain of the soldiers who guard the gates, and two local Mandarins had been to the scene of the disturbance; that they had seized several of those who were plundering the premises, and would have them punished. He then sent for chairs, and we returned under escort.

'When we reached the house, the scene was such as baffled description. A pile of half-burned reeds showed where one of the attempts to fire the premises had been made; strewn about everywhere were the remains of boxes and furniture broken and smouldering – but no trace of inhabitants within.'

After a long and agonizing search it was with unspeakable thankfulness he learned that some at any rate of the party were hiding in a neighbour's house. The darkness of the night had favoured their escape from their own burning premises. Taken from one room to another as the danger of discovery increased, they had finally been left without a glimmer of light in the innermost apartments.

'Mr. Reid lay groaning with pain,' wrote Emily Blatchley, 'the poor tired children wanted to sleep and we dared not let them, as at any moment we might have to flee again. Mrs. Taylor was almost fainting from loss of blood; and I now found that my arm was bleeding from a bad cut, and so painful that I could not move it, while most of us were stiff and sore with bruises.'

Then it was that suspense about Taylor and Duncan was hardest to bear. In the darkness and silence, the uncertainty was terrible.

'I cannot attempt to describe to you our feelings,' Maria wrote. 'But God was our stay, and He forsook us not. This confidence He gave me, that He would surely work good for China out of our deep distress.

'At last, after a much shorter time than it appeared to us, we heard my husband's voice outside the door, which had been barred for greater safety. He told us that the rioters had all been driven out, and he thought we might venture back to our own rooms, for there would be a guard around the premises. How our hearts went up to God in thanksgiving that He had spared us to each other!

'For the remainder of the night we were in quiet, though for some of us there was no sleep. Early in the morning the guard retired, and the people began to come in again to plunder. Again my husband had to go to the *yamen*, and again commenced a season of anxiety similar to, though in some respects more trying, than the night before. Once more my room became our sanctuary, till just when it seemed as if in another minute the crowd would be upstairs, the alarm was given that the Mandarin had come, and his soldiery soon dispersed the people.'

It was *thankfulness* more than anything else that filled the hearts of that little company, wounded and suffering as they were, on the boats that took them to Chinkiang. The Mandarins had insisted on their leaving for a time, that the house might be repaired and the people quietened; and with no thought of compensation, still less of revenge, the missionaries looked forward to a speedy return. Homeless and despoiled of almost everything, they rejoiced in having been counted worthy to suffer 'for the sake of the Name', and their hearts were cheered as they recalled the protecting care of God. Their lives had been spared as by a miracle and even the money and more important Mission papers were safe, though the room in which they lay had been open to the rioters.

Upon reaching Chinkiang, great was the kindness received from the foreign residents. Though the community was small, they managed to put up all the refugees. Here, in the midst of the debris from the riot, the Taylors set to work at once on business and correspondence, having nine or ten stations and many fellow-workers to think of as well as the party with them.

It was a dark hour indeed that was coming upon the leader of the Mission, a period so painful in some of its aspects that even the sufferings of the riot seemed little in comparison. To begin with, a resident at Chinkiang, with the kindest intentions, wrote stirring accounts to the Shanghai papers, and public feeling demanded that action, prompt and decisive, should be taken by the British authorities. This brought the Consul-General and later on the Ambassador himself into the matter. A gunboat was sent up to Chinkiang, and there was much coming and going of British officers and blue-jackets.

These proceedings caused grave concern to Taylor. While grateful for the Consul-General's desire to help, how much rather would he have gone back at his own risk to live down unfriendliness and opposition by patient continuance in well-doing. Detained in Chinkiang week after week, he saw the difficulty grow only more serious. Meanwhile he was faced with distressing complications of another sort in his own circle, for it was at this time the group of five left him, and he was conscious of the questions that would be asked by friends of the Mission at home.

A letter to Mr. Berger written even before this happened showed how the true character of the work was more and more unfolding itself to his mind. With Maria bearing so bravely her share of the burdens, it had meant much to him when he wrote:

It is most important that married missionaries should be *double* missionaries – not half or a quarter or eight-part missionaries. Might we not with advantage say to our candidates: 'Our work is a peculiar one. We aim at the interior, where the whole of your society will be Chinese. If you wish for luxury and freedom from care, *do not join us*. Unless you intend your wife to be a true missionary, not merely a wife, home-maker, and friend, *do not join us*. She must be able to read and be master of at least one Gospel in colloquial Chinese before you marry. A person of ordinary ability may accomplish this in six months, but if she needs longer there is the more reason to wait until she has reached this point before you marry. She must be prepared to be happy among the Chinese when the duties of your calling require, as they often will, your temporary absence from home. You, too, must master the initial difficulties of the language and open up a station, if none be allotted to you, before you marry. With diligence and God's blessing you may hope to do this in a year or so. If these conditions seem too hard, these sacrifices too great to make for perishing China, *do not join our Mission*. These are small things to some of the crosses you may be permitted to bear for your dear Master.'

China is not to be won for Christ by self-seeking, ease-loving men and women. Those not prepared for labour, self-denial, and many discouragements will be poor helpers in the work. In short, the men and women we need are those who will put Jesus, China, souls first and foremost in everything and at all times: life itself must be secondary – nay, even those more precious than life. Of *such* men, of *such* women, do not fear to send us too many. Their price is far above rubies.

The riot and all that grew out of it did but emphasize these considerations and deepen Taylor's thankfulness for many of the fellow-workers already given him. He rejoiced in the devotion to Christ which had led them to cast in their lot with such a Mission, and in the practical way they were adapting themselves to their surroundings. It was not only obvious to him but to others, how effective was Maria's unconscious influence. One of the younger workers who on their arrival in China had early been moulded by her strong though gracious personality, wrote:

> How impressed I was with her calm, holy, happy appearance, as well as her Christian carriage! She, with Mr. McCarthy and a Chinese helper, had come seven days' journey from Hangchow to meet our party. She gave us the warmest welcome and every assistance possible, but it was evident that she had no mercy on fastidiousness as to food or any other matters.

Her one desire now, in spite of all that had happened at Yangchow, was to return to that city and win a way to darkened hearts for the saving love of Christ.

It was with thankfulness that news was at last received of an amicable settlement of the Yangchow matter. A stone tablet was placed at the entrance to the Yangchow house, stating that the foreigners were there with the full recognition of the authorities. Quite a function was arranged to reinstate the party; and Taylor wrote, 'The result of this case will probably be greatly to facilitate work in the interior.'

It was, however, the family life and friendly spirit of the missionaries that disarmed suspicion and gradually won its way among the people. They could not but be touched when the children were brought back after all that had taken place, and the arrival of a fourth son made a favourable impression, calling forth the congratulations of Chinese neighbours.

> 'In this again,' Maria wrote to her friend at Saint Hill, 'God has given me the desire of my heart. For I felt that if safety to my infant permitted, I would rather it were born in this city, in this house, in this very room than in any other place.'

The landlord of the inn (a Mr. P'eng) and two others who had befriended the missionaries in the riot were by this time candidates for baptism; and when before the end of the year the Chinkiang house was also in their possession, Taylor might well write, 'Once again we raise our Ebenezer – "Hitherto hath the Lord helped us".'

The Yangchow difficulties were far from ended with this satisfactory settlement, however, for the action of the consular authorities[1] gave rise to a storm of indignation at home. Missionaries were making trouble as usual. The country would be involved in war before the Government had even time to consider the matter! It seems almost incredible as one looks back upon it, that so much misrepresentation could have found its way into the

[1] The only appeal of any kind that Hudson Taylor had made to the consular authorities had been a verbal message on August 22, and a pencilled note the following morning informing them of the situation.

daily papers, and that for a period of four or five months Hudson Taylor and his doings could so largely have occupied the public mind. From the 'connected narrative' in *The Times* of December 1, 'explaining' the whole situation, to the discussion in the House of Lords on March 9 – in which, after a heated declamation, the Duke of Somerset urged that all British missionaries should be recalled from China – the matter seems hardly to have been absent from the public mind. Needless to say, the brunt of all this fell upon Mr. Berger. He wrote

> The excitement, indeed I may almost say storm, seems bursting over us now. *The Times* is very severe and incorrect in some things. Whether to reply to the false statements I scarcely know. At present the Yangchow outrage is the all-absorbing subject.
>
> January 13, 1869: It rejoices our hearts that you are again at Yangchow. The late riots have led to such an immense increase of correspondence and claims upon me, that I must guard against breaking down entirely.
>
> February 25: We are just back from Bristol, where we found many dear friends who remembered and inquired most affectionately after you and Mrs. Taylor. The sympathy expressed for you and those with you in the late trial was great and very sweet; and none spoke more warmly of you than dear Mr. Müller.
>
> I asked for his opinion respecting the appeal to the British Consul, and you would have rejoiced to have heard him repudiate the spirit of judging you, or of fault-finding. He said he would never have spoken to me on the subject, had I not asked him for his judgment: after which he said that, had poor George Müller been in such circumstances, he cannot tell what he might have done; still he thought the more excellent way would have been to trust in God. That we must not set up what *we* think the more excellent way, as a rule for others, he quite agreed with me. Finally, Mr. Müller only allowed me, upon my request, to refer to his opinion with the understanding that it was that we might help each other in serving the Lord, and not in any spirit of fault-finding or condemning you.
>
> March 11: The Yangchow matter is before the House of Lords, and I hope to send you a copy of *The Times* ere long. You can scarcely imagine what an effect the matter has produced in the country. Thank God I can say, 'None of these things move me'. I believe He has called us to this work, and it is not for us to run away from it or allow difficulties to overcome us. Be of good courage, the battle is the Lord's.

One result of all these difficulties was, not unnaturally, a falling off in the income of the Mission, so that for the first time Taylor was faced with serious shortness of funds in China. This would have been much more the case if the Lord had not laid it upon the heart and put it into the power of George Müller largely to increase his gifts. He had been sending regularly to several members of the Mission sometimes as much as £25 a quarter; and now, within a day or two of the Yangchow riot (long before he heard of it), he wrote to Mr. Berger asking for the names of others who were thoroughly satisfactory in their work whom he might add to his list. Mr. Berger sent him six names from which to choose, and his choice was to take them all.[1] This was not only a substantial help, it was a great encouragement, for it meant added sympathy and prayer on the part of one who knew the way to the Throne. And more and more Taylor was feeling the need of just such fellowship. Constantly under pressure of strain and stress as he was, his spiritual life had hardly kept pace with the demands upon it. Outwardly it may not have seemed so.

> 'Our hearts were much drawn to Mr. Taylor,' said one of the fellow-workers constantly with him, 'by seeing his gentle, humble, tender spirit under the administrative trials of those early years.'

But 'the heart knoweth its own bitterness', and the load Hudson Taylor was carrying was almost more than he could bear. It was not the work with all its difficulty and trial: when consciously in communion with the Lord these seemed light. It was not shortness of funds, nor anxiety about those dearest to him. It was just – himself: the unsatisfied longing of his heart; the inward struggle to abide in Christ; the frequent failure and disappointment. So bitter was this experience that even when it was left far behind he could never forget it. This it was that made him always sympathetic with younger workers in their spiritual conflicts, quick to see and make the most of every opportunity to help them. Fellowship with God was to him a great reality, a great necessity. He had known much of it; much too of the terrible void of losing it. 'Like a diver under water without air, or a fireman on a burning building with an empty hose', he found himself face to face with heathenism and all the claims that pressed upon him, but alas! too often out of touch with Christ.

Just at this time the pages of the *Revival* (later the *Christian*) were largely occupied with a genuine holiness movement destined, in the providence of God, to lead to the Keswick Convention with its world-wide influences for good. Finding its way to all the stations of the Mission, this paper was bringing the subject of a deeper spiritual life prominently before its readers, and not a few, like Taylor himself, were hungering for a fuller experience of the possibilities it set forth, which they saw to be in accordance with the Word of God. It was the life of habitual victory over sin, the life that is in deep reality 'Not I, but Christ', for which their hearts longed.

Life was too busy as a rule for Taylor's correspondence to reveal much of the crisis through which he was passing, but early in 1869 he found himself alone on a journey which gave opportunity for one of the old-time letters to his mother.

[1] George Müller later increased his gifts even more, and for some years sent nearly £2,000 annually to the C.I.M.

I have often asked you to remember me in prayer, and when I have done so there has been much *need* of it. That need has never been greater than at the present time.

My own position becomes continually more and more responsible, and my need greater of special grace to fill it; but I have continually to mourn that I follow at such a distance and learn so slowly to imitate my precious Master. I cannot tell you how I am buffeted sometimes by temptation. I never knew how bad a heart I had. Often I am tempted to think that one so full of sin cannot be a child of God at all; but I try to throw it back, and rejoice all the more in the preciousness of Jesus, and in the riches of that grace that has made us 'accepted in the beloved'. Beloved He *is* of God; beloved He *ought* to be of us. But oh, how short I fall here again! May God help me to love Him more and serve Him better. Do pray for me. Pray that the Lord will keep me from sin, will sanctify me wholly, will use me more largely in His service.

It was six months after writing this letter that he himself received one which proved to be God's channel for the illumination he needed. The letter came from John McCarthy in Hangchow, and reached him at a time when life was specially full and busy. There it lay amid a pile of accumulated correspondence that awaited his return from attending a fellow-missionary dangerously ill. We do not know if he was alone as he read it: we do not know just how the miracle was wrought. But 'as I read, I saw it all. I looked to Jesus; and when I saw, oh how joy flowed!'

The whole story of his own extremity and deliverance was poured out in a letter to his sister Amelia,

October 17, 1869: The last month or more has been, perhaps, the happiest of my life; and I long to tell you a little of what the Lord has done for my soul. I do not know how far I may be able to make myself intelligible about it, for there is nothing new or strange or wonderful – and yet, all is new! In a word, 'Whereas I was blind, now I see'.

Perhaps I shall make myself more clear if I go back a little. Well, dearie, my mind has been greatly exercised for six or eight months past, feeling the need personally, and for our Mission, of more holiness, life, power in our souls. But personal need stood first and was the greatest. I felt the ingratitude, the danger, the sin of not living nearer to God. I prayed, agonized, fasted, strove, made resolutions, read the Word more diligently, sought more time for retirement and meditation – but all was without effect. Every day, almost every hour, the consciousness of sin oppressed me. I knew that if I could only abide in Christ all would be well, but I *could not*. I began the day with prayer, determined not to take my eye from Him for a moment; but pressure of duties, sometimes very trying, constant interruptions apt to be so wearing, often caused me to forget Him. Then one's nerves get so fretted in this climate that temptations to irritability, hard thoughts, and sometimes unkind words are all the more difficult to control. Each day brought its register of sin and failure, of lack of power. To will was indeed present with me, but how to perform I found not.

Then came the question, 'Is there *no* rescue? Must it be thus to the end – constant conflict and, instead of victory, too often defeat?' How, too, could I preach with sincerity that to those who receive Jesus, 'to them gave he power to become the sons of God' (i.e. God-like) when it was not so in my own experience? Instead of growing stronger, I seemed to be getting weaker and to have less power against sin; and no wonder, for faith and even hope were getting very low. I hated myself; I hated my sin; and yet I gained no strength against it. I felt I *was* a child of God: His Spirit in my heart would cry, in spite of all, 'Abba, Father': but to rise to my privileges as a child, I was utterly powerless. I thought that holiness, practical holiness, was to be gradually attained by a diligent use of the means of grace. I felt that there was nothing I so much desired in this world, nothing I so much needed. But so far from in any measure attaining it, the more I pursued and strove after it, the more it eluded my grasp; till hope itself almost died out, and I began to think that, perhaps to make Heaven the sweeter, God would not give it down here. I do not think I was striving to attain it in my own strength. I knew I was powerless. I told the Lord so, and asked Him to give me help and strength; and sometimes I almost believed He would keep and uphold me. But on looking back in the evening, alas! there was but sin and failure to confess and mourn before God.

I would not give you the impression that this was the daily experience of all those long, weary months. It was a too frequent state of soul; that toward which I was tending, and which almost ended in despair. And yet never did Christ seem more precious – a Saviour who *could* and *would* save such a sinner!

Sometimes there were seasons not only of peace but of joy in the Lord. But they were transitory, and at best there was a sad lack of power. Oh, how good the Lord was in bringing this conflict to an end!

All the time I felt assured that there was in Christ all I needed, but the practical question was how to get it *out*. He was rich, truly, but I was poor; He was strong, but I weak. I knew full well that there was in the root, the stem, abundant fatness; but how to get it into my puny little branch was the question. As gradually the light was dawning on me, I saw that faith was the only prerequisite, was the hand to lay hold on His fullness and make it my own. *But I had not this faith.* I strove for it, but it would not come; tried to exercise it, but in vain. Seeing more and more the wondrous supply of grace laid up in Jesus, the fullness of our precious Saviour – my helplessness and guilt seemed to increase. Sins committed appeared but as trifles compared with the sin of unbelief which was their cause, which could not or would not take God at His word, but rather made Him a liar! Unbelief was, I felt, *the* damning sin of the world – yet I indulged in it. I prayed for faith, but it came not. What was I to do?

When my agony of soul was at its height, a sentence in a letter from dear McCarthy was used to remove the scales from my eyes, and the Spirit of God revealed the truth of *our oneness* with *Jesus* as I had never known it before. McCarthy, who had been much exercised by the same sense of failure, but saw the light before I did, wrote (I quote from memory):

'But how to get faith strengthened? Not by striving after faith, but by resting on the Faithful One.'

As I read I saw it all! 'If we believe *not*, he abideth faithful.' I looked to Jesus and saw (and when I saw, oh, how joy flowed!) that He had said, '*I* will never leave *you*'.

'Ah, *there* is rest!' I thought. 'I have striven in vain to rest in Him. I'll strive no more. For has He not promised to abide with me – never to leave me, never to fail me?' And, dearie, *He never will*!

But this was not all He showed me, nor one half. As I thought of the vine and the branches, what light the blessed Spirit poured direct into my soul! How great seemed my mistake in having wished to get the sap, the fullness *out* of Him. I saw not only that Jesus would never leave me, but that I was a member of His body, of His flesh and of His bones. The vine now I see, is not the root merely, but all – root, stem, branches, twigs, leaves, flowers, fruit: and Jesus is not only that: He is soil and sunshine, air and showers, and ten thousand times more than we have ever dreamed, wished for, or needed. Oh, the joy of seeing this truth! I do pray that the eyes of your understanding may be enlightened, that you may know and enjoy the riches freely given us in Christ.

Oh, my dear sister, it is a wonderful thing to be really one with a risen and exalted Saviour; to be a member of Christ! Think what it involves. Can Christ be rich and I poor? Can your right hand be rich and the left poor? or your head be well fed while your body starves? Again, think of its bearing on prayer. Could a bank clerk say to a customer, 'It was only your hand wrote that cheque, not you,' or, 'I cannot pay this sum to your hand, but only to yourself'? No more can your prayers, or mine, be discredited *if offered in the Name of Jesus* (i.e. not in our own name, or for the sake of Jesus merely, but on the ground that we are His, His members) so long as we keep within the extent of Christ's credit – a tolerably wide limit! If we ask anything unscriptural or not in accordance with the will of God, Christ Himself could not do that; but, 'If we ask anything according to his will, he heareth us, and . . . we know that we have the petitions that we desired of him.'

The sweetest part, if one may speak of one part being sweeter than another, is the *rest* which full identification with Christ brings. I am no longer anxious about anything, as I realize this; for He, I know, is able to carry out *His will*, and His will is mine. It makes no matter where He places me, or how. That is rather for Him to consider than for me; for in the easiest positions He must give me His grace, and in the most difficult His grace is sufficient. It little matters to my servant whether I send him to buy a few cash worth of things, or the most expensive articles. In either case he looks to me for the money, and brings me his purchases. So, if God places me in great perplexity, must He not give me much guidance; in positions of great difficulty, much grace; in circumstances of great pressure and trial, much strength? No fear that His resources will be unequal to the emergency! And His resources are mine, for *He* is mine, and is with me and dwells in me. All this springs from the believer's oneness with Christ. And since Christ has thus dwelt in my heart by faith, how happy I have been! I wish I could tell you, instead of writing about it.

I am no better than before (may I not say, in a sense, I do not wish to be, nor am I striving to be); but I am dead and buried with Christ – aye, and risen too and ascended; and now Christ lives in me, and 'the life that I now live in the flesh, I live by the faith of the Son of God, who loved me, and gave himself for me'. I now *believe* I am dead to sin. God reckons me so, and tells me to reckon myself so. He knows best. All my past experience may have shown that it *was* not so; but I dare not say it *is* not now, when He says it is. I feel and know that old things have passed away.

I am as capable of sinning as ever, but Christ is realized as present as never before. He cannot sin; and He can keep me from sinning. I cannot say (I am sorry to have to confess it) that since I have seen this light I have not sinned; but I do feel there was no need to have done so. And further – walking more in the light, my conscience has been more tender; sin has been instantly seen, confessed, pardoned; and peace and joy (with humility) instantly restored; with one exception, when for several hours peace and joy did not return – from want, as I had to learn, of full confession, and from some attempt to justify self.

Faith, I now see, is 'the *substance* of things hoped for', and not mere shadow. It is not *less* than sight, but *more*. Sight only shows the outward forms of things; faith gives the substance. You can *rest* on substance, *feed* on substance. Christ dwelling in the heart by faith (i.e. His word of promise credited) is *power* indeed, is *life* indeed. And Christ and sin will not dwell together; nor can we have His presence with love of the world, or carefulness about 'many things'.

And now I must close. I have not said half I would, nor *as* I would had I more time. May God give you to lay hold on these blessed truths. Do not let us continue to say, in *effect*, 'Who shall ascend into heaven? that is, to bring Christ down from above'. In other words, do not let us consider Him as afar off, when God has made us *one with Him*, members of His very body. Nor should we look upon this experience, these truths, as for the few. They are the birthright of every child of God, and no one can dispense with them without dishonour to our Lord. The only power for deliverance from sin or for true service is Christ.

CHAPTER 16

Jesus Does Satisfy

(1869–1871)

TO MARIA the new life that had come to her husband and many of their fellow-workers was a joy not unmixed with wonder. The experiences they were finding as something new had long been her secret of victory and peace. 'It was just resting in Jesus,' as she expressed it, 'and letting Him do the work' – a little sentence, but one that really lived out, made her life the strength to the Mission that Taylor had often realized it to be. And now husband and wife were one in a new way, and helpers of each other's faith.

That such blessing should be tested by increasing trials is not to be wondered at. Inwardly and outwardly the period upon which they were entering was to be one of unprecedented distress. In the work they were to experience the power of the adversary as never before, while in personal matters new and deep sorrows awaited them. But for the preparation of heart which unconsciously to themselves had thus been made, things would have gone very differently both with Hudson Taylor and with the Mission.

> The shadow of a cross falls deep and broad;
> With Thee I enter, tremblingly, the shade:
> Whence this new light which brightens round me, Lord?
> 'The fellowship of suffering,' He said.

To begin with, the time had come for breaking up that happy family life which meant so much to the Taylors. They dared not risk another summer for their elder children in China, and the delicate health of Samuel, who was only five years old, made it clear that he should go with his brothers and sister. This meant separation from four of their little flock, leaving them with only the baby born after the Yangchow riot. For some time it was a question as to whether the mother should not go herself, but the necessity for this seemed obviated when Emily Blatchley volunteered to take her place in caring for the children. To part from her was almost like giving up a daughter, so devoted had she been in sharing all their experiences. But she truly loved the children, and it meant that Maria might remain in China. Plan as they might, they could not see far ahead, and could only trust the little party to the care of Him whose love was infinitely wiser and more tender than their own. Taylor wrote to his mother,

You can enter somewhat into our feelings as this dark cloud draws near. Sometimes it seems, for a while, to take all one's strength and heart away, but God does and will help us. It is so good of Him to have given us to know more than we ever have known of His heart, His love, His gift, His joy, before calling us to take this step. And there are many mercies connected with this trial. Miss Blatchley's love and self-sacrifice we can never repay. I am sure you will do what you can to help her and you will specially pray for my dear Maria. When all the bustle of preparation and the excitement of departure are over, then will come the trying time of reaction. But the Lord, whose work calls for the separation, can and will support her.

Very painful it was, as the time drew near for the parting, to see the child about whom they were most concerned get worse. Or was it only that his chronic trouble had increased, and that with care the voyage would set him up again? Taking the opportunity of apparent improvement, the family set out from Yangchow, but hardly had they got clear of the city when the little invalid showed signs of a relapse. All night long they watched beside him, doing everything that could be done under the circumstances. But at dawn the following morning he fell into a deep sleep, and passed without pain or fear to the Better Land.

Before a driving storm the parents crossed the river, there more than two miles wide, to lay their treasure in the little cemetery at Chinkiang, and then went on with the others to Shanghai. A few weeks later, after taking them all on board the French mail which was to sail at dawn the following morning, Taylor wrote at midnight to Mr. Berger:

I have seen them awake, for the last time in China. Two of our little ones we have no anxiety about; they rest in Jesus' bosom. And now, dear Brother, though the tears will not be stayed, I do thank God for permitting one so unworthy to take any part in this great work, and do not regret having engaged and being engaged in it. It is *His* work, not mine nor yours: and yet it is ours – not because we are engaged in it, but because we are His, and one with Him whose work it is.

This was the reality that sustained, and more than sustained them. Never had there been a more troubled summer in China than that on which they were entering.

'Politically, we are facing a crisis. If our Government continues their present, I had almost said *mad* policy, war must result. In the meantime our position is becoming always more embarrassing. You can scarcely judge how intricate our path seems at times.'

And yet in the midst of it all, with a longing for their little ones that was indescribable, they never had had more rest and joy in God.

'I could not but admire and wonder at the grace that so sustained and comforted the fondest of mothers,' Taylor wrote as he recalled it afterwards. 'The secret was that *Jesus* was *satisfying* the deep thirst of heart and soul.'

Maria was at her best that summer, borne up, it would seem, on the very tempest of troubles that raged about them. Sickness was rife in the Mission, and before they could reach Chinkiang after parting from the children, news came to them of a young missionary being there at the point of death. After days and nights of nursing, her husband was almost too weary to bear up, when in the courtyard below he heard sounds of an unexpected arrival. Who could it be at that hour of night, and where had they come from? No steamer had passed up-river, and Chinese boats would not be travelling after dark. Besides it was a wheelbarrow that had been trundled in. A long day's journey on that springless vehicle a woman had come alone, and soon he saw the face of all others he could have longed to see. He had thought them far away, but Taylor, who could not leave the boat on account of another patient, had consented to Maria's pressing on alone to give what help she could.

'Suffering though she was at the time and worn with hard travelling,' he recalled, she insisted on my going to bed and that she would undertake the nursing. Nothing would induce her to rest.

' "No," she said, "you have quite enough to bear, without sitting up any more at night. Go to bed, for I shall stay with your wife whether you do or not." '

Nothing but prayer brought the patient through, just as nothing but prayer saved the situation in many an hour of extremity that summer.

'We had previously known something of trial in one station or another,' Taylor wrote to the friends of the Mission, 'but now in all simultaneously, or nearly so, a widespread excitement shook the very foundations of Chinese society. It is impossible to describe the alarm and consternation of the Chinese, when first they believed that native magicians were bewitching them, or their indignation and anger when told that these insidious foes were the agents of foreigners. It is well known how in Tientsin they rose and barbarously murdered the Romish Sisters of Charity, the priests, and even the French Consul. What then restrained them in the interior, where our brothers were alone, far from any protecting human power? Nothing but *the mighty hand of God,* in answer to united, constant prayer, offered in the all-prevailing name of *Jesus.* And this same power kept *us* satisfied with Jesus – with His presence, His love, His providence.'

It is easy to read, but only those who have passed through like experiences can have any idea of the strain involved. The heat of the summer was excessive, which added to the unrest of the Chinese population. Women and children had to be removed from several of the stations, and for a time it seemed as though the Chinese Government might insist on their leaving the country altogether. The accommodation of the little house at Chinkiang was taxed to its utmost, and so great was the excitement, even there, that no other premises could be obtained.

Yet the troubles of the time were not allowed to interfere with as much work among the people as was possible. Maria reported in a letter to Emily Blatchley:

> We have been holding classes on Sundays and two or three evenings in the week, having two objects specially in view: first, to interest the Chinese, those who can read, in searching the Scriptures, and those who cannot, in learning to do so; and secondly, to set an example to the younger members of the Mission. It may be a practical proof to them of the importance we attach to securing that people learn to read and understand for themselves the Word of God.

As for Taylor, his letters reveal not so much the endless difficulties as the full tide of blessing that carried him through all. To one fellow-worker, for example, he wrote in the middle of June after a careful letter about Yangchow affairs:

> And now I have the very passage for you, and God has so blessed it to my own soul! John 7. 37-39: 'If any man thirst, let him come unto me and drink.' Who does not thirst? Who has not mind-thirsts or heart-thirsts, soul-thirsts or body-thirsts? Well, no matter which, or whether I have them all – 'Come unto Me and' remain thirsty? Ah, no! 'Come unto Me and *drink*.'
>
> What, can Jesus meet my need? Yes, and more than meet it. No matter how intricate my path, how difficult my service, no matter how sad my bereavement, how far away my loved ones, no matter how helpless I am, how hopeless I am, how deep are my soul-yearnings – Jesus can meet all, all, and more than *meet*. He not only promises me drink to alleviate my thirst. No, better than that!
>
> 'He who trusts me in this matter (who believeth on Me – takes me at my word) out of him shall *flow*. . . '
>
> And not mere mountain torrents, full while the rains last, then dry again . . . but 'out of his belly shall flow rivers' – rivers like the mighty Yangtze, ever deep, ever full. In times of drought brooks may fail, often do; canals may be pumped dry, often are; but the Yangtze *never*. Always a mighty stream; always flowing, deep and irresistible!
>
> ' "Come unto me and *drink*",' he wrote in another June letter. 'Not, come and take a hasty draught; not, come and slightly alleviate, or for a short time remove one's thirst. No! "*drink*", or "*be drinking*" constantly, habitually. The cause of thirst may be irremediable. One coming, one drinking may refresh and comfort; but we are to be ever coming, ever drinking. No fear of emptying the fountain or exhausting the river!'

How sorely the lesson would be needed by his own heart in days that were drawing near, he little knew when writing; for unknown to him Maria's strength was failing. It was not easy to be much alone that summer, but prayer became her very life, and in a new sense her refuge.

'It often comforts me about the children,' Emily Blatchley wrote some months later, 'to remember how much she prayed for them. I have seen her at night, when she thought all were sleeping, with head bowed, kneeling for a long, long time on the bare floor. And when I picture her so, I always feel that she was praying most especially for you and the dear children.'

Far away were those little ones now, and she longed with all a mother's longing to know of their being safely sheltered somewhere in England. With thankfulness amid the trials of that hot season she thought of the Berger home, Saint Hill – the cool green walks and pleasant lake, the lawns around the house and the atmosphere of love within – and pictured the little travellers welcomed there. Her own heart meanwhile was filled with a new love and joy as, on July 7, her fifth son was born.

But an attack of cholera had greatly prostrated her, and lack of natural nourishment told upon the child. When a Chinese nurse could be found, it was too late to save the little life, and after one brief week he died.

'Though excessively prostrate in body,' Taylor wrote, 'the deep peace of soul, the realization of the Lord's own presence, and the joy in His holy will with which she was filled, and in which I was permitted to share, I can find no words to describe.'

She herself chose the hymns to be sung at the little grave.

Weak as she was, however, it had not yet occurred to them that for her too the end was near. The deep mutual love that bound their hearts in one seemed to preclude she thought of separation. She was only thirty-three. There was no pain up to the very last, though she was weary, very weary. A letter from Mrs. Berger had been received two days previously, telling of the safe arrival at Saint Hill of Emily Blatchley and the children. Every detail of the welcome and arrangements for their well-being filled her heart with joy. She knew not how to be thankful enough, and seemed to have no desire or thought but just to praise the Lord for His goodness. Many and many a time had Mrs. Berger's letters reached their destination at the needed moment; many and many a time had her loving heart anticipated the circumstances in which they would be received, but never more so than with this letter.

'And now farewell, precious Friend,' she wrote. 'The Lord throw around you His everlasting arms.'

It was in those arms she was resting. At daybreak on Saturday, July 23rd, she was sleeping quietly, and Taylor left her for a few moments to prepare some food. While he was doing so she awoke, and serious symptoms called him to her side.

By this time it was dawn, and the sunlight revealed what the candle had hidden – the deathlike hue of her countenance. Even my love could no longer deny, not her danger, but that she was actually dying. As soon as I was sufficiently composed, I said:

'My darling, do you know that you are dying?'

'Dying!' she replied. 'Do you think so? What makes you think so?'

I said, 'I can see it, darling. Your strength is giving way.'

'Can it be so? I feel no pain, only weariness.'

'Yes, you are going Home. You will soon be with Jesus.'

My precious wife thought of my being left alone at a time of so much trial, with no companion like herself, with whom I had been wont to bring every difficulty to the Throne of Grace.

'I am so sorry,' she said, and paused as if half correcting herself for the feeling.

'You are not sorry to go to be with Jesus?'

Never shall I forget the look with which she answered, 'Oh, no! It is not that. You know, darling, that for ten years past there has not been a cloud between me and my Saviour. I cannot be sorry to go to Him; but it does grieve me to leave you alone at such a time. Yet . . . He will be with you and meet all your need.'

But little was said after that. A few loving messages to those at home, a few last words about the children, and she seemed to fall asleep or drift into unconsciousness of earthly things. The summer sun rose higher and higher over the city, the hills, and the river. The busy hum of life came up around them from many a court and street. But within one Chinese dwelling, in an upper room from which the blue of God's own heaven could be seen, there was the hush of a wonderful peace.

'I never witnessed such a scene,' wrote one who was present, a few days later. 'As dear Mrs. Taylor was breathing her last, Mr. Taylor knelt down – his heart so full – and committed her to the Lord; thanking Him for having given her, and for the twelve and a half years of happiness they had had together; thanking Him, too, for taking her to His own blessed presence, and solemnly dedicating himself anew to His service.'

It was just after 9 a.m. when the quiet breathing ceased, and they knew she was 'with Christ, which is far better'.

Now that the joy of life on its human side was gone and there was nothing left but aching loneliness and silence, would the Saviour's promise prove true now? 'My thirsty days are all past,' Hudson Taylor had felt and said and written that very summer, rejoicing as never before in the promise, 'He that cometh to me shall never hunger; and he that believeth on me shall never thirst'. Under the pressure of continued difficulty on every hand, health began to give way, and, sleepless at night, he found himself scarcely able to face the suffering, not to speak of the labours, of each new day. If ever the reality of the power of Christ to meet the heart's deepest need was put to the test of experience it was in this life, swept clean of all that had been its earthly comfort – wife, children, home, health to a large extent – and left amid the responsibilities of such a Mission and such a crisis, far away in China.

'How lonesome,' he recalled, 'were the weary hours when confined to my room. How I missed my dear wife and the little pattering footsteps of the children far away in England! Then it was I understood why the Lord had made that passage so real to me, "Whosoever drinketh of the water that I shall give him *shall never* thirst". Twenty times a day, perhaps, as I felt the heart-thirst coming back, I cried to Him:

' "Lord, you promised! You promised me that I should never thirst."

'And whether I called by day or night, how quickly He always came and satisfied my sorrowing heart! So much so that I often wondered whether it were possible that my loved one who had been taken could be enjoying more of His presence than I was in my lonely chamber.'

The letters he wrote during those days tell their own story:

I cannot describe to you my feelings; I do not understand them myself. I feel like a person stunned with a blow, or recovering from a faint, and as yet but partially conscious. But I would not have it otherwise, no, not a hair's breadth, for the world. My Father has ordered it so – therefore I know it *is*, it must be best, and I thank Him for so ordering it. I feel utterly crushed, and yet 'strong in the Lord and in the power of his might'. Oft-times my heart is nigh to breaking but, withal, I had almost said, I never knew what peace and happiness were before – so much have I enjoyed in the very sorrow.

I think I sent you a few weeks ago a copy of some notes on John 7.37; precious thoughts they have been to me. I now see more and deeper meaning in them than then. And this I know: only a thirsty man knows the value of water, and only a thirsty soul the value of the Living Water.

I could not have believed it possible that He could *so* have helped and comforted my poor heart.

By the end of August the youngest of Taylor's children, the only one left to him in China, was seriously ill. The only hope of saving him it seemed was to take him to Ningpo. There the baby must be left, for fellow-missionaries were so ill that he had to accompany them to Hong Kong. It was hard to leave his sick child at such a time even in the hands of the kindest of friends, but by doing so a missionary's life was saved, and the journeys between Shanghai and Hong Kong provided the change and comparative rest he himself so greatly needed.

His children in England – the little daughter of three years old, and the boys of eight and nine, were constantly on his heart.

You do not know how often Papa thinks of his darlings, and how often he looks at your photographs, till the tears fill his eyes. Sometimes he almost fears lest he should feel discontented when he thinks how far away you are from him: but then dear Jesus, who never leaves him, says: 'Don't be afraid. I will keep your heart satisfied. You know it was your Father in Heaven who took them to England, and who took Mamma to her little Noel, Samuel, and Gracie in the Better Land.' Then I thank Him, and feel so glad that Jesus will live in my heart and keep it right for me.

I wish you, my precious children, knew what it was to give your hearts to Jesus to keep every day. I used to try to keep my own heart right, but it would be always going wrong; and so at last I had to give up trying myself, and accept Jesus' offer to keep it for me. Don't you think that is the best way? Perhaps sometimes you think: 'I will try not to be selfish, or unkind, or disobedient.' And yet, though you really try, you do not always succeed. But Jesus says, 'You should trust that to Me. I would keep that little heart, if you could trust Me with it'. And He would too.

Once I used to try to think very much and very often about Jesus, but I often forgot Him: now I trust Jesus to keep my heart remembering Him, and He does so. This is the best way.

To keep their confidence and love himself, even at so great a distance, he toiled many an hour long after body and mind craved rest. Returning to Shanghai, for example, amid other letters penned in his comfortless third-class quarters were the following:

My darling Treasures – It is not very long since my last letter, but I want to write again. I wonder if you will try to write to me a little answer? I have been thinking tonight – if Jesus makes me so happy by always keeping near me, and talking to me every minute or two though I cannot see Him, how happy darling Mamma must be! I am so glad for her to be with Him. I shall be so glad to go to her when Jesus thinks it best. But I hope He will help me to be equally willing to live with Him here, so long as He has any work for me to do for Him and for poor China.

Now, my darling children, I want you to love Jesus very much, and to *know* that *He* really does love you very much. He likes us to talk to Him. When I am walking alone, I often talk aloud to Him. At other times I talk to Him in my heart. Do not forget, my darling children, that He is *always* with you. Awake or asleep, at home or elsewhere, He is *really* with you though you cannot see Him. So I hope you will try not to grieve so constant and kind a Friend.

And to Emily Blatchley:

Try to explain these most sweet and practical yet simple truths to the children, and to draw out their desire for these things. 'Out of the mouths of babes and sucklings thou hast perfected praise.' In all your intercourse with friends of the Mission, seek to deepen their realization of the value of Christ, and of our union with Him. Should you succeed in interesting them in China or in the Mission, your efforts may end there; but if you minister blessing to their souls, they will the better enter into Christ's command and purposes toward China, and will be more likely to become helpers in prayer, and not less so pecuniarily. After all, what we want is not money but power. Doubtless it is in answer to many prayers that my own soul has been so sustained under sore trial. Seek prayer for us, and we shall have all things: let it be lacking, and our very blessings may become a snare.

Hastening to Ningpo on his return, in the hope of being able to take his youngest child with him to Chinkiang, he found him desperately ill with croup, and scarcely expected to live. This was a sore trial. But Mission affairs were urgent, and as soon as there was improvement, leaving him in the care of Dr. Parker, Taylor pressed on to Hangchow, where the church was prospering under the faithful ministry of Pastor Wang. Seven evangelists were at work in the surrounding districts. Detained there by medical duty, it was a refreshment to Taylor to see something of old friends, including the McCarthys and Jennie Faulding, who had been almost a member of his own family from the time of their sailing for China. Four years of steady work in Hangchow had developed in her rare sweetness of character and depth of spiritual experience. Though still only twenty-seven, she was a most efficient missionary, and her schools were prospering both as regards numbers and results. Several of the boys had committed to memory the entire New Testament, with the exception of two Gospels, and not a few had become earnest Christians, one later marrying the daughter of Wang Lae-djün and becoming his co-pastor.

Meanwhile there was no lessening of the pressure of outward difficulties. The Chinese authorities, knowing that Europe was involved in war, took no steps to allay anti-foreign feeling. The long strain of excitement and danger told on the nerves, and even the spiritual life, of lonely missionaries and an inland station was abandoned. The last day of the year was set apart as usual for prayer and fasting, in arranging for which Taylor wrote to the members of the Mission:

The present year (1870) has been in many ways remarkable. Perhaps every one of our number has been more or less face to face with danger, perplexity and distress; but out of it all the Lord has delivered us. Personally, it has been alike the most sorrowful and the most blessed year of my life, and I doubt not that others have to a greater or lesser extent had the same experience. We have put to the proof His faithfulness, His power to support in trouble and to give patience under affliction, as well as to deliver from danger. We have had great cause for thankfulness in one respect: we have been so placed as to show the Chinese Christians that *our* position as well as theirs has been, and may be again, one of danger . . . to look from 'foreign power' to God Himself for protection.

I trust we are all fully satisfied that we are God's servants, sent by *Him* to the various posts we occupy. We did not come to China because missionary work here was either safe or easy, but because *He* had called us. We did not enter upon our present positions under a guarantee of human protection, but relying on the promise of *His* presence. The accidents of ease or difficulty, of *apparent* safety or danger, of man's approbation or disapproval, in no wise affect our duty. Should circumstances arise involving us in what may seem special danger, I trust we shall have grace to manifest the reality and depth of our trust in Him, and by our faithfulness to our charge *prove* that we are followers of the Good Shepherd who did not flee from death itself. But if we would manifest this calmness *then*, we must seek the needed grace *now*. It is too late to look for arms and begin to drill when in presence of the foe.

The pressure of work on Taylor at this time was great. He was overwhelmed with correspondence, accounts and all manner of detail in addition to the general direction of the work. But for C. T. Fishe, who had now been twelve months in China, he could not have got through at all, and it was with thankfulness he saw his way at the close of the year to appointing him Secretary to the Mission on the field.

Well was it that such help came when it did, for Taylor had borne all and more than he had strength for physically. Flooded though his soul had been with joy in the Lord, the poor body had suffered, and he had to learn more than ever before of the close and often humbling connection between the one and the other. A badly deranged liver made him sleepless and brought on painful physical depression. This was increased by lung trouble which caused not only pain but serious difficulty in breathing. And time did not lessen the desolation. After the home life in which he had delighted, it was a change indeed to be one of a bachelor household, with one or two young men for his only companions and his youngest child still in Ningpo. His suffering condition made him the more conscious of outward loneliness, yet in it all he was proving the sustaining power of the Word of God. Passages which already had meant much to him unfolded new depth and meaning, and in the very darkness permitted for a time, he was making more his own treasures which through coming years he was to pour out for others.

He came to see fresh power and beauty in the promises from our Lord's own lips which had already been made so vital in his experience. 'Whosoever drinketh of the water that I shall give him', stood out in letters of light as he saw the full bearing of the original. The force of *continuous habit* expressed by the present tense of Greek verbs flooded the passage with new meaning, over against his long-continued and increasing need.

'Do not let us change the Saviour's words,' he often said in later years. 'It is not "Whosoever has drunk", but "Whosoever drinketh". It is not of one isolated draught He speaks, or even of many, but of the continuous habit of the soul. Thus in John 6.35 the full meaning is, "He who is habitually coming to me shall by no means hunger, and he who is believing on me shall by no means thirst". Where many of us err is in leaving our drinking in the past, while our thirst continues present. What we need is *to be drinking* – yes, thankful for the occasion which drives us to drink ever more deeply of the Living Water.'

CHAPTER 17

Not Disobedient to the Heavenly Vision

(1872–1874)

MARCH WINDS, tossing the big elms at Saint Hill and sweeping round the house that had so warmly welcomed Taylor on his return from China, did but make the fireside more home-like when at length he had time to sit down quietly and talk over with the Bergers all that was on their hearts. Six years almost had elapsed since the outgoing of the 'Lammermuir Party'. The Mission, which up to that time had had but two stations and seven members, now numbered more than thirty workers, in thirteen central stations at an average distance of 100 miles apart, with the Bergers giving themselves to its service at home. The task however had proved too much for their strength and must be committed to other hands. But who was to take their place?

The need for the change had come so suddenly that Taylor had no plans in view. The work in China was now a large one, entailing an expenditure of about £300 a month. His own health was much impaired by those six strenuous years, and rest of mind and body would have been welcome in view especially of a speedy return to the front. But the home base could not be neglected. Unequal as he felt to the task, there was nothing for it but to take up the entire responsibility himself, looking to the Lord to liberate him when and as He should see fit.

'The change about Mr. and Mrs. Berger's retiring has tried me a good deal,' he wrote to a member of the Mission in China early in 1872. 'I love them so dearly! And it seems another link severed with the past in which my precious departed one (who is seldom absent from my thoughts) had a part. But His word is, "Behold, I make all things new".'

Writing to his parents, a few weeks later, Taylor used notepaper bearing the modest heading.

China Inland Mission,
6 Pyrland Road,
Newington Green, N.

It was a far cry from Saint Hill to a little suburban street on the outskirts of London, such as Pyrland Road was in those days. For more than twenty years the entire home-work of the Mission was to be carried on from this centre. The weekly prayer meeting was held in the downstairs rooms, two of which could be thrown together by opening the communicating doors; and a bright London lad found his way there one day. Many years later, as a member of the Mission in China, he recalled his first impressions:

'A large harmonium stood at one side, and various Chinese articles were arranged in other parts of the room, but beyond this there was little either of furniture or decoration. Between a dozen and twenty people were present.

'Mr. Taylor opened the meeting by giving out a hymn, and seating himself at the harmonium led the singing. His appearance did not impress me. He was slightly built, and spoke in a gentle voice. Like most young men, I suppose I associated power with noise, and looked for great physical presence in a leader. But when he said, "Let us pray", and proceeded to lead the meeting in prayer, my ideas underwent a change. I had never heard anyone pray like that. There was a simplicity, a tenderness, a boldness, a power that hushed and subdued one, and made it clear that God had admitted him into the inner circle of His friendship. He spoke with God face to face, as a man talketh with his friend. Such praying was evidently the outcome of long tarrying in the secret place, and was as a dew from the Lord. I have heard many men pray in public since then, but the prayers of Mr. Taylor and the prayers of Mr. Spurgeon stand all by themselves.

'The meeting lasted from four to six o'clock, but seemed one of the shortest prayer meetings I had ever attended.'

Longing to press forward with the great task before the Mission, it must have been difficult indeed for Taylor to curb himself to the routine of office work as the days and weeks went by. He was not in haste to rush into new arrangements, having no indication as to what might be the mind of the Lord. But when prayer for the right helpers seemed to bring no answer, and the work to be done kept him busy morning, noon and night, it would have been so easy to be impatient or discouraged! But in the dark days of 1870 he had learned some deep lessons about waiting for, as well as waiting upon God.

The place at Taylor's side that had been so empty was now taken by one fitted in every way to be a help and comfort. Jennie Faulding, by God's blessing the life of the women's work in Hangchow, had been obliged to come home on furlough, and travelling by the same steamer – other arrangements having fallen through at the last moment – Taylor found the regard he had long felt for her developing into something more than friendship. The marriage had not been long delayed, and he was thankful for the children to see as much of her as possible before she returned with him to China. But though it was the home of a bride, the arrangements at Pyrland Road were just as simple as at Coborn Street in the early days.

As they prayed and planned for advance to the unreached interior of

China, standing before the large map in the sitting-room, their hearts were moved by the thought – How are these Christless millions to be reached?

'Have you faith to join me in laying hold upon God for eighteen men to go two and two to those unoccupied provinces?' asked Taylor at one of the prayer meetings.

They knew what he meant, and then and there covenanted with one another to pray daily in definite faith for this, until the Lord should bring it to pass.

It was about this time that, from unexpected quarters, guidance began to come as to the future management of the home side of the Mission. A friend, Richard Hill, suggested the formation of a Council of Christian friends, not to take any responsibility with regard to the management of affairs on the field, but to divide among themselves the home work of the Mission, thus setting Taylor free to return to China.

This suggestion, reinforced by Hill's offer to become Hon. Secretary to such a Council, proved a seed thought. The more Taylor considered it, the more he saw that it was simply an enlargement of the plan upon which the C.I.M. had been worked from the beginning. A Council, not a Committee of Management, could undertake many of Mr. Berger's former responsibilities. Taylor was purposing to leave Emily Blatchley in charge of his children at Pyrland Road. Intimately acquainted with the work both at home and in China, she would be of the greatest assistance to the Council, and would be able to keep up the prayer meeting and provide a centre for returning missionaries. Passing through her hands the daily correspondence could be attended to, and only necessary letters forwarded to the Secretary, while the Council would deal with candidates and with funds, keeping in touch with the friends of the Mission through its *Occasional Paper*. After some weeks of thought and prayer, therefore, he wrote to Richard Hill on the 1st August:

> Could you take tea with us on Tuesday next about 6 p.m. and spend the evening? I would ask one or two friends interested in the work, and Mr. George and Mr. Henry Soltau, to join us, and we might have some quiet prayer and conversation about the Mission and those whose co-operation it would be well to seek; after which, perhaps, we might see our way to further action more clearly. It seems to me that a little time thus spent would be helpful, before asking many either to meet or to join us in the proposed Council.

Quietly, thus, the way opened. The meeting was held and the Council practically formed that night, August 6, 1872.

After an absence from China of a year and three months, Taylor was prepared to find matters needing a good deal of attention. It had not been possible to leave anyone in charge of the whole work, none of the members of the Mission having sufficient experience to fit them for such a position. On arrival, the travellers learned that although there was cause in the southern stations especially for encouragement, the need for Taylor's presence was even greater than they had anticipated. Duncan of Nanking had been obliged, through failing health, to relinquish the post he had so bravely held and even then was on his way home, as it proved, to die. The absence of the Judds on furlough had left the work in the Yangtze valley with little supervision, and it was important to send someone to take charge without delay. Transferring themselves and their belongings to a Chinese boat, Hudson and Jennie Taylor set out forthwith for Hangchow. Warm was the welcome that awaited them in the old home from many who owed their spiritual life, under God, to the one who returned to them now as a bride. McCarthy's six years in China qualified him for larger responsibilities, and leaving Hangchow to Pastor Wang, he willingly undertook the difficult work on the Yangtze.

Meanwhile Taylor set out to visit all the stations, in some of which sickness and trial of various sorts had told on those who remained, while Chinese leaders had grown cold, some having even lapsed into open sin.

'Though things are very sadly, they are not hopeless; they will soon look *up*, with God's blessing, if looked after,' he wrote.

In his confidence he went on, prayerfully and patiently, until he had visited every station and almost every out-station in the Mission. Not content with this, he sought out the Chinese workers in each place, so that the evangelists, colporteurs, teachers and Biblewomen, almost without exception, came under his influence.

It was work carried on under special difficulties, for he had all his correspondence and directorial duties to attend to at the same time. It meant constant travelling, through summer heat as well as winter cold, and involved long separations from Jennie, who could not always accompany him. At times they were together in stations that needed an extended visit; or she would stay on where there was sickness, to give help in nursing or among the women. How glad they were of his medical knowledge in those days! for it gave opportunity for really serving their fellow-workers as well as the Chinese Christians. Needless to say it added to Taylor's burdens, as when he reached a distant station on the Yangtze to find eighty-nine letters awaiting him, and took time to send, the very next day, a page or more of medical directions about 'A-liang's baby' – A-liang being a valued helper at Chinkiang.

Such an outpouring of heart and life could not but tell.

'The Lord is prospering us,' he wrote to his parents in July; 'and the work is steadily growing, especially in that most important department, *native help*. The helpers themselves need much help, much care and instruction; but they are becoming more efficient as well as more numerous, and the future hope for China lies, doubtless, in *them*. I look on foreign missionaries as the scaffolding round a rising building; the sooner it can be dispensed with the better – or rather, the sooner it can be transferred to other places, to serve the same temporary purpose.'

After nine months in the Yangtze valley, Taylor turned his attention to the southern stations, in the province of Chekiang. When there the unexpected tidings reached him of the complete breakdown of Emily Blatchley's health. Apart altogether from sorrow in the thought of her removal was the serious question as to how her place was to be filled. Gifted, devoted, and with some experience, matters had tended more and more to come into her hands. Not only was she keeping the mission-house going, and the weekly prayer meeting; she was editing and sending out the *Occasional Paper*, dealing with correspondence to a considerable extent, and caring for the children whom she had received as a sacred charge from their mother, the friend she had supremely loved. All this made it difficult indeed to see how her place could be filled; and Taylor, unable for the present to return home, could do nothing.

Already, in addition to the burdens upon him in China, he was tried and perplexed by the irregularity as well as diminution of supplies from home. It was but natural that Mr. Berger's retirement should continue to be felt in these and other ways. The work had grown up in his hands. To the friends and supporters of the Mission he seemed almost as much a part of it as Taylor himself. His extensive business had given him a familiarity with financial and practical matters that was invaluable, and the needs of the workers in China were upon his heart day and night. This could not be so to the same extent with other friends, no matter how interested and anxious to help. The members of the C.I.M. Council, moreover, were all new to their responsibilities. They did what they could, with no little sacrifice and devotion, but they had experience to gain.

Meanwhile it was in China that the difficulties of the situation were most acutely felt. Taylor did what was possible by correspondence; and irregularities that could not be dealt with in that way had just to be taken to the Lord in faith and prayer. Comparatively small though the Mission was in those days, there were fifty buildings to be kept up and 100 workers provided for, including Chinese helpers. There were all the children besides, in families and schools, making fully 170 mouths to feed daily. Travelling expenses were also a serious item, with a work extending to five provinces and furloughs involving the expensive journey to England. Altogether, Taylor's estimate of £100 a week as a working average could not be considered extravagant. Indeed, it was only with most careful planning and economy that the work could be carried on vigorously upon that sum.

But there were many weeks and even months in which little or nothing was forwarded to him for the general purposes of the Mission. Funds were not coming in plentifully at home, and many gifts – such as those of George Müller and W. T. Berger – were sent to individual workers. This left but little for the general fund, from which home expenses had to be met as well as the current outlay for all but specially supported workers in China.

And now, in addition to this long-continued shortness of funds and all the other difficulties of the work, had come the keen personal sorrow of Emily Blatchley's illness. Concern about his children, too, was very real. Who was caring for them, or how they would be provided for if their almost mother were taken, he did not know. And before he could be with them again, many months *must* elapse.

It would be little cause for wonder if, amid such distresses, Taylor's longing after the multitudes yet unreached had abated; but the really significant thing is that he had never lost the vision. It did but become, if anything, more commanding.

On the first day of January, 1873, he wrote to Emily Blatchley:

> I want you to pray daily that God will direct us as to which provinces we should attempt, and how. We have the almighty God with us; the all-wise Counsellor to guide; the indwelling Spirit to give efficacy to the preached Word. Ask for me more simple trust in Him, and boldness to attempt great things. Try to get friends to promise and seriously endeavour to pray *daily* about the opening up of new provinces to the Gospel. Christ *must* speedily be proclaimed in them: how and by whom we must ask Him.

Meanwhile, he was learning to value more than ever the co-operation of Chinese fellow-workers, and was full of plans for developing and using them to the utmost.

> 'I am aiming at such organization of our forces as will enable us to do more work with fewer foreign missionaries,' he wrote to his parents in April. 'I *hope* I may be able, ere the year closes, to commence a college for the more thorough training of our native helpers. Long desired, there seems more probability of our attaining this than heretofore.'

To place two Chinese helpers in each governing city of a district, with colporteurs in centres of less importance, all under the supervision of an experienced missionary, was the plan kept steadily in view, beginning with the capitals of provinces and departments. It was essential, therefore, to develop the Chinese workers, as well as obtain missionaries of the right kind.

Men of faith, with a personal knowledge of God as the Hearer and Answerer of prayer; men of stamina to rough it, and to live as he did in closest contact with the people, were the missionary helpers he longed and prayed for.

'We are going on into the interior,' he wrote to a member of the Council somewhat later. 'If any one is not prepared to rough it, he had better stay at home at once.'

And to another: 'The only persons wanted here are those who will rejoice to work – really to labour, not to dream their lives away; to deny themselves; to *suffer* in order to *save*.'

Hastening to Shanghai to meet a party of new workers, Taylor's mind was full of these things, and he was not altogether sorry for the lack of a receiving home, though it involved some inconveniences. It was his purpose to secure such a home on this visit, for the Mission was growing so large as to need a business centre at the coast. But in the meanwhile he put up at a Chinese inn, glad of the opportunity of seeing what the young men were made of.

Early that November morning the new arrivals had set out to enquire for Taylor. They learned that the leader of the Mission was in Shanghai, and had probably gone down to the steamer to meet them. They turned back therefore, and on the way Judd, who had travelled back to China with them, exclaimed, 'There is Mr. Taylor!'

'We looked,' wrote one of his companions, 'but could only see a Chinaman on a wheelbarrow. The barrow stopped and the figure advanced toward us. It was a good thing that there was someone to do the introducing, for we should never have recognized Mr. Taylor. The weather was cold, and he had on a wadded gown and jacket. Over his head he wore a wind-hood with side pieces which fitted close to the face, leaving nothing but a medallion-shaped opening for nose, eyes and mouth. In his hand he grasped a huge Chinese umbrella, which he carried in true native style, handle foremost. In his wadded clothes he looked almost as broad as he was long, and to our foreign eyes was the oddest figure we had ever seen. He said he had made arrangements for the ladies and Mr. Judd to stay with friends in the French Settlement, and, turning to Henry Taylor and myself, added:

'"After we have been to the vessel, perhaps you will accompany me to my hotel."'

Little realizing what was in store for them, the young men cheerfully agreed.

'Turning up a side street at right angles to The Bund, Mr. Taylor threaded his way among the crowds till he stopped at the door of a native post office. Passing through the front part of the office, he led the way to a small door secured by a Chinese lock. This he opened and invited us to follow him up the stair. It was pitch dark and very narrow, but we stumbled up till we came to a door which he entered. We followed him, and found ourselves in the "hotel". It consisted of a room about twelve feet square, innocent of any adornment, and containing a square table, a small skin-covered box, and a Chinese food-basket. Along one side was a raised dais, on which, if I remember aright, was spread a Chinese coverlet. A window opened out on to the street, but it had paper of grimy hue instead of glass, and did not count for much in the way of illumination.

'Mr. Taylor very courteously asked us to be seated, and after making enquiries as to our voyage, produced a Bible. He read the seventeenth chapter of the Gospel by John, and asked what we thought was the meaning of the words, "That the love wherewith thou hast loved me may be in them, and I in them". I do not remember what we said, but I was distinctly impressed with the fact that he asked us. Reading over, we knelt down and had prayer together, when he commended us to the Lord who had brought us to China.

'Such was our first meeting with Mr. Taylor in China. We took to Chinese dress, Chinese food, Chinese ways as a duck to water!'

Leaving the young men at Nanking to their studies in charge of the Judds, Taylor hastened back to Chekiang. The twelve millions of that province, small though it was among the provinces of China, lay heavily on his heart. Far from overlooking, in his growing concern for the interior, needs more immediately around him near the coast, he was stirred with sorrow and shame over the great, waiting fields so easily accessible, that yet had no labourers. Writing to Richard Hill from one of the southern stations in January (1874), he said:

The work is now greatly extending, and I hope will yet do so. If the Lord spare me, and permit me to labour here a year or two more, I trust there will be no county left in this province in which we have not preached Christ, either by located or itinerant labours. At present there are many such. Of the sixty-three *Hsien* cities in this province (each governing a county) fifteen have workers for Christ resident in them. Ten have been opened by us, five by others; forty-eight remain unopened. In one of them I have just rented a house; to another I hope to send a couple of men tomorrow. If they succeed in obtaining an opening, there will still be four *Fus* and forty-six *Hsiens* – *fifty cities in all* to be possessed for Christ. And in the meantime, how many precious souls will have passed beyond the reach of the Gospel! The Lord help us to be faithful. The claims of my family at home on the one hand, and the claims of the perishing heathen here on the other, cast me in an agony upon the Lord: 'Lord, what wilt *thou* have me to do?'

The position was indeed a perplexing one. There was need for his presence in England, but the state of funds made it almost impossible for him to leave the workers on the field. And all the while his sense of responsibility deepened for the multitudes around him, so dark, so needy, so accessible! In his letter of January 26 to Hill, he continued:

Last week I was at Taiping, one of the unopened cities I have referred to. My heart was greatly moved by the *crowds* that literally *filled* the streets for two or three miles, so that we could hardly walk – for it was market day. We did but little preaching, as we were seeking a place for permanent work, but I was constrained to retire to the city wall and cry to God to have mercy on the people, to open their hearts and give us an entrance among them.

Without any seeking on our part we were brought into touch with at least four anxious souls. An old man found me out, I know not how, and followed me to our boat. I asked him in, and enquired his name.

'My name is Dzing. But the question which distresses me, and to which I can find no answer, is – What am I to do with my sins? Our scholars tell us that there is no future state, but I find it hard to believe them.'

'Do not believe any such thing,' I replied, 'for there is an endless future before every one of us. One must either burn for ever in hell fire, or rejoice for ever in heavenly bliss.'

'Then what *can* I do; what am I to do with my sins?'

Gladly then I told him of a living, loving God – our Father in Heaven; pointing to various proofs of His fatherly love and care.

'Yes!' he interrupted, 'and what are we to do to recompense such favour, such goodness? I do not see how it is to be recompensed. Our scholars say that if we worship Heaven and Earth and the idols at the end of the year, it is enough. But that does not satisfy me.'

The poor old man told me of all the idols he worshipped, and was quite overwhelmed to think that in doing so he was sinning against the true and living God. It takes time for the mind to grasp such a total reversal of all it has believed for well-nigh seventy years. When my companions returned he listened again to the wonderful story of the Cross, and left us soothed and comforted – yet evidently bewildered – to think over all he had heard, more than glad to know that we had rented a house and hoped soon to have Christian colporteurs resident in the city.

Little wonder such an experience brought to a crisis the exercise of mind through which Taylor had been passing. Two women in the same city, and a young man, had shown similar earnestness in learning from his Chinese companions the way of Life. Multitudes from the surrounding towns and villages would come on market-days to the little 'Gospel Hall', and there the enquirers would be taught until they in their turn could become teachers of others. Just the same work needed doing in all the fifty cities throughout the province that still remained without the message of salvation. And oh, the great Beyond! Must he hold his hand, and refrain from going forward as the way opened, on account of financial straitness, or the needs that seemed to call him home?

God's resources, he was assured, were equal to the occasion. What was required of him was to honour Him with a full trust. In his Bible he wrote the record of what he did that day.

Taichow, January 27, 1874: Asked God for fifty or 100 additional Chinese evangelists, and as many foreign superintendents as may be needed, to open up the four *Fus* and forty-eight *Hsiens* still unoccupied in Chekiang; also for the men to break into the nine unoccupied provinces. Asked in the Name of Jesus. I thank Thee, Lord Jesus, for the promise whereon Thou hast given me to rest. Give me all needed strength of body, wisdom of mind, grace of soul to do this Thy so great work. Amen.

It was not until many years later, when Taylor could look back over all the way in which the Lord had led him, that he was impressed with the fact that every important advance in the development of the Mission had sprung from or been directly connected with times of sickness or suffering which had cast him in a special way upon God. It was to be so now; as though a deeper preparedness of spirit were needed, before he could be trusted with the answer to this prayer.

There was quite enough, as far as outward experiences went, to account for the serious illness that overtook him before he could get back to his temporary quarters at Fenghwa. In the depth of winter he had been almost incessantly on the road for weeks past, bearing an unusual strain even for him, physically and mentally. Then came the news that the Crombies were threatened with the loss of their children. This meant hard travelling over mountain passes deep in snow; and before he could return a messenger had come in haste from a more distant station with news of a whole family down with smallpox.

Taylor set out once more to cross the mountains. It was a desperate business facing January storms on those heights, more than one of which could only be scaled by steps literally cut in the rock. Anxieties pressed sorely upon him with regard to Emily Blatchley and his children at home, as well as in connection with the shortness of funds in China.

'Well, the Lord reigns,' he had written to his mother from a wretched inn on the road. 'Trials cannot rob me of this unchanging source of joy and strength.'

But the overtaxed physical powers at length gave way, and his patients were no sooner convalescent than Taylor himself went down with fever, and was so ill as to be hardly able to get back to Fenghwa. The interval, from the time when they were out of danger until he could safely leave them, he had employed in the evangelistic journey which brought him in touch with old Dzing, and led to the definite prayer recorded above.

And now, how unpromising seemed the sequel to that step of faith! Week after week he lay in helplessness and suffering, able to do nothing but wait upon the Lord. Of all that in His providence was drawing near, Hudson Taylor was unconscious. He only knew that God had given him to see something of the purposes of His heart; that he was sharing in some measure the compassions of Christ for the lost and perishing, and that the love of which he felt the yearnings was His own infinite love. That that love, that purpose, would find a way to bless, he could not doubt. So he just prayed on – holding in faith to the heavenly vision; ready to go forward when and as the Lord should open the way. Never had advance seemed less possible. But in the Bible beside him was the record of that transaction of his soul with God, and in his heart was the conviction that even for the inland provinces – the western branch of the mission he longed to plant, as a stepping-stone to the far interior – God's time had almost come.

And then, as he lay there slowly recovering, a letter was put into his hands that had been two months on its way from England. It was from an unknown friend, a Mrs. Grace of Wycombe, Buckinghamshire, who had only recently become interested in the Mission.

'My dear Sir,' the somewhat trembling hand had written early in December, '*I bless God*, in two months I hope to place at the disposal of your Council, for *further* extension of China Inland Mission work, £800. Please remember, for *fresh* provinces.'

The very secrets of his heart seemed to look back at him from that sheet of notepaper. Even before the prayer recorded in his Bible, the letter had been sent off; and now, just when it was most needed, it had reached him with its wonderful confirmation.

From his sick-room back to the Yangtze valley was the next step, and those spring days witnessed a happy gathering at Chinkiang. Over a year of patient, plodding work in China had done much to improve the situation he had found on arrival. In almost all the stations, new life was coming to the little companies of believers, and the young missionaries, who had made good progress with the language, were eager for pioneering work. As many as could leave their stations came to meet Taylor for a week of prayer and conference, before he and Judd set out to seek, up the great river, a home for the new Western Branch.

It was not any improvement in the state of funds that accounted for the new note of joy and confidence.

'I feel no anxiety,' he wrote to his mother on the 1st May, 'though for a month past I have not had a dollar in hand for the general purposes of the Mission. The Lord will provide.'

To Jennie he had written during April, 'The balance in hand yesterday was sixty-seven cents! The Lord reigns: herein is our joy and confidence.' And when the balance was still lower, 'We have twenty-five cents – and all the promises of God.'

One thing that concerned Taylor more at this time than shortness of supplies was the fear lest, in their desire to help, friends at home should be tempted to make appeals in meetings, or even more personally, for funds. To one and another he wrote very earnestly on the subject, begging that this might not be done. The trial through which they were passing was no reason, to his mind, for changing the basis on which they had been led to found the Mission. In acknowledging one of George Müller's generous contributions he had written early in April:

> The work generally is *very* cheering, and we feel happier than ever in the Lord and in His service. Our faith never was so much tried: His faithfulness never so much experienced.

This position was to him far more safe and blessed, as long as the trial was permitted, than the alternative of going into debt or making appeals to man. How truly this was the case may be seen from the following letter to a member of the Council, written just after the Conference at Chinkiang (April 24):

> I am truly sorry that you should be distressed at not having funds to send me. After living on *God's faithfulness* for many years, I can testify that times of want have ever been times of special blessing, or have led to them. I do beg that never any appeal for funds be put forward, save to God in prayer. When our work becomes a begging work, it dies. God is faithful, must be so. He has said: 'Take *no* thought (anxiety) for your life, what ye shall eat, or what ye shall drink, nor yet for your body, what ye shall put on. . . . But seek . . . first (to promote) the kingdom of God, and (to fulfil) his righteousness, and *all these things shall be added unto you*.'
>
> It is doubting, beloved brother, not trusting that is tempting the Lord.

At this very time, it is interesting to notice, the Taylors were themselves giving largely to the work in various ways. A considerable proportion of all they received for their own use was passed on to fellow-workers, and a property yielding an income of £400 a year, which had recently come to Jennie from a relative, was joyfully set apart for the Lord's service. The intimate friend to whom Taylor was writing had questioned the wisdom of this course, which led to one of the few references he ever made to the subject. Anxious that their position should not be misunderstood, he continued in this letter:

> As to the property my dear wife has given to the Lord for His service, I most cordially agreed with her in the step, and do so now. I believe that in so doing she has made hers for ever that which was her Master's, and only entrusted to her so to use. It is not a modern question, this of principal or interest, endowment or voluntary support, and we cannot expect *all* to see alike on the subject. We might capitalize the

annual income of the Mission, and use only the interest; but I fear the income would soon be small, and the work not very extensive.

But you may, I think, be mistaken as to our . . . intention, as well as with regard to the nature of the property. The whole cannot be realized, half of it being reserved to provide annuities. At present all we have is about £400 of annual interest, payable in varying quarterly sums. We do not propose to put either principal or interest into the General Fund (though we might be led to do so), but to use it, equally avoiding stint or lavishness, as the Lord may direct, for special purposes not met by the General Fund. We are neither of us inexperienced, unacquainted with the value of money, or unaccustomed either to its want or possession. There are few more cool and calculating, perhaps, than we are; but in all our calculations we calculate on God's faithfulness, or seek to do so. Hitherto we have not been put to shame, nor have I any anxiety or fear lest we should be in the future.

CHAPTER 18

The Faithfulness of God

(1874–1877)

IT WAS a memorable day for Hudson Taylor when he set out with Judd to follow the mighty Yangtze to Hankow, the metropolis of mid-China and the farthest outpost of Protestant missions. Northward, westward, southward of it stretched the nine unopened provinces, from the tropical jungles of Burma to the barren steppes of Mongolia and the snowy ramparts of Tibet.

'My soul yearns, oh! how intensely,' he wrote at this time (June 1874), 'for the evangelization of the 180 millions of these unoccupied provinces. Oh, that I had a hundred lives to give or spend for their good!'

Not until he had seen Judd in possession of suitable quarters at Wuchang across the river from Hankow where the London Missionary Society and the Wesleyan Mission were already at work did he return to England. Here the need for him was great indeed. Strange and sorrowful was the homecoming in October, to find Emily Blatchley's place empty, the children scattered, the Saturday prayer meeting discontinued, and the work almost at a standstill. But, even then, the lowest ebb had not been reached. When on his way up the Yangtze a fall had severely shaken Taylor. Extreme pain in the back disabled him for several days, and even when the ankle was well he still needed the help of crutches. Concussion of the spine often develops slowly; and it was not until he had been at home a week or two that the rush of London life, with constant travelling by train and omnibus, began to tell. Then came gradual paralysis of the lower limbs, and the doctor's verdict that consigned him to absolute rest in bed.

The outlook did not brighten as the year drew to a close. Taylor was less and less able to move and at last could only turn from side to side with the help of a rope firmly fixed above him. At first he had managed to write a little, but now could not even hold a pen. Yet with the dawn of 1875 a little paper found its way into the Christian press entitled:

'APPEAL FOR PRAYER
On behalf of more than a hundred and fifty millions of Chinese.'

It briefly stated the facts with regard to the nine unopened provinces; that friends of the C.I.M. had long been praying for men to go as pioneer evangelists to these regions; that recently £4,000 had been given for the purpose; and that among the converts in the older stations of the Mission were some from the far interior, who were earnestly desiring to carry the Gospel to the districts from which they had come.

'Our present, pressing need,' it continued, 'is of more missionaries to lead the way. Will each of your Christian readers at once raise his heart to God, and spend one minute in earnest prayer that God will raise up, this year, eighteen suitable men to devote themselves to this work?'

It did not say that the leader of the Mission was to all appearances a hopeless invalid. It did not refer to the fact that the £4,000 recently given had come from his wife and himself, part of their capital, the whole of which they had consecrated to the work of God. It did not mention that for two and a half years they and others had been praying daily for the eighteen evangelists, praying in faith. But those who read the appeal felt the influence of these things and much besides, and were moved as men are not moved by sayings and doings that have not their roots deep in God.

Before long Taylor's correspondence was largely increased, as was also his joy in dealing with it – or in seeing, rather, how the Lord dealt with it and with all else that concerned him.

'The Mission had no paid helpers,' he wrote of this time, 'but God led volunteers, without pre-arrangement, to come in from day to day to write from dictation, and thus letters were answered. One of the happiest periods of my life was that period of forced inactivity, when one could do nothing but "rejoice in the Lord" and "wait patiently for him", and see Him meeting all one's need. Never were my letters, before or since, kept so regularly and promptly answered.

'And the eighteen men asked of God began to come. There was first some correspondence; then they came to see me in my room. Soon I had a class studying Chinese at my bedside. In due time the Lord sent them forth, and then dear friends began to pray for my restoration. The Lord blessed the means used and I was raised up. One reason for my being laid aside was gone. Had I been well and able to move about, some might have thought that *my* urgent appeals rather than God's working had sent the eighteen men to China. But utterly laid aside, able only to dictate a request for prayer, the answer to our prayers was the more apparent.'

When he was so far recovered that the physicians wished him to sit up for an hour or two daily, he could scarcely find time to do so. Every moment was taken up with interviews, with correspondence through his willing helpers, and with care for the work in China. The weekly prayer meeting was now held in his room, and the Council gathered from time to time at his bedside.

By this time a marked change had come over the spirit of the scene at

Pyrland Road. Instead of a deserted house, many were coming and going. The first party of the Eighteen had already sailed, and candidates overflowed all the accommodation available for their reception. Another house, indeed, had to be taken for this purpose, for in answer to the 'Appeal for Prayer' published in January, no fewer than sixty offers of service were received during the year. How important Taylor felt it that no hasty decisions should be made may be judged from the following letter used in his correspondence with candidates at this period. If their response to this faithful statement of the case warranted the hope that they would work happily in the Mission, they were invited to spend a longer or shorter time at Pyrland Road for personal acquaintance.

While thankful for any educational advantages that candidates may have enjoyed, we attach far greater importance to spiritual qualifications. We desire men who believe that there is a God and that He is both intelligent and faithful, and who therefore trust Him; who believe that He is the Rewarder of those who diligently seek Him, and are therefore *men of prayer*. We desire men who believe the Bible to be the Word of God, and who, accepting the declaration "All power is given unto me", are prepared, therefore, to go to the remotest parts of the interior of China, expecting to find His arm a sufficient strength and stay. We desire men who believe in eternity and live for it.

The Mission is supported by donations, not subscriptions. We have, therefore, no guaranteed income, and can only minister to our missionaries as we ourselves are ministered to by God. We do not send men to China as our agents. But men who believe that God has called them to the work, who go there to labour for God, and can therefore trust Him whose they are and whom they serve to supply their temporal needs, we gladly co-operate with – providing, if needful, outfit and passage money, and such a measure of support as circumstances call for and we are enabled to supply. Our faith is sometimes tried, but God always proves Himself faithful, and at the right time and in the right way supplies all our need.

One-third of the human family is in China, needing the Gospel. Twelve millions there are passing beyond the reach of that Gospel every year. If you want hard work and little appreciation; if you value God's approval more than you fear man's disapprobation; if you are prepared to take joyfully the spoiling of your goods, and seal your testimony, if need be, with your blood; if you can pity and love the Chinese, you may count on a harvest of souls now and a crown of glory hereafter 'that fadeth not away', and on the Master's '*Well done*'.

You would find that, in connection with the China Inland Mission, it is no question of 'making the most of both worlds'. The men, the only men who will be happy with us, are those who have this world under their feet: and I do venture to say that such men will find a happiness they never dreamed of or thought possible down here. For to those who count 'all things' but dross and dung for 'the excellency of the knowledge of Christ Jesus my Lord', He does manifest Himself in such sort that they are not inclined to rue their bargain. If, after prayerfully considering the matter, you still feel drawn to engage in such work, I shall be only too glad to hear from you again.

Young men and women who came to Pyrland Road on probation, encouraged rather than daunted by the spirit of the above letter, soon found occasion to rejoice in God as the Hearer and Answerer of prayer. Such, for example, was the experience in May when Taylor, casting up the amounts received from the 4th to the 24th of the month, found that they came to a little over £68.

'This is nearly £235 *less* than our average expenditure in China for three weeks,' he added. 'Let us bring the matter to the Lord in prayer.'

That very evening the postman brought a letter which was found to contain a cheque to be entered 'From the sale of plate', and the sum thus realized and sent to the Mission was £235 7s. 9d. Little wonder that prayer was turned to praise at the next noon hour.

Quite as remarkable was another experience that soon followed. It was early in June, and Taylor was returning from a memorable convention on Scriptural holiness. Waiting for his train at the station, he was accosted by a Russian nobleman who had been attending the meetings, and who on learning that Taylor was going to London suggested that they should find seats together.

'But I am travelling third class,' said the missionary.

'My ticket admits of my doing the same,' was the courteous reply. Presently Count Bobrinsky took out his pocket-book with the words:

'Allow me to give you a trifle toward your work in China.'

Glancing at the bank-note as he received it, Taylor felt there must be some mistake – it was for no less than £50.

'Did you not mean to give me £5?' he said at once. 'Please let me return this note: it is for fifty.'

'I cannot take it back,' replied the other, no less surprised. 'It was £5 I meant to give, but God must have intended you to have fifty; I cannot take it back.'

Impressed with the incident, Taylor reached Pyrland Road to find a prayer meeting going on. A remittance was about to be sent to China, and the money in hand was short by £49 11s. of the sum it was felt would be required. This deficiency was not accepted as inevitable. On the contrary, it called together those who knew of it for special prayer. £49 11s. was being asked for in simple faith, and there upon the office table Taylor laid his precious bank-note for £50. Could it have come more directly from the Heavenly Father's hand? 'Whoso is wise and will observe these things, even they shall understand the lovingkindness of the Lord.'

New wine must have new bottles. Taylor saw that all the life and blessing that had come with the appeal for the Eighteen needed more adequate representation. The production of an illustrated monthly was a great undertaking, for those were not the days of illustrated papers such as we have now, and *China's Millions* when it appeared was quite an innovation. Its up-to-date pictures and reports of pioneer journeys, conversions, progress in the older churches, and above all the devotional articles from Hudson Taylor himself, came to be looked for by friends old and new. It was through its pages that he shared a new conception of the scope and meaning of faith that had come to him in 1870, the year of bereavement. It was just in his usual reading, as he often related, that he was struck with the words, '*Ekete pistin Theou*'. How strangely new they seemed! 'Have (or hold) the faithfulness of God:' surely it was a passage he had never seen before? Turning to the corresponding words in English he read (Mark 11. 22): 'Have faith in God'. Ah, *that* was familiar enough; and something within him whispered, 'the old difficulty!' How gladly would he have an increase in faith in God, if only he knew how! But *this* seemed entirely different. It laid the emphasis on another side of the matter in a way he found surprisingly helpful. It was not 'have' in your own heart and mind, however you can get it, 'faith in God', but simply 'hold fast, count upon *His faithfulness*'.

'Let us see that in theory we hold that God is faithful; that in daily life we count upon it; and that at all times and under all circumstances we are fully persuaded of this blessed truth.'

And now, just five years later, the subject was filling his mind. China seemed as inaccessible as ever, despite the Treaty of Tientsin, ratified in 1860. Passports, besides being practically unobtainable, meant little or nothing of protection, and the European who would venture far from the beaten track had to take his life in his hand. After nearly seventy years of Protestant work in China, only thirty-nine centres were occupied by representatives of all societies. But the appeal for the eighteen pioneers had gone out, and the men were being given. In the fourth issue of *China's Millions,* which dwelt upon the definite plan before the Mission for evangelizing all the inland provinces, he wrote:

Want of trust is at the root of almost all our sins and all our weaknesses; and how shall we escape it but by looking to Him and observing His faithfulness? The man who holds God's faithfulness will not be foolhardy or reckless, but he will be ready for every emergency. The man who holds God's faithfulness will dare to obey Him, however impolitic it may appear. Abraham held God's faithfulness and offered up Isaac, 'accounting that God was able to raise him . . . from the dead'. Moses held God's faithfulness and led the millions of Israel into the waste, howling wilderness. 'And what shall I more say? for the time would fail me to tell' of those who, holding God's faithfulness, had faith, and by it 'subdued kingdoms, wrought righteousness, obtained promises . . . out of weakness were made strong, waxed valiant in fight, turned to flight the armies of the aliens'.

Satan, too, has his creed: Doubt God's faithfulness. 'Hath God said? Are you not mistaken as to His commands? He could not really mean just that. You take an extreme view, give too literal a meaning to the words.' How constantly, and, alas, how successfully are such arguments used to prevent whole-hearted trust in God, whole-hearted consecration to God! How many estimate difficulties in the light of their own resources, and thus attempt little and often fail in the little they attempt! All God's giants have been weak men, who did great things for God because they reckoned on His being with them.

For ten years this had been, in the main, the attitude of the Mission, when in the spring of 1876 the first anniversary services were held to report progress. Taylor was by this time well enough to move about with the help of a strong walking-stick, and it was with joy that he pointed out on the large map twenty-eight stations in five provinces in which churches had been gathered – 600 converts having been baptized from the beginning. Of these, more than seventy were devoting their lives to making known the Gospel, and in them lay the chief hope of the future, specially in regard to the evangelization of the unreached interior. Sixty-eight missionaries had been sent to China, of whom fifty-two were still connected with the Mission. Means for their support had never failed – though that also which is 'more precious than . . . gold' had not been lacking, 'the *trial* of your faith'. Without a collection or an appeal of any kind for funds, £52,000 had been received, and the Mission was not and never had been in debt.

How much of prayer and practical self-denial lay behind these facts the Report did not reveal, but the candidates at Pyrland Road could have supplied some details not lacking in interest. Preparing, themselves, to face danger and sacrifice in the work to which the Lord was calling them, it meant everything to have the encouragement of their leader's example.

Of his first visit to Pyrland Road, while Taylor was still an invalid, one wrote:

He led me to his study, which was also the 'office' of the Mission. It was the back room on the ground floor, largely occupied with packing-cases. Near the window, which looked out on the dreary back gardens, was a writing-table littered with papers. In front of the fireplace where a fender is usually found was a low, narrow, iron bedstead, neatly covered with a rug. Taylor lay down on his iron bedstead and eagerly plunged into a conversation which was, for me, one of life's golden hours. Every idea I had hitherto cherished of a 'great man' was completely shattered: the high, imposing airs, and all the trappings were conspicuously absent; but Christ's ideal of greatness was then and there so securely set in my heart, that it has remained through all the years. I strongly suspect that, by his unconscious influence, Mr. Hudson Taylor did more than any other man of his day to compel Christian people to revise their ideas of greatness.

He never used his position as Director of the Mission to purchase for himself the least advantage or ease. However hard his lot might be in China, every missionary knew that Hudson Taylor had suffered in the same way, and was ready to do so again. No man could suspect, at any time, that while he himself was bearing the cross, his leader, under more favourable circumstances, was shirking it.

And now he was going back to China to speed the pioneers, as he fully hoped and expected, on their far inland journeys. A gracious answer to the prayers of many years had made this possible, in the coming of his sister Amelia and her husband, Benjamin Broomhall, into the home department of the work.

How real was the faith involved in joining the Mission, when at length the way opened, may be judged from the fact that they had by that time a family of ten growing boys and girls. But this was perhaps one of their chief qualifications. Number 2 Pyrland Road soon radiated an atmosphere that made it for many a long year the best loved centre of the Mission.

Early in September, 1876, Taylor set out again for China, notwithstanding the war-cloud that hung heavily over the eastern horizon. Negotiations that had dragged on for months, subsequent to the murder of a British official in China, had come at last to a stalemate. Nothing would induce the Chinese Government to give satisfaction of any sort for the murder of Mr. Margary; and the British Ambassador, having exhausted diplomatic resources, was on the point of retiring to the coast to put the matter into the hands of the Admiral. It seemed impossible that war could be averted, and there were many among the friends of the Mission who strongly advised against Taylor's going out.

'You will all have to return,' they said. 'And as to sending off pioneers to the more distant provinces, it is simply out of the question.'

It was indeed a critical juncture. But in the third-class cabin of the French Mail, as in the prayer meetings at Pyrland Road, fervent supplication was going up to God that He would overrule the crisis for the furtherance of His own great ends. With Him it is never too late. At the last moment, utterly improbable as it seemed, a change came over the Peking Foreign Office. More alive to the situation than his fellows, the Viceroy Li Hung-chang hurried to the coast, overtaking the British Ambassador just in time to reopen negotiations; and there, at Chefoo, was signed the memorable Convention which threw open the door of access at last to the remotest parts of China. Foreigners were at liberty to travel in any part of the Emperor's dominions and did so under his protection. Imperial proclamations were to be posted in every city, giving publicity to these arrangements; and for a period of two years British officials might be sent inland, specially to see that this clause was carried out. This was the news that awaited Taylor on his arrival in Shanghai, the agreement having been signed within a week of his leaving England; and already three parties of the Eighteen had set out and were well on their way to the interior.

> 'Just as our brethren were ready,' he wrote, 'not too soon and not too late the long-closed door opened to them of its own accord.'

As a matter of fact, representatives of the C.I.M. were the first, and for years almost the only, foreigners to avail themselves of this great opportunity. Far and wide they travelled, crossing and recrossing all the provinces of the interior, and penetrating even into eastern Tibet. 30,000 miles were thus traversed in the next eighteen months, Scriptures and tracts being everywhere sold or distributed, and friendly relations almost uninterruptedly maintained.

Permanent localized work was the object kept in view. To this end itineration had to be patiently pursued; and even when inquirers were gathered and a district seemed full of promise, it was often long before it was possible to settle.

But there were times, too, when disturbing news reached the Mission centre in Chinkiang. On one occasion, George Nicoll, himself recently driven out of I-chang, was in the room with Taylor when a budget of letters containing news of serious rioting in two different stations was brought in. Standing at his desk to read them, Taylor mentioned what was happening and that immediate help was necessary. Feeling that he might wish to be alone, the younger man was about to withdraw when, to his surprise, someone began to whistle. It was the soft refrain of Hudson Taylor's best-loved hymn:

Jesus, I am resting, resting, in the joy of what Thou art . . .

Turning back, Nicoll could not helping exclaiming, 'How *can* you whistle, when our friends are in such danger!'

'Would you have me anxious and troubled?' was the long-remembered answer. 'That would not help them, and would certainly incapacitate me for my work. I have just to roll the burden on the Lord.'

Day and night that was his secret, 'just to roll the burden on the Lord'. Frequently those who were wakeful in the little house at Chinkiang might hear, at two or three o'clock in the morning, the soft refrain of that favourite hymn. Taylor had learned that, for him, only one life was possible – that of resting and rejoicing in the Lord under all circumstances, while *He* dealt with the difficulties inward and outward, great and small.

Second only to his longing for the evangelization of the inland provinces was the desire that possessed him at this time for unity and blessing in the Conference of missionaries, convened for May, 1877, to be held in Shanghai. There were still some months before the Conference, and this interval Taylor was seeking to make the most of.

'There is one very important matter to pray about,' he wrote to Jennie in February – 'the forthcoming conference. It *will* be *a power*: shall it be for good or evil? This rests much with us, through the use of believing prayer. Unless there is a great outpouring of God's Holy Spirit, very much harm may result: very much has already resulted from preliminary discussions. Nor are *we* likely to pass without attack if some have their way. But our God is an *almighty* Saviour, and my hope is in Him. If His Spirit be poured out, evil will be kept in check; and if we ask for it, will it not indeed be so? Let us pray, then, much for this – pray daily for this, that division and discord may not prevail instead of unity and love.'

But Taylor not only prayed; he did all that in him lay to promote the unity he felt to be of such importance, and to remove misunderstandings. It was hardly to be wondered at, as he was the first to recognize, that the C.I.M. should have come in for a large share of criticism. Its aims and methods never had been popular, and its new departure in the direction of widespread evangelization was of the nature of an experiment. Because the pioneers were young, at the beginning only of their missionary life, it was argued that it could not be right to use them in work so difficult and important. Undoubtedly they *were* ignorant and inexperienced as compared with older missionaries, especially with the able men to be found in the foremost ranks of other societies. No one would have been more thankful than Taylor to have seen such workers take the field. But they were all needed, more than needed in their actual posts. There was no suggestion that some or any of *them* should be set free, though China was accessible at last, from end to end, to preachers of the Gospel. Was, then, no one to go because they could not send the best? Taylor had good reason to believe that these young workers had been given in answer to prayer, and that the hand of God was in the coincidence of their being ready on the spot, when the Gates of the West were thrown open. If only their critics, and they were many, could come nearer – could meet and know the men in question, and hear from their own lips of the wonderful opportunities God was giving – objections, he had no doubt, would give place to sympathy. But how was this to be brought to pass?

A leader less humble, perhaps, less truly taught of God, might have brushed aside unfriendly criticism, absorbing himself in what he felt to be his own work. But years of self-effacing discipline had not been in vain. Keenly as Taylor felt the attitude of opposition, he knew that those whose views differed most widely from his own might have just as sincere a desire for the advancement of the Kingdom of God. He had grasped, moreover, something of the real, indissoluble oneness of the body of Christ: that it is not that the eye *should not* say to the hand, 'I have no need of thee' – it *cannot*. On the contrary, whatever it may say or feel, of the body it is and must remain. The bearing of this principle upon the position of the C.I.M. he saw with increasing clearness. As a hand, this pioneering effort might reach out a certain distance beyond the rest of the body; but if it would go further, *the body must go too:* there could be no other way. Where is there room for independence in a living organism, every part of which is bound up with the whole? A large part, and not the easiest part of his work as he was learning, must consist in the humble, patient endeavour to carry his brethren with him in any new departure to which he was constrained of God.

These thoughts in mind, Taylor went on from Chinkiang, as soon as he was able, to the new centre of the Mission at Wuchang. Judd had just set out with one of the pioneers for the far-off capital of Kweichow, and his place had to be filled. There were problems also to consider as to how to keep in touch with distant workers, so as to reach them regularly with supplies. For several weeks Taylor had the benefit of experienced help, while McCarthy was preparing to walk right across China to Burma, accompanied by the faithful soldier evangelist, Yang Ts'üenling. Difficult as it was to spare him, Taylor rejoiced in the project almost as much as if he were going himself, and many were the hours of consultation and prayer they had over the whole forward movement.

Remembering their own spiritual difficulties, they felt the importance of providing help for younger workers whose strenuous life exposed them to so much of trial and temptation. The thought of calling together as many of the pioneers as possible for a week of conference had long been in Taylor's mind, and in sending off recent parties he had arranged that they should return for books and money at a given time. And now as he considered the matter with McCarthy, they saw in such a reunion the possibility of just the *rapprochement* needed with workers of other societies. The missionary community in Hankow, across the river, was considerable, and if united meetings could be arranged, much might be done to promote mutual understanding, and prepare the way for the larger Conference in Shanghai.

The response this suggestion met with from the London and Wesleyan Missions was so encouraging that Taylor could not but feel that, already, prayer was being answered; and he determined to seek opportunities for closer intercourse, especially with those whom he knew to be critical toward the C.I.M.

For this reason he was glad rather than otherwise to find himself delayed in Hankow one evening until it was too late to recross the river. Before he could reach the other side the city gates would be shut, and without bedding, etc., he could not very well go to an inn. It was necessary, therefore, to seek hospitality; and this Taylor did by calling upon a missionary with whom he was but slightly acquainted, and who took a very unfavourable view both of himself and the C.I.M. Quite simply he explained the circumstances, asking whether it would be convenient to put him up for the night. Christian courtesy admitted but one reply, and the sense of having done a kindness opened the way for friendly intercourse. Taylor being as good a listener as he was a talker, his host found himself drawn into conversation even upon spiritual things. A cordial friendship resulted; the missionary in question taking an early opportunity of letting it be known that he had had 'no idea Mr. Taylor was so good a man'.

Down the Yangtze more or less the same experience was repeated, as Taylor visited the river stations, and where missionaries of other societies were to be found, he took time to see something of their work.

> 'There are such openings in China as there never have been and as are not likely to recur,' he wrote. 'Just while the effect of the Imperial proclamations lasts (and this will largely be over in a very few months) we can do in weeks what would have taken months or years before. I see God's hand in bringing me here just now, on this and many other grounds.'

Meanwhile the long-closed gates were opening indeed. In the north and far north-west, the pioneers held on their way; McCarthy was already nearing the western province of Szechwan, larger than the whole of France and far more populous; Judd and Broumton had been prospered in renting premises in the capital of Kweichow, the first permanent Mission centre in any of the nine unoccupied provinces, while from Bhamo, in Burma, Stevenson and Soltau had made extended journeys into the Kachin hills, from which two or three hours' descent would have brought them into Chinese territory.

With high expectation Taylor returned to Wuchang to meet the pioneers as they gathered for their little conference. From the far inland provinces they came, as well as from the river stations – seventeen C.I.M. workers in all, to be joined by a dozen or more of the Hankow missionaries. As always in times of special need, a day was set apart for prayer and fasting. They were one in the longing for an outpouring of Divine blessing that should sweep away all coldness and deadness in their own hearts, all criticism and misunderstanding; an enduement with 'power from on high' for the great work to be done.

Wonderful in the days that followed was the answer to these prayers. The story the young evangelists had to tell, simple though it was, called forth deepest sympathy. The hopefulness of these inexperienced workers, their enthusiasm and genuine confidence in God as able and willing to do the impossible, were contagious as well as cheering.

Three weeks later came the Shanghai General Conference, and Taylor turned to the difficult task awaiting him at the coast. The paper he had to read was upon 'Itineration Far and Near, as an Evangelizing Agency', and as *The Celestial Empire* recorded, it 'secured the deepest interest of his audience'. Dr. Griffith John's opening address with its searching, powerful appeal for a life in the Holy Spirit struck the right note for a conference which culminated in a call 'to the Mission boards, colleges and churches of the world' for men and women to meet the great opportunity of the day: 'The most important step China missions have yet taken', Taylor wrote. The parting, after two weeks of fellowship, had no discordant note. Even the Chinese dress of C.I.M. missionaries had ceased to offend, and the forward movement they represented had passed into the confidence and prayerful sympathy of most if not all present.

The forty weeks of his expected absence from England were nearing an end, but not so the work to be done in China. None of the older centres of the Mission had yet been visited. After the conference he set out, therefore, on a thorough visitation of the Chekiang stations, accompanied most of the way by a travelling companion whose presence proved especially welcome among the women.

Miss Elizabeth Wilson, whom he was escorting to Wenchow, had by this time been more than a year in China. Though scarcely beyond middle age and full of energy, her silvery hair brought her the advantage of being considered 'old' among a people with whom such an appellation was an honour, and her coming to China at all was rather a wonder to other foreigners. But Taylor knew the whole story. He had met her long before, as a girl on a visit to London, and had learned of her earnest desire to give her life to missionary work. But at that time she was needed in her Westmorland home, and when her parents became invalids the cherished hope had to be hidden in her heart.

> 'Years went on,' as Taylor said in speaking of her, 'and this loving daughter never let her parents suspect that she was making any sacrifice on the one hand, yet never recalled the gift she had given to the Lord for missionary service on the other.
>
> 'Ten, twenty, thirty years passed away ere the Lord set her free; but the vow of twenty was as fresh in her heart at fifty as when first it had been offered. Within three weeks of the death of her surviving parent, she wrote to our headquarters in London of her desire to spend the remainder of her days in missionary work in China.'

Very illuminating it was to him now to see the welcome with which the

Christian women received this unexpected visitor. With their Romanized New Testaments wrapped in coloured handkerchiefs (the precious book it had cost years of labour to provide) they walked miles on tiny feet to meet the travellers, and begged in place after place that the 'Elder Sister' might stay among them, that they as well as the men might have someone to teach them the things of God.

Much though there was to encourage in connection with this five-month journey, there were also little churches that greatly needed quickening. As they travelled on, a plan was revolving in his mind for helping them, which he saw fulfilled before leaving for home. A conference was convened in Ningpo for *Chinese* leaders, similar to the united meetings for missionaries in Shanghai, and the attendance exceeded even his expectations. Three English and three American societies were represented, the delegates coming from all parts of the provinces, and the meetings were entirely in Chinese. When he was in the midst of preparations for the return to England – taking with him a difficult party to care for: one sick mother, one newly widowed, and several ailing children – he left everything to come himself and take part in the Conference, as if it were the only concern upon his mind.

It was one of the most interesting conferences I have ever attended, and we were both surprised and delighted at the ability displayed by our Chinese brethren. When it is remembered that all these men were themselves, but a few years ago, in heathen darkness, we cannot but feel encouraged, and look for yet greater things in the future.

CHAPTER 19

He Goeth Before

(1877–1880)

JOYFUL was the reunion just before Christmas when Taylor reached home after this fourth visit to China. He had been away almost sixteen months, and the little ones of two and three years old could not remember him. The elder brothers and sister were fast growing up, and an adopted daughter had been added to the family, the doubly orphaned child of Duncan, the pioneer missionary of Nanking. The Christmas season was full of gladness for Taylor that year.

He had not much time to spend with the children, however, for he had come home deeply impressed with the need for immediate reinforcements. Twenty-four men and at least six women were urgently wanted, and for that number he was praying – thirty new workers to go out if possible in the following year (1878). Among the candidates awaiting his arrival, several were ready to go forward, and Taylor was soon absorbed in farewell meetings, which brought him in contact with many friends.

'I am praying for an increase of £5,000 a year in our income,' he wrote to a senior member of the Mission in February, 'and for £2,000 extra for outfits and passages. Will you daily join in this prayer? We are daily remembering you all by name before the Lord.'

Meanwhile grievous news was coming, mail by mail, of the terrible famine in North China. In January it was estimated that six million people were starving, and the united efforts of the Chinese Government and of the foreign Relief Committee were wholly inadequate to cope with the disaster. In public meetings and through the press, Taylor was making known the facts, with the result that funds were coming to the C.I.M. freely for use in relief work. But more than money was needed. Not only were tens of thousands dying of starvation; thousands more were being sold into slavery – girls and young women literally taken away in droves by cruel traffickers from the south. Children were perishing in multitudes who might be gathered into orphanages and saved for time and eternity, and everywhere the poor suffering women were accessible as never before. Surely the time had come when missionary *women*, as well as men, should be found at the front in the newly opened provinces of inland China.

But where was the woman who could take the lead? To go to that famine-stricken region, two or three weeks' journey from the coast, was no easy matter. Someone with experience was needed; someone with a knowledge of the language, fitted to help and care for younger workers. In China there was no one in the C.I.M. circle free and suitable; and at home? Ah, that was where light began to come – but at what a cost!

Yes, there was one who undoubtedly combined the qualifications necessary. Experienced, prayerful, devoted, with a knowledge of the language and the confidence of her fellow-workers, Jennie could give just the help required. But how could she be spared from home? How could he let her go so soon after their long parting? And if the sacrifice was great for him, who shall say what it meant to the mother's heart? At first, indeed she could not see it to be called for. Her husband in poor health and overwhelmed with work surely needed her, to say nothing of the children. Could it be right to leave him, even if the family were provided for? The struggle, if not long, was desperately hard; but for her, as for him, only one issue was possible. A little worn brown notebook tells the rest; and it is the same wonderful story that every truly Christian heart has known, of God's own Word meeting the inward need, the need so deep as to be voiceless even to Him, but none the less understood.

Point by point all her difficulties were met, her questions answered until she knew beyond a doubt that it was God Himself who had need of her out there in China. And, even then, His tender care went further. He knew the inward shrinking, the hours of testing that must come. She wrote of it later,

> I felt like Gideon. I wanted some fleeces to confirm my faith, and as a token for those who would have me remain at home. I asked God to give me, in the first place, money to purchase certain requisites for outfit, as we had none to spare; and further, to give me liberally, as much as £50, so that there might be money in hand when I went away.

The very next afternoon (Thursday) a friend called to see her, and before leaving said:

'Will you accept a little gift for your own use, to get anything you may need for the journey?'

And the sum put into her hand was £10 – just the allowance made by the Mission at that time towards the cost of outfit.

No one knew, not even Taylor, about the fleeces; and with a wondering heart she waited. Several days passed without the further answer to her prayer. Perhaps the Lord was withholding it that she might trust Him without so much confirmation?

Somehow I felt He would provide at the right time, and was very happy – realizing that He is my Helper, and that in going I should learn more of Him and find His strength made perfect in my utter weakness.

Glancing next morning over the letters she came on one from Barnsley. Lo, it was from Taylor's parents enclosing a cheque for £50! Overwhelmed with joy and thankfulness, she ran to his study: but he was not alone.

When I returned, he was reading your letter, and considering how the Lord would have the money applied. He knew we needed it, but never takes anything for ourselves that is left optional.

'Oh,' I said, 'that £50 is mine! I have a claim on it that you do not know of.' And I told him all the circumstances.

So we accept it with warmest thanks to you, and with gratitude to God. I had said to the Lord: '£50 just now would be worth more than a fortune to me at another time. It would be a guarantee of all other needs being met.' I feel it is such tender consideration for my weakness to send it; and you and dear father may be assured, when I am far away, that the memory of this gift will be a continual strength and help to me.

Meanwhile, Amelia Broomhall, when she heard of the proposed step, was deeply moved. With the care of the Mission house and candidates, as well as her own family of four boys and six girls, it would have been easy and true to think that her hands were full. But hers was the love that 'never faileth', and in a busy, practical life she knew the secret of so waiting upon God as to have her strength daily renewed.

'If Jennie is called to go to China,' she said without hesitation, 'I am called to care for her children.'

This provision, which would mean that the little ones could remain with their father, and the home-life be carried on as usual, was even more than Jennie had asked. But there was yet more. The very day before she left England, accompanied by several new workers, a letter came to hand from an old friend expressing warm sympathy with the object she had in view. It contained a gift toward the orphanage she hoped to found; and to her surprise on looking at the cheque, it proved to be for a *thousand pounds*. 'Please enter it anonymously,' he wrote. 'It does not represent any superabundance of wealth, as my business affairs will miss it. But if you, for Christ's sake, can separate, I cannot give less than this.'

When Jennie Taylor set out from Shanghai to go to the inland province of Shansi, two younger women accompanied her, travelling under the experienced escort of Mr. Baller. Never before had foreign women attempted to go so far inland, and with their work in the famine-stricken region, a little light began to shine for the women and children of that vast, waiting world – the 180 millions of the far interior. When the news reached Taylor by cablegram he wrote,

> I cannot tell you how my heart and prayers go with you all. *The Lord be glorified in this movement.* I do thank God for giving me such a wife as alone could satisfy my heart – one to whom the Lord Jesus is more than husband; to whom His work is more than love and enjoyment here. I *know* He is blessing and will bless our dear children; I *know* He is blessing and will bless you; I *know* He is blessing and will bless me too, and the work. And I am glad to think I am not selfishly, for my own help or enjoyment, depriving you of the eternal fruit of what you are now sowing. What will not the harvest be!

For himself, meanwhile, the sacrifice involved was very real. As long as Amelia could come in and out freely from her home next door, he did not feel the burden of family care; but when his own children developed whooping cough, calling for the isolation of his household, more responsibility naturally fell to his share. In addition to very full days of work, he had many an anxious night of watching by little bedsides from which the mother was absent.

The answer to the petition for thirty new workers in the current year was at the same time bringing added burdens.

That he was deeply feeling the responsibility of leadership in a mission which had already grown beyond the desires and hopes with which it was founded is evident from a letter to Jennie.

> I have been praying very much this morning for a wise and understanding spirit, and for largeness of heart, and organizing capacity. The Lord make me equal to increasing claims.

That summer he had an unexpected holiday – the first he had taken, apart from sea voyages, during the twelve years since the formation of the Mission. At the invitation of friends, who generously met the expense, he joined their family party in the Engadine for two or three weeks. It was the first time he had been in Switzerland, and many letters tell of the delight with which he drank in the beauty of lake, mountain, and Alpine flowers, and the glacier air which seemed to give him new life. Even there Mission matters followed him – as many as twenty-five letters being received one day, most of which required answers. Comparative leisure enabled him to write freely to Jennie, whose absence he was specially feeling amid those beautiful scenes.

> Every day I look at the little Bible marker you gave me, with the words 'For Jesus' sake', and I am thankful for the reminder. It is not for your pleasure or mine that we are separated, nor for money-making, nor for our children's sake. It is not

even for China, or the missionaries or the Mission: no – *for Jesus' sake. He* is worthy! And He is blessing you, and is making the people I meet so kind to me, one and all.

Many were the problems thought out and prayed over in those mountain solitudes. A critical time had come, he could not help feeling, in the history of the Mission. Prayer had been wonderfully answered, and the whole interior opened up to the work of evangelists; but now the step had to be taken of sending women inland, to follow up what had been begun. In praying for the first twenty-four 'willing, skilful labourers' on the sands at Brighton, he had hardly contemplated this. If it had caused an outcry when *men* were sent to face the loneliness and dangers of life in the far interior, what would happen when he encouraged women, single or married, to do the same? Then there were questions connected with the home organization of the growing work.

But most of all it was with the Lord Himself those hours of soul-refreshing silence were occupied. To a Swiss member of the Mission he wrote:

May God keep you, and not only keep you – *fill* you more and more, and keep you running over with the living waters. The one thing, I judge, to bear in mind is that it has 'pleased the Father that *in him* should all fulness dwell'. Apart from Him we have nothing, are nothing, cannot bring forth any fruit to God. He will not give some of His riches to you and some to me, to use and live on away from Himself. But *in* Him *all* is ours. With Him there is a constant feast for us. To know Christ as the Bridegroom is most blessed; to be not betrothed and having occasional visits, but married. 'I *am* with you alway', 'I will *never* leave thee', 'I will not fail thee, nor forsake thee' – such are now His messages of love to us.

Upon the many meetings that awaited Taylor's return to England in September we must not dwell, nor upon the remarkable answers to prayer that facilitated the outgoing of all the thirty asked for and given in 1878. Twenty-eight new missionaries actually sailed before the close of the year, and several others were accepted to follow shortly. Not one really suitable candidate was declined for lack of funds, though some had to be told that there was not a penny in hand to send them out. But again and again the Lord's provision came earmarked, so to speak, to meet the special need. The very day one October party sailed, for example, Taylor wrote to two young men of much promise, accepting them for work in Shansi. Although he had nothing, as he frankly told them, toward the expense of passages and outfits, he invited them to come to London with a view to an early departure. These communications were posted at 5.15 p.m. and by nine o'clock delivery that same evening, a letter was received from Lord Radstock enclosing, among other gifts, the sum of £100 *to send two new workers to the famine-stricken province of Shansi*. Thus, even before the young men could set out in faith for London, the money needed was in hand and the way open for them to go forward.

And in matters more perplexing than finance, help was given that cleared the way for Taylor's own return to China. Benjamin Broomhall was appointed General Secretary. Amelia continued to care for the outgoing and returning missionaries and the seventeen children, and McCarthy, in addition to deputation work, undertook the sub-editing of *China's Millions*.

There was still no lack of difficulties to be met both in England and in China. On the journey out, he became so seriously ill that a Singapore doctor doubted whether he could reach Hong Kong alive. Was it at that time that Jennie, far away in Shansi, had the curiously vivid dream, in which she saw him ill and needing her urgently? The work she had undertaken for the famine orphans was now well established and her companion able to carry on, and with two missionary married couples at the capital, Taiyuanfu, there was no longer the same need for her presence. The dream, fitting in with other elements of guidance, decided her to cross the mountains and return to Shanghai to await his arrival there.

At first, in the joy of reunion, he was full of plans for visiting the stations and helping the new missionaries who had been sent out (thirty-four in number) during his recent visit to England. But the strain of all that had to be attended to was more than he could bear, and within a fortnight he was so ill that again life itself was hanging in the balance. The physician consulted had little hope, unless he could at once be removed to a more bracing climate. Summer was coming on, and it was useless to attempt to remain anywhere in the Yangtze valley. The northern port of Chefoo, with its freedom and freshness, he recommended as the best available refuge: but how to get there was the difficulty.

It was an anxious journey for Jennie, from the Monday evening when they went on board, through the long hours of Tuesday – moving slowly in a damp sea-mist, while the fog-horn droned its melancholy sound – to Wednesday morning when they arrived and had nowhere to go.

Lying there in the little boat while his companions went in search of quarters,[1] Taylor little imagined all that his illness and forlorn arrival were to mean of help and comfort for his fellow-labourers! He had come to China full of hope for extension, especially in the field of women's work. His wife had proved that the interior of that land was no less accessible to women missionaries than to men; and having sent her first, he felt the more free to encourage others in following her example. It was a great task that lay before him, a great responsibility; and here he was, laid aside, able to do

[1] Hudson Taylor and his wife were accompanied on this journey by J. J. Coulthard, one of the party just arrived from England who acted as Taylor's secretary and afterwards became his son-in-law.

nothing! He did not know it, but months were to elapse before he would leave that silent shore again.

The silent shore – how much help it was to afford in the practical problem of reaching the far interior with the Gospel! Scattered homes, missionary homes, centres of light and love among the people, were what he longed to see all over inland China. But what about the little children sent in love to such homes? What about the need that must arise in the not distant future for schooling that should not separate them wholly from the influence of parents who must remain in China? What about the needs of those parents and others throughout the Mission, for rest and refreshment from time to time, and for a health resort in cases of illness like his own? All this Taylor could foresee but dimly, nor did he then imagine the extensive and complete equipment of buildings that was to arise on that far sweep of shore – the hospital, sanatorium, schools of the Mission; the bright, breezy centre of young life from which incalculable influences for good were to flow. The Lord knew, foresaw and planned it all.

In the home of a Christian customs house officer, meanwhile, Jennie Taylor had met with a cordial welcome. He and his wife were given to hospitality, and had room for visitors. The missionary party soon found themselves received into a real home, as paying guests.

Few could remember a hotter season in China than the summer that followed. Work such as Taylor had planned down in the Yangtze valley would in all probability have cost his life; and the illness of one and another made him long to share with them the very real benefit he was deriving from Chefoo. Several of the newly arrived young missionaries were sent for first of all, and an unused building known as 'The Bungalow' was called into requisition.

Then came the news that far away in Wuchang Mr. and Mrs. Judd were breaking down under the strain of their work and the overpowering heat. 'Come up here if you can,' wrote Taylor, telling them how wonderfully Chefoo was answering in his own case. So Judd took his suffering wife and five little boys to the northern port. To see the children playing on the beach was almost as much joy to Taylor as to their own parents, and he longed to bring the same relief to other fellow-workers and their families.

Meanwhile, he was so much better that he felt he must go down to Chinkiang to see about certain rather surprising developments. For while he had been laid aside, unable to do anything in the matter most upon his heart, the Lord Himself had been working. His time had come, indeed, for opening the door of faith to the long-waiting womanhood of the recently entered provinces. It was the pioneers themselves who broke the ice. After repeated journeys, the far interior did not seem to them so very different from inland districts near the coast. They were quite at home among the people, and saw the advantage of having some settled stations. What more natural than that they should wish to be married, and take the first foreign women to those outlying regions as their own home-makers and fellow missionaries? Thus when Taylor came down in August to the Yangtze valley, one young couple had already started for the far north-west, and others were preparing for similar journeys.

A busy month was spent in Shanghai and Chinkiang, with visits to Yangchow, where Taylor was altering the old premises to fit them for more aggressive work.

'It does seem so homelike,' he wrote of the latter place. 'How I should like to settle there for the remainder of my days and be a missionary again!'

In letter after letter to Jennie he spoke of being so thankful he had come; of seeing the Lord's hand manifestly working in the removal of difficulties and the solution of problems; of his purpose to go on to Hankow, despite the fresh heat-wave that could not last long, etc. Then came a break in the correspondence, and for the fourth time in as many months it looked as though his work was to be cut short, his earthly service ended. Dysentery returned with the overpowering heat, and very near the spot where his loved ones lay sleeping Hudson Taylor came once more to the borderland.

But the life that had not yet attained its widest usefulness was still prolonged. Nursing him day and night with the utmost devotion, Rudland managed to get the patient down to Shanghai and on board the coasting steamer, not leaving him till he was safely back in Chefoo once more. Once there the bracing air again did wonders, and Taylor was lured into spending much time out of doors by a new project that almost thrust itself upon him.

Delighting day by day in that long sweep of sandy shore, he and his fellow-workers could not but see how much it would mean to the Mission to have a sanatorium there, and some day, perhaps, a school for missionaries' children. How well it would suit them – that retired hilly spot with its fresh-water stream! But, for the time being, they could only pray. They did not often go over there even, knowing how prices might soar if any interest were shown in a possible purchase. But one day Taylor and Judd were walking over the ground when a farmer came up and, to their surprise, asked if they wanted to buy land.

He was offering the very bean-field about which they had just been speaking and at no unreasonable price, as they soon discovered.

'Then and there the bargain was struck,' recalled Judd. 'I never knew a piece of business settled so easily. The money was paid and we got the field, with a gully and fresh water running down beside it. Then neighbouring farmers were willing to sell theirs as well; and we bought all we wanted at a remarkably fair price.'

Neither Taylor nor Judd had any experience in house building, but they employed men to quarry stone out of the gully, make bricks from the surface soil and utilize the wrecks of two ships for doors, beams, floors and furniture. A house with some ten rooms was erected, the first simple structure of what was to become the well-known Chefoo school in which the children of C.I.M. missionaries in China received their education from kindergarten until college years; with adjacent hospital and holiday home for parents.

Far in the future, however, were these developments as the year 1879 drew to a close. As soon as health was re-established, Taylor set out for the advance post of the Mission at Wuchang. The young couples who had left for the interior some months previously were now in their distant homes, beginning work for the first time among the women of the western and north-western provinces. Now the time had come to take a step which cast him more than ever in faith upon the living God. What, send women – unmarried women, young and defenceless – into all the dangers and privations, the hardship and loneliness of life in the far interior of China? Let them take those perilous journeys of weeks and months at a time, and condemn them to isolation in crowded cities, hundreds of miles from any other foreigner? The responsibility was great indeed, and keenly he felt it. He was but a servant, however, not the Master. And if women were waiting to go at the Master's call, surely the time had come to help them rather than hinder.

Travelling by mule-litter with Coulthard from Chefoo to the Grand Canal, Taylor had leisure for thought and prayer over the situation. The younger missionary never failed to see, if he woke early enough, the little candle burning that told of the older man's quiet hour over the Word of God.

When at length Taylor reached Wuchang, a number of C.I.M. people were there for various reasons, with Mr. and Mrs. Baller in charge. Daily they met for Bible reading and prayer, the needs of the lonely workers at the distant outposts burdening their hearts. A thousand miles up the Yangtze, George Nicoll and his wife had just reached Chungking, where she was the only foreign woman in the great province of Szechwan. Mr. and Mrs. George Clarke had gone on further – another seventeen days' journey to the capital of Kweichow, where Broumton was holding the fort alone. This latter post was very distant, very isolated and Trench, on his next evangelistic journey, was to call in and see the little party. Yes, he could act as escort, if there were women willing and ready to go. And there were. Mrs. William McCarthy, newly widowed, whose husband had been designated to that very province, only asked to give her life to what was to have been their united task; and Miss Kidd was more than willing to accompany her. So the week of meetings was followed by one of busy preparation.

'Such a venture of faith as it was!' said Coulthard, looking back with more understanding than he or any of the young missionaries could have had at the time. 'The last meeting to commend them to God was deeply solemn. Mr. Taylor no doubt felt it as we could not. We never thought of danger; but he realized what might be involved, and his heart was moved accordingly.'

The route decided upon lay across Hunan, turbulent and anti-foreign; and in addition to the Chinese Christian woman who had volunteered to accompany the missionaries, Baller was to be spared to reinforce the party. This practically exhausted the resources of the station, and when a call came for the help of women in quite another direction, no foreign escort was available. Miss Fausset, a young worker with true courage, was ready to go at once to the help of Mrs. King; but it meant a three months' journey by houseboat, without coming to a single place at which there were foreigners, and there was no one save Miss Wilson to accompany her.

Then it was that advancing years and silvery hair came to their own in a new way; for Miss Wilson's venerable appearance, from the Chinese point of view, made it possible for the ladies to travel without foreign escort, and they were quite prepared to undertake the journey with the Lord alone as their Protector. It is easy to write the words, easier still to read them with passing interest; but only those who have known from experience what such journeys meant in the early days can at all appreciate the situation. Taylor knew; yet he encouraged these brave women, and assumed the responsibility of letting them go.

Not lightly, however, or at little cost did he go through with this matter. No one of experience being left in the Mission house, he engaged the boat himself and made all arrangements, even to packing food-baskets and rolling up their bedding with his own hands. Delayed after they had gone on board, he spent the first night with them among the crowded shipping at the mouth of the Han – sharing the only available cabin with Miss Wilson's protégé, a leper lad rescued at Yangchow, who had become an earnest Christian and proved invaluable as a helper.

Seeing that the vegetable oil, which was all they had been able to procure for cooking, made their food unpalatable, Taylor went ashore next morning and was gone some time.

'When he returned,' wrote Miss Fausset, 'he was carrying a basket on his arm in which were sweet potatoes, eggs and lard. One never could have thought a little lard capable of doing so much good, or making so enduring an impression!'

When the boatmen really started (March 1, 1880) Taylor still remained on board till they got well out on the Han; then after a time of prayer, while the attention of the missionaries was occupied, he slipped into his little *sampan* and was gone. Never were travellers more faithfully escorted than by his prayers. Day and night he went with them in spirit, as they had the comfort of knowing, and Miss Fausset could never forget the earnestness with which he said on meeting her again:

'I have prayed for you thousands of times.'

As news began to come from distant stations in which these and other pioneers were winning their way to the homes and hearts of the people, Taylor wrote to his mother,

> I cannot tell you how glad my heart is to see the work extending and consolidating in the remote parts of China. It is worth living for and worth dying for.

CHAPTER 20

The Rising Tide

(1880–1885)

BACK in the terrible days of the Taiping Rebellion, Captain Yü of the Imperial army was stationed for a short time in Ningpo. While there, he fell in with preachers of 'the Jesus Doctrine', and learned something of the teachings of Christianity. Naturally a thoughtful, religious man, he could not but be impressed, but the little he had heard left him with no clear knowledge of the way of salvation. Fifteen long years went by without bringing him further light; but he was seeking, groping after the truth, and doing all in his power to win and help others to win 'the favour of Heaven'.

Among a sect of reformed Buddhists strongly opposed to idolatry he had found kindred spirits, and was giving all his time to going from place to place as their accredited agent, though without remuneration. His preaching was necessarily rather negative than positive – denouncing the folly and sin of idol-worship, and proclaiming the existence of one true, supreme Ruler of the universe, the only God who should be worshipped, but of whom he could tell his hearers practically nothing.

He was growing an old man before, in an inland city (Kin-hwa-fu), he met a foreign missionary. Dr. Douthwaite had come over from his station on the Tsientang river, and with Pastor Wang Lae-djün was preaching daily in a newly opened Gospel hall. Here the devout Buddhist heard in all its fullness the glad tidings of salvation – heard, believed, and found himself a new creature in Christ Jesus. After his baptism a year later (1876) he went down to Chü-chow-fu to be under Dr. Douthwaite's care, for medical treatment, and the latter was rejocied to see how much progress he had made in knowledge of the Word of God.

> 'I well remember how, after we had been reading the Scriptures and praying together,' he wrote, 'Yü earnestly entreated me to let him go out as a preacher of the Gospel.
>
> ' "I have led hundreds on the wrong road," he said, "and now I want to turn them to the Way of Truth. Let me go. I ask no wages; I do not want your money. I only want to serve the Lord Jesus." '

Three weeks later this ardent missionary, sent out with the prayers of the little church at Chü-chow-fu, returned with his first convert. He had crossed the watershed between Chekiang and the adjacent province of Kiangsi, and in the beautiful district of Yüshan had visited some of his former disciples. One of these it was who accompanied him now – a cheery farmer, also named Yü, who was himself to become an earnest soul-winner. Dr. Douthwaite recalled of this farmer,

> He seemed to be just boiling over with joy.
> 'For forty years I have been seeking the Truth,' he said, 'and now I have found it!'
> Then he earnestly requested to be at once baptized.
> 'Oh,' I replied, 'we cannot go so fast!'
> 'No,' he urged, 'let me be baptized *now*. I am an old man and have come three days' journey. I may never be able to travel so far again. I believe everything you have told me about the Lord Jesus. There is no reason why I should not be baptized today.'
> On further enquiry, I myself could see none; so I baptized him and he went away rejoicing.
> But he did come back, bringing with him six or seven neighbours (Feb. 1877). They, too, definitely expressed their faith in Christ, saying that from what they had heard they were convinced that idolatry was false and sinful, and were prepared to give it up. After a few months' testing, I had the joy of receiving them, too, into the church.

The ex-Captain meanwhile, continuing his labours, had been led to another man from the same district whose heart the Lord opened. Travelling to Yüshan one day, carrying his few belongings, he had joined company with a stranger who soon became interested in his conversation. Perceiving the old 'Teacher' to be a good man, Farmer Tung insisted on relieving him of his bundle of bedding, etc., as they tramped along together mile after mile. So fully did the story of the life, death and resurrection of Christ meet the young man's need, that from that day he too was not only a believer in Jesus but a preacher of the Gospel. On visiting his village (Tayang) some months later, Dr. Douthwaite was surprised to find the courtyard of the house filled with an orderly assembly of people waiting as if for a meeting. Stools, chairs, baskets, inverted buckets, whatever could be used as a seat had been requisitioned, and the company consisted of women as well as men – all eagerly expectant. They were waiting, he found, for him to address them; and on asking how such an audience had been gathered at short notice, he was still more interested to learn that had he *not* been coming the meeting would have been held just the same. It was their custom to come together every evening in Farmer Tung's house or courtyard, to sing hymns and pray and read from the Word of God; and in villages far and near, for miles around, the Good News had been made known.

Hudson Taylor himself, in 1877, had met some of these converts, and now, in the summer of 1880, during a visit to the Mission centres in Chekiang, he decided to cross into the neighbouring province of Kiangsi, and return to the Yangtze by way of the Kwangsin River.

Upon his visits to Farmer Tung and the newly opened out-station at Yüshan we must not dwell; but in the light of those lives touched with the love of Christ, the darkness of all that lay around them and beyond was felt the more. Did the vision come to him then, as he passed the cities day after day that were to witness a chain of Mission centres unique in China, staffed entirely by women; the vision of girls then free and happy in far-off Christian homes, quietly laying down their lives in loving, self-sacrificing service for the upbuilding of the kingdom of God in human hearts? Whether he saw it or not, there was One who knew why Hudson Taylor had been brought to the Kwangsin River; One who knew where to find the treasures of love ready to be outpoured in His service from many a woman's heart.

And all the while in distant provinces, hundreds of miles farther north and west, a beginning was being made. Strange and new as was the presence of foreign women in the great inland cities they now called home, it was no more so than the experiences that were coming to them.

> 'For nearly two months past,' Mrs. Nicoll wrote from Chungking in Szechwan, 'I have daily seen some hundreds of women. Our house has been like a fair. Often while getting one crowd out at the front door another has found its way in at the back.'

How much she needed help may be imagined; for, without a Christian woman anywhere within reach, the only person she could fall back upon was a member of their household who, being an old man, was tolerated among the guests in the inner courtyard. As the summer wore on she had to get up at three o'clock in the morning to obtain quiet for Bible study or letters. The busy day that followed rarely brought opportunity for rest; and more than once she fainted from weariness in the midst of her visitors, returning to consciousness to find the women fanning her, full of affection and concern.

Among many well-to-do women who were her friends was one elderly lady who cared for her like a mother. From time to time, knowing how weary she must be, this lady would send round her sedan chair with an urgent request for Mrs. Nicoll to return in it immediately. If she succeeded thus in getting her away from the Mission house, she would put her on the most comfortable bed in her own apartment, send out all the younger women, and sit down herself to fan her until the tired missionary was fast asleep. Then she would prepare an inviting meal and on no account let her go home until she had had a good dinner.

That was the surprise, the unexpected encouragement that everywhere awaited these first women who went – the people were glad to see them, were eager, often, to hear their message, and showed not only natural curiosity and interest, but real heart sympathy. Even crossing the desperately anti-foreign province of Hunan, for example, Miss Kidd could write of friendly women wanting to detain them.

'Why do you go to Kweichow?' they said in several places: 'we too want happiness and peace. Stay here and be our teachers.'

Their experiences on reaching Kweiyang were no less encouraging.

> 'We find the people most friendly,' Mrs. McCarthy wrote during the following summer, 'and we go in and out without the least inconvenience. As we walk about, we get many invitations to sit down and drink tea.'

With Miss Wilson and Miss Fausset it was just the same in their distant northern province. Arrived in Hanchung-fu they found George King and his wife in the midst of an absorbing work. God had a people in that place, and it was all the missionaries could do to keep up with developments that before long gave them an unusually bright little church of over thirty baptized believers. One of these, an elderly woman who seemed all on fire with love to Christ, never wearied of accompanying Miss Wilson to the surrounding villages.

About six months later Mr. and Mrs. Parker came up, on their way to a still more distant sphere. They were bound for Kansu, the farthest north-west of all the provinces, where, with its Muhammadan and Chinese population of ten millions, G. F. Easton was the one solitary witness for Christ. Five months only after their arrival Mr. Parker wrote (June 2, 1881):

> 'I doubt whether there is a lane or courtyard in the city where a visit from my wife or Miss Wilson would not be welcomed. Three candidates are waiting to be baptized.'

Thus at point after point in the far interior, prayer was being answered and the seemingly impossible brought to pass. 'Do love the Chinese women,' Hudson Taylor had said to Miss Wilson when she first went out. 'Whatever is your best time in the day, give that to communion with God; and *do love the Chinese women.*' This was the power that was telling now on hearts that were learning through human love, unknown before, the wonder of the Love that 'passeth knowledge'.

'What is this strange, warm feeling we have when we come here to you?' said a group of visitors to one of the first women missionaries in Honan. 'We never feel it anywhere else. In our own mothers' homes we do not feel it. Here our hearts are *k'uan-ch'ao* – broad and peaceful. What is it warms them so? We have never felt it before.'

But such service was not without its cost. While there was much to encourage – for by the end of 1880 the pioneers were rejoicing in sixty or seventy converts gathered into little churches in the far inland provinces – there was much also to call for faith and patience and the spirit of those who overcame 'by the blood of the Lamb' and 'loved not their lives unto the death'. First to go to the women of western China, Emily King was the first also to be called to higher service. But before her brief course ended – the one precious opportunity in which she had given her all – she had the joy of seeing no fewer than eighteen women baptized on confession of their faith in Jesus. Dying of typhus fever in her far-off home (May 1881), this it was that raised her above the sorrow of leaving her husband desolate, and their little one but five weeks old without a mother. The Man of Sorrows was seeing of 'the travail of his soul' among those for whom He had waited so long! And she was satisfied.

This it was that strengthened the mother's heart by a little lonely grave, when in that same month of May Mrs. George Clarke went on from Kweichow, in which she had been the only woman missionary, to the still more distant and difficult province of Yünnan. The sisters who had come to her help were able by that time to carry on the work; and the precious child who had filled her hands as well as her heart had been taken to a safer, better Land.

> 'The Lord has been leading us by a painful path,' the father wrote. 'Doubtless He saw best to take our dear boy to Himself, to send us to Yünnan; for if he had been spared we should not have thought of leaving Kweichow. Now, where is the married couple who can go as well as we?'

Forty days' journey westward lay the city in which a house was waiting; and Yünnan with its twelve millions was without a resident missionary, or anyone at all to bring to its women and children the glad tidings of a Saviour's love. Kneeling beside that little grave, the mother consecrated herself afresh to God for this work, and went on to the loneliness and privations she knew so well, to do in a second great province of western China what she had already been doing in Kweichow. And though only two and a half years later she too was called to her reward, the fruit of that life, the answer to her many prayers, lived on.

From the snow-capped mountains that reminded her of her own Switzerland, on which she loved to watch the sunset glow, in later years hundreds upon hundreds of the neglected tribespeople came to the Saviour she so truly loved and served. And in the two provinces where she pioneered the way as the first woman missionary, a church numbering more than 8,000 spread across to the Burma border forty years after her death, and went on increasing.

Shortly before Mrs. Hudson Taylor had left home (May 1878) to lead in this pioneer movement, a special Prayer Union had been formed in England 'to seek blessing upon the 125 millions of heathen women in China'. The circular setting forth the objects of the Union was headed with the promise: 'If two of you shall agree on earth as touching anything that they shall ask, it shall be done for them of my Father which is in heaven' (Matt. 18. 19). Daily prayer for those labouring among them was the condition of membership; and who shall say how much the safety, happiness and success of the first women workers to go to the far inland provinces was due to the united, definite prayer focused thus upon their labours?

The work of the C.I.M. pioneers was extensive and thorough-going. 'Other missionaries are doing a good work, but they are not doing *this* work,' wrote Alex. Wylie of the London Missionary Society early in the 1880s. 'They are opening up the country, and this is what we want.' And one of Her Majesty's Consuls included, in the same year, the following statement in his official report from Hankow:

> Always on the move, the missionaries of this society have travelled throughout the country, taking hardship and privation as the natural incidents of their profession and, never attempting to force themselves anywhere, they have made friends everywhere; and while labouring in their special field as ministers of the Gospel, have accustomed the Chinese to the presence of foreigners among them. Not only do the bachelor members of the Mission visit places supposed to be inaccessible to foreigners, but those who are married take their wives with them and settle down with the good will of the people in districts far removed from official influence, and get on as comfortably and securely as their brethren of the older Missions under the shadow of the Consular flag. This Mission has, at the same time, shown the true way of spreading Christianity in China.

In the course of six years of almost uninterrupted travelling James Cameron traversed every province in China except Hunan, even reaching Mongolia and Tibet. John McCarthy had gone on foot through the three south-western provinces, preaching everywhere as he went, while George Clarke and Edward Fishe were evangelizing in Kwangsi, still farther south and until then wholly unreached. Broumton, once Kweiyang was occupied, was set free to travel again, and visited with others nearly every city in eastern Yünnan. On the west J. W. Stevenson and Henry Soltau, who had been in Burma, crossed the hills to unite the advance guards of the Mission coming from east and west, and then proceeded to the coast, the first Europeans to travel from the Burmese frontier right through to Shanghai. Taylor was at Wuchang when they reached the Yangtze, whence he had seen off another large party, including women, bound for western China.

Hardly had they started before Adam Dorward appeared, fresh from five and a half months of pioneering. Hunan was graven on his heart, and he had just commenced the self-sacrificing labours that for eight years he continued almost without intermission, giving his life at last in hope of the blessed results seen later. Little wonder that a crying need began to be felt, rising out of these developments – the need for reinforcements to follow up such labours and enter many a widely opened door!

This then was the state of things when Jennie Taylor was obliged to return to England, after more than three years' absence (October 1881), and Taylor set out from Chefoo, now his headquarters, for a conference with several of the pioneers at Wuchang. Dorward was there from Hunan, Parrott and Pigott from the north, Trench and Miss Kidd from the far south-west and other workers from central China. Just a family party they seemed, overjoyed to have Taylor with them, quite unconscious of what was to be the outcome. There had been little or no pre-arrangement about these meetings. As Taylor came up-river, he brought with him one and another who seemed to need refreshment, and Coulthard's bachelor house-keeping was taxed to the utmost. But a spirit of prayer prevailed. And shortly after the conference had begun, Hudson Taylor wrote:

> God is giving us a happy time of fellowship together, and is *confirming us in the principles on which we are acting.*

That one little sentence, taken in connection with the crisis to which they had come, lets in a flood of light on the important sequel to those days of fellowship at Wuchang. For unconsciously, perhaps, to the younger members of the Mission, it *was* a crisis, and more was hanging in the balance than Taylor himself could realize. After years of prayer and patient, persevering efforts, a position of unparalleled opportunity had been reached. Inland China lay open before them. At all the settled stations in the far north, south, and west, reinforcements were needed, whole provinces as large as kingdoms in Europe being at last accessible to resident as well as itinerant missionary work. Not to advance would be to retreat from the position of faith taken up at the beginning. It would be to look at difficulties rather than at the living God. True, funds were low – had been for years, and the workers coming out from home were few, while several retirements had taken place in China. Difficulties were formidable; and it was easy to say, 'All these things are indications that for the present no further extension is possible'. But *not* to go forward would be to throw away opportunities God had given, and to close, before long, stations that had been opened at great cost. This, surely, could not be His way for the evangelization of inland China.

What then was to be done? What answer must be given to the pioneers who were writing and eagerly looking for help? There are several different ways of working for God, as Taylor reminded the little company.

> One is to make the best plans we can, and carry them out to the best of our ability. This may be better than working without plan, but it is by no means the best way of serving our Master. Or, having carefully laid our plans and determined to carry them through, we may ask God to help us, and to prosper us in connection with them. Yet another way of working is to begin with God; to ask His plans, and to offer ourselves to Him to carry out His purposes.

This then was the attitude taken up. Day by day the needs of the whole work were laid before the Lord, guidance being sought as to His will in connection with them.

> Going about it in this way, we leave the responsibility with the Great Designer, and find His service one of sweet restfulness. We have no responsibility save to follow as we are led; and we serve One who is able both to design and to execute, and whose work never fails.

It was only gradually it came to them – for it seemed too big a thing for faith to grasp. Walking over the Serpent Hill in the midst of Wuchang, Taylor was counting up with one of his fellow-workers how many men and women it would really take to meet the most pressing claims. Station after station was considered, their thoughts quickened meanwhile by the scene outspread before them – the homes of no fewer than two million people being gathered at that confluence of the mighty Yangtze with the Han. Thus it was the thought dawned, overwhelming almost in its greatness. Fifty to sixty new workers? Why, the entire membership of the Mission was barely 100! But fifty or sixty, at the lowest computation, would be all too few. '*Other seventy also*', came to Taylor's mind: 'the Lord appointed other seventy also, and sent them. . . .'

They did not run away with the new idea all at once. Several prayer meetings and quiet consultations were held before they came to feel liberty and confidence in asking the Lord for seventy new fellow-workers. Three years was agreed upon as the period in which the answer should be looked for, as it would hardly be possible to receive and arrange for so many new workers in a shorter time.

'If only we could meet again and have a united praise meeting when the last of the Seventy has reached China!' said one.

'We shall be widely scattered then,' said another with a practical turn of mind. 'But why not have the praise meeting now? Why not give thanks for the Seventy before we separate?'

So the meeting was held, and those who had joined in the prayer joined in the thanksgiving also, with which the answer was received – in faith.

From that time on the prayer for reinforcements was taken up throughout the Mission. In the scene of his early labours at Ningpo, Hudson Taylor drafted an appeal to the home churches which in due course was signed by seventy-seven members of the Mission in China. The sense of responsibility that lay behind it, as well as its quiet confidence in God, may be judged from the following extracts:

> Souls on every hand are perishing for lack of knowledge; more than 1,000 every hour are passing away into death and darkness. Provinces in China compare in area with kingdoms in Europe, and average between ten and twenty millions in population. One province has no missionary; in each of two other provinces there is only one missionary and his wife resident; and none are sufficiently supplied with labourers. Can we leave matters thus without incurring the sin of blood-guiltiness?

After requesting prayer for more workers 'in connection with every Protestant missionary society on both sides of the Atlantic', the needs of the C.I.M. were specially referred to.

> A careful survey of the spiritual work to which we ourselves are called has led us to feel the importance of immediate and large reinforcements, and many of us are daily pleading with God in agreed prayer for forty-two additional men and twenty-eight additional women. We ask our brothers and sisters in Christ at home to join us in praying the Lord of the Harvest to thrust out this 'other seventy also'. We are not anxious as to the means for sending them forth or sustaining them. *He* has told us to look to the birds and flowers, and to take no thought for these things, but to seek first the kingdom of God and His righteousness, and that all these things shall be added unto us. But we *are* concerned that only men and women called of God, fully consecrated to Him, and counting everything precious as dross and dung 'for the excellency of the knowledge of Christ Jesus my Lord', should come out to join us; and we would add to this appeal a word of caution and encouragement, to any who may feel drawn to offer themselves for this blessed work. Of *caution*, urging such to count the cost; to wait prayerfully on God; to ask themselves whether they *will* really trust Him for *everything*, wherever He may call them to go. Mere romantic feeling will soon die out amid the toilsome labour and constant discomforts and trials of inland work, and will not be worth much when severe illness arises and perhaps all the money is gone. Faith in the living God alone gives joy and rest in such circumstances. But a word also of *encouragement*, for we ourselves have proved God's faithfulness and the blessedness of dependence on Him. He is supplying and ever has supplied all our need. And if not seldom we have fellowship in poverty with Him who for our sakes became poor, shall we not rejoice if the Day prove that we have

been, like the great missionary Apostle, 'poor, yet making many rich; as having nothing, and yet possessing all things'? He makes us very happy in His service, and those of us who have children desire nothing better for them, should the Lord tarry, than that they may be called to similar work and similar joys.

(Shortly before this was written, Hudson Taylor had welcomed his eldest son to China.)

What should we not expect from 1882 after this beginning, with the prayer for the Seventy being taken up in such a spirit throughout the Mission? Should we not confidently look for a rising tide of spiritual blessing both at home and in China, and that Taylor especially, as representing the movement, should be led on from strength to strength? Perhaps a deeper knowledge not only of the 'acts' but of the 'ways' of God would modify such expectations, and lessen the surprise with which one finds the reality to have been very different. In England as in China, difficulties did not lessen. Working to the limit of his powers, Benjamin Broomhall was not able to report any decided increase either of funds or of service. Eleven new workers were sent out, but three only of the number were men, when five times as many had been hoped for. So great was the trial as to shortness of supplies that Taylor could scarcely wonder at the retirement of one and another from the Mission whom he knew to be loosely attached to its principles. Government posts were to be had at a salary of £50 a month, in which it was easy to think that exceptional opportunities for usefulness would be found. Most disturbing of all, the work in some important stations seemed to be going back rather than forward.

Faith was thus thrown into the crucible in many ways. Weaknesses were brought out with startling clearness – need of spiritual power, of organization, of leaders of more calibre. With answered prayer on the one hand as to the opening up of inland China, and a growing faith for large reinforcements on the other, they were forced to a realization of the utter inadequacy of existing arrangements to carry on the work even as it was. In and through it all, Taylor himself was assailed by depression, loneliness and forebodings.

Yet there were gleams of brightness, all the more welcome for the shadows, and some outstanding experiences that told of a deepening work of God. Memorable among these was the Conference lasting for several days at Anking in June. Seven months had now elapsed since in a similar gathering the decision had been reached to ask in faith for seventy new fellow-workers, and to this little company on their knees at Anking came a wonderful confirmation of their convictions as to that purpose.

'We have had a day of united fasting and prayer today,' Taylor wrote on June 30, 'and a wonderful time of blessing it has been. The Holy Spirit seemed so to fill us this morning that several of us felt as if we could not *bear* any more.'

One cannot but trace the rising tide of spiritual blessing that began to make itself felt, to the waiting upon God of this and of other special meetings toward the close of the year. Taylor paid another visit to the district in which a few months previously he had found so much to discourage. Then he had written of his efforts being all or 'nearly all in vain, so far as this part of the work is concerned'. Now, baptized afresh with a spirit of love, he found his way to hearts that had seemed closed against him, and a work of grace was the result, that was not only to save valuable workers from being lost to the Mission, but was to set them in its front rank as soul-winners.

It was at Chefoo that the later months of the year were spent and some of its most important work accomplished and Taylor began to see his way at length to returning to England. Faith was encouraged by definite answers to prayer in the matter of funds. Early in October, for example, they were looking with special expectancy for the home remittance.

> We were at table, when we received our letters (the home mail); and when on opening one of them I found, instead of seven or eight hundred pounds for the month's supplies, only £96 9s. 5d, my feelings I shall not soon forget!
>
> I closed the envelope again and, seeking my room, knelt down and spread the letter before the Lord, asking Him what *was* to be done with less than £97 – a sum it was impossible to distribute over seventy stations in which were eighty or ninety missionaries, including their wives, not to speak of about 100 Chinese helpers, and children to be fed and clothed in our schools. Having first rolled the burden on the Lord, I then mentioned the matter to others of our own Mission in Chefoo, and we unitedly looked to Him to come to our aid; but no hint as to our circumstances was allowed to reach anyone outside.
>
> Soon the answers began to come – kind gifts from local friends who little knew the peculiar value of their donations, and help in other ways, until the needs of the month were all met without our having been burdened with anxious thought even for an hour. We had similar experiences in November and again in December; and on each occasion, after spreading the letter before the Lord and leaving the burden with Him, we were 'helped'. Thus the Lord made our hearts sing for joy, and provided through local contributions in China for the needs of the work as never before or since.

Encouraged in this way, the little circle at Chefoo were the more prepared for Taylor's suggestion that they should unite in asking some definite 'token for good' of the same sort to strengthen faith at home. Letters received had shown how really concerned were some of the workers and friends of the Mission as to the appeal for the Seventy. It had been kept in the background as much as possible, just because it seemed too great an advance to contemplate at such a time; and Taylor, who by no means ignored the difficulty, felt it laid on his heart to ask the Lord to put His seal upon the matter in a way that could not be mistaken. It was at one of the daily prayer meetings at Chefoo, on or about February 1st, 1883, and the few who were present were conscious of much liberty in laying their request before God. Recalling the occasion Taylor wrote,

> We knew that our Father loves to please His children. What father does not? And we asked Him lovingly to please us, as well as to encourage timid ones at home, by leading some one of His wealthy stewards to make room for a large blessing for himself and his family by giving liberally to this special object.

No account of that special prayer meeting had been written home, nor could a letter of that date have reached London until the end of March. But at Pyrland Road on *February 2nd* a sum of £3,000 was received for work in China.

Meanwhile Taylor was on his way back to England and, on landing at Marseilles, took the opportunity of visiting the Bergers at Cannes.

> The April *China's Millions* there came to hand, and I found in the list of donations this £3,000, acknowledged under the date of February 2, with the text, 'Ask of me, and I will give thee the heathen for thine inheritance, and the uttermost parts of the earth for thy possession', as follows:

Father..	£1,000
Mother	1,000
Mary	200
Rosie	200
Bertie	200
Amy	200
Henry	200
	£3,000

> It was most striking to see how literally God had fulfilled our prayer, and led His faithful steward to *make room for a large blessing for himself and his family*. Never before was a donation sent to us in such a way, and never since, save on one occasion, a year and five months later, when a donation for the same fund is entered thus in *China's Millions:*

Father..	£200
Mother	200
Mary	100
Rosie	100
Bertie	100
Amy	100
Henry	100
Baby	100
	£1,000

A beautiful instance, this, of a father who seeks that each member of his family should have 'treasure in heaven'.

Reaching home at the end of March, Taylor soon noticed the new position accorded to the Mission in the esteem of the Christian public. The eight years of Benjamin Broomhall's unwearied labours had told especially in the direction which was his forte – that of inspiring confidence and making friends. In many parts of the country people were wanting to hear of the achievements of the pioneers, and how they had effected a settled residence inland. Meetings, therefore, soon claimed the leader of the Mission.

'When he was speaking,' one recalled, 'you could be quite sure that, whatever else he might say, he would make no plea for funds. His great desire was that no funds should be diverted from other societies to the China Inland Mission. Nothing gave him more genuine pleasure than to speak well of other Missions.

'Oh, the dignified way in which his life of faith was lived out, the reality of it all! Instead of wanting to get anything out of you, he was always ready to give to you.'

At a conference in Salisbury no reference was made to the China Inland Mission. It was for *China* that lives were consecrated and money flowed in. In spite of there being no collection, people emptied their purses, stripped themselves of their jewels, handed over watches, chains, rings and the like, and gave their lives to God for His service.

Fifteen or sixteen offers for the mission field were the result, and a whole jewelry case was sent in next day. People had received so much that they felt they could give anything.

Fully as were Taylor's time and strength occupied in these ways, he was quietly seeking light upon how to prepare for the larger growth that was coming in the Mission. In August he sent out a carefully considered letter to all the members, stating what was proposed and asking their judgment.

Our home arrangement of assisting the Director by a Council may be introduced in China; the members of that Council may themselves be Superintendents of districts, in which capacity they may in their turn be assisted by district Councils of our missionaries. In all this no new principle will be introduced, yet our work will be rendered capable of indefinite expansion while maintaining its original character. Many local matters can thus be locally considered and attended to without delay, and local as well as general developments will be facilitated. I have hitherto had the opportunity of conferring only with those of our number who might be within reach, and that at irregular intervals. The plan I now propose will, through the district Superintendents, bring me into conference with all our missionaries of experience, and will secure an increasingly effective supervision of the whole work.

Meanwhile, away in China, Dr. Harold Schofield, stricken with a malignant fever, had laid down his life after only three years on the mission field. On the face of it there seems little connection between that fact and the special developments of 1883 and 1884. Why recall Harold Schofield's short-lived service, brilliant and self-sacrificing though it undoubtedly was? Only this – that Schofield died *praying*. During all the later months of his life his chief preoccupation had been prayer. For this he would leave wife and children, denying himself rest and recreation, and making time at any cost for waiting upon God. And the petition he urged with special fervency was that God would touch the young life of our universities, and raise up men of gifts and education for His work among the heathen. There was no Student Christian Federation in those days, no Volunteer Movement in any of the colleges. Himself a distinguished prizeman, who had taken more than £1,400 in scholarships, he knew well the value of thorough mental training; and remembering all that had been said in his own case about 'sacrifice of brilliant prospects', he prayed for a new spirit to come over Christian thinking, more in harmony with Him who 'made himself of no reputation' that dying souls might live.

The prayers of those last months had not been in vain. News of his death, though cabled to England, did not reach Taylor immediately, but *that very day* a letter came to him in the north of England that one cannot but connect with Dr. Schofield's prayers. It was from a young officer in the Royal Artillery asking for an interview, signing the name that, little as either of them could suppose it, was in due course to replace Hudson Taylor's own. D. E. Hoste writing from Sandown Fort in July, Stanley P. Smith coming up from Trinity College and his exploits on the river, these and the others who joined them making the well-known 'Cambridge Seven',[1] whose going out awakened a new spirit indeed throughout the universities of the United Kingdom and America, and through them of the world – what were they but the answers to those sacred pleadings in which a believing heart had entered into fellowship with God?

It came about very naturally. In his *History of the Church Missionary Society*, Dr. Eugene Stock speaks of 'the extraordinary interest aroused in the autumn of 1884 by the announcement that the captain of the Cambridge Eleven and the stroke oar of the Cambridge boat were going out as missionaries'. When the news reached Edinburgh it deeply stirred a group of medical students who for some months had been burdened about the indifference to spiritual things in the university, especially among their fellow medicals. A series of remarkable meetings had just been held at Oxford and Cambridge in which Hudson Taylor and several of the outgoing party

[1] D. E. Hoste, Stanley P. Smith, C. T. Studd, Montagu Beauchamp, W. W. Cassels, C. P. Polhill, A. T. Polhill.

had won the sympathies of the undergraduates for foreign missions as never before. Could they not come to Edinburgh also?

'Many had heard of Stanley Smith,' wrote Professor Charteris, 'and to everyone who knew anything of cricket the name of Studd was familiar. And so the word went round our classrooms, "Let us go and give the athlete missionaries a welcome!"

'The men gathered – about 1,000. Smith would have made his mark as an orator anywhere. Studd has not the gifts of an orator, but he never went more straight at the mark in the cricket field than he did in his narrative of the way God had led him for years, from stage to stage of the Christian life, until he was ready to forsake father and mother, home and friends, because of his love for his Redeemer.

'The students were spellbound. Those two speakers were so manly – types indeed of handsome, healthy manhood – were so happy, spoke in such unconventional style, that when they had done, hundreds of students crowded round them to grasp their hand, followed them to the train by which they were going right off to London, and were on the platform saying "God speed you", when the train steamed away.'

As further meetings were planned, it was becoming clear to Taylor that the hand of God was in the movement. He had seen the influence of the Seven not over students only, but over leaders of Christian life and thought.

'The gift from God of such a band to the China Inland Mission,' wrote the Editorial Secretary of the C.M.S., 'was a just reward to Mr. Hudson Taylor and his colleagues for the genuine unselfishness with which they had always pleaded the cause of China and the world, and not of their own particular organization, and for the deep spirituality which had always marked their meetings. And that spirituality marked most emphatically the densely crowded meetings in different places at which the seven men said farewell. They told, modestly and yet fearlessly, of the Lord's goodness to them, and of the joy of serving Him; and they appealed to young men, not for their Mission, but for their Divine Master. No such missionary meeting had ever been known as the final gathering at Exeter Hall on February 4, 1885. We have become familiar since then with meetings more or less of the same type, but it was a new thing then.'

It was not in public gatherings, however, that these men were knit to their leader and the Mission with which they had cast in their lot. It was behind the scenes in quiet hours the work was done, and chiefly in times of prayer at Pyrland Road, as on the last day of 1884. There was no disguising on these occasions the poverty, as far as material resources were concerned, of the Mission that had closed its latest balance sheet with only £10 in hand – '£10 and all the promises of God'. But how small a matter this seemed with the presence of the Lord Himself so consciously felt!

When Taylor left London three weeks later to go ahead to Shanghai, some of the party were again in Scotland, rejoicing to tell of all the wealth they were finding in deeper fellowship with Christ, which so far outweighed anything of worldly advantage they were laying down. And in a blinding snow-storm, as he crossed France alone, the traveller's heart was full of praise for news received only that morning from the northern capital: '2,000 students last night – wonderful times! It is the Lord.'

CHAPTER 21

Days of Blessing

(1885–1886)

As he neared Shanghai some weeks later, Hudson Taylor was very conscious of the responsibilities that lay before him. He hoped to give effect, on this sixth visit, to the plans for organization that had been maturing in his mind, by appointing someone who could be associated with himself as Deputy Director, as well as Superintendents to help recruits. Any delegation of his authority was apt to be regarded with misgivings, however. The family feeling in the Mission had been very precious to its early workers, who were accustomed to dealing with him direct about every matter in which advice and help were needed. Much more difficulty lay in the way of associating others with himself in these responsibilities than he had anticipated; but the appointment of Superintendents for a number of provinces, and the better ordering of business and financial matters, were part of the outcome of his labours in 1885.

It was not until the close of the year that he saw who could be his Deputy. Then, with an exceptional record of varied and useful service behind him, Stevenson returned to China, landing on Christmas Eve after an absence of ten and a half years in Burma and elsewhere.

> 'The Rev. J. W. Stevenson has, I am thankful to say, accepted the position of Director's Deputy,' Taylor wrote in March (1886) to the members of the Mission. 'He will assist, *D.V.*, by visiting for me many places I cannot reach; will represent me in my absence from China, and deal with all questions brought before him by the Superintendents requiring immediate determination. I feel sure you will all share with me in thankfulness to God for this appointment, and feel that it is one of the most important steps in advance that we have recently been able to make.'

Shortly after sending out this letter he set off to visit a centre in Chekiang, and decided to cross the watershed into the neighbouring province of Kiangsi and return by the Poyang Lake. Hoping that the complete change of boat life would help to restore strength to one of the Yangchow missionaries who had been dangerously ill, he arranged for her and several younger women workers to accompany him.

Thus, then, the months of May and June (1886) brought to that long-waiting district the loving hearts and earnest, prayerful lives that were to become its channels of Divine blessing. Six years had passed since Taylor on his previous visit had met the converts gathered in through the labours of Captain Yü in the neighbourhood of Yüshan. The little out-stations he had visited then among the hills and down the river were out-stations still, and had rarely seen even a passing missionary. Recently, however, a young worker, a girl of only twenty, had come to spend a few days' holiday in that beautiful region. She stayed with the evangelist and his wife, sleeping in an attic to which she climbed by a ladder-like stair. But neither this nor any other consideration could keep visitors away, and from morning till night her room was besieged by women and children. Warm-hearted Agnes Gibson welcomed them all, and spent her much-needed 'holiday' in telling the old, old story.

The result was that Taylor found a marked change in the Sunday services. On his previous visit the Christians had been all and only men; and so bitter was the opposition of their women-folk that they had even rented a room for themselves, where they might read and pray undisturbed. Now, however, the women were as much in evidence as the men, and a deputation of the latter waited upon him to point the moral.

'We want a missionary of our own,' they said, 'and we want a *woman*. If one visit of a week could bring about such a change, what might not be accomplished if we had a lady-teacher all the time?'

This was unanswerable. As he travelled down the Kwangsin river and saw the welcome with which the women missionaries travelling with him were received everywhere, he realized that the time had come, and that the Lord had sent His own messengers. Going forward therefore in faith, he arranged for three of them to return with an older worker, and settle down among the Chinese Christians, making the evangelization of this populous region their life-work. Within the first year of women's work on the Kwangsin river forty-two additional converts were baptized, and eventually in a complete chain of ten central stations and sixty out-stations, women were the only foreign missionaries.

Returning to Shanghai after six weeks' absence, Taylor arrived on the very last day of an option obtained upon a building site in the Settlement, admirably situated for the purposes of the Mission. The price, however, was almost £2,500, and he had not money in hand to justify the purchase. If lost, the opportunity would never recur; yet what was to be done?

One thing at any rate was possible: the whole matter could be laid before the Lord in definite, united prayer, with the assurance that He would deal with it in the way that was best. This then they did at the noon prayer meeting (June 14) when no outsiders were present; and then and there the answer was given.

Among the party just arrived from home was one who had been interested in China through John McCarthy's meetings in Scotland two years previously. Large business responsibilities rested upon him at that time, and it was not until he could see how these were to be cared for that he felt free to join the China Inland Mission. Unexpected delays in his coming out had coincided with delays in Taylor's northern journey, so that the two met in Shanghai on the very day in question, met one might almost say in that prayer meeting. The outcome was a gift sufficient to cover the purchase of the entire property, followed (though that was a later thought) by the still larger gift of all the buildings necessary to make it the most complete and serviceable of headquarters. It was a wonderful provision, a wonderful answer to prayer, and a wonderful anticipation of the enlargement in the Mission that was at hand.

For seven years Taylor had been planning to visit Shansi. Once he had even set out, only to be recalled by claims at the coast. But now the better organization of the Mission permitting an absence of several months from Shanghai, he hoped to strengthen the work in regions lying farther inland. Each station to be visited had its problems, but greatest of all was the question how to evangelize the vast population to which the missionaries now had access. To bring help and encouragement to these lonely toilers was his chief object, and to confer with them about the organization of the Chinese Church, which in some places was growing rapidly. It was also his hope to establish a Church of England district in the great western province of Szechwan, a matter which had long been under consideration. In the Rev. W. W. Cassels the Mission had for the first time one qualified to take the lead in such an enterprise, and Szechwan with its sixty-eight millions had as yet only two centres in which Protestant missionaries were to be found. Cassels with four others of the Cambridge party had been gaining experience in Shansi and they went up to Taiyuan-fu, the capital, to meet Taylor for a few days of conference from their centres, full of the problems that press upon young missionaries in the midst of a large and growing work.

Some echoes of the conference may be gathered from suggestions made by Taylor as to the relation of the missionary to his work:

> How can we secure the development of strong, healthy, Christlike native Christians unless we are living strong, healthy, Christlike lives ourselves?
>
> What the spiritual children will be depends on what the spiritual father is. The stream will never rise higher than its source, but it will not fall far short of it, circumstances permitting. The hardness of heart which is a hindrance to the Gospel is not that of the hearers; it is the hardness of this heart of mine.

On the need for contact, close and real, not only with the Lord Himself but with those whose good we seek, he dwelt with insistence.

There is power in drawing near to this people. A poor woman in Chengtu, when she heard of Mrs. Riley's death, said: 'What a loss to us! *She used to take hold of my hand* and comfort me so.' If you put your hand on the shoulder of a man, there is power in it. Any Christian, full of the Holy Ghost, may often impart blessing thus. Contact is a real power that we may use for God.

It is not preaching only that will do what needs to be done. Our life must be one of visible self-sacrifice. There is much sacrifice in our lives of which the Chinese cannot know. That will not suffice. They must *see self-sacrifice* in things they cannot but understand.

It was in that city (Taiyuan-fu) where the blood of martyrs was to be so freely shed that Taylor dwelt much upon the necessity for sacrifice, and the certainty not only that persecution must come, but that it would be overruled for blessing.

There is no better way of proving to the world that the devil's power is not so great after all than by letting him have his fling, and showing in the midst of it what a triumph over him the believer has in Christ. Just as Jesus, by dying, conquered him who had the power of death, so frail, feeble martyrs, many of them women, were able to show that all the power of pagan Rome could do *nothing* against those who were filled with Christ. Hence there were many conversions in the very arena, and the blood of the martyrs proved itself to be indeed the seed of the Church. Their foes thought they had succeeded; it was even announced in their edicts that Christianity was defunct; but it was paganism that tottered.

We need not be afraid of persecution. *It is coming; it is sure to come.* Only let us have such success as to make the people fear the abolition of their customs, and we shall see severe persecution. But are we to fear lest the Gospel should triumph sufficiently to bring such results about?

With all his desire that the gifts of the Chinese Church should be developed, Taylor was keenly conscious of the danger of allowing education, medical work or any other auxiliary to usurp the foremost place.

To substitute medicine for the preaching of the Gospel would be a profound mistake. If we get the idea that people are going to be converted by some educational *process*, instead of by a regenerative re-creation, it will be a profound mistake. Let all our auxiliaries be auxiliaries – means of bringing Christ and the soul into contact – then we may be truly thankful for them all. Let us exalt the glorious Gospel in our hearts, and believe that *it* is the power of God unto salvation.

In its practical influence on Christian character, Taylor felt that the truth of the Second Coming – the personal return of the Lord Himself to reign upon earth – was of paramount importance.

You will often read in missionary reports that the people have turned to God from idols, to serve the living and true God, but not in one out of ten do you hear anything about their waiting for His Son from Heaven (1 Thess. 1.9).

Well do I remember the effect, when God was pleased to open my own heart to this great truth that the Lord Jesus was coming again, and that He might come *at any time*. I had not many books, but it sent me to see if I could give a good account of *all* I had, and also of the contents of my little wardrobe. The result was that some of the books disappeared before long, and some of the clothing too. It was an immense spiritual blessing to me.

Very practical, too, was his attitude as to the fullness laid up for us in Christ.

God is willing to give us all we need, as we need it. He does not equip for life-service *all at once*. . . . And whatever the sufficiency of Christ is for *us*, there is the same sufficiency in Him for our converts.

Refreshed in spirit, the workers from the south of the province hastened back to their stations after this week of meetings, Taylor and his companions following a few weeks later. They arrived in Hungtung on July 30th to find the Hungtung Christians assembled in force for the conference at which Mr. Hsi, the ex-Confucian scholar, was to be ordained, while others were appointed deacons and elders. These men, full of their first love and zeal, had been sounding out the message of salvation far and wide. What it was to Taylor to meet them and see for himself the inspiring work of which he had heard, may be better imagined than described. It was a wonderful meeting, that first day of the conference, when he and Mr. Hsi took the Sunday morning service between them.

'There cannot have been fewer than 300 listeners in the court,' wrote Stanley Smith. 'It made our hearts glad to think of Mr. Taylor's joy as he saw those earnest worshippers, and in that sight *some* outcome of years of prayer that has known no ceasing, and labour that has known no respite; above all, it raised our hearts to Him who in that gathering was seeing further of the travail of His soul and being satisfied.'

It was not easy to get Mr. Hsi to accept the position to which the leader of the Mission wished to appoint him, so deep was his sense of unworthiness. But when it was pointed out that Taylor was but confirming what was manifestly a Divine appointment, he could no longer demur. From that Saturday until the Ordination Service of the following Monday he gave himself to fasting and prayer, literally touching no food; and the sense of the presence of God with him was deeply solemnizing.

'Mr. Hudson Taylor, inviting the brethren working in the district to unite with him in the laying on of hands,' Stanley Smith recorded, 'after a few words of fervent prayer, set him apart to be a watcher over and feeder of the sheep of God. Mr. Hsi was ordained pastor of no particular district. He has done such an extensive work and been so owned of God, that it was thought best that he should be free to go anywhere for the work of God in these parts, knowing well how he would be welcomed by all the churches. Mr. Song was then set apart as Chinese pastor of the Pingyang church.'

The appointment of two elders and of sixteen deacons followed, after which over seventy baptized believers united in the Communion Service led by Pastor Hsi.

One day's journey farther south – at Pingyang-fu – another conference was held, with the ordination of Ch'ü, the fervent and scholarly evangelist of the Ta-ning district, and the appointment of five deacons. After that Taylor had to turn his face westward for the long journey to Hanchung-fu.

A brief visit first to Pastor Hsi's home, ten miles across the plain, gave him the opportunity of seeing more of this remarkable man and the Opium Refuge work for which he was responsible. Accompanied by quite a party, Taylor arrived in the cool of the day.[1] Everything was beautifully arranged for their coming, the guest hall being fitted up as a state chamber, and the courtyard on which it opened covered with an awning that it might do duty as a chapel. Here the principal meetings were held, the joy on all faces reflecting the golden characters of welcome above the guest hall, shining out from their crimson background – '*Ta Hsi Nien*', or 'Year of Great Happiness'.

Perhaps the most moving part of the visit to Taylor was the account he heard of the opening of a Refuge in one of the cities he had passed on his journey through the province. The place had long been on Pastor Hsi's heart, though he little anticipated the way in which his desire to commence work there was to be granted. Having no means in hand that he could use for the purpose, he prayed the more earnestly day by day at family worship that the Gospel might be given to the Christless population of Hwochow.

'We have prayed very often for that city,' his wife said at length, 'is it not time to *do* something there?'

'Gladly would I,' responded her husband, 'but money is lacking. I have nothing to use for the purpose, and renting houses is expensive.'

'How much would it require?' was her next question. And on hearing his reply she went away and said no more about it.

But she too could not forget Hwochow; and next morning it was an unadorned little figure that came up and laid some packages on the table after family worship.

[1] Dr. Edwards, Stevenson, Stanley Smith, and Beauchamp were with him, as well as his son, Herbert Taylor, who had been his companion all the way from Shanghai.

'I think,' she said, 'that God has answered our prayers about that city.'

Missing something in her appearance as well as being surprised at her words, Pastor Hsi opened one of the packets, to find nothing less than all her jewellery – the gold and silver ornaments, bracelets, rings, and even hair-pins so indispensable to a Chinese lady and that form her marriage dower.

'You cannot surely mean,' he began, 'you cannot do without –"

'Yes, I can,' she said joyfully. 'I can do without these: *let Hwochow have the Gospel.*'

And with the money they had brought, the Refuge had been opened and a good work begun.

It was hard to leave such fruitful fields ready for the reaper and go on to where there was no sign of harvest. Studd and Beauchamp were going on with Taylor to take part in opening up the Church of England district he hoped to arrange for in Szechwan, and Cassels was to follow shortly. During twenty-four travelling days not a single Mission station was passed, because in all that populous region there was none.

Taylor's cheerfulness and power of endurance greatly impressed his fellow-travellers. Hearing him singing on one occasion when they were very hungry, and catching the words 'We thank Thee, Lord, for this our food', Beauchamp could not but inquire where the food was.

'It cannot be far away,' was the smiling reply. 'Our Father knows we are hungry and will send our breakfast soon: but *you* will have to wait and say your grace when it comes, while *I* shall be ready to begin at once!'

And so it proved; for just ahead they met a man with ready-cooked rice to sell, which made an excellent meal.

But the soul never went hungry. A box of matches, a foreign candle, and his Bible in four small volumes were included in Taylor's travelling kit whatever else had to be left behind.

> 'He would invariably get his quiet time an hour before dawn,' Beauchamp wrote, 'and then possibly sleep again. When I woke to feed the animals I always found him reading the Bible by the light of his candle. No matter what the surroundings or the noise in those dirty inns, he never neglected this. He used to pray on such journeys lying down, for he usually spent long times in prayer, and to kneel would have been too exhausting.'

With regard to the denominational position of the Mission, Taylor had written as early as 1866 (a few weeks only after the arrival of the *Lammermuir* party), in reply to an inquiry from the Rev. W. Muirhead of the L.M.S., Shanghai:

> Those already associated with me represent all the leading denominations of our native land – Episcopal, Presbyterian, Congregational, Methodist, Baptist and

Paedobaptist. Besides these, two are or have been connected with the 'Brethren' so-called. It is intended that those whose view of discipline corresponds shall work together, and thus all difficulty on that score will be avoided. Each one is perfectly at liberty to teach his own views on these minor points to his own converts; the one great object we have in view being to bring heathen from darkness to light, from the power of Satan to God. We all hold alike the great fundamentals of our faith, and in the presence of *heathenism* can leave the discussion of discipline while together, and act as before God when in separate stations.

For the moment, the outlook was not encouraging. The travellers had reached Hanchung when they learned that a serious riot had taken place at Chungking – one of the only two centres in Szechwan at which Protestant missionaries were working. At the same time tidings received from the coast made it clear that he must return to Shanghai as soon as possible. Mission affairs required his presence, and he was still a month's journey from civilization in the shape of a foreign steamer. But though he had to leave the actual pioneering in Szechwan to others, a day was set apart for fasting and prayer, when Taylor united with the Hanchung circle in seeking the guidance of the Holy Spirit and a fresh baptism of love and power upon those who were to go forward and who did, in fact, occupy eastern Szechwan before the end of the year.

CHAPTER 22

The Hundred

(1886–1888)

The Mission was still very young. It had been founded little more than twenty years, and out of a total of 187 no fewer than 110 were junior missionaries. Nearly two years had passed since Taylor had come out in advance of the Cambridge Seven, but the way was not yet clear for his return to England. The chief object before him was the formation of a Council in China, and the year 1886 was drawing to a close when the Superintendents of the various provinces gathered for the first meeting. J. W. Stevenson, in his new capacity as Deputy Director, had just returned from an inland journey, full of enthusiasm over what he had seen in the northern provinces. Coming freshly into responsibilities that Taylor had been bearing for years, he brought with him an accession of hope and courage.

'We all saw visions at that time,' he himself recalled. 'Those were days of Heaven upon earth; nothing seemed difficult.' It was this spirit of faith and expectancy which launched the Mission upon a new enterprise in which to prove again the faithfulness of God. Up in Shansi it had begun, when Stevenson had written from the capital:

> We are greatly encouraged out here, and are asking and receiving definite blessings for this hungry and thirsty land. We are fully expecting at least 100 fresh labourers to arrive in China in 1887.

It was the first suggestion of the Hundred. Ardent and full of confidence in God, Stevenson kept the matter to the fore on his return to Shanghai nd in the Council Meetings, but Taylor seems at first to have shared the general impression that this was going rather too fast. 100 new workers in one year, when the entire staff of the Mission was less than twice that number – why, even if the men and women were forthcoming, think of the additional expenditure involved!

'Yes,' urged the Deputy Director, 'but with needs so great how can we ask for less?'

That was difficult to answer. For fifty central stations and many outstations in which resident missionaries were needed, not to speak of China open from end to end, made 100 new workers even in one year seem but a small number.

Such was the atmosphere of faith and prayer that the thought could strike root. Before long Taylor was writing home quite naturally:

> We are praying for 100 new missionaries in 1887. The Lord help in the selection and provide the means.

A little later he was working at accounts, etc. with a view to leaving for England as soon as possible, when an incident occurred that fanned expectancy to a flame. He was dictating to his secretary, walking up and down the room as was his wont, when he repeated in one of his letters what he had written above: 'We are praying for and expecting 100 new missionaries to come out in 1887.' Did he really mean it? Stevenson saw the secretary, a young man who was himself to be one of the Hundred, look up with an incredulous smile. 'If the Lord should make windows in heaven', that look seemed to say, 'then might this thing be.' Hudson Taylor saw it too, and immediately caught fire!

> 'After that, he went beyond me altogether!' recalled Stevenson. 'Never shall I forget the conviction with which he said:
>
> ' "If you showed me a photograph of the whole Hundred, taken in China, I could not be more sure than I am now."
>
> 'Then I sent out a little slip throughout the Mission: "Will you put down your name to pray for the Hundred?" and cabled to London with Mr. Taylor's permission: "Praying for a hundred new missionaries in 1887".'

Thus the step was taken, and the Mission committed to a programme that might well have startled even its nearest friends. Yet it was in no spirit of rashness or merely human energy. Far too deeply had Taylor learned the lessons of experience to embark upon such an enterprise without the assurance that he was being led of God. To an inner circle of friends he wrote in December:

> Will you help us in prayer as often as you can? This movement will involve great responsibility and much toil, time, and expense. Much correspondence about the candidates will be needed; much prayer and thought about which of them to accept and which to decline. The labour of arranging for and attending farewell meetings, to secure the prayers of at least six congregations for each party that comes out, will be great. Outfits and passages for 100 people will come to £5,500, and travelling expenses for many of them from distant parts of Great Britain and Ireland, as well as the cost of board in London, will materially add to this sum. The money, much of it, will come to our office at Pyrland Road in small gifts, each calling for a letter of thanks, which will involve additional help in correspondence, etc. So we shall have much need of Divine guidance, help, and strength, all of which He will supply, but for which He will be enquired of.

Am I wrong then in asking your prayers for myself and for those who will be associated with me in this important work? As I look forward in faith and think of the 'willing, skilful' men and women who are coming – of the barren fields they will help to till, of the souls they will be the means of saving, and above all of the joy of our Redeemer in this movement and its widespread issues – my heart is very glad, and I think yours will be too.

It was this vision, this spirit of joy that upheld him through all the wonderful and strenuous days of 1887. And what a year it was! It was preceded by two days of prayer – 'We need two days at least. We have much to praise for, but Satan will be busy, and we must be prepared by living near to God.' With growing courage Taylor and those associated with him were led to pray for £10,000 of additional income, as necessary to meet the increased expenses; and that it might be given in large gifts, so that the home staff should not be overwhelmed with correspondence. The year ended with the last party of the Hundred on their way to China, all expenses met, not ten but eleven thousand pounds of extra income having been received, *the whole coming in just eleven gifts!*

That, briefly, is what happened, but it did not all come about so simply. 'We want workers, not loiterers,' was one of the first things Taylor wrote after his return to England, and he certainly set an example by his own unparalleled labours throughout that year. With brief intervals for correspondence and Council meetings he was travelling and speaking all the time. The letters he wrote during the year averaged thirteen or fourteen for every day of the twelve months, Sundays excepted. And these were not business notes, or mainly to do with his programme of meetings. They were many of them long, thoughtful letters to Stevenson about the direction of affairs in China; answers to correspondence sent on to him from the field, which required careful consideration; and replies to people who consulted him about spiritual and other difficulties, having been helped through the meetings.

Three visits to Ireland and four to Scotland, an extensive campaign on the subject of World Evangelization, and attendance at no fewer than *twenty* conventions for the deepening of spiritual life, in most of which Taylor spoke repeatedly, were but part of his outward activities. Besides these there were farewell meetings in churches of all denominations, as party after party went out, and frequent addresses in drawing-rooms or from the pulpit to the circles the young missionaries represented. Then the Council was so busy with those who came before them in London, that they had occasionally to meet twice and three times a week, to get through the work.

'We were in Glasgow last week,' wrote Jennie Taylor in March, 'holding one, two, or three meetings every day; and my husband had conversations with forty candidates.'

And in Edinburgh, at the very time she was writing, he was dealing with twenty more. At one meeting in the Scottish capital, so deep was the interest that 120 people definitely offered themselves for foreign missionary work, to go or stay as God might lead.

At Pyrland Road, meanwhile, Benjamin Broomhall was no less busy and encouraged. Invited to breakfast with a friend in London early in the year he found himself one of several guests who had at heart the interests of the kingdom of God. Conversation turning on the C.I.M., Broomhall took from his pocket a letter which had touched him deeply. It was from a poor widow in Scotland who, with only a few shillings a week to live upon, frequently sent gifts for the work in China. She could do without meat, she said, but the heathen could not do without the Gospel. Very real was the self-denial that lay behind the simple words, and very real the prayers with which the modest gifts were accompanied. This it was, doubtless, that led to results from that letter far beyond anything the writer can have asked or thought.

At the close of the meal, the host said that all he had ever given to the work of God (and he had given much) had never cost him a mutton-chop. His interest had been chiefly in home missions, but he wanted now to forward the evangelization of China. And to Broomhall's surprise, he then and there promised £500 for the work of the C.I.M. A little further conversation round the table led to similar promises from three of the guests, while another who had been unable to come, upon hearing what had transpired made up the sum to £2,500. And on the twenty-first anniversary of the sailing of the *Lammermuir* party, a letter from Mr. Berger came as a token for good, bringing a gift of £500 – the second or third he had given – toward the outgoing Hundred.

No wonder Hudson Taylor began his address at the Anniversary Meetings by recalling the quaint saying of a well-known coloured evangelist: 'When God does anything, He does it handsome!' That very morning another cable had been received from China, announcing a donation of £1,000 toward the expenses of the Hundred – fifty-four of whom were already either sent out or accepted. Up to that time all who were ready among the accepted candidates had gone forward, and Taylor could with confidence say:

> God is, in this matter of funds, giving us signs that He is working with us; that this work is pleasing to Him, and that therefore He is prospering it. He will give the whole Hundred, and He will provide for them.

It was about the beginning of November, when Taylor had the joy of announcing to the friends of the Mission that their prayers were fully answered – all the Hundred had been given and the funds supplied for their passages to China.

'Six times that number offered,' wrote Dr. Eugene Stock in the *History of the Church Missionary Society*, 'but the Council, faithful to its principles, declined to lower the standard, and rejected five-sixths of the applicants; yet the exact number of one hundred – not ninety-nine nor a hundred and one, but 100 actually sailed within the year. Still more significant of God's blessing is the fact that, seven years later, seventy-eight of the Hundred were still on the C.I.M. staff; and of the remainder, five had died, and most of the others were still labouring in China, though in other connections. Does the whole history of Missions afford quite a parallel to this?'

At the end of December Taylor returned to London, and wrote his last letter of the year to Stevenson.

I have assured the friends that there will be a big Hallelujah when they, the crowning party of the Hundred, reach Shanghai! It is not more than we expected God to do for us, but it is very blessed; and to see that God does answer, in great things as well as small, the prayers of those who put their trust in Him, will strengthen the faith of multitudes.

Among many visitors to Pyrland Road toward the close of the year of the Hundred came Henry W. Frost, one who in a special way was to be identified with the enlargement of Taylor's influence and the sphere of the Mission. Finding Taylor still away in Scotland, he took a room nearby, and quietly gave himself to studying the work of which he had heard enough to bring him across the Atlantic. In spite of the pressure of those days, the Broomhalls welcomed the young stranger, giving him every opportunity to become acquainted with the inner life of the Mission, and all he saw only deepened the desire with which he had come. Of this he was writing to Taylor in the middle of December:

About five months ago I began correspondence with Mr. Broomhall from America, my home, concerning going to China. As the result of that correspondence I am now at Pyrland Road, and have been here long enough to satisfy myself concerning the spiritual standing of the China Inland Mission, and to confirm my own desire of connecting myself with it. But I came to London with a larger purpose in view. It has been laid on my heart for many months past to talk with you and Mr. Broomhall about the establishment of an American Council that might work as a feeder of men and money for China, on the same principles of faith that have made the China Inland Mission so favourably known. Meeting Mr. Forman in Glasgow I found that he, too, had been praying for something of the same kind for a long time, and that Mr. Wilder, his companion, had also had the matter laid on his heart.

From his meetings in Scotland, bringing to a successful issue the work of that memorable year, Taylor returned just as simple, quiet, natural as ever, to banish in a moment any apprehension his visitor had felt as to the interview. A little note from Glasgow, 'fragrant with the love of Christ', had prepared the way for what proved an important conversation.

'Fear did indeed vanish on that occasion,' wrote Henry Frost, 'for I found him at leisure from himself, and most gentle and kind. From that hour my heart was knit to this beloved servant of God in unalterable devotion.'

But though their intercourse resulted in an abiding friendship, it seemed to the one who was building much upon it to have failed in its object. His interest in the Mission was warmly appreciated and his desire to work with it welcomed, but Taylor could not see his way to the establishment of an American branch. It would be, he suggested, far better for Frost to start a fresh organization on the lines of the C.I.M. if he pleased, but something that would be native in its inception and development; for a transplanted mission, like a transplanted tree, would have difficulty in striking root in the new soil. Needless to say this was a great disappointment.

'On reaching my lodgings,' the visitor recalled, 'I had one of the most sorrowful experiences of my life. At the threshold of my room, Satan seemed to meet me and envelop me in darkness. I had come over 3,000 miles only to receive to my request the answer, No. But this was not the worst of it. I had had positive assurance that the Lord had Himself guided me in my prayer, and had led me to take the long journey and make the request that had been made; but now I felt I could never again be sure whether my prayers were or were not of God, or whether I was or was not being guided of Him.'

Only those who have passed through similar experiences can know what such a test of faith meant, and how real was the victory when eventually he was enabled to trust where he could not understand. This restored 'something of soul-rest', and Frost went back to America leaving the issues with the Lord.

The matter did not end there, however. Frost had learned that Taylor was returning to China before long, and that if invited to do so he might travel by way of America. This he made known to the Conveners of the Bible Study Conference at Niagara-on-the-Lake and to D. L. Moody, with the result that invitations began to reach Taylor to visit the great new world.

Meanwhile, in England, the latter was unremitting in his labours. The widespread interest aroused by the outgoing of the Hundred brought more openings for meetings than he could possibly accept, and very stimulating to faith were the facts he had to tell.

'What a wonderful year it has been, both for you and me!' he wrote to Stevenson early in 1888. 'Satan will surely leave no stone unturned to hinder, and we must not be surprised at troublesome difficulties coming up; but greater is He who is for us than all who can be against us.'

The certainty of opposition, definite and determined, from the powers of darkness seems to have been much before him, and the question of funds for the largely increased work was one that could not be ignored. He had written a few weeks previously,

You must continue very earnestly in prayer and secure the prayers of our friends generally, that God will magnify His Name and adequately sustain the work with funds. Nothing is clearer to me than that in obtaining a hundred for this year we have obtained at least a second hundred. To send them out and sustain them will require *another* £10,000 of additional income; and in times like these it is a tremendous rise from a little over twenty to forty thousand pounds annually. One is so glad that God has Himself asked the question, 'Is anything too hard for the Lord?' But we must not forget that He will 'be enquired of by the house of Israel, to do it for them'. If we get less prayerful about funds, we shall soon get sorely tried about funds. Thank God, there is no need to be less prayerful. We can well afford to be more prayerful, and to God be the glory.

At the Annual Meetings in May 1888, he said, 'Suppose He should not work in the way He has done, by sending in tens of thousands of pounds? Well, then, we can do without it. We cannot do without Him, but we can do without any "it" in the world. If only we have the Lord, that is sufficient.'

It was a summer day toward the end of June when the S.S. *Etruria* put out to sea. Taylor was finding, almost with surprise, that parting from those he loved best did not become any easier. A long while might elapse before he could return, and the very uncertainty was painful.

'As I walked the deck last night,' he wrote to Jennie, 'I found myself singing softly, "Jesus, I am resting, resting in the joy of what Thou art" – such a comfort when feeling desolate, and feeling your desolation! No one comforts like He does.'

'Few know what is betwixt Christ and me,' wrote the saintly Rutherford; and little can his fellow-passengers on that Atlantic voyage have realized what lay behind the quiet exterior of the missionary on his way for the seventh time to China. Yet the sweetness was felt, and the power; and by no one more than the young American who was on the New York landing stage to meet him. There was about Henry Frost's spiritual nature a quality that responded in an unusual way to much of which he could be, as yet, but dimly conscious in the life of Hudson Taylor. It was with joy at any rate that he received the party, including Mr. and Mrs. Reginald Radcliffe, and escorted them to his father's home in Madison Avenue.

Of the three months that followed it is difficult to write, not for lack of information but because of the very fullness of the records and the importance of events that took place. Who could have foreseen that, arriving in America in July, little known and with no thought but to take part in a few conferences on his way to China, Taylor would leave again in October, widely loved and trusted, laden with gifts, followed by prayer, and taking with him a band of young workers chosen out of more than forty who had offered their lives for service in the Mission? If the going out of the Hundred in the preceding year had been a striking evidence of the hand of God working with him, what shall be said of this unexpected movement, deeply affecting Christian life in the Eastern States and Canada?

Only two summers before had the Student Volunteer Movement been called into being, but already it had attained remarkable proportions. Over 2,000 undergraduates had signed the declaration: 'I am willing and desirous, God permitting, to become a foreign missionary.' All this, it seemed, had a direct connection with the China Inland Mission. 'The story of the Cambridge band, particularly the account of the visits of a deputation of these students to other British universities, with their missionary message, made a profound impression on us,' wrote Charles Ober, one of the early leaders. 'Here really was the germ thought of the Student Volunteer Movement.' If he had been aware of this, however, Hudson Taylor had no thought of anything growing out of his visit to America in regard to the China Inland Mission.

> 'I was glad to come when my way was providentially opened,' he recalled, 'I wanted to see Mr. Moody, and had heard of over 2,000 students wishful to consecrate their lives to God's service abroad. The American societies, I thought, are not quite in a position to take up these 2,000, and perhaps if we tell them about God's faithfulness they will find it written in their Bibles not "be sent" but "go". I believe in verbal inspiration, and that God could have said "be sent" if He had wished it, instead of "go". I hoped I might be able to encourage some to "go".'

As to bringing forward the work of the Mission with a view to developing an American branch, nothing was further from his thoughts. Had he not told Frost only a few months earlier that he had no guidance in that direction, sending him back from England perplexed and disappointed? And if it was not in Taylor's purpose, still less was it anticipated by those to whom his personality and message came as so new a force that summer at Northfield. The Student Conference was in full swing when he and his companions arrived and, met by D. L. Moody himself, were driven out to his beautiful home. 400 men from ninety different colleges filled the Seminary buildings, and overflowed in tents on the far-reaching campus backed by hills and woods. The afternoon was kept entirely free for recreation.

'Delegates should come fully equipped for bathing, tennis, baseball, football, hill-climbing and all other outdoor exercises,' ran the official invitation. 'They should also bring their own reference Bibles and a good supply of notebooks.'

Morning and evening the spacious auditorium was filled for devotional meetings and Bible study. It was an inspiring assembly, including many pastors, professors, Y.M.C.A. secretaries, and leading philanthropists. The corps of speakers was able and representative, and Moody, who presided, was at his best. But it was in the young men themselves the inspiration lay – such power, such possibilities! Hudson Taylor could not but be moved by such an audience, and to him the students seem to have been attracted in a special way.

'With the exception of my own father,' said Robert Wilder many years later, 'Mr. Taylor was the man who was the greatest spiritual help to me. When he came to Northfield and appealed on behalf of China, the hearts of the delegates burned within them. And he not only made the needs of the mission field very real; he showed us the possibilities of the Christian life. The students loved to hear him expound the Word of God. He was a master of his Bible, and his sympathy and naturalness attracted men to him. His addresses were so much appreciated that Mr. Moody had to announce extra meetings to be held by him in the afternoons – so many of the students were anxious to hear more from the veteran missionary. Eternity alone can reveal the results of that life, and the effect of his words upon our Student Movement. What impressed us undergraduates was not merely the spirituality of Mr. Taylor, it was his common sense. One asked him the question: "Are you always conscious of abiding in Christ?"

' "While sleeping last night," he replied, "did I cease to abide in your house because I was unconscious of the fact? We should never be conscious of *not* abiding in Christ."

'When asked, "How is it that you can address so many meetings?" he said to us: "Every morning I feed upon the Word of God, then I pass on through the day messages that have first helped me in my own soul."

' "You can work without praying, but it is a bad plan" was another of his sayings, "but you cannot pray in earnest without working". And "Do not be so busy with work for Christ that you have no strength left for praying. True prayer requires strength."

'It was not, however, the words only of Mr. Taylor that helped us, it was the life of the man. He bore about with him the fragrance of Jesus Christ.'

It was not until Taylor had been nearly a month in America that it began to dawn upon him that there was a larger purpose concerning this visit than any he had in view. His increasingly full programme had brought him, a few days previously, to a conference at Niagara-on-the-Lake, a special feature of which was the large number of ministers present, Canadian as well as American, of various denominations. Taylor was only able to speak twice, having to pass on to Chicago for other meetings, but the impression made was profound. Personal love to the Lord Jesus as typified in the Song of Solomon, and faith in God (or the faithfulness of God rather, upon which faith is to lay hold), were his subjects, and he scarcely made any reference to China or the Mission. Frost wrote later,

> One of the leading evangelists present confessed that the addresses had come to him almost as a revelation, and many others shared this feeling. Hearts and lives were brought into an altogether new relationship to God and Christ, and not a few, in the joyfulness of full surrender, quietly but finally offered themselves to the Lord for His service anywhere and everywhere.

Of this and subsequent happenings Taylor knew nothing. His visit to Chicago ended, he had come east again to Attica, a lovely village in the state of New York, where Mr. Frost senior and his son had their summer homes. The son was expected on the midnight train from Niagara, and Taylor was at the station to meet him, but little thinking of the news he had to bring.

Unexpected developments had taken place at the Niagara meetings after Taylor's departure. Disappointed at not hearing more from him on the subject of foreign missions, the Conference all the more welcomed the addresses of Reginald Radcliffe and Robert Wilder, for which the way had been well prepared. Burning words were spoken by the veteran evangelist and the young volunteer on the responsibility of each succeeding generation of believers to obey the great command, 'Go ye into all the world and preach the gospel to every creature'. He had learned, Wilder told them, the secret of how to work for the Lord *twenty-four hours a day,* and to keep on doing so all the year round. It was a lady who had made the discovery. When asked how it was possible –

'I work twelve hours here,' she replied, 'and when I have to rest, my representative in India begins her day, and works the other twelve.'

'We want many from the Niagara Conference to work twenty-four hours a day like this,' he urged. 'Christian friends, you who cannot go, why not have your own representatives on the foreign field?'

This was a new idea, but seemed so reasonable that Radcliffe was kept busy answering questions as to how much it would take to support a worker in the China Inland Mission. $250 a year (£50) he thought would suffice,[1] and a meeting was appointed to see what was to be the practical outcome. Dr. W. J. Erdman was in the chair, but the occasion was not one for much direction or control.

[1] This proved inadequate however, as it made no allowance for incidental and travelling expenses, house rent, and the like.

'After singing and prayer,' he wrote, 'the Secretary, who had in mind the general guidance of the meeting, suddenly found himself entirely emptied of every idea and preference, and the Spirit of the Lord came upon the believers present. The rest of the hour was filled with voluntary praises, prayers and consecration of young men and women to service in the foreign field. It was a meeting never to be forgotten, and money for the China Inland Mission came in without advertisement or urging on the part of any.'

But even this experience was surpassed next day when the Conference reassembled.

'As I reached the Pavilion,' wrote Henry Frost, to whom gifts and pledges of money sufficient for the support of two missionaries had been given the previous evening, 'I found that people had become intoxicated with the joy of giving, and that they were seeking another opportunity for making free-will offerings for the Lord's work in China. A number were standing up, pledging themselves to give a certain amount toward the support of a missionary, and some were saying that they wanted to work twenty-four hours a day by having a missionary all to themselves. Again promises and money came flowing in until, this time, I had scarcely a place to put them. There I stood in the midst of the assembly – without ever wishing it or thinking such a thing could be – suddenly transformed into an impromptu Treasurer of the China Inland Mission. And afterwards, upon counting what had been given, I found enough to support not two missionaries but actually *eight*, for a whole year, in inland China.'

Returning to his room that summer morning Frost could not but remember the sorrowful experience through which he had passed in London, when he had wondered whether he could ever know that prayer was really answered, or be assured of the guidance of God again. The faith that had sustained him then was being exchanged for sight, and as he poured out his heart in wondering thankfulness he realized how safe and good it is 'not only to wait upon God, but also to wait for Him'.

This then was the story he had to tell, when upon reaching Attica at midnight he found Taylor on the platform to meet him.

'I kept my secret, however,' he continued, 'until we reached my father's house and Mr. Taylor's bedroom. Then I described to him how after his departure from Niagara the Spirit had swept over the Conference; how the offerings had been given and put into my hands to pass on to him; and how they had been found to amount to a sum sufficient to support *eight* missionaries for a year in China.

'Quietly he listened, and with such a serious look that I confess, for once in my life, I was disappointed in Mr. Taylor. Instead of being glad, he seemed burdened. If I remember rightly, he did just say "Praise the Lord", or "Thank God", but beyond this there was nothing to indicate that he accepted the news as good news, as I had anticipated. For a few minutes he stood apparently lost in thought, and then said:

'"I think we had better pray."

'Upon this we knelt beside the bed, and he began to ask what the Lord meant by all that had taken place. It was only as he went on pleading for light that I commenced to understand what was in Mr. Taylor's mind. He had realized at once that this was a very marked providence, and that God had probably brought him to America for other purposes than simply to give a few addresses on his way to China. He had inquired from me how the money was to be used, and I had replied that it was designated, by preference, for the support of North American workers. From this he saw that the obligation was laid upon him of appealing for missionaries from North America – a heavy responsibility, in view of all that it involved. It was becoming clear to him, as to me, that my visit to London and appeal for a branch of the Mission to be established on this continent had been more providential than was at first recognized.'

Unexpectedly a crisis had arisen, fraught, as Taylor could not but see, with far-reaching results. The problem that faced him, after little more than three weeks in America, was no simple one, and as yet the man at his side, young and retiring as he was, had not been recognized as the providential solution.

'I think we must have an American branch of the Mission,' Taylor wrote to Stevenson. 'Do not be surprised if I should bring reinforcements with me.'

The conclusion to which Taylor was thus being led was strongly confirmed on his return to Northfield. D. L. Moody advised his appealing at once for workers, and introduced him to some of his own students who were feeling called to China. But even then it was with fear and trembling that he went forward. The Mission had always been interdenominational, but twenty-one years of experience had made its leader cautious. 'I never felt more timid,' he said a year later, 'about anything in my life.' But once his mind was made up, the appeal was a strong one.

'To have missionaries and no money would be no trouble to me,' was the way he put it; 'for the Lord is bound to take care of His own: He does not want me to assume His responsibility. But to have money and no missionaries is very serious indeed. And I do not think it will be kind of you dear friends in America to put this burden upon us, and not to send some from among yourselves to use the money. We have the dollars, but where are the people?'

One by one prepared men and women responded to the call. When the first three were accepted, Taylor began to be relieved about the funds in hand. Their passages had been promised independently, but their support for the first year would use a considerable part of the money contributed at Niagara 'if things went smoothly'. But from this point of view, things did not go at all smoothly. Parents, friends, or the churches to which they belonged claimed the privilege of sustaining these workers. When as many as eight had been accepted, the original fund was still untouched, and the further they went the less chance there seemed of getting to an end of it. Consecrated money, Taylor remarked, was something like the consecrated loaves and fishes, there was no using it up!

But all the while, out of sight, there was a quiet force of prayer at work that went far to account for the wonderful things that were happening. Taylor and his party were so carried forward on a tide of interest and enthusiasm that it was all they could do to keep up with their programme, and prolonged seasons of prayer – save for his early morning hour – were impossible. But in the retirement of that country home at Attica a man was on his knees, prevailing with God. A serious illness that threatened the life of his father kept Henry Frost from travelling, and when not required in the sick room he had more leisure than usual for thought and prayer. He saw, with the clearness of a listening soul, the way in which things were tending. Money continued to come to him for the support of missionaries in China, and in the middle of August he sent out a circular letter to the contributors asking 'many and fervent prayers' that the right persons might be chosen, and that some might be ready to sail without delay, that the opportunity of Hudson Taylor's escort might not be lost. To the latter he wrote also:

> Please very specially remember the C.I.M.'s relation to America. I dare not seek to influence you, yet I ask most earnestly that you will consider the question, Will it not be well to establish a branch here?

Meanwhile Taylor, as he moved about, was increasingly impressed with the spirit and enterprise of American Christians, and with the interest in China awakened among them. By the middle of September the number of applicants to join the Mission had risen to over forty. In Hamilton he found a band of young people who seemed prepared in a special way for his message. From the Secretary of the Y.M.C.A. he learned that they were united in earnest prayer that seven of their number might be privileged to go as missionaries to China, and among the party that sailed with him a few weeks later were four young women and three men from the Hamilton Christian Associations, the Secretary himself following by way of Europe.

The culminating experience of the American visit was the farewell meeting in Toronto.

> 'Sunday night, September 23, 1888, saw the greatest and most enthusiastic gathering ever held in Toronto up to that time,' wrote one who was present. 'The place was the Y.M.C.A., the hour 8.30 p.m., just after the evening services in the churches. One might say that the cream of Toronto's religious life was gathered there, to hear the Rev. J. Hudson Taylor and the men and women accepted by him for work in

China. The power of God was manifest in a wonderful way, and as a result a great and abiding impetus was given to foreign missions.'

Writing after the meeting, Mrs. Reginald Radcliffe reported,

The Y.M.C.A. Hall was so full that an overflow meeting had to be held, and hundreds went away unable to get in. On Monday Mr. Taylor had to leave for Montreal, but it was arranged for the missionary party and their friends to meet at nine the following evening, to take the Lord's Supper together, going from the church to the station. It was said that from 500 to 1,000 people were at the station, singing and cheering. Finally my husband led in prayer, the great concourse repeating the words aloud after him . . . and slowly the train moved away.

Surely not the least remarkable of the converging providences by which Taylor was led to go forward was the generous, devoted co-operation of Henry Frost. He was ready to assume whatever responsibility Taylor gave him, and an incident happened in Toronto which confirmed Taylor's assurance that he was being guided by God. They had come prayerfully to the conclusion that a temporary Council should be formed until, after consultation with friends in London and Shanghai, more permanent arrangements could be made. Mr. Sandham of the Christian Institute undertook the responsibility of Hon. Secretary in Canada, with Frost occupying a similar position in the United States. But the time was short in which to arrange for a Council.

In an upper room at the Institute Taylor was in conference with the two men. It was the day after the farewell meetings which had moved Toronto so profoundly, and that very day he was to leave for Montreal. The names of some who were felt suitable to join a provisional Council were before him, but he had no time to arrange interviews with them. He was about to ask the others to act for him when a knock was heard at the door. Great was the surprise of those within when the visitor proved to be one of the men in question. Hardly had Taylor explained to him the circumstances and received his assurance of willing co-operation, however, before another knock came, and a second of those whose names had been mentioned appeared. He, too, was glad to serve on the Council, and they were all feeling impressed with the hand of God in the matter, when yet another visitor came seeking Sandham. It seemed almost too wonderful to be true when the third of the friends entered whom Taylor had desired to meet before leaving – especially when it transpired that two of the three had not been in the building for months, and had no idea that he was there. 'They were indeed sent by the Lord,' was Henry Frost's comment, 'and we were never disappointed in the choice He had made.'

CHAPTER 23

With Wings as Eagles

(1888–1889)

CROSSING the Rocky Mountains by Canadian Pacific was an inspiring experience to Taylor. The greatness of the country as it unrolled before him was in keeping with the greatness of the possibilities he had felt among Canadian as well as American Christians for the rapid, world-wide extension of the kingdom of God. Nevertheless, the consciousness was much with him of the certainty of opposition from the powers of evil. For years the Mission had been carried forward on a wave of unparalleled success. During the period of the Seventy its membership had doubled, and since then it had more than doubled again, without the addition of this latest party. And what opportunities for enlargement did not their coming suggest? But experience had taught him that for every time of prosperity and blessing one of special trial was in store, though even he can hardly have anticipated how long and testing the conflict now before them was to prove.

Even before they came in sight of China it began, as in Yokohama news was received of the death from hydrophobia of the headmaster of the Chefoo School, who in protecting his boys from a mad dog had himself been bitten; and that also of Adam Dorward, the devoted pioneer of Hunan. On landing in Shanghai he learned not only of the death of a young worker of much promise, but that in the Mission home to which he was taking his fellow-travellers another was even then nearing the end of life's journey.

A few weeks later these trials were surpassed by the arrival of the saddest party ever received from England. On the voyage out one of the new workers had had a shock which resulted in temporary insanity, and on landing her condition was that of acute mania. No asylums were to be found in China, even in the foreign Settlements, and she had to be cared for in the already crowded premises the Mission was renting in Shanghai.

'There is absolutely nothing to be done,' wrote Taylor, 'but to bear the trial, while using proper means, and wait on God. Our house has been a hospital; it is now an asylum. All that this means the Lord only knows. The night and day strain are almost unbearable, but I know the Lord's ways are right, and I would not have them otherwise. So whatever time and care the case claims must be given, and it must be pleasing to the Lord for us to be so occupied.'

Meanwhile a telegram had been received from Hong Kong telling of the serious illness of William Cooper, returning from furlough, and at the same time of another worker in an inland station being struck with black smallpox, from which she died six months later.

> 'It was a dark and trying time that winter,' recalled Stevenson. 'There had been so much success, such rapid extension. We were going ahead full sail set, before a favourable breeze. Ballast was needed, though at the time we could not see it.'

There was scarcely a grey head in the Mission in those days, and under his enthusiastic leadership as Deputy Director in China everything had seemed possible. Was there a danger perhaps, of growing too fast for the spiritual well-being of the work or the faith of its supporters?

> 'We might be lifted up, perhaps, or lose spiritual life and power,' wrote Hudson Taylor, 'if success were unaccompanied by discipline.'

Even more serious than the troubles in China were the anxieties that pressed upon him from another quarter. Friends of the Mission in England, it appeared, including some of the London Council, were concerned about the steps taken in America. No one had as yet foreseen the adaptability of the Mission, on account of its special form of government, to relations of an international character. The principle of control on the field – the direction of the work not from a distance but by experienced leaders in China – could not but constitute Shanghai the headquarters of the Mission rather than London, making it possible for Taylor or his representatives there to work with auxiliary Councils in any part of the world, just as with the original Council at home. This natural application of one of the cardinal principles of the Mission came as a surprise, however, to those who had hitherto never dreamed of such developments. Even the necessity for the China Council had hardly yet been fully conceded; and that it should come to occupy a central position, with affiliations in America and perhaps elsewhere practically independent of the mother country, caused great consternation. Some felt they might have to resign from the Council rather than consent to it.

The position was a critical one for the leader of the Mission. More sure he could not be as to the guidance given in America. Step by step he had been led, almost compelled, to accept the party that had accompanied him, and to appoint as Secretaries and provisional Council those who had been so remarkably provided. Go back upon it he could not, without going back upon what he had assuredly gathered to have been the will of God. But how go forward at such a cost?

'The Cross does not get comfortable,' is one revealing sentence in a letter of this winter, 'but it bears sweet fruit.' How truly it was so in Taylor's experience may be gathered from recollections of Stevenson, who was much with him during that 1888–89 period.

Everything seemed crowded into those terrible months. I do not know what we should have done without Mr. Taylor, but oh, the look on his face at times!

One thing that deeply touched me at this time was his evident and intense longing to walk uprightly before God. He would go all lengths to do the right thing and put away misunderstandings. Early this spring, when our troubles were at their height, he was burdened about the lack of cordiality between ourselves and two former members of the Mission who were still in Shanghai. The trouble had arisen during one of Mr. Taylor's absences in England, but he could not leave it with simply – 'They were wrong, and we did what we could at the time.'

He wrote a note saying he would be glad to call upon them and talk matters over, greatly desiring that any bitterness of feeling might be removed. On the 4th March, I remember, he spent a long evening with them, going over the whole story. It must have been very painful, for their attitude was far from conciliatory, but it ended right. He was able to have prayer with them, and friendship was restored.

Oh, his was a life that stood looking into – searching through and through! Get a man like Mr. Taylor, and you could start *any* mission tomorrow. He walked with God; his life bore the light all through. And he was so gracious and accessible! Day or night, literally at all hours, he was ready to help in sickness or any trouble. For self-denial and practical consecration, one could not but feel, he stood alone.

A sheet of notepaper bearing a few lines in Taylor's writing reveals, perhaps, more than anything else the secret of his inward life at this time. Found between the pages of his diary, it brightens the record with unexpected radiance. From the brief entries in the book itself one learns little; but that well-worn paper, used evidently as a marker and moved on from day to day, what does it not reveal?

Lord Jesus, make Thyself to me
A living, bright Reality;
More present to faith's vision keen
Than any outward object seen;
More dear, more intimately nigh
Than e'en the sweetest earthly tie.

Was it not the answer to this daily prayer that made endurance possible? 'I see no light as to the future of home arrangements; but I see God, the living God; and I love Him all the more for this trial – and *trust*.'

It was with a deep sense of the gravity of the situation that Taylor set out for England again when it became evident that home difficulties could not be settled by correspondence. There was no spirit of self-confidence in the letter he wrote to Stevenson when nearing Aden:

It is so solemn to feel that one may go out as Samson did, unconscious that the Lord has left one, to win defeat and captivity and blindness. May the Lord keep me and keep you very near Himself. All our service will be worse than useless without that. The solemnity of our position makes me tremble.

From the very day of his arrival, however, he found that God Himself had been working to make a continuance of happy relations possible. He wrote at the end of the month,

I think that all may now be put right, and that great good will result from our great trial.

And a few weeks later:

July 4: It is impossible not to see in these things the good hand of our God in answer to many prayers. I do not think things have been so cordial for years. In all this there is abundant cause for gratitude and praise.

Thus the storm-clouds began to roll away, and when a visit to America seemed necessary to strengthen the relations between the oldest and newest departments of the work, he went armed with a cordial letter of welcome to the Toronto Council from the Council in London. Of the quickened hopes stirring within him, and the way in which he was pressing on to know more of the wonder-working power of God, some impression may be gained from a letter to Jennie before leaving Queenstown Harbour (July 6):

Darling, I do want our whole life to be an ascending plane – not resting in anything we have learned or felt or attained, but a pressing on and up. God has been faithful to us, as far as we have gone out on His promises and have trusted His faithfulness; but how little we have done so!

What would a great Sovereign think of a proposal to add 100 soldiers in the course of a year to his army of invasion in a country like China? We must get on to a higher plane of thought altogether, and of prayer, if we are to walk worthy of God and deal in any sensible way with the world's crying need. Let us ask in faith for such workers for every department as shall be fit and able to deal worthily with their work at home, in America, in China, and for such an enduement of power as shall make the feeblest mighty.

Do we not want more really to meditate on God; to gaze on Him; to take in what we are even now competent to take in of His greatness, His resources, His assurances and promises? Dwelling thus on Him, should we not be enabled to grasp more of the heights and depths of His character and purposes, and be more ready and able to do *His* will? May He, darling, in our separation, become all the more to us, that we may first be more to Him, and then through Him to our work and to each other.

In the little town of Attica two other hearts had been learning similar lessons, hearts united in an equally deep bond of love. Circumstances had changed a good deal for Henry Frost and his wife since Taylor's previous visit, but their home seemed, if anything, more attractive than before. The marriage gift of his father, it had been beautified by the addition of panelled wooden ceilings, to replace the plaster ones which had fallen in the lower rooms, a detail that was to have a good deal to do with the direction of their lives at this time. With every comfort in their surroundings, a large circle of friends and nothing but happiness in their children, there seemed little of earthly good left to desire. But an unseen Hand was stirring up this nest, and Taylor's second visit found them in the midst of strange experiences.

Their income, which had hitherto been amply sufficient, had suddenly been cut off through the failure of a flourishing business. At his father's express desire, Frost had given up his own business some years previously, to devote himself entirely to evangelistic work. The father was well able to supply the needs of the family, and rejoiced to have fellowship in this way in his son's service for the Lord. But now, to his sorrow, this was no longer possible. To have gone back into secular employment would have greatly curtailed Henry Frost's usefulness as an evangelist, and would have necessitated his giving up much active participation in the work of the C.I.M. This he could not feel to be the will of God, after all the way in which he and Taylor had been led, and it practically came to be, as he expressed it, a question, 'Which father are you really trusting?'

Outside the immediate family no one knew of their position, and the Frosts saw it to be a special opportunity for putting to the test not their faith only but the definite promises of God. A few months previously they had determined never, under any circumstances, to go into debt. Amid the apparent comfort of their surroundings, therefore, they found themselves directly dependent upon their Heavenly Father even for daily bread. Searching as well as precious were the experiences through which they were learning more of His infinite faithfulness, but their joy in God was growing deeper and their desire to be wholly engaged in His service stronger, although they little anticipated the sacrifice that would be involved.

Meanwhile the interest in China and sympathy for the China Inland Mission were increasing. This was evident from the welcome both Taylor and Frost received at the Niagara Conference. The gifts of 1888 for the support of American workers were largely exceeded, and many new friendships were formed while old ones were strengthened.

Taylor's chief object in coming over being the settlement of the work upon a permanent basis, he gave much time to meetings with the Council and intercourse with its individual members. The number of the latter was increased, and Sandham finding it necessary, on account of many engagements, to retire from the position he had held, Henry Frost was invited to assume the sole responsibility as Treasurer and Secretary, making his home in Toronto.

So this was what it had all been leading to! In view of recent experiences, he was himself prepared for a life of faith with regard to temporal supplies; but he knew that his wife would feel giving up their lovely home very keenly, on account of the children.

'One day as I was in the parlour, resting,' he wrote of this critical time, 'my wife, unknown to me, was waiting upon God in her own room for guidance. While thus engaged she was led to open her Bible and to read in the book of Haggai; and she had not read long in this portion of Scripture before she had the light for which she had been so earnestly seeking. A moment later I heard her coming to me across the library and hall. She stepped to my side, and without a word laid her open Bible on my knee, pointing as she did so to the fourth verse of the first chapter of Haggai. I looked at the words indicated and read as follows:

' "Is it time for you, O ye, to dwell in your cieled houses and this house lie waste?"

'It was not necessary that my wife should say anything to explain her meaning; the lesson was self-evident. One look in her face showed me that the Lord had won the victory for her, and one look at the ceiling overhead settled the question finally for myself. From that hour, though it was not an easy thing to do, we were united in our desire to give up our home, in order that we might have part in the building of that spiritual house, the temple of Christ's body, which we knew the Lord was waiting to see completed.'

Gladly would Taylor have made it possible for the step to be taken without financial difficulty; but while he could give them enough for the actual move, there was little over. The contributions at Niagara and in other centres, while amounting to thousands of dollars, were almost all designated for individual missionaries, and could not be drawn upon. About £50 given to Taylor for his own use he felt free to pass on, but 'Beyond this,' he said quite frankly, 'I can promise you nothing. You will have to look to the Lord for supplies, as we do in England and in China.' Recollecting his own reactions Frost wrote later,

I confess that Mr. Taylor's words did not at first suggest an inviting prospect. To move my family and belongings, to take a home in a strange city, to invite a large number of candidates into that home, to supply their needs and our own and to carry on the work of the Mission with little more than $250.00 was certainly not a promising arrangement from an earthly standpoint. But recent experiences had given me to understand that there was a factor in the case not to be left out, and which being reckoned upon altered the proposition. That factor was the Lord Himself. $250.00 was anything but a large sum with which to begin such an undertaking; but $250.00 *with the Lord* was all that we could need. Thus, so far as finances were concerned, I soon felt prepared to accept Mr. Taylor's offer.

Could he have foreseen the many and wonderful answers to prayer that were to bring to the American branch of the Mission over half a million dollars within the next seventeen years, and place at his disposal property to the value of $40,000 more, he might have gone forward with less fear and trembling!

Cheered and strengthened by many tokens for good, Taylor left America in August, to carry out a full programme of meetings, which included a visit to Sweden before the close of the year. The interest that had grown to considerable proportions in that country owed not a little to Hudson Taylor's unconscious influence over a young stranger whom he met one busy day in Paternoster Row in London. He had gone out of his way to show the Swedish visitor courtesy, and later they met at an important meeting in connection with the outgoing of the Seventy.

> 'We had a conversation after the meeting,' Mr. Holmgren recalled, 'and Mr. Taylor talked to me in a very kind way, by which my heart was drawn out to him. He seemed to be full of love.'

Visits to Pyrland Road deepened the interest, and Holmgren returned to Sweden as a staunch friend of the China Inland Mission. First as editor of a religious weekly, then as pastor of one of the leading churches in Stockholm, he did all that in him lay to awaken Swedish Christians to a sense of responsibility for the unevangelized millions of China, among whom they as yet had no representatives. Eric Folke, an Upsala graduate, deeply conscious of a call from God to that great field, could find no Swedish society to send him there. Going independently, he was welcomed at the C.I.M. in Shanghai, and passed on to its training home at Anking for the study of the language. Six months later he wrote to Holmgren of his desire to work in association with the Mission, and a Committee was formed in Stockholm to facilitate the going out of others to join him.

For some time this representative group of friends had been urging Taylor to visit Sweden. Tied for time as he was by the second General Missionary Conference in Shanghai, at which he had promised to preach the opening sermon, it was not easy to spare a month for this purpose; but the Committee was needing advice as to their work in China, which was to be carried on in close affiliation with the C.I.M.

The whole thing was coming about so naturally that he can hardly have realized the widening that was taking place in his personal ministry and the connections of the Mission, which was yet to be linked with deeply prayerful movements in many Continental centres as well as in America and Australasia. With the Niagara Conference of the previous year the new movement had begun, and to the present summer may be traced the larger vision, which was to lead to outward development. Taylor himself was growing with the growing work. After the recent difficulties which had so tested and strengthened faith in God, he was full of longing 'to grasp more of the heights and depths of His character and purposes, and be more ready and able to do His will'. And now, even before he could pay his promised visit to Sweden, a fuller revelation of that will had come.

Conscious of a new call from God, a new urgency about the work to which his life was given, Hudson Taylor was ready for the important openings his northern journey afforded.

'We seldom address fewer than two to five thousand people daily,' he wrote toward the close of the visit, in which he was accompanied by his second son. 'Even in small places we have large audiences. Hundreds could not get in last night: and some had come thirty miles to the meeting. May great and lasting blessing be the result.'

In Sweden as elsewhere it was the spirit of the man that added weight to what was said. Seen through the eyes of Holmgren, who travelled with them, this was if anything the more eloquent message.

Everywhere the people were drawn to Mr. Taylor. He showed much love and affection, which also was returned. It was a joy to see how the children gathered round him in the families we visited, although they could not understand what he said. He spoke very friendly to them and patted their heads.

Mr. Hudson Taylor felt much gladdened by his visit to Sweden. He gained many friends; and still today when his name is mentioned before those who heard him, their faces are lit up with joy. He also was very simple, and without pretensions. On leaving Linköping, for example, he was specially tired. He had had several meetings the day before, and had risen early in the morning. There had already been a meeting at eleven o'clock, and at six there should be another in a town sixty miles away. On the way to the station, Dr. Howard Taylor said to his father:

'You are very tired now. Let me take a second class ticket.'

In so gentle a way Mr. Taylor answered: 'Well, it is the Lord's money, you know; we had better be very careful about it.'

Which answer made a great impression on me. I have many times since heard this word repeat itself in my ears: 'It is the Lord's money: we had better be very careful about it'.

Lastly, I may mention an incident which also made a great impression upon my mind, and which shows his trust in God. The Committee had intended to meet Mr. Taylor's expenses and those of his son for their journey by taking collections at the meetings. When I met them in Gothenburg I told Mr. Taylor this. Then he looked at me, and with a smiling face said:

'Well, I have a rich Father, you know. I will ask Him about it. But I do not think this thought is quite according to His will. He is sure to provide for me; and I feel that what is gathered by collections ought to be used for the Swedish Mission.'

I felt very much touched, and if I had had money I should gladly have paid all the expenses of his travels in Sweden. But as to his trust that these would be provided, I said to myself, 'That is all very well in England; but in Sweden it is not the same.'

I parted from Mr. Taylor at Christiania. He crossed for England and I returned to Stockholm. In his first letter he said:

'A few days after we had come to England I received a letter from someone in Sweden, I do not know from whom. A cheque was enclosed for £50, and the writer said that this money was to meet my expenses and those of my son for our journey in Sweden, and if anything was left over I might use it as I liked. If you know who has sent it, please give them my warm thanks.'

I did not know at all from whom it was; but I felt very much ashamed and humiliated for my unbelief. At the same time I could not restrain my thanksgivings to the Lord for His faithfulness, and that His power is *just the same* in Sweden as in England.

The burden on Taylor's heart all through this Swedish visit, if burden it could be called, was the deeper apprehension that had come to him one Sunday a few months previously of the meaning of the Divine command, 'Go ye into all the world, and preach the gospel to every creature'. It was Jennie's birthday and they were spending it in her father's home at Hastings. Did it recall that other memorable Sunday, on the sands at Brighton, when he had met the crisis of his life, and had yielded himself to God for the evangelization of inland China?

What he saw now, in the light of the Holy Spirit's teaching, was a meaning so great, so comprehensive, in those few simple words – among the last that fell from the ascending Saviour's lips – that it seemed as if he heard them for the first time.

'I confess with shame,' he wrote a few months later, 'that until that moment the question, What did our Lord *really mean* by His command "Preach the gospel to every creature"? had never been raised by me. I had laboured for many years, as have many others, to carry the Gospel further afield; had laid plans for reaching every unreached province and many smaller districts in China, without realizing the plain meaning of our Saviour's words!'

'*To every creature*'? And the total number of Protestant communicants in that great land was only 40,000. Double the number, treble it, to include adherents, and suppose each one to be a messenger to eight of his fellow-countrymen– even so, only *one million* would be reached. '*To every creature*': the words burned into his very soul. But how far was the Church, how far had he been himself from taking them literally, as intended to be acted upon! He saw it now, however; and with Hudson Taylor there was but one course – to obey.

How are we going to treat the Lord Jesus Christ with reference to this command? Shall we definitely drop the title Lord as applied to Him, and take the ground that we are quite willing to recognize Him as our Saviour, so far as the penalty of sin is concerned, but are not prepared to own ourselves 'bought with a price', or Him as having any claim to our unquestioning obedience? Shall we say that we are our own masters, willing to yield something as His due, who bought us with His blood, provided He does not ask too much? Our lives, our loved ones, our possessions are our own, not His: we will give Him what we think fit, and obey any of His requirements that do not demand too great a sacrifice? To be taken to Heaven by Jesus Christ we are more than willing, but we will not have this Man to *reign* over us?

The heart of every Christian will undoubtedly reject the proposition, so formulated; but have not countless lives in each generation been lived as though it were proper ground to take? How few of the Lord's people have practically recognized the truth that Christ is either *Lord of all,* or is *not Lord at all*! If we can judge God's Word as much or as little as we like, then *we* are lords and He is the indebted one, to be grateful for our dole and obliged by our compliance with His wishes. If, on the other hand, He is Lord, let us treat Him as such. 'Why call ye me, Lord, Lord, and do not the things which I say?'

So, all unexpectedly, he came to the widest outlook of his life, the purpose that was to dominate the closing decade of its active service.

CHAPTER 24

The Coming Thousand

(1889–1892)

NOT a mere human project but *a Divine command* was what Taylor saw in the words, 'To every creature', that autumn day by the sea. They came to him with all the urgency of a royal mandate that brooks no delay. It was a question of duty, and no time was to be lost. 'If we begin at once,' he realized afresh with straitened heart, 'millions will have passed away ere we can reach them.'

But begin what? Begin a definite, systematic effort to do just as the Master said – to carry the glad tidings of salvation to every man, woman and child throughout the whole of China. Nothing if not practical, Taylor set himself forthwith to consider, not whether the attempt should be made, but simply – *how*? And as he thought and prayed he came to see, first of all, that *it could be done*. There was no impossibility about the matter. Armies of scores of thousands could be sent to the ends of the earth for the sake of material conquest, and the Church had at her command resources fully equal to the obligations laid upon her.

Very simply it occurred to him, about the vast population to be reached: a million is a thousand thousands: given 1,000 evangelists, each one teaching 250 people daily, and in 1,000 days 250 millions would have the offer of Divine mercy. Surely a task that could, at this rate, be accomplished in little over *three years* should not be thought of as chimerical or beyond the resources of the Christian Church!

Many objections, he knew, could be raised to this calculation. To begin with some might think it impossible for an individual worker to reach as many as 250 people daily; or that, if they could, such an offer of the Gospel would accomplish little. Taylor could not but remember, however, the work he had himself done in early years, and especially the many months spent with William Burns in the thorough systematic evangelization in districts in which there were no settled missionaries. They had not found it difficult to reach 500 to 1,000 people daily – preaching in all the streets of a given town or city, and entering every shop with books and tracts. As night came on they would repair to a previously announced tea-shop, where interested hearers could meet them for conversation, and any who wished to learn more were invited to their boats for further talk and prayer. As to results, he in common with many others could recall, among the brightest converts they had ever known, not a few who had truly given their hearts to Christ the first time they ever heard of Redeeming Love. 'And if one offer of the Gospel is insufficient,' he urged, 'what shall we think of *none*?'

Thus it was that in the December *China's Millions* an earnest, practical paper entitled 'To Every Creature' made its appearance, outcome of the deep soul-exercise of that October day. Its plea was for immediate action, first in the realm in which every believer may have power, the realm of prayer. What part the C.I.M. might take in the forward movement Taylor did not attempt to determine. It was the united, simultaneous action of all the societies that alone could put 1,000 evangelists in the field without delay.

Travelling out to China for the second General Missionary Conference, he was thankful for the opportunity the gathering would afford for bringing forward the matter.

'We cannot take hold of this thing in earnest,' was his conviction, 'without getting more than 1,000; and oh, the enlargement, the enrichment that would come in the train of such a movement! Could China be blessed alone? Would not the whole world necessarily share in the blessing? For we could not be blessed on the field without our home churches being brought into it; and if they were filled with spiritual life, every land would be thought of and cared for. The Church is well able to evangelize the whole world and to do it with rapidity.'

When face to face with his audience at last – that responsible body of men and women representing all the Protestant societies at work in China – his heart overflowed the bounds of his written address.

I do not know that we are told anywhere in the Bible to try to do anything. 'We must try to do the best we can' is a very common expression; but I remember some years ago, after a remark of that kind, looking carefully through the New Testament to see under what circumstances the disciples were told to *try* to do anything. I did not expect to find many instances, but I was surprised not to find any. Then I went through the Old Testament, very carefully, and I could not find that the Lord had ever told Old Testament believers to try to do anything. There were many commands that appeared impossible to obey, but they were all definite commands: and I think we all need to set ourselves, not to try to obey our Lord as far as we can, but simply *to obey* Him.

If as an organized Conference we were to set ourselves to obey the command of the Lord to the full, if as an act of obedience we were to determine that every district, every town, every village, every hamlet in this land should hear the Gospel, and that speedily, and were to set about doing it, I believe that the Spirit would come down in such mighty power that we should find supplies springing up we know not how. We should find the fire spreading from missionary to flock, and our Chinese fellow-workers and the whole Church of God would be blessed. God gives His Holy Spirit to them that obey Him. Let us see to it that we really apprehend what His command to us is, now in the day of our opportunity – this day of the remarkable openness of the country, when there are so many facilities, when God has put steam and telegraph at the command of His people for the quick carrying out of His purposes.

The Conference appealed for the Thousand – a thousand men within the next five years, for all forms of missionary work in China. Taken by representative leaders of American and Continental as well as English Societies, this united action could not but have weight with all sections of the Church at home on either side of the Atlantic.

'We make this appeal,' they wrote, 'on behalf of 300 millions of unevangelized heathen; we make it with the earnestness of our whole hearts, as men overwhelmed with the magnitude and responsibility of the work before us; we make it with unwavering faith in the power of the risen Saviour to call men into His vineyard, and to open the hearts of those who are His stewards to send out and support them, and we shall not cease to cry mightily to Him that He will do this thing, and that our eyes may see it.'

Meanwhile, in other scenes and unexpected ways, the hand of God was working. Simultaneously, though independently of each other, four ministers in Melbourne had been much exercised about China's spiritual need and claims. To each of them came the conviction that Australian Christians ought to be doing something towards the evangelization of the greatest heathen country in the world, and the heathen country nearest their own shores. Of the four, two were Episcopalians, one a Presbyterian and one a Baptist. After some weeks, when they discovered that the burden was one they shared in common, the friends met together for prayer, and it was not long before they found that the Lord was calling one of their number to give his own life to the work. His place could be filled at home, but few were thinking of the greater need beyond.

Missions to the New Hebrides and New Guinea, as well as in some parts of India, were receiving the support of Australian Christians at this time, but partly in consequence of racial prejudice against the Chinese in their midst, nothing was being done for the vast and populous land from which they came. Yet it was evident that these merchants, market gardeners, and laundry-men represented a strong sagacious people, capable of wonderful response to the redeeming love of Christ. Thus when the curate at Caulfield, near Melbourne, desired to go as a missionary to China, it was necessary to seek a connection with one of the societies in the old country. This led to a correspondence with the China Inland Mission; to the acceptance of Parsons and his sailing for Shanghai shortly before the conference which had brought Taylor from England, and also to the earnest desire on the part of his friends in Victoria that a local Council should be formed, to work in connection with the C.I.M. as did the Councils in Toronto and elsewhere.

Nor was this all – for in the neighbouring island of Tasmania similar results had been arrived at, though in a different way. A young missionary who had gone out from England as an Associate of the Mission was obliged, through failing health, to return to Launceston about the time that Taylor was writing *To Every Creature*. In the church of which George Soltau was then the pastor, her influence was telling. China in all its need was still the burden on her heart, and as she spoke of it in meetings, with the love and zeal of one who was following in the footsteps of the Master, many were moved with the same spirit. The result was that gifts began to flow in and offers of service.

To Taylor, in the midst of the conference, all this was full of encouragement. If in China they were being led to ask great things for the Lord's work He was certainly showing, under the Southern Cross, that He could open up fresh channels of supply. The new headquarters of the Mission also, to which he had been welcomed on landing, encouraged thoughts of development. Commenced as he was leaving China little more than a year previously, these ample premises were completed just in time for his return, and to receive the members of the Mission, eight of whom gathered for the conference and for the C.I.M. meetings which followed. The opening of the hall for prayer and public services, and the wedding that took place a few days later, when the generous donor of land and buildings married a fellow-member of the Mission – all the bridal party being in Chinese dress – attracted many friends, and called attention to the wonderful provision the Lord had made for the needs of the growing work.

Upon the C.I.M. conference we must not dwell, nor upon the subsequent Council Meetings, when for three weeks the leaders of the Mission were occupied with problems of the work and with preparation for future developments. A cable to Melbourne authorizing the formation of the proposed Council had put matters in train for Taylor's visit to the Australian states, and by the end of July he found himself free to set out.

On his arrival open doors awaited him on every hand, and friends old and new were generous with help and sympathy. Beginning in Melbourne, where at first the meetings were not large, Taylor had time to become personally acquainted with the members of the Council, and both there and in Tasmania it was noticed how he laid himself out to help these and other friends in the duties they had undertaken. Of a meeting in the drawing-room at Mount Pleasant to consider the important question of candidates, one who took part wrote:

> Never can I forget how helpfully Mr. Taylor led us on to see the needs, so that we suggested the rules to be made and the line to be taken by the Council, wholly

unaware at the moment of how he was guiding our thought. But that was characteristic of Mr. Taylor! the grace of our Lord Jesus Christ so overflowing, that those who listened were for the time being scarcely conscious of the wisdom and power behind his words.

His simplicity and the naturalness of all he said and did impressed many. As the meetings became better known, large buildings were filled with eager hearers; but he was still the same, and as free from self-consciousness as a child. One occasion was long remembered in Melbourne, when a large Presbyterian Church was crowded, the Moderator himself occupying the chair. In eloquent, well-chosen phrases he enlarged upon what had been accomplished in China through Hudson Taylor's instrumentality, finally introducing him to the audience as 'our illustrious guest'.

Quietly Taylor stood for a moment, and then began his address by saying in a way that won all hearts: 'Dear friends, I am the little servant of an illustrious Master.'

Children were drawn to him, just as in Sweden, and indeed wherever he went. After a meeting in Government House, Hobart, it was just like him to return with pleasure to the nursery of the home in which he was entertained, a few miles out of the city.

'He was just beautiful with little ones,' wrote his hostess. 'He took each child in our home, and kneeling with them apart, presented them one by one to his Heavenly Father for definite blessing. Two of those children are now engaged in missionary work, one in India and one in China.'

It was the latter, little Edith, only three years old at the time of Taylor's visit, who remembered him with special affection. A year or two later, when she achieved the triumph of knitting a doll's garment, nothing would do but that it must be sent to China, to Hudson Taylor – " 'Cause I love him so!"

But it was on those of ripe experience that he made the most impression, and the deeper the spiritual life the more it responded to his own. His host in Melbourne wrote:

He was an object lesson in quietness. He drew from the Bank of Heaven every farthing of his daily income – 'My peace I give unto you'.

'Keswick teaching' as it is called was not new to me at that time. I had received those glorious truths and was preaching them to others. But here was *the real thing* – an embodiment of 'Keswick teaching' such as I had never hoped to see. This impressed me profoundly – here is a man almost sixty years of age, bearing tremendous burdens, yet absolutely calm and unruffled. Oh, the pile of letters! any one of which might contain news of death, of shortness of funds, of riots or serious trouble. Yet all were opened, read and answered with the same tranquillity – Christ his reason for peace, his power for calm. Dwelling in Christ he partook of His very being and resources, in the midst of and concerning the very matters in question. And he did this by an act of faith as simple as it was continuous.

Yet he was delightfully free and natural. I can find no words to describe it save the Scriptual expression '*in God*'. He was 'in God' all the time, and God in him. It was that true 'abiding' of John 15. But oh, the *lover-like* attitude that underlay it! He had in relation to Christ a most bountiful experience of the Song of Solomon. It was a wonderful combination – the strength and tenderness of one who, amid stern preoccupation, like that of a judge on the bench, carried in his heart the light and love of home.

More than sixty applied to join the Mission before the time came for Taylor's return to China, and many others were profoundly influenced who found their life-work in India and elsewhere. Such, for example, was the young evangelist who felt quite annoyed when he saw in the local paper an announcement of Taylor's Hobart meetings. He had no sympathy at that time, no patience even, with those who advocated foreign missions; being convinced, through certain preconceptions, that the whole idea was mistaken and unscriptural. Charles Reeve was an earnest Bible student, however, and when drawn to the meetings in spite of himself the first thing he noticed was that the speaker was certainly dealing faithfully with the Word of God. Indeed as he listened, Reeve felt that he had never heard the Bible more truly expounded, though the conclusions he could not escape ran counter to his strongest convictions up to that hour. For it was on the back seat of that hall, as Taylor's earnest voice went on, that the call of God came to him, and the Poona and Indian Village Mission of today, with its band of devoted workers, is the outcome.

The best of the meetings were naturally the last, when Taylor was surrounded by the young volunteers who were returning with him to China. He had had no hesitation in letting it be known that he was praying for 100 fellow-workers from Australasia, and the large number who had already come forward awakened the deepest interest. When the Council arranged for a day of prayer and conference for ministers only, to meet Hudson Taylor, no fewer than forty attended; and the same evening the Melbourne Town Hall witnessed an enthusiastic gathering of 3,000 people to bid farewell to the party.

The party was to sail in October. The vessel was delayed, however, owing to a strike of dock labourers, and an invitation for meetings in Queensland, which he had had to decline, recurred to Taylor's mind. He little knew how much prayer there had been behind that invitation, or the outgoings of heart with which the Queensland vicar and his wife thought of great, dark China, far away. Their home was attractive and their work congenial, but the appeal of the Shanghai Conference had reached them, and Mr. Southey noted that ordained men were specially asked for. His health was not very robust, and with three young children to think of, it might well have seemed that he was doing all he could, by earnestly forwarding the cause of missions at home. But this did not satisfy his conscience before God.

'I cannot help feeling,' he wrote to Taylor when he heard that the latter was really coming, 'that some of the Ipswich ministers ought to go to the heathen. In a town of eight or nine thousand inhabitants – of whom not quite two-thirds are Protestants – there are nine Protestant churches with ten ministers; and not one of the churches is ever really full. It is not from any wish to change that I write this. I am only anxious to do my Father's will. I am perfectly willing to stay in Queensland if it is His will, and I am willing if it be His will to go to the heathen. There is plenty to do here. Spiritual religion in all the churches is at a sadly low ebb, and there is but little missionary zeal. So that I may truly say that there is work for a child of God here; but it does seem that there is more among the heathen.'

Few experiences ever touched Taylor more deeply than the visit to this happy, delightful home, which the parents were so ready to forsake for the love that is stronger than any earthly tie. Southey, when he met him that early summer morning, was for a moment disappointed. He had heard and thought so much about the veteran missionary that he unconsciously expected someone of imposing appearance; and when a single passenger alighted from the express and came toward him, he could hardly believe it was the visitor expected. Some years later he wrote,

On reaching home, I mentioned this feeling of disappointment to my wife, adding, however, 'I am sure he is a good man'. But she was of quicker discernment than I, and after a little chat with our guest came and said, 'Look at the light in his face'.

And truly Mr. Taylor did have the light of God in his face. So constantly did he look up to God, and so deep was his communion with God, that his very face seemed to have upon it a heavenly light. He had not been many hours in the house before the first sense of disappointment gave place to a deep reverence and love, and I realized as never before what the grace of God could do. Often and often had I longed to go to Keswick, but now God in His love had sent Keswick to me, and I was permitted not to listen to beautiful teaching, but to see the beauty of a life lived in abiding fellowship with the Lord Jesus. In the house he was all that a guest should be, kind, courteous, considerate, gracious. He at once fell into the routine of the household, was punctual at the meal table, studied to give the minimum of trouble, and was swift to notice and to express his thanks for every little service rendered. We could not help noticing the utter lack of self-assertion about him, and his true because unconscious humility. About the Lord and His grace and faithfulness he spoke freely; about himself and his service he said nothing. Only by questioning did we learn anything of his own labours or experiences, but when he was thus drawn out, how much he had to tell!

While he was with us the question of our going to China was discussed, and though from the very first he seemed to feel that our offer was of the Lord, yet he took pains to set before us the whole facts of the case. The climate, the discomforts, the absence of medical help, the necessity of parting from the children, etc., were fully gone into. He certainly did not lead us out by withholding from us the real facts; and more than once after walking up and down our garden, which seemed to have a great charm for him, he said to my wife, 'You won't have a garden like this in China!'

But the refuge in God that they would have, and the certainty of His sustaining grace, was confirmed to them by all they saw of their visitor, and had not a little to do with the step of faith which gave to China two of its truest helpers and to the Mission, ultimately, its Home Director for Australia and New Zealand.

Wonderful were the developments of that winter, both before and after Taylor's return to China. Arriving on Sunday, December 21st, he had the joy of finding Jennie awaiting him. Arrangements had at last been possible to free her from home responsibilities, and she had long felt that her place was at his side. Absent nine years from China, she saw great changes, great advance on every hand, and her presence seemed to double Taylor's capacity for work and happiness in it. There was need of all he could do and be that winter, to keep pace with the unprecedented growth of the Mission. Great had been the joy in 1887 when 100 new workers had come out within twelve months; but now, in *half* that time, *a hundred and thirty-one* were received in Shanghai for the C.I.M. alone. Sixty-six of them, indeed, arrived in little over three weeks – a new thing on any mission field! And the sources of supply were no less remarkable than the numbers.

Far away in northern Europe, the little pamphlet *To Every Creature* had fallen into the hands of a devoted evangelist, the Rev. F. Franson – Swedish by birth but a naturalized American – who had worked for seven years with D. L. Moody. Always keen about foreign missions, its appeal for absolute loyalty to the Lord Jesus Christ and unquestioning obedience to His great command fired a soul whose zeal could not but move others. Twice had Franson been in prison for his uncompromising earnestness in preaching the Gospel; and now, with a burning heart, he carried this new crusade throughout the region where he then was, which happened to be northern Germany. In Barmen missionary interest was specially developed. The China Alliance Mission was the result, and wishing to work on the lines of the C.I.M., its leaders entered into correspondence with Taylor. It was not long before its first representatives sailed for China as associates of the China Inland Mission; but Franson, by that time, had entered upon another campaign, among the Scandinavian churches in America.

Well-known throughout the States, he had no lack of openings, and he proceeded on the plan of encouraging the Lord's people 'to give support each church to one missionary'.

'This plan has proved to be a very good one,' he continued. 'I have succeeded very well. Not only have this party their support secured, but another expedition of some ten will leave Omaha twelve days later than this one. We arrange it so that we do not send any who has not been used of God to blessing for souls. A good many have offered themselves but have been refused, some on the ground of insufficient health, some on the ground of incapability for mission work. A very great interest has been created all over America among Scandinavians, through my personal visits and the visits of these missionaries.'

Chosen men and women of devoted spirit, their intention was, as Franson explained, to do itinerant work; 'that is to be of the Thousand Mr. Taylor has prayed to the Lord about – to do just that work'.

They are prepared to go from place to place preaching the Gospel, distributing tracts and Bibles, as the Lord may lead for at least three years, and not to marry during this time, or even get engaged. I suppose it best that they procure Chinese clothes as soon as they arrive.

Their desire was to be associated with the C.I.M., just as the Swedish and German Alliance Missions were, and to be under the direction of Taylor and his representatives no less than that of their own leaders. It was a large contribution, as it proved, to the ranks of the Mission.

One February morning Stevenson was on the long verandah of the Mission house when two healthy-looking young men presented themselves at the main entrance.

'They must be the Scandinavians,' said the Deputy Director, going to meet them. He had just been speaking of Franson's party.

'How many are you?' was a necessary question in view of providing accommodation.

'We are thirty-five,' came the astonishing reply, 'and there are ten more, or perhaps fifteen, who will be here next week.'

The Scandinavian Fifty had hardly gone singing on their way when riots began to break out all along the Yangtze valley. In place after place mission premises were destroyed, and though the fury of the people was specially directed against the Romanists, all foreigners were more or less imperilled. Even in Shanghai it seemed uncertain whether the authorities would be able to restrain looting and violence, and little sleep was to be had on more than one hot summer night because a riot was expected before morning.

For five long months, from May to October, the excitement continued, notwithstanding an Imperial proclamation which had a good effect. Gradually the anti-foreign feeling died down for the time being, and normal conditions were restored.

Meanwhile burdens of a different nature were pressing more and more heavily. With a Mission embracing so many workers, widely scattered over a vast territory, all to be counselled, guided, sustained by prayer, supplied with means and many of the necessities of life, it was inevitable that much of care, if not anxiety, should come upon its responsible head in Shanghai.

Often had the question of funds to be brought to the Lord at this time, for it was one that was causing Taylor considerable exercise of mind. With a rapidly growing and encouraging work on the field, the income received in England had been falling for two or three years. Believing as he did that every gift to the Mission was the outcome of a Divinely given impulse, Taylor could not but search his own life again and again, and prayerfully consider every aspect of the work to see whether there might be anything hindering the blessing of the Lord in this respect. His heart was kept in peace about it and about all the pressure that was upon him, but apart from the daily miracle of sustaining grace it would have been far otherwise.

And there were other trials that led to even deeper exercise of heart and mind. The relation of the work in China to the Council at home had not yet passed beyond the experimental stage, in which questions were apt to come up that were difficult of settlement. The whole idea of the Mission in this connection – government on the field rather than from a distance – was so new and contrary to received traditions that it was no wonder it had to win its way gradually and in face, at times, of criticism and questioning. To Taylor with his thorough grasp of the problems to be dealt with, nothing could be clearer than that the control of affairs in China must be vested in men of expert knowledge, leaders in whom their fellow-missionaries would have confidence, able to deal with matters effectively on the spot. It was easy to see that in the home centres the Directors and Councils must be free to apply the principles of the Mission to their own problems and decide their own line of action in accordance with them; but it needed time and experience to make it equally plain that the China administration must be upon the same footing. In principle this had been conceded from the first; but it was one thing to have confidence in Taylor's management as long as matters were in his own hands, and quite another to transfer that confidence to the China Council. Yet this was a cardinal point in the organization he was building up.

'Mr. Berger is quite right,' he wrote in this connection (May 1891), 'that the supreme question is that of final headship, and it is equally clear to me that it can only be vested in China.'

There could be no question of compromise upon so vital an issue.

'We may make mistakes in China,' he wrote again (Aug. 28), 'and no doubt mistakes have been made in the past; but evils far more serious would result from abandoning what I am convinced are God-given lines for the C.I.M.'

Much as it would have meant to him therefore, amid all the pressure of this period, to have had the full and sympathetic concurrence ultimately secured in these matters, there was nothing for it but to wait upon God and to wait His time.

'The Lord doubtless has His purpose in permitting it,' he wrote to Stevenson at the close of the year 1891, 'and to learn any lesson He may have to teach us is more important than getting rid of the trouble.'

What could have been more encouraging under the circumstances than just the outpourings of spiritual blessing, both in the spring of the year and at its close, with which the Lord was pleased to cheer His servants in Shanghai? No one could relieve Taylor of burdens that pressed the heaviest, but others might be channels of Divine grace through which the entire Mission should be refreshed.

Such a channel was Henry Frost, now paying his first visit to China. Arriving with a party from Toronto in February, he stayed until well on in the summer, making a considerable journey round the nearer stations. A conference of American workers gathered in Shanghai to meet him proved a time of real spiritual help.

Early in the autumn Cassels of the Cambridge Seven arrived from his far western province to attend the Council Meetings, and the Misses Newcombe of the C.M.S. – soon to lay down their lives for Christ's sake – came up from Foochow on a visit. All these brought blessing to the resident staff and the many coming and going in the Mission house. They spoke much of the life that is 'No longer I but Christ' in practical reality, but best of all *they lived it*. And is there anything else so sure to awaken hunger in other hearts?

'There is a real spirit of prayer and quickening in the home here, praise God!' Jennie Taylor wrote on November 7.

Then a great uplift was given, as the year drew to a close, by the coming of a C.M.S. party with Mr. and Mrs. Heywood Horsburgh from England. These beloved friends had the sorrow of losing a precious child in Shanghai, but from stricken hearts only love and blessing flowed to others. The tide of spiritual life was deepening, and before they left for their new sphere,

1,500 miles up the Yangtze, several conversions had taken place in the C.I.M. hall and on a British man-of-war lying in the river.

After that came a wonderful time, in which one and another were brought face to face with a question which revealed the heart's deepest need and opened up a whole world of blessed possibility. One young worker from the interior, for example, unavoidably detained in Shanghai, was present at these meetings, and stirred with a sense of need and longing as never before. Four years in China had taught her something of the joy and blessing to be found in deeper fellowship with the Master, but something also of the deadening influences of heathenism, the power of evil within as well as around her, and the blank despair of seeking to help others when her own soul was out of living touch with Christ. How she longed for 'the exchanged life', the life she saw in others, but knew not how to attain. Praying in an anguish no one suspected for light and help, it was the last Sunday before Christmas when a word was spoken that, under God, brought deliverance and made all things new. After the evangelistic service in the C.I.M. hall, an entire stranger – a Christian seaman – came up to her and said earnestly:

'Are you filled with the Holy Ghost?'

Filled with the Holy Ghost? She remembered no more of the conversation, but that question burned deeper and deeper into her heart. This, then, was the explanation of all the inward failure, the sorrow that seemed unavailing, the purposes that came to nothing. God had made a provision, given a Gift that she had never definitely accepted. She knew that the Holy Spirit must be her life in a certain sense, for 'if any man have not the Spirit of Christ, he is none of his'. And yet, just as certainly, she knew that she was *not* 'filled with the Spirit', and was experiencing little of His power.

But how afraid she was of being misled, of running into error and mistaking emotion for reality! The Word of God was full, now she came to study the subject, of the personality and power of the Holy Spirit. The Acts of the Apostles – what was it but the acts of the Holy Ghost, transforming and quickening lives just as she knew she needed to be quickened and transformed? O yes, why had she never seen it? It was indeed the Holy Spirit she needed; the fullness of the Holy Spirit, to make unseen things real to her and impossible things possible. And there stood out in Gal. 3. 13, 14 the words:

'Christ hath redeemed us from the curse of the law, being made a curse for us . . . that we might *receive* the promise of the Spirit *through faith*.'

What was she doing with the infinite Gift purchased at such a cost? She saw that just as Christ is ours by the gift of God, and yet we have each one personally to receive Him, so with the Holy Spirit. She saw that He too was a Person, just as real as the Lord Jesus, and to be just as truly welcomed by faith into the heart that cannot do without Him as a living link with the risen, glorious Lord. All the rest that can be told is that she took the step, though with fear and trembling – scarce knowing what it meant – and trusted the Holy Spirit to come in and possess her fully, just as she had trusted the Lord Jesus to be her Saviour. Feeling nothing, realizing nothing, she just took God at His word, and then and there asked that the promise might be fulfilled, 'When he is come (to you) he will reprove (or convict) the world of sin, and of righteousness, and of judgment'. Her chief sorrow for many months had been that she seemed to have little power for soul-winning, and hardly knew of any who had been brought to Christ through her instrumentality. It was Christmas week, and believing that a real, a definite transaction had taken place alone in that quiet room, she asked in faith that God would give her to see the proof of it in actual conversions *every day that week*, in connection with meetings that were being held.

And every day that week the prayer was answered. More than twenty people, young and old, sailors, visitors, and residents in Shanghai, it was given her to help to a definite decision for Christ, while the joy and liberty of her own heart were so manifest that others could not but long for and seek the same blessing.

> 'God is working in our midst,' Jennie Taylor wrote in April, 1892, 'emptying and humbling one and another, and filling with the Holy Spirit. We are having frequent meetings full of liberty and power.'

On the 16th of that month the Council, which was in session, was suspended, a minute being passed to record that,

> Instead of meeting for conference, the China Council united with the members of the Mission in Shanghai in seeking for themselves, the whole Mission in China and the Home Councils, the filling of the Holy Spirit.

In answer to prayer the blessing spread. From distant stations letters that took weeks in coming told of individual missionaries, and whole groups in some cases, transformed by the same renewing power, while from the young men's training home came the tidings that not one of the students remained unblessed. In a circular letter to the members of the Mission, Taylor wrote:

> Here in Shanghai there have been some very hungry hearts, and praise God He has been fulfilling to them the promise 'He satisfieth the longing soul, and filleth the hungry soul with goodness'; with the result that there have been more conversions in connection with our work here, in a few months, than for several years previously – some fifty persons, sailors and residents as well as servants, having accepted Christ. From other places too we are hearing of quickening and ingathering, which we trust may be as droppings before the showers we need.

The supreme want of all missions in the present day is the manifested presence of the Holy Ghost. Hundreds of thousands of tracts and portions of Scripture have been put into circulation; thousands of Gospel addresses have been given; tens of thousands of miles have been traversed in missionary journeys, but how small has been the issue in the way of definite conversions! We as a Mission have much need to humble ourselves before God. There has been a measure of blessing among us and souls have been saved, but where are the ones that chase a thousand, or the two that put ten thousand to flight? Where are the once-thirsty ones, now filled, from whom flow rivers of living water?

Few of us, perhaps, are satisfied with the results of our work, and some may think that if we had more, or more costly machinery we should do better. But oh, I feel that it is *Divine power* we want and not machinery! If the tens or hundreds we now reach daily are not being won to Christ, where would be the gain in machinery that would enable us to reach double the number? Should we not do well, rather, to suspend our present operations and give ourselves to humiliation and prayer for nothing less than to be filled with the Spirit, and made channels through which He shall work with resistless power?

Souls are perishing *now* for lack of this power. God is blessing *now* some who are seeking this blessing from Him in faith. All things are ready, if we are ready. Let us ask Him to search us and remove all that hinders His working by us in larger measure. If any of us have been tempted to murmur, to think or speak unkindly of fellow-workers; if light conversation or jesting 'which are not convenient' have been indulged in; if we have allowed less important things to take time and attention that God's direct work should have had; if our Bibles or secret prayer have been neglected, let us confess the evil before God and claim His promised forgiveness, carefully avoiding such occasions of weakness for the future. And having sought the removal of all hindrances and yielded ourselves up in fresh consecration, let us accept *by faith* the filling, and definitely receive the Holy Ghost, to occupy and govern the cleansed temple.

Before the close of the year, deliverance was given in the matters of difficulty that had necessitated Taylor's return to England. When it seemed that unanimity could not be reached by discussion of the problems, the whole time was given at more than one Council Meeting to united waiting upon God. After that the change was very marked. With certain concessions on Taylor's own part, liberty for the China administration was fully and finally secured, and early in 1893 it was evident that this prolonged period of trial was passing away.

As to the financial trial of the period, there had been times of straitness in China when special prayer was called forth, times when the members of the Mission had been drawn to one another in quickened love and sympathy, and had learned fresh lessons of the overruling care of God. Such, for example, was the December day in 1891 when £2,000 was urgently needed for general purposes, and the cable announcing the month's remittance was due to arrive from England. Taylor and his wife were at work in the study as usual, a junior member of the Mission being with them when the telegram was brought in. With a brief pause for silent prayer he opened and read it, read it aloud, forgetful perhaps of the young worker to whom the moment was one of almost breathless suspense.

'A hundred and seventy pounds.'

'One thousand seven hundred, perhaps?'

'No: a hundred and seventy.'

In the silence that followed it seemed to the one who listened as if the heavens had fallen, or a chasm of measureless blackness had opened at her feet. A hundred and seventy pounds, and a pressing need of two thousand! Nearly 500 missionaries, and no further cable for a month!

How did he know just what that young heart was experiencing? How could he be so at leisure from himself, so sure of God and at rest in Him that his first thought was for the faith of another? Turning in his chair, Taylor held out his hand with fatherly kindness:

'Now you will watch,' he said, and there was even a touch of joyous confidence about the words. 'You will watch and see *what God will do*.'

A special opportunity for God to work and for faith to triumph – this was the immediate attitude, fully justified by the events that followed. The deficiency was not made up by any outstanding gift on this occasion, but in many directions the hand of God was seen. Larger remittances than usual were received from Australia and other centres, while unexpected help was forthcoming in China, so that by the end of the month an average remittance had been sent to all the stations with more than an average sense of the love and care of Him who 'abideth faithful', who even when our faith wavers 'cannot deny himself'.

CHAPTER 25

Can Ye Drink of the Cup?

(1893–1895)

NEVER since that October day in 1889, when the thoughts had come to Taylor that found expression in his pamphlet *To Every Creature,* had the subject of a widespread evangelistic campaign throughout the whole of China been absent from his heart. Despite the many grave difficulties that had attended missionary work in China since then, as though the appeal of the Shanghai Conference for 1,000 missionaries had aroused all the opposition of the powers of evil, he was assured that the purpose was of God, and had lost none of his first sense of responsibility to do all that in him lay to carry it into effect. Travelling, thinking, speaking, planning new premises to replace the long inadequate quarters at Pyrland Road, encouraging his fellow-workers by visits to the Continent, he quietly kept in view the larger reinforcements that would be needed for a Forward Movement to carry the Gospel to 'every creature' in China.

With a diminishing income in England and responsibilities already heavy in China, it might have seemed anything but seasonable for fresh advance. But the heart of the Mission was glowing with fresh blessing and Taylor felt the time had come. With the enlarged staff at Pyrland Road, much in the way of development seemed possible. A visit to Germany in April and another in August had convinced him that many valuable workers for China might be added to those who had already gone out from Barmen as associates of the Mission. He saw his way to organize a thorough campaign throughout England, Scotland, and Ireland, specially with a view to calling forth young men for missionary service. The newly published *Story of the C.I.M.* was being widely read; funds were encouraging, no less than £10,000 having been received in little over a month for new undertakings; and with the exception of a brief visit to America for the second Student Volunteer Conference, Taylor was looking forward to a steady spell of work at home such as he had not had since the days of the Hundred.

Just at that time a little cloud no bigger than a man's hand warned him that he was needed in China. It concerned the welfare and usefulness of one or more valued members of the Mission; and Taylor's warm love for them personally, as well as his sense of responsibility for the work, decided him to go on from America to Shanghai to deal with the matter. While regretting the break in his programme at home, it seemed that only a brief absence would be necessary, and he allowed his name to stand as one of the speakers at Keswick for the following summer.[1]

The Student Conference at Detroit was memorable, when John R. Mott, Robert E. Speer, and other leaders fresh from college gave evidence of the gifts which were so remarkably developed in worldwide work for God.

> 'Our chief and only burden,' John Mott had written to Taylor in urging him to come over, 'is that it may be a markedly spiritual convention. God has been with you in other gatherings, as well as in your regular work, and we have faith to believe that you would be a channel of great spiritual blessing in this continent and through it to the world, if you are at Detroit. Have we not a right to expect that God will do mighty things during these days, if we comply with His conditions?'

And He did do mighty things, through various instrumentalities. Never to be forgotten was one early morning hour when the great hall was filled with students only, who had come together because they were hungry for definite, abiding blessing. The message was the same that had brought help to many in Shanghai two years previously; and as then, heart after heart discovered God's provision to meet all depths of failure and need. Years of devoted service on many a mission field were to bear witness to the spiritual transactions of that hour.

A few weeks later, the matter having been prospered that had brought Taylor to Shanghai, he was about to leave again for home, eager to help in calling out men for the Forward Movement, when all unexpectedly he found himself claimed in quite another direction. Far away in the north of China complications had arisen which threatened the recall of all Scandinavian missionaries to the coast. A little band, unconnected with the C.I.M., had recently commenced work in a devoted spirit, but on lines so foreign to Chinese ideas of propriety that grave and growing danger was the result. The workers themselves were too inexperienced to realize the state of affairs, but passing travellers had carried the tidings to Peking and the Swedish Foreign Office was on the point of taking action. Of this, warning was received by Taylor, and though he had nothing to do with the missionaries in question he could not but see how seriously the Scandinavian associates of the C.I.M. might be affected. To those who knew of the situation it seemed providential that the Director of the Mission was in China, as no one could have greater influence in the matter, or be more likely to command the confidence of the authorities in Peking.

But how, even if he gave up his return to England, could he reach those

[1] Hudson Taylor and Jennie sailed for New York on 14 February, 1894, accompanied by Geraldine Guinness, whose marriage to Dr. Howard Taylor took place on their arrival in Shanghai.

far-off stations in time to be of use save by travelling through the entire summer? It was already the end of April. In a few weeks the hot season would begin, and the journey was one that involved three or four months of overland travel. Railways there were none at that time in the inland provinces, and after the wheelbarrow stage must come even rougher travelling on springless carts. Exposure to the burning sun and tropical rains of midsummer were serious indeed, not to speak of the difficulty of obtaining food when villages are deserted during the harvest season.

'It may cost your life,' he was warned.

'Yes,' was the reply, 'and let us not forget – "We *ought* to lay down our lives for the brethren".'

After this there was nothing more to be said, but he did not travel alone. Jennie would not be left out, his doctor son with his bride accompanied them, and with J. J. Coulthard, Taylor's son-in-law, the family party numbered five.

They left Hankow in May, and traversing five provinces visited all the mission stations along the route. For the rest, excepting Sundays, it was fourteen hours daily on the road, all through the blazing heat, everywhere meeting crowds of accessible, friendly people. The long weeks of the cart journey were specially painful for Taylor, who had a sensitive back from concussion of the spine. But it was all well worth it from his point of view as he saw the signs of progress in all regions, in the work nearest to his heart – especially on the vast and populous Sian plain. When he had crossed it eight years previously, travelling with Montagu Beauchamp from Pastor Hsi's district to Hanchung, no light-centres had broken the darkness all around them for hundreds of miles. Now, station after station had been opened, and in the capital – long one of the most anti-foreign cities in China – the Scandinavian workers were gathered whom he had come so far to meet.

It was a wonderful change, all due under God to the devoted lives of a little group of pioneers, long homeless, scorned, and persecuted, for Christ's sake and the Gospel's. When Thomas Botham first went over from Hanchung, things were so hard that even he was discouraged. Yet he could not give up the task to which he felt himself called.

'I am willing to walk in the dark with God,' he said to his Superintendent, himself one of the first pioneers in the province.

'In the dark with God,' replied Easton; 'why, dear Brother, in Him, with Him is "no darkness at all".'

It was a good word with which to begin work on the Sian plain, and much he and his companions had need of it! The young men naturally took it for granted that they must obtain a settled dwelling. Not so, however, the people of the plain. No one would rent them a house, and every effort in that direction aroused intense opposition. At last it came to them – 'the command is "Preach the gospel". Let us go everywhere and do that, and leave the rest with God. If He wants us to have a house He will give it, and give it in such a way as not to hinder His work.'

Twenty-two governing cities, sixty market towns and innumerable villages formed their parish – a district extending over 12,000 square miles, in which they were the only missionaries – and from end to end of it they were met with little but opposition. All they could do was to move from place to place, staying as long as possible in any inn willing to receive them, preaching on the streets, and seeking by Christlike humility and love to recommend the Gospel. It was work that told, and they were willing for the cost.

When Botham married, his bride, herself a missionary, had already been two years in China, and gladly shared with him in the hardships of his life.

> 'I never feel so happy as when with all my worldly goods on one donkey, and my wife on another, I set out to carry the Gospel to some new place on the Sian plain,' he wrote.

So liable were they to riots and disturbances that the little company had to divide, and scarcely ever dared to be more than two in a city at the same time.

But their wanderings were not aimless. They were literally carrying out the Master's word, 'When they persecute you in this city, flee ye into another'; but they took good care, as Botham put it, to 'flee in a circle', so that coming back from time to time to the same places, the people became used to seeing them.

To this district the leaders of the Scandinavian Fifty had been sent, and arriving just as these devoted lives were beginning to bear fruit, they were ready to take advantage of the changed conditions. Station after station was opened with little difficulty, and the new workers, being men of faith and prayer, were enabled to hold their own even in the capital itself. Many a missionary had sought to obtain footing in that important city, but it was reserved for Holman and his guitar to win the day. Surrounded by a crowd bent on mischief that had invaded his premises, he pleasantly asked the people if they would like to hear him sing. Taken by surprise they listened, as with musical voice and instrument he poured forth Swedish melodies. He was so quiet and friendly that they began to feel ashamed; and finally, as he went on singing – crying to God in his heart for deliverance – the crowd gradually melted away.

It was to the city thus opened that Taylor's party came for the conference where definite arrangements were entered into with regard to the Swedish associates. A district, including the capital and extending north-west into the province of Kansu, was set apart for them under the general supervision of Botham, one of their own leaders being appointed missionary-in-charge. It was a great joy to Taylor to see how those in Sian-fu had grown and developed during the short time, little more than three years, that they had been in China, and to find that though he had to suggest restrictions that might have seemed irksome, the ties were but drawn the closer that united the Scandinavian Alliance workers with the C.I.M.

In the neighbouring province it was encouraging to meet Folke and his fellow-workers of the Swedish Mission in China. Beyond this point the travelling was by moonlight, to escape the intense heat (120° in the carts) which had almost cost Taylor's life in coming from Sian. Setting out toward evening, it was a comfort to feel that before the sun rose again a good stage would have been accomplished, though dangerous characters other than wolves were to be met with in the mountains or in the shelter afforded by tall-growing crops. Stopped one night in the shadow of an arch or shrine, they found that two men had accosted the foremost cart.

'Do you carry foreign travellers?' was the question which startled them.

A moment later, however, the situation was explained by the inquiry in a cultured English voice, 'Is this Mr. Taylor's party?'

Pastor Hsi and D. E. Hoste! Miles had they walked out together to meet the expected visitors, and warm indeed was the welcome with which they received Taylor once again, just where Hoste had parted from him eight years previously.

It was a week later when, the Pingyang-fu Conference being over, Taylor was free to accept Pastor Hsi's hospitality and spend a day or two in his home. Having been there before, what was his surprise on arrival to be driven in through courtyard after courtyard, past house and farm buildings, till an open space was reached that looked like a threshing floor. There stood an ample table covered with a clean white cloth and other preparations for a 'foreign' meal. Overhead a brown awning, supported on a dozen or more wooden masts, formed a sheltering roof, and in the background a building (could it be a barn?) stood with open doors. To this Taylor and his party were led – and lo, a royal pavilion, a whole suite of apartments, beautifully arranged, clean, cool, and ready for use!

With growing astonishment they explored its resources, touched by evidences of loving thoughtfulness on every hand. The central dining-room gave access to a large sleeping apartment on one side, and to a couple of smaller chambers on the other. All were comfortably furnished and most inviting. Lamps were ready on the tables, fresh straw mats completely covered the floors, new bamboo curtains as well as coloured hangings protected doors and windows, new white felt rugs were laid over fine white matting on each of the beds. The tables were spread with red covers, and neatly laid in the centre of each was a square of green oil-silk, beautifully rich in colour. Brass basins, shining like mirrors, were placed upon little stands ready for use, with clean white towels and new cakes of the best Pears' soap! The whole place, in a word, was so clean and attractive, so polished and radiant, that they could hardly believe their eyes.

And there stood Pastor and Mrs. Hsi eager to see if they were pleased, but disclaiming gratitude or remonstrance.

'It is nothing. It is altogether unworthy. Gladly would we have arranged far better for our Venerable Chief Pastor and his family.'

Nothing could exceed the love and joy of that welcome, in which the whole household took part. Pastor Hsi himself brought hot water for washing, and kept the cups filled with tea. He hastened the midday meal, covering the table with good things, and insisted on waiting in person, lest his helpers should not be quick enough to anticipate every wish. His eyes filled with tears as Taylor tried to thank him, and he said,

'Sir, what have you suffered and endured that we might have the Gospel! This is my joy and privilege. How could I do less?'

Harvest days had come in southern Shansi, of which Taylor had seen the promise, and the outlook was full of encouragement. Far away from the Western Chang village events were transpiring, however, that were to have an important bearing on Taylor's movements. Hastening to complete the matter he had in hand, the leader of the Mission was anticipating a speedy return to England to take up the Forward Movement he had reluctantly left in February. But there is an unseen Leader whose great ends are served by all happenings and in ways we should least devise. The very day Hudson Taylor spent in the delightful hospitality of Pastor Hsi's home, July 25, witnessed the outbreak of war between China and Japan, and by the time he reached Shanghai it was evident that he could not absent himself from the scene of danger. All thought of leaving for England now had to be abandoned, and the visit to China that had already lengthened out from weeks to months was prolonged indefinitely.

With the close of the Japanese War in April 1895 came the close also of the period in which the thousand missionaries were looked for in response to the appeal sent out by the Shanghai Conference of 1890. As chairman of the committee to report results, Taylor was able to state that not 1,000 only but 1,153 new workers had been added to the missionary staff in China during that time. And yet, as he pointed out, it was far from final, in the sense of having attained the end in view. A great step forward had been taken, but it left the primary duty – that of making known the Gospel 'to every creature' in China, in obedience to the Master's great command – still unfulfilled. Out of the eleven to twelve hundred new missionaries, only 480 were men; and this number, divided among the forty-five societies which had sent them, would give only an average of ten to each. Clearly, as many of these societies were working in provinces on or near the coast, the addition of even this large number hardly affected the situation in the great waiting world of inland China. It was for these unreached millions that he still pleaded with renewed urgency.

> 'An important crisis in China's history has been reached,' he wrote on behalf of the committee. 'The war just terminated does not leave her where she was. It will inevitably lead to a still wider opening of the empire and to many new developments. If the Church of Christ does not enter the opening doors, others will, and they may become closed against her. Time is passing. If a thousand men were needed five years ago, they are much more needed now.'

But the effect upon missionary work of the tragic events which had transpired was to be serious and far-reaching. Five years yet remained of Taylor's active service, years which raised unparalleled difficulties in the way of carrying out the project so much upon his heart. China had entered at last upon the troubled period of transition from her exclusive policy of centuries to the reluctant but inevitable acceptance of her place in the great family of nations. The change was not one that could take place easily; and the weakening, through loss of prestige, of the Imperial Government at Peking let loose forces of disorder in many parts of the country. Shortly after the above letter was written Taylor began to hear of riots, persecutions, and rebellion, from the coast right out to the borders of Tibet. Sitting quietly at breakfast on Sunday, June 1st, a telegram was put into his hands which brought the startling tidings:

> Riot in Chengtu (capital of Szechwan). All missions destroyed: friends in *yamen*.

This was followed by another and another, until within ten days he learned of destruction in all but one of the central stations of the Mission in that province. At the same time bitter persecution broke out against the Christians in the Wenchow district, one of the oldest and most fruitful in the Mission. Tidings kept coming of homes attacked and pillaged, families fleeing for refuge to the Mission compound, and a work that had taken long years to build up threatened with complete devastation.

Nor were these the most serious issues. They were symptomatic of general excitement and unrest and loss of confidence in the ruling powers. Secret societies were everywhere active, and a great Muhammadan uprising was reported from the north-west, where C.I.M. missionaries were the only foreigners. The disbanded soldiers – still armed and with arrears of pay due in many cases – were a serious menace, and with hundreds of fellow-workers in inland stations, Taylor had evident cause for concern.[1]

Over 1,000 miles from Szechwan and kept in suspense for weeks until letters could reach him, Taylor was specially exercised about the Church of England district in which the work had been full of promise. No lives were actually lost in Szechwan, however, and not a few of the missionaries who had taken refuge with the local Mandarins were allowed to return before long to their dismantled dwellings. To their great joy they found in some places that the converts had been witnessing so faithfully that new inquirers had enrolled their names and were coming regularly for instruction. In Paoning the Christians had braved all danger, and coming to the wall of the *yamen*, had sought to reassure their missionary friends by calling out fearlessly: 'We are all here! Not one of us has gone back.'

In a lonely station among the hills the house where the women missionaries lived was guarded night after night by Christian men who, unknown to them, volunteered for the task; and a woman of position in the district was so concerned for their safety that she came twenty miles on her crippled feet to make inquiries, finding far more than she sought, for her heart was drawn to living faith in the Saviour of whom she thus heard for the first time.

Even when the worst came – the tragedy that was to make this summer memorable in the long conflict between light and darkness – it was immediately and wonderfully overruled for good. Hardly could any missionary then in China forget the awe with which the news was received of the cold-blooded murder of the Rev. Robert Stewart with his wife and child and eight fellow-workers of the Church Missionary Society. Taylor was at Chefoo when it happened, engaged upon buildings for the growing schools, and was not slow to realize the full significance of the event. Never before had the protecting hand of God been so far withdrawn as to permit of such a sacrifice. Instances had occurred in which Protestant missionaries had laid down their lives one or two at a time, but they had been few and far between, and no women had hitherto been among the number. Now mother and children had alike been attacked, and most of the sufferers were young, unmarried women. Gathered at a hill station for rest during the great heat, they had fallen a prey to the plottings of a secret society which apparently hoped to involve the Government in trouble. Whatever the cause or ultimate results, the realization came home to many a heart that a new era had dawned that day, August 1, and that a great price might yet have to be paid for the triumph of the Gospel in China.

[1] At the end of March 1895 the Mission numbered 621 members, settled in 122 central stations, ninety of which were in the eleven formerly unoccupied provinces.

At that very time, unknown to those who were praying for China, but not to Him who was watching over all, another little band was in utmost peril, far in the heart of that great land. After a preparatory stage of several months the Muhammadan Rebellion had swept down upon the city of Sining on the borders of Tibet, where the Ridleys, their infant child, and Hall were the only foreigners. Ten thousand Muhammadans lived in the suburbs round the city, and it was a terrible night when, contrary to vows and protestations, they turned upon their Chinese neighbours, and amid scenes of fearful carnage threw in their lot with the rebels. Already the city was filled with refugees, and the missionaries were working night and day to care for the wounded. Led by a beggar who knew the healing virtue of their medicines, they had found in the Confucian temple hundreds of women and children who had made their escape from burning villages and the horrors perpetrated by their enemies. Groans and wailing were heard on every hand, and in the twilight of that summer evening they saw a mass of human suffering that was appalling. Burned from head to foot and gashed with fearful sword-cuts, scores of these poor creatures lay dying with not a hand to help them, for no one would go near even with food and water.

Then the missionaries understood why they had felt so definitely that they ought to stay on in the city, when they might have made good their escape. This was the work for which they were needed, the work that was to open hearts to the Gospel as years of preaching had not done. With heroic courage they gave themselves to the task, and throughout all that followed never ceased their ministrations. Amid scenes passing conception they cared for the wounded of both sides – first in the seven months of Muhammadan frenzy, when the Chinese were falling before them in thousands, then in still more awful months of Chinese retaliation. With no surgical instrument but a pen-knife and hardly any appliances but such as could be obtained on the spot, they performed hundreds of operations, and treated over 1,000 cases of diphtheria, not to speak of the dressing of wounds that occupied them from early morning till late at night. Neither Ridley nor Hall had had medical training, and though Mrs. Ridley was experienced in sickness she was not a qualified nurse. Operations without chloroform that would have daunted many a strong man she bravely took her part in, and they never once lost a life by cutting an artery in the extraction of bullets, etc. Cotton wool and oil for burns, and common needles and silk for sewing up wounds they were able to buy in the city, as also the sulphur with which they treated diphtheritic patients. A foreign razor helped out the pocket-knife in surgical cases.

But for the help of a four-footed friend Mrs. Ridley could never have got through at all. Their servants left them at the beginning of the siege, and with the baby she was nursing and all the household work on her hands, she alone could attend to a large proportion of their patients, the women and girls. Full gallop her brave little donkey would go through the busy streets the people gladly making way for the mother whose baby was waiting at home!

Once only her heart failed her – in the midst of an attack upon the city, when it seemed as though all hell were let loose, and that at any moment the defences might fall. She was fully alive by that time to what it meant to be at the mercy of Muhammadan hordes. Had not infants been brought to her, scores of them, mutilated by their savagery? Alone in the house that night, her husband and Hall being out amid the panic-stricken people, a wave of terror swept over her. It was Dora, little Dora she thought of. For themselves it did not matter – but oh, her baby! Her happy, smiling, always contented treasure! How could she bear to see . . .? But as she knelt beside the sleeping infant and cried to God, the Presence which is salvation so wrapped her round that all else receded and was forgotten.

'He gave me the assurance then,' she said, 'that no harm should come to us.' And though it was many a long month before fighting and massacre were over, that agonizing dread never returned.

To Taylor, far off in Shanghai, such knowledge as he had of the situation was peculiarly distressing. Neither letters nor money could be sent to these fellow-workers, and for months together no tidings of them were received. A remittance forwarded in the spring had got through before the siege commenced, but it was spring again when the next came to hand. Relief expeditions sent by the Government failed to reach the city, more than 1,000 soldiers losing their lives in the attempt. It was well Taylor did not know that Ridley had almost succumbed to an attack of diphtheria, that smallpox was raging in the city, and that neither bread nor coal was to be purchased at any price. A winter of seven months had to be faced, with the temperature below zero much of the time, and so small was their supply of fuel that they had to eke it out with manure, and even so could only afford a fire at meal-times. Had he seen and known it all, Taylor's solicitude could hardly have been greater, however; and so much was that little group upon his heart that not infrequently he rose two and three times at night to pray for them.

Prayer was answered in their desperate situation. God raised up friends for them, supplied their need when money was useless and kept them strong in faith, so busy helping others that they had little time to think of themselves. An official (the Governor's Secretary) living in the same street gave nineteen *taels* toward the medical work, which purchased oil, wadding, and material for bandages; and his wife, knowing that Mrs. Ridley had no time for cooking, invited her to run in whenever she could for meals. Another lady used to send batches of bread from time to time, and when in the straitness of the siege she could no longer do so, she begged that her cook might make bread for the Ridleys from their own flour.

No one guessed how hard up they really were, because Chinese families in their position would always have reserve stores of grain. When the flour was running low therefore, they had to take very literally the promise, 'Trust in the Lord and do good; so shalt thou dwell in the land, and verily thou shalt be fed.' Hardly welcome under the circumstances was a visit from one of the city magnates; for, being alone in the house, Ridley had to light the fire and prepare tea, excusing as best he could his poor hospitality.

Too polite to make any comment, the visitor was taken aback by his discovery, and going straight to the head Mandarin informed him that the foreigners who were doing so much to help others were without a servant of any kind. Four soldiers were immediately pressed upon Ridley to attend him and look after his 'animals', with the result that he was obliged to explain his circumstances and that he really could not provide them with food.

Busy among his patients next morning, what was his surprise to see two men enter the courtyard each carrying a large sack of grain. These were set down amid the delighted onlookers, the bearers explaining that the Prefect had sent 200 lb. of wheat as a small recognition of the virtuous labours of the missionaries. Presently two more soldiers came and carried the sacks to the mill, bringing back the flour. Long before that supply could be exhausted, a procession of six men in uniform appeared, each with his sack of wheat, which was also ground and returned in the shape of 600 lb. of flour! So that without asking help of any save of God alone, those children of His, so isolated and resourceless, were not only provided for but were enabled to feed many of the starving around them until the siege was over.

Meanwhile Hudson Taylor was making every effort to reach them with supplies. He knew they must be still alive because of the burden of prayer on his heart for them day and night, but for months there was no other encouragement to hope. Not until 1896 dawned did the longed-for message come that Sining was relieved and communication re-established, and even then the reign of terror was prolonged by the Chinese retaliation. Almost two years in all the fearful business lasted, 80,000 people being actually massacred, not to speak of soldiers killed in battle or frozen upon the mountains. But through it all the missionaries stayed at their post, proving themselves the friends of Chinese and Muhammadans alike, and winning love and confidence that brought wonderful opportunities for the Gospel. All the country was open to them. Wherever they went they found known and unknown friends, and the work they could not overtake emphasized afresh the need for large and immediate reinforcements. But that belongs to a later period.

Anxiety about Sining was at its height when, in the middle of October, tidings reached Taylor in Shanghai that added a poignant element to the already full cup of 1895. Troubles and dangers had followed one another in quick succession, but so far without loss to the Mission. Now it was cholera that had visited one of the nearer stations, carrying off a whole group of Chinese Christians and foreign missionaries. Nine deaths in all had taken place in ten days, leaving the bereaved community sorely stricken.

And there were circumstances that made the news peculiarly distressing. Well did Taylor remember the young husband and wife he had welcomed to China only a few months previously, whose record in the Soldiers' Home at Litchfield proved them to be soul-winners of exceptional value, and the brave Scots workers they had joined in the Wenchow district, who had stood the brunt of the persecution already referred to in this chapter, sheltering in their home scores of the suffering Christians. Could it be that of the four only one was left, and that to her had come the double bereavement of losing husband and child?

Not so long before, it seemed, she had arrived in China, having put off her marriage with the full consent of her fiancé, that they might each give themselves to learning the language and becoming useful as missionaries before beginning life together. The rule of the Mission in this respect had meant, for them, real sacrifice, for they had long been engaged and were everything to each other. But amid the loneliness of those first days in China, she looked as well as lived the message engraved on the simple brooch she wore: 'Jesus does satisfy.'

Married after two years to Alexander Menzies, home had been to them a little bit of heaven, and their joy in one another had deepened with the coming of their baby boy. And now the letter lay before Taylor in which the mother tried to comfort *him* in her overwhelming grief.

> 'It is just possible,' she wrote from Wenchow, 'that you may have heard of the honour that my God and Father has put upon me. Yes, He has trusted me to live without my beloved husband and darling child. They are not, for God has taken them.'

Briefly she told the circumstances, sparing Taylor most of the touching details: the father reaching home from a journey to find himself just in time for the funeral of his little son; the short, sharp fight for life after life on the Mission compound; three schoolgirls taken, a man, a woman, and the missionaries caring for them to the last, regardless of their own danger; then her husband the first to go, followed by Mr. and Mrs. Woodman within a few hours of each other.

'It would have been so easy for me to have joined my treasures,' she continued, 'but our Father has willed it otherwise. My treasures are gone and I am left alone – yet not alone: "Nevertheless, I am *continually* with thee".

'Dear Mr. Taylor, God has taken His workmen, but He will carry on His work. I do not know what He has in store for me, but I do know He will guide the future as He has the past. I long more than ever to do His blessed will. He has taken my *all*: now I can only give Him what remains of life. He has indeed emptied me! May it be only to fill with His love, compassion and power.'

So the sweet fragrance went up to God, and the life more than ever given to the Chinese witnessed, as words never could, to the blessed reality – 'Jesus does satisfy'. Thus it was all over the field: sorrow worked blessing; trials of faith resulted in deeper confidence; the bond of love and unity in the Mission was strengthened, and a spirit of prayer was called forth that prepared the way for more of God's own working.

It was during this year, while the war with Japan was still going on, that Pastor Wang Lae-djün came up to Shanghai to see Taylor. In the old home at Hangchow, he and his family had united in making an offering to the Lord. Declining a settled salary that he might be on the same faith basis as the members of the Mission, Wang Lae-djün had yet been enabled to lay by for his only child a sum which to people in their position was considerable. His daughter's husband had long been his co-pastor in the Hangchow church, but while his gifts would have brought them affluence in a business career, it was all they could do to educate their large family on the income he received in connection with the C.I.M. But neither Pastor Ren nor his wife would consent to accept the savings of their father's lifetime.

How large a sum it seemed – $1,000! No: it must not be given to them or their children. The Lord had always provided for their needs, and would still provide. It was far too precious for any but Himself; and to Him they would unitedly give it. The object of Pastor Wang's visit was that the money which meant so much to him and his was to be used, through the Mission, for sending out evangelists to carry the glad tidings to those who had never heard.

To the old Pastor it was wonderful to see the extensive premises of the Mission in Shanghai, and hear of the progress of the work throughout the far inland provinces, remembering the early beginnings in the little house by the Ningpo canal to which his missionary friend had brought home his bride. Deeply their hearts were still united in the supreme longing that the Lord Jesus should see of the travail of His soul and be satisfied through the gathering in to Him of the fullness of His redeemed from among the millions of China. And as he looked back over the year with its sorrows and trials, Hudson Taylor observed that a larger number of converts had been baptized in 1895 than in any previous year.

CHAPTER 26

Even So, Father

(1895–1902)

It was hardly to be wondered at that Taylor's physical powers, so long taxed to the utmost in the interests of the Mission, should begin to fail under the strain of periods such as this of his ninth visit to China. Little by little the scaffolding of his life was being taken down from about the work he had prayed into being. Not that those nearest to him recognized it. He himself had it steadily in view, and rejoiced in the growing usefulness of others, and the way in which provision was being made for leadership in days to come.

The internal organization slowly developed, and was working well throughout the Mission. More and more the C.I.M. was saving expense and caring for its workers through the business department, and in nothing was the practical value of its principles more evident than in the provision made in this and other ways for coming needs. Refusing none who seemed truly called of God, whatever their nationality, denomination, or previous training, the Mission had been given men and women with every sort of qualification for usefulness. If all had been theologians or members of learned professions, how could the practical working of so large and varied an organization have been provided for? As it was, when need arose for the formation of a diocese in Western China, there was a Bishop to be found in the ranks of the Mission. There were Superintendents for great districts. There were financial experts for the management of complicated money matters; stenographers to help with the burden of correspondence; competent heads for postal, shipping, and business offices; an architect and land surveyor for building operations; doctors and nurses to care for their fellow-missionaries as well as for medical work among the people; and qualified teachers for posts at Chefoo. All these workers, each indispensable in their own department, were equally members of the Mission and called to spiritual service in China.

Of the appointment of Cassels to the diocese of West China, Dr. Eugene Stock wrote in his *History of the Church Missionary Society:*

> The China Inland leaders heartily entered into the plan, and Archbishop Benson, who took a warm interest in it, appointed, at the suggestion of the C.M.S. Committee, and with all his usual graciousness, the head of the C.I.M. in Szechwan to be the

new bishop. This was the Rev. W. W. Cassels, one of the Cambridge Seven of 1885, in whose goodness and wisdom all parties had learned to repose confidence. The first public announcement was made at the great Saturday missionary meeting at the Keswick Convention of 1895, and drew forth much prayerful interest and sympathy. The C.M.S. guaranteed the episcopal stipend, and Mr. Cassels came on to the Society's roll of missionaries, while fully retaining his position in the C.I.M. He was consecrated on St. Luke's Day, October 18, 1895, together with Dr. Talbot, the present Bishop of Rochester; and he sailed on that day week for China.

When Bishop Cassels reached China to take up his new responsibilities, Taylor missed the expected pleasure of meeting him in Shanghai. Broken down after a visit to Wenchow, to which he had gone immediately upon hearing of the deaths through cholera, he had been obliged to take a few weeks' rest. This gave opportunity for a boat journey to several of the Chekiang stations, and for refreshing intercourse with Henry Frost, who was again in China. They went to the beautiful district of Chuchow, occupied by the Barmen Associates of the Mission, and completed the arrangements for handing it over to these fellow-workers - an important step in the direction of division of the field. But Taylor was still so unfit for any pressure of work on his return to Shanghai that it was with thankfulness they looked forward to the visit to India he was to pay before long.

A former member of the Mission, Miss Annie Taylor, who had made a remarkable journey through Tibet, was urgently needing help with a band of inexperienced workers she had been the means of calling out. They were in northern India, hoping to gain an entrance from the Darjeeling district to that closed land, and Taylor was to speak at the first Christian Student Conference in Calcutta on his way to join them. An unexpected gift received for their own use made it possible for his wife to accompany him, which in his poor state of health was no little comfort. It would have enabled them also to travel second class by French mail, had they chosen to spend it all upon themselves. But there were fellow-workers to think of; and though third class meant separation in the cabins for men and women respectively, they were thankful for berths near the doors which were not far apart. Then at Hong Kong, Taylor was able to write the following letter, among others, to Shanghai:

After completing our arrangements here and making up our accounts, I find we have a margin that will allow of our providing the £10 we spoke of as desirable for your expenses beyond Melbourne. As the Mission funds were low when we left, we are very thankful to be able to send this. I had rather no one knew of the little gift.

I find the kind gift received in Wenchow more than covers my wife's travelling expenses; and having come to Hong Kong cheaply, we have the joy of being able to enclose a cheque for 100 *taels* towards your journey. Please do not let any one know of this, but cash the cheque yourself at the bank.

Few things are more precious in the records that remain than the frequency of such acts of loving ministry, at a cost that no one knew of save the Lord Himself, to whom first and most of all their gifts were offered.

But though prospered in their visit to India, and much refreshed by intercourse with workers in that great field, Taylor was in no condition to face a summer in China, and an absence of more than two years from England made it desirable for him to be again in touch with the home work.

Great were the changes that had taken place with the new headquarters of the Mission at Newington Green now completed. Knowing they would arrive from Paris during the Saturday prayer meeting, the Taylors avoided mentioning the train by which they were coming, so that no thought of giving them a welcome might disturb the meeting. Leaving their cab at the entrance they walked up the private road from the busy London thoroughfare to the open door of the hall for meetings, over which, carved in stone, stood out the words which meant so much in the history of the Mission – 'HAVE FAITH IN GOD'. Entering quietly, they remained at the back of the room while prayer was going on, so that not until the meeting closed was it generally known that Mr. and Mrs. Taylor were present. The warmth of the welcome they then received was added to by some Continental delegates of the World's Evangelical Alliance who were staying at the Mission house. The new premises were spacious enough to contribute to the realization of one of Taylor's cherished ambitions: that of being able, in measure, to discharge the debt of the Mission for hospitality in many lands, by receiving – whether in London, Shanghai, or elsewhere – those of the one great family to whom a home away from home might be a convenience.

Here then, in the summer of 1896, Taylor settled down for the last period, little as anyone realized it, of his active service in connection with the work in England. Their children being scattered, he and Jennie no longer needed a home of their own, and though they might have been glad of more privacy at times, they were thankful for the closeness of touch with their fellow-workers afforded by the daily life of the Mission house.

Effective leadership at the home end left Taylor free for the larger issues claiming thought and prayer, for conference with Stevenson and the Council, and for visits to Norway, Sweden, and Germany for personal intercourse with the representatives of affiliated Missions.

> My aim is to get every part of the work into such a condition that it can be carried on without me, and with this in view I visit different branches of it in turn. We are specially asking God to give us an increased number of efficient leaders, and to preserve the lives and health of those we already have.

The Forward Movement, which had been for a time in abeyance, was still the chief burden on his heart. Wherever he went he kept it to the front, pleading for full consecration to Christ in view of His unconditional command 'Preach the gospel *to every creature*'. Busy indeed was the winter (1896–1897) after his return from the Continent, when he was strong enough to travel constantly and address meetings in all parts of the country. Never had invitations been more cordial or the hearts of the Lord's people more open to him. Many who remembered his missionary appeals in the days of their childhood had grown to maturity, and those who remained of his first friends and supporters were, like himself, far on in life's pilgrimage. No voice had quite the ring for them of his voice; no one was more welcome in conference or among the churches of all denominations that had known him for so long. It was as always the need of others that occupied him most – the desire not to get but to give, to bring all whom he could influence into the rest and joy of abiding fellowship with Christ.

'There are many hearts, everywhere, wanting to know more of the fulness of Christ,' he wrote before a visit to Germany in the spring of 1897. 'Ask with us a fresh anointing for this service of love.'

Tired with the winter's work, he was glad to accept Mr. Berger's invitation to the south of France for a quiet week or two before proceeding to Germany for the months of March and April. In addition to the Barmen Mission, whose workers Taylor had recently visited in China, there was a newer movement at Kiel which he was glad to strengthen. Started as a branch of the C.I.M. and subsequently developed as the Liebenzell Mission, this work was destined to great usefulness, and both its leaders and those of the older Barmen Mission gave Taylor a cordial welcome and many opportunities for speaking about China.

In Berlin their meetings were chiefly under the auspices of the Y.M.C.A., which had invited them for a student conference. Generously entertained by Count Pückler, they were kept busy for ten days in the capital, some of the meetings doing much to deepen friendly relations. The C.I.M., as they discovered, was none too favourably regarded in certain quarters. Its interdenominational basis did not commend it to leaders of Societies connected with the State Church, and the accounts that had reached them of its growth and faith principles were hardly credited. It was, thus, in a somewhat uncertain frame of mind that prominent ministers and secretaries gathered in the drawing-room of Mrs. Palner Davies (*née* Baroness von Dungern) to meet the visitors, interested specially in seeing what sort of person 'the renowned Hudson Taylor' might be.

'The stranger who stood in our midst,' wrote the Baroness, 'was not of an imposing appearance, and his fair curly hair made him look younger than he really was.'

The time was largely given to questions through interpretation, and as hostess she was naturally anxious. She was conscious, as Taylor could not be, of the critical attitude of not a few present, who regarded him as rather a free lance in the sphere of missions. That as leader of the C.I.M. he received workers from various denominations was the first point on which explanation was desired.

Only recently the Mission had accepted a number of highly educated and well-gifted young men who were members of the State Church. How, then, were they able to work together with Methodists and Baptists, etc.? Mr. Taylor replied that, in our chief aims, we are all one in Christ; and that the workers can be distributed so that each denomination is able to retain its particular order of Church government. 'Only recently,' he stated, 'we have been glad to welcome an English bishop (one of our own number) for Western China, so that our missionaries from the State Church are not lacking the care of a spiritual guide and head. The great work of the mission field, which is a call to us all, overrides theological differences, and our motto remains, "All one in Christ . . .".'

Just when the Director of the Gossner Mission had shaken his silver-white head and remarked to his neighbour in an undertone, 'Such a mixture of Church and Sectarians would be impossible with us,' Mr. Taylor continued:

'It is remarkable how the Lord Himself has chosen His instruments, so that even the most insignificant, in His hand, are able to be "to the praise of His glory". Surely it goes as in creation: there are strong and beautiful oak trees, but there are also little flowers of the meadow; and both the oak and the flower have been placed there by His hand. I myself, for instance, am not specially gifted, and am shy by nature, but my gracious and merciful God and Father inclined Himself to me, and I who was weak in faith He strengthened while I was still young. He taught me in my helplessness to rest on Him, and to pray even about little things in which another might have felt able to help himself.'

Instances were mentioned from his early experiences – such as the giving away of his last half-crown, the only coin he possessed in the world, when he was living alone in lodgings and scarcely knew where the next meal was to come from. To know God for himself as the Hearer and Answerer of prayer had been the preparation, in view of his life-work, that he felt all-important.

Thus I experienced, quite early, how He is willing to help and strengthen and to fulfil the desire of those who fear Him. And so in later years, when I prayed the money came.

He then told how the passage, 'Owe no man anything save to love one another', had raised the question in his mind, 'Are we entitled to make exceptions in work for the Kingdom of God, and continuously to sigh under the oppression of debt?' His own conclusion had been that the words meant just what they said: that God is rich enough to supply 'all our need' as it arises, and that He likes to do so before we run into debt much better than afterwards; and he gave instances to show how, trusting Him to fulfil His own Word, and neither spending money before it was received nor making appeals for help, the 700 missionaries of the C.I.M. were actually sustained.

'Will you please tell us,' was then asked, 'whether it is true that after you had moved a large audience by putting the need of missionary work to their hearts, and someone arose to make a collection, you went so far as to hinder it?'

'I have done so more than once,' replied Mr. Taylor. 'It is not our way to take collections, because we desire to turn aside no gifts from other Societies. We receive free-will offerings, but without putting any pressure upon people. After such a meeting they can easily find opportunity, if they wish, to send their gifts – which so far has been done freely.'

'We have heard,' remarked a clergyman, 'that in that way some quite large sums are sent in; but *we* aim at training our congregations to systematic giving.'

'That is a very important matter,' answered Mr. Taylor. 'However, one is led so, while another is led otherwise. Each must act according to his light. As I said before, for my weakness' sake the Lord has acknowledged my way of working and praying, but I am far from advising anyone to copy me. You do well to train individuals, to train the whole Church to systematic giving.'

Other questions were still raised, until I at length interposed, saying that Mr. Taylor had promised to be present at another meeting that same evening, and it might be well to spare his strength. He had been standing, by his own request, while for over an hour we had been sitting comfortably round him. Just then a sunbeam touched his face, so full of joy and peace, bringing a brightness as from above – and I could only think of Stephen, who saw Heaven opened and Jesus at the right hand of God. One present bowed his head, covering his eyes with his hand, and I heard him whisper: 'We must all take shame before this man.'

'Yes,' the white-headed Professor replied to my suggestion, 'you are quite right; we will not trouble our friend any further.' And rising he crossed the room, put his arm round Mr. Taylor's neck and kissed him.

Summer days in England, after Taylor's return from the Continent, found him more than ever occupied with meetings. Not that he was equal to the strain, but funds were low for the general purposes of the Mission, and he was never one who could pray without working to the limit of his powers. That limit was reached before the Keswick Convention, however. Suffering severely from neuralgia and headache, he was obliged to cancel his engagements and accept the doctor's verdict – complete rest, and absence from the Mission for several months to come.

The wonderful air of Davos, in Switzerland, proved just the tonic he was needing, and there in the early autumn he heard of an answer to prayer that helped to confirm his recovery. He had been much exercised about a financial difficulty that had arisen, due in part to the arrangements for special support in the new branches of the Mission. To deal with it, he would have to visit America as well as China and perhaps Australia, and he was planning such a journey, when a gift of no less than £10,000 for the general fund relieved the situation and sent him rejoicing on his homeward way.

And there was more to follow. The generous donor had been in failing health for some time, but it was a shock to hear of his death within a few days of the above-mentioned gift, and almost more so to learn that he had bequeathed to the C.I.M. a fourth part of his residuary estate for evangelistic and education work. £10,000 a year for ten years or longer – for the money was to be paid in instalments – what might it not accomplish? Articles under the title of 'The Forward Movement' began to appear in *China's Millions* and before the year 1897 was out he was on his way to Shanghai, full of longing to see the inauguration of an evangelistic effort that might spread throughout all the provinces.

He saw with perfect clearness, however, the dangers to which so large an accession of means exposed the Mission, and deeply felt the need for an increase of spiritual power. Not with silver and gold could precious souls be won, or men and women fitted to be messengers of the Cross of Christ. A fresh baptism of the Holy Spirit, the Spirit of Calvary and Pentecost, was the supreme need, and for this he prayed as never before. And he did more than pray. Knowing how much blessing had been given through 'winter missions' in India, he approached the leaders of the Keswick Convention about similar work among the Christians in China. It was not the C.I.M. only that was upon his heart. More and more it was to Chinese Christians that he looked for the evangelization of China. He longed to see the 80,000 communicants of all Protestant churches quickened with new life and fired with zeal for the salvation of their fellow-countrymen.

> 'We are not immediately appealing for new workers,' he continued with regard to the China Inland Mission, although the Forward Movement was the object most of all upon his heart, 'our first need is to prepare for them in China, and the most important preparation of all is a spiritual one.'

One year and nine months now lay before Hudson Taylor of this last period of his active service in China (Jan. 1898 to Sept. 1899). He as little as those about him realized it to be the last, though for several months after his arrival ill-health confined him more or less to his room. However one cannot but be conscious now of the finishing touches God was putting to the life labours of His servant. He was present at all the Council Meetings of this period, with one exception. Seven times the leaders of the Mission gathered to meet him, and he came in touch, through them, with a large part of the work. The important question of the Forward Movement was dealt with in ways that told of God's own working.

Quite apart from previous planning, experienced workers had met in Shanghai from England, America, the Continent of Europe, and the interior of China, and after the January and April Council Meetings all was arranged for a beginning to be made in the accessible province of Kiangsi, with its ninety-nine governing cities, capitals of counties, in very few of which the Gospel was as yet being preached.

The tide of spiritual blessing, too, was rising, even before the arrival of the Keswick deputation. He who delights to use 'the weak things' had found a cleansed and empty vessel which He was pleased to fill to overflowing with His own Spirit.

'I go forth in conscious weakness,' Miss Soltau in charge of the Women's Department in London had written of her visit to China, 'feeling my need of His abundant life for the untried way.'

Drawing on the promised fullness, she had begun the journeys which were to occupy thirteen consecutive months, taking her over 6,000 miles in all, to forty-four mission stations, in every one of which she was made a blessing.

Then came the Keswick deputation to China. The Rev. Charles Inwood, fresh from a wonderful time of blessing on the Continent, was accustomed to speaking through interpretation and was just the teacher needed. From autumn to early summer he and Mrs. Inwood laboured without intermission as Henrietta Soltau was doing, their united service covering almost the entire period of Taylor's visit.

He meanwhile had improved in health and even before Inwood's arrival had been able to take several journeys. While detained in Shanghai he had met over 200 members of the Mission, and subsequently in visits to Chefoo and the new hill-station at Kuling had had opportunity for ministry to a large circle. But his letters went further still, carrying much of the blessing that sustained him and which he thankfully realized to be accessible to all.

'Go forward in the strength of the Lord, and in the sufficiency that comes from Him alone,' he wrote to one who needed encouragement, 'and thank Him for your conscious insufficiency, for when you are weak, then He can be strong in you.

'Do not let any self-consciousness prevent your being at God's disposal for any message He may want you to give at any time, to anyone. Never mind what people think about you.' [1]

[1] Written from Kuling, Sept. 2nd, 1898.

No pains seemed too great if he could lead a soul into fuller blessing, and not least, his own children. To his daughter he wrote,

> Now the heart can no more be filled with two things at the same time than a tumbler can be filled with both air and water at the same time. If you want a tumbler full of water to be filled with air, it has first to be emptied of the water. This shows us why prayer to be filled with the Spirit is often gradually answered. We have to be shown our sins, our faults, our pre-possessions, and to be delivered from them. Faith is the channel by which all grace and blessing are received; and that which is accepted by faith, God bestows in fact. Being filled does not always lead to exalted feeling or uniform manifestation, but God always keeps His word. We have to look to His promises or rest in them, expecting their literal fulfilment. Some put asking in the place of accepting; some wish it were so, instead of believing that it is so. We have never to wait for God's giving, for God has already 'blessed us with all spiritual blessings in heavenly places in Christ'. We may reverently say, He has nothing more to give; for He has given His *all*. Yet, just as the room is full of air, but none can get into the tumbler save as far as the water is emptied out, so we may be unable to receive all He has given, if the self-life is filling to some extent our hearts and lives.

Gradually, as 1898 wore on, the outlook with regard to social and political conditions became increasingly disquieting. While souls were being saved in larger numbers than ever before and spiritual blessing given, the political unrest and the bitterness of feeling due to the aggressions of foreign powers were hastening a crisis the nature of which was but too evident. 'If the Spirit of God work mightily we may be sure that the spirit of evil will also be active,' Taylor had written on his way out to China, and the counter-move he had anticipated was taking serious form. Too hasty attempts on the part of the young Emperor to introduce reforms had thrown the country into a ferment; a powerful rebellion had broken out in Western China in the spring of the year; local uprisings and riots were of frequent occurrence; and finally the Dowager Empress had resumed the reins of government, consigning the helpless Emperor to virtual imprisonment in 'the inner apartments'. This had taken place in September, and now in quick succession drastic measures were being taken to reverse the policy of recent years and to curtail the pretensions of foreigners. Needless to say, this sudden change of front on the part of the Government encouraged anti-foreign feeling throughout the country; and as almost the only Europeans in the interior were missionaries, it was against them particularly that hostilities were directed. The situation was fraught with peril, and could not but give rise to serious apprehensions.

That for thirty-two years God had so watched over the Mission that no life had ever been lost through violence or accident or in travelling was a very real comfort to Taylor. Indeed there had grown up in his mind a restful confidence in God that He *would* thus protect His servants in the Mission, especially defenceless women, working alone in their stations, at a distance often from the nearest missionaries. He rejoiced in their faith and devotion no less than in the blessing that rested on their labours. At this very time (1898–99) despite persecution and threatened danger, 250 converts were received into church membership in the women's stations on the Kwangsin River, while 1,000 inquirers were under instruction as candidates for baptism. Such was the result from the labours of a few young women in a few brief years.

> They are weak enough for God to use, and they believe in being filled with the Holy Ghost. They seek a blessing with fasting and prayer, and they do not seek in vain. The people feel that there is power in connection with their work.

To a woman also had been given success in the difficult and dangerous task of effecting a settled residence in Hunan, so long the most anti-foreign province in China. With a single native helper and a Chinese woman-companion she had walked quietly over the border from Kiangsi, under the very eyes of the soldiery sent to guard the frontier, but who never dreamed of connecting those dusty wayfarers with the dreaded foreigner they were to intercept! During his recent visit to England Taylor had received a letter from this brave Norwegian worker saying that the Lord Jesus had taken up His abode in the hearts of some of the people over the border, and that if *she* should be put out, *He* could not be – for hearts that have once received Him are not likely to give Him up. But a new day had dawned for Hunan. Miss Jacobsen was not put out. On the contrary, the Rev. George Hunter, Dr. Keller and others were so prospered in similar efforts that this very period of uneasiness and trouble witnessed the opening of centre after centre, until the C.I.M. alone had *four* settled stations in the province.

By this time Taylor was on his way up the Yangtze to the far west of China. Despite the rebellion in Szechwan which was still in progress, and the unquiet state of the country everywhere, Charles Inwood and his wife were to attend the conference of West China missionaries to be held at Chungking in January 1899, and the Taylors had decided to accompany them.

Every possible arrangement was made for the comfort of the travellers at the various homes and business centres of the Mission; but not all the loving care of fellow-workers could keep from him the heavy tidings received at Hankow of the first martyrdom in the ranks of the C.I.M. Away in the distant province of Kweichow the tragedy had occurred, when William S. Fleming, from Australia, had been murdered with his friend and helper, P'an, a convert from the Black Meo tribe they were seeking to evangelize. In trying to protect the latter, Fleming's own life had been sacrificed; and while thanking God for the spirit in which he had met his brief but terrible end, Taylor realized with a straitened heart something of what it meant that such an event should have happened.

> 'How sad the tidings!' he wrote to Stevenson November 22; 'blessed for the martyrs but sad for us, for China, for their friends. And not only sad, but ominous! It seems to show that God is about to test us with a new *kind* of trial: surely we need to gird on afresh "the whole armour of God". Doubtless it means fuller blessing, but through deeper suffering.'

His own way now was increasingly hedged about with difficulty. The conference at Chungking, attended by seventy to eighty missionaries of various societies, was followed by serious illness again, and although on the return journey to Shanghai he regained a measure of strength, the summer had to be spent either on the hills or at Chefoo. He was concerned that men for the Forward Movement seemed to be volunteering so slowly. Some had been sent out and some had offered from the ranks of the Mission in China, including his own youngest son, but their number fell far short of even the first twenty, though the money to sustain them was waiting in abundance. Contrasted with former experiences, such as the answers to prayer in connection with the Seventy and the Hundred, this seemed the more remarkable and could not but confirm Taylor's life-long conviction that in God's work the silver and the gold, though very necessary, are of secondary importance. He was to some extent reconciled to patience by the disturbed state of the country, for things seemed to be going from bad to worse politically. The anti-foreign movement fostered by the Dowager Empress was growing in power, and it might be long before normal conditions were restored. Meanwhile a promised visit had to be paid to Australia and New Zealand, and then to New York for the Ecumenical Missionary Conference. This journey, Taylor hoped, would greatly help the Forward Movement, as well as call forth much prayer for China.

Events were moving with startling rapidity, however, to the *dénouement* of 1900. He was still in the midst of his campaign in Australia when the Dowager Empress put forth the inflammatory edict with which that fateful year opened. Posted up in every city of importance, those burning words lost nothing through the free translation given by scholars to the great mass of the illiterate. It was seen to be war to the death, and the secret society of patriotic 'Boxers', pledged to the extermination of all foreigners, flourished under Imperial protection till the movement spread like wildfire throughout the land.

By this time Taylor and his party, which included his son and daughter-in-law, had crossed the Pacific to California, and were on their way to New

York, where they were among the speakers expected at the Ecumenical Conference. From all parts of the world representative missionaries and others gathered for this great occasion, and much prayer was made for China, where the situation was becoming desperate. After the conference Taylor remained on for further work, but concern about the state of things in China and an overfull programme proved too much, and brought about a rather serious breakdown.

England was reached in June, and under a feeling of urgency that she hardly understood, Jennie Taylor arranged for the continuation of their journey to the quiet spot among Swiss mountains where her husband's health had been so wonderfully restored some years previously. He was quite unfit for meetings or correspondence, and consented to the course that offered best prospect of recovery, thankful to leave the work in London, as in Shanghai, so well provided for. At Davos they had found warm friends in an English lady and her husband, Mr. and Mrs. Hofmann, who received visitors in a homelike *pension* at moderate charges. Simply writing to say they were coming, the travellers set out – a few days only before the prayer meeting at Newington Green, at which Mrs. Hofmann herself was present, when the first announcement was made of the terrible events even then transpiring in China. Had the Taylors delayed for that meeting or for a reply from the Villa Concordia, they probably would never have reached the shelter of that quiet home, for when the telegrams began to come they could not have left London. The Boxers had already entered Peking, and the work of destruction was begun. Hundreds of Christians were massacred, and war openly entered upon by the Chinese authorities. The Foreign Legations were in a state of siege, and Imperial decrees had gone out commanding viceroys and governors everywhere to support the rising.

Hearing that Taylor would already be at Davos, Mrs. Hofmann hastened back to do all in her power to help and comfort in that time of sore distress. And there it was the blow fell, and telegram after telegram was received telling of riots, massacres, and the hunting down of refugees in station after station of the Mission – until the heart that so long, in joy and sorrow, had upheld these beloved fellow-workers before the Lord could endure no more. 'I cannot read,' he said when things were at their worst; 'I cannot think; I cannot even pray; but I can trust.'

With the relief of the Legations and the flight of the Court from Peking, the Boxer madness began to pass away, and Li Hung-chang was called again to the helm, to pilot his distracted country through the complications with foreign powers. But before that time the China Inland Mission had a martyr roll of over fifty of its members, while not a few who survived had suffered even more than those whose lives had been laid down. Fifty-eight in the C.I.M. alone perished in that terrible crisis, besides twenty-one children of the Mission, martyred with their parents or dying under sufferings the latter were enabled to survive. But in all the correspondence of the period not one bitter feeling can be traced against their persecutors, not one desire for vengeance or even for indemnification. The spirit of that tender mother who – dying after weeks of brave endurance on the journey to Hankow, having lost one little one by the way and witnessed the prolonged sufferings of others – whispered to her husband, 'I wish I could have lived, I wish I could have gone back there to tell the people more about Jesus', seemed rather to animate all hearts.[1]

When with returning strength Taylor was able to bear more detailed knowledge of what had taken place, not one page of journals or letters did he spare himself as these came to hand. Tears overflowed as he read last letters from two women missionaries written only the day before they met death alone in their distant station.

'Oh, think what it must have been,' he said when able to command his voice, 'to exchange that murderous mob for the rapture of *His* presence, *His* bosom, *His* smile.

'They do not regret it now,' he continued rather brokenly. ' "A crown ... that fadeth not away." "They shall walk with me in white, for they are worthy." '

'We thank God for the grace given to those who have suffered,' he wrote in December replying to a letter of sympathy sent from Shanghai, and signed by 300 members of the Mission. 'It is a wonderful honour He has put upon us as a Mission to be trusted with so great a trial, and to have among us so many counted worthy of a martyr's crown. Some who have been spared have perhaps suffered more than some of those taken, and our Lord will not forget. How much it has meant to us to be so far from you in the hour of trial we cannot express, but the throne of grace has been as near to us here as it would have been in China.'

Prevented from being himself in China and feeling that his own life might be cut short at any time, Taylor cabled out in August, appointing D. E. Hoste as Acting General Director of the Mission. This was no hasty step taken in an emergency. For years he had been looking to the Lord for guidance as to his successor, and had seen with thankfulness Hoste's growing fitness for the position. There had been no uncertainty in Taylor's mind, even before he left China, as to the answer to his prayers; and though the appointment of Hoste was not made public until some months later, when Stevenson's approval and that of the London and China Councils had been

[1] *A Thousand Miles of Miracle in China,* a touching record of personal experiences during the Boxer crisis by A. E. Glover.

cordially expressed, Taylor had the comfort of knowing that an important step had been taken to safeguard the interests of the whole work.

As to the difficult question of compensation, Taylor had from the first advised that no claim should be made by the Mission, and that even if offered, none should be accepted for injury to life or person. Later on when, besides a heavy indemnity and other punitive measures, retribution of a fearful character was inflicted by certain of the Powers, he went further, fully agreeing with the Councils that indemnification for Mission property also should be declined, though individuals were left free to accept compensation for personal losses if they so desired. This action, though criticized in certain quarters, was warmly approved at the British Foreign Office and by its Minister in Peking, who sent a private donation of £100 to the Mission in expression of his 'admiration' and sympathy.

It was not until the following summer (1901) that Taylor was obliged to abandon his cherished hope of returning to China. Even a visit to England proved too much of a strain, and just before his seventieth birthday he returned to Switzerland, thankful for the relief of the simple retired life which enabled him and Jennie to serve the Mission still by prayer and correspondence.

Glad to be near their friend Mrs. Berger, it was by the Lake of Geneva they made their home at length, in the hamlet of Chevalleyres above Vevey. No railway climbed the hillside then nearer than the village and castle of Blonay, whose grey old tower looked out on a scene of ever-changing beauty. Further up toward the wooded heights of the Pleiades an attractive though simple *pension* was found among meadows and orchards. Entering at the back, from the level of the road, the south rooms on the ground floor were raised a storey above the garden. This was just what Jennie was seeking. A little sitting-room and bedroom, with a front balcony and a closed-in verandah toward the sun-rising, offered just the accommodation needed; while the moderate charge of four and a half francs a day included meals served in their own apartment.

Little by little, as their stay was prolonged, the *pension* became quite a resort for English guests, many friends coming for longer or shorter visits because the Hudson Taylors were there.

'It was not so much what he *said* but what he *was* that proved a blessing to me,' wrote one. 'His strong faith, quietness, and constant industry, even in his weakness, touched me deeply. To see a man who had been so active compelled to live a retired life, unable to pray more than fifteen minutes at a time, and yet remaining bright and even joyous, greatly impressed me. Not one single complaint or murmur did we ever hear from his lips. He was always cheerful – rejoicing in the flowers by day and studying the stars at night.'

One reason for the quiet happiness of those days was that changes and partings were over, and the two who had known so much of separation could be together at last and have time to enjoy one another's society. At first they were able to be out a good deal together, delighting in little excursions by rail and steamer and in the long, patient climbs that ended in a glorious outlook from some favourite height. By degrees it came to be others who accompanied Taylor in his longer walks, however, Jennie finding sufficient excuse for staying oftener at home. But always – writing at the table or knitting by the window – she was ready for their return with the welcome cup of tea and cheery news of visitors or letters. Then there were long hours in developing the photographs taken and studying the flowers gathered. The keenness of Taylor's pleasure in these simple enjoyments as well as his delight in nature and the everyday intercourse of friendship were remarkable. His capacity for happiness was like that of an unspoilt child. Time never hung heavy on his hands; and while unable for any but easy reading, his love for the Word of God remained the same.

Until the autumn of 1902 Hudson Taylor retained his position as General Director of the Mission, but when Hoste arrived from China Taylor felt that the time had come for laying down responsibilities for which he was no longer equal. Many problems were pressing in connection with the reconstruction and rapid development of the work. The seed sown in tears and watered with blood was giving promise of an abundant harvest. The blessing of God had signally rested on the appointment made two years previously, and knowing he had the full concurrence of all the Directors and Councils, Taylor resigned to Hoste the full direction of the Mission.

The change had come about so gradually that to many it was hardly felt, but it was evident to those who saw below the surface that Taylor deeply and painfully felt his inability to labour as formerly. The true joy of life, he said once, was to do all for Jesus' sake. Sacrifice and labour were alike sweet when it was for Him. Then he added after a pause, 'But it's hardest of all to do *nothing* for His sake.'

CHAPTER 27

His Way is Perfect

(1903–1905)

Two glad services are ours,
  Both the Master loves to bless;
First we serve with all our powers,
  Then with all our feebleness.
Nothing else the soul uplifts
  Save to serve Him night and day;
Serve Him when He gives His gifts,
  Serve Him when He takes away.

It was in this spirit that Taylor met the last great sorrow of his life. In the remote Swiss hamlet Jennie was drawing near the end of her earthly pilgrimage. She had been confined to bed for a few weeks in that summer of 1904, and the end came quietly. A last gift to the Mission of £100 as 'a thank-offering for mercies received and expected'; a few days so peaceful and tender that those about her caught the reflection in those deeply shining eyes of a Presence to them unseen, and then the silent crossing of the swift, dark river.

'No pain, no pain,' she said repeatedly, though for some hours the difficulty in breathing was distressing. Toward morning, seeing her husband's anguish:

'Ask Him to take me quickly,' she whispered.

Never had he had a harder prayer to pray; but for her sake he cried to God to free the waiting spirit. Five minutes later the breathing became quiet – and in a little while all was peace.

But for him the desolation was unutterable. On the wall of the little sitting-room hung a text, the last purchase they had made together, and many a time during the days that followed did he look up through his tears to the words in blue, shining out from their white background:

'*Celui qui a fait les promesses est fidèle.*'

'My grace is sufficient', had been almost her last words to him, and then 'He will not fail'. Upon this certainty he rested now in the desolation he had so little strength to endure, remembering her constant joy in the will of God and that, as he recalled again and again, 'She never thought anything *could* be better'.

He was not without congenial society at Chevalleyres that winter. Not only was his niece, Mary Broomhall, with him, but some old friends from Toronto made a stay of several months and entered into all his interests. A decided improvement in health encouraged him to hope that with the spring he might even think of returning to China; and the desire gaining ground, it was arranged that he should do so, travelling by way of America accompanied by his son and daughter-in-law.

How short the time was to be, and how full of precious experiences, no one anticipated. Only six weeks lay before him in China, but frail though he was for the long journeys undertaken, there was no sign that the end was near, and least of all did he himself expect it.

Landing at Shanghai on the 17th April (1905), he was welcomed by a representative company at the Mission house, for the Spring Council Meetings were in session. Hoste and Stevenson were there together with some who had come through the worst of the Boxer outbreak, and Meadows, whose association with Taylor went back to the old days of the Ningpo Mission, had come up from Chekiang. The flowers that filled his rooms, the comforts forethought had provided, and the letters of love and sympathy that flowed in, all revealed the love and veneration in which he was held.

Easter was spent at Yangchow, home of so many memories! From the new Mission house near the hills at Chinkiang it was an easy walk to the cemetery overlooking the river, where in the long ago years that seemed somehow not far away he had laid his heart's best treasures. There the names of four of his children were engraved beside their mother's; and the memories were sweet rather than sorrowful, for the partings were long since past and reunion must be at hand. To a group of young workers just setting out for inland stations he spoke a few words of loving counsel:

> It is a great privilege to meet many of you here. I have met many here in days gone by. My dear wife died by me here. In spirit our loved ones may be nearer to us than we think; and HE is near, nearer than we think. The Lord Jesus will never leave nor forsake us. Count on Him; enjoy Him: abide in Him. Do, dear friends, be true to Him and to His Word. He will never disappoint you.
>
> 'You may be tired often and lonely often,' he said to one in parting, 'but the Lord knows just how much each cup costs. Look to Him; He will never disappoint you.'

Steamer to Hankow was an easy stage that brought him once again to that busy centre of the Mission at which there was so much coming and going for the far interior. Here the welcome was just as warm as at Shanghai, and old friends of other Societies gathered round him with every token of affection. Dr. Griffith John, still in the ripeness of his strength, was there and seemed to remember Taylor's love of music, singing hymn after hymn with all the old Welsh fire. Dr. W. A. P. Martin too, came over from Wuchang to join the circle, the missionary life of the three together amounting to no less than 156 years.

The journey to Hankow having been accomplished in safety, Taylor felt encouraged to go a little farther and make trial of the new railway running northward to Peking. If he could only reach one or two of the stations in Honan, it would be so good to be right in the interior again!

'Once before on just such a May morning we had left Hankow on the same journey,' wrote one of his companions, 'but then it was by barrow, and many a weary day lay between us and our destination. Now, two weeks of strenuous travelling was replaced by a run of twenty-four hours. It was a wonderful change, and as we glided swiftly over the iron road we felt as if there must be a rude awakening. But no, it went on and on, fresh surprises meeting us at every point, until only six hours after leaving Hankow we steamed through the long tunnel under the mountains between Hupeh and Honan, and found ourselves once again in that familiar province.'

A visit at Yencheng, a station to which the railway brought them, was followed by one to the neighbouring station though it involved an overland journey. A night, indeed, had to be spent in an inn, which was an outstanding experience for its strangeness and yet familiarity – just an ordinary wayside inn like so many hundreds Taylor had known in earlier days.

After he had gone to rest a touching little incident happened, which he did not hear of until morning. It was between ten and eleven at night when a Chinese Christian, who had heard in his village not far away of Taylor's being in the inn that night, arrived. He had come over after his long day's work to pay his respects to the Venerable Chief Pastor. It was explained that Taylor was now sleeping; that the journey had tired him very much, and that it would hardly do to awaken him.

'Never mind, never mind,' said the visitor. Then, fumbling with something he was carrying, he pushed a little bundle through the paper window.

'Why, what is this?' he was asked.

'Oh, nothing! It is only my poor little intention. It is my duty to provide for the Venerable Pastor while he is near our village.'

It was 200 cash, money the man had brought for Taylor's expenses at the inn.

As heavy rains came on, an easier method of returning to the railway was suggested. Hour by hour the river rose behind the Mission house, until with a good current boats were going downstream cheerily. On one of these the journey was made, and instead of parting when the railway was reached, Taylor decided to go right on to a station where his daughter (Mrs. Coulthard) had been the first woman missionary.

And so, just a step at a time, the way opened until he had visited five of the centres in Honan, meeting with the missionaries from as many others. To his son and daughter-in-law the latter part of the journey was of special interest, as the two stations to which he travelled by sedan chair they had had a part in opening. Every tree and house looked just as they had seen them scores of times, until they neared the first of the two cities (Chenchow-fu) and there something unusual arrested their attention.

On the main highway a crowd of men and boys were gathered near a table, standing in the sunlight, with several bright gleaming objects held up in their hands. They were the Christians from Chenchow-fu who had come out to meet the travellers. The table was spread with refreshments; the glittering objects shining in the sun were four large golden characters (*Nui-ti en-ren,* Benefactor of Inland China) held up to greet Taylor – the motto to be fixed on a banner they were preparing to present when he arrived.

When they reached the house inside the city they found the whole court-yard covered in, with a broad platform arranged at one end, draped in red, and welcome written large on everything. Taylor was much among the Christians during the days spent there, and spoke to them once or twice by interpretation. At a Christian Endeavour meeting they were all presented with silver badges, and enrolled as members of the Chenchow branch. Taylor was very pleased with the way in which it was done, and wore the sign of membership on his coat right on to the end.

Some of the Christians at Taikang hired a cart and came to Chenchow, a whole day's journey, to meet the travellers. On the way they passed a letter-carrier who said that Taylor was not well and that he would have to turn back without visiting their city. Upon this the Taikang friends were greatly distressed, and stopped in the middle of the road to pray that the Lord would strengthen him and help him to undertake the journey.

'O Lord, what have we done,' they said, 'that the Venerable Pastor should come thousands of miles from the other side of the world, and after months of travelling stop short just one day's journey from our city? O Lord, we too are his little children! Help him to come on and visit us.'

Great was their joy a few hours later, when they reached Chenchow, to find a baptismal service in progress, with Taylor taking part, and to hear that he had already made up his mind to go on to Taikang next day!

Taylor and his party found themselves at Chowkiakow for a Sunday, and as it happened, Sunday, May 21st. The Christians came to know it was his birthday, and prepared a beautiful scarlet satin banner to present to him, bearing the inscription '*O man greatly beloved*'. One after another they rose and made little addresses to Taylor, some of them very heart-moving.

It was Friday, May 26th, when the party reached Hankow once more, the thirty-ninth anniversary of the sailing of the *Lammermuir*. Only eight days were left of his earthly pilgrimage, five in May and three in June – and then the 'far more exceeding and eternal weight of glory'.

After a quiet Sunday in Hankow he set out on the last journey he was to take, though none could know it then. He had decided to go by steamer to Changsha, capital of the province of Hunan, which he had never visited. First of the far inland provinces the Mission had attempted to enter, it had been the last in which settled residence had been obtained, and for more than thirty years Taylor had borne it specially upon his heart in prayer.

As they crossed the far-reaching lake and steamed up the river, passing well-built cities, beautiful pagodas and temples, rich plains covered with ripening crops, and noble mountain ranges near and distant, he could not but think of all the toil and prayer of years gone by, of buried lives and dauntless faith, richly rewarded at last in the change that was coming over the attitude of the people. Until eight or nine years previously, there had not been one Protestant missionary settled in the province. None had been able to gain a footing. No fewer than 111 missionaries were to be found there now, connected with thirteen societies, working in seventeen central stations and aided by a strong band of Chinese helpers.

It was Thursday afternoon, June 1st, when they reached the capital, Changsha, and were welcomed by Dr. and Mrs. Keller. On the following day it rained all the morning, but after lunch, sedan chairs were called and Taylor was taken to the T'ien Sin Koh, a lofty building on the highest point of the city wall. He climbed to the second storey and was delighted with the wonderful view of mountains, plain and river, and afterwards went to see the site for a new hospital.

On Saturday, he did not go down to breakfast, but was dressed and reading when his tray was taken up. He was to speak to the Chinese friends that morning, many of whom had just read *A Retrospect* translated into Chinese. Mr. Li the evangelist responded to Taylor's words, and expressed the love and joy with which they welcomed him to Changsha.

That afternoon a reception had been arranged to give all the missionaries in the city an opportunity of meeting Taylor. It was cool and pleasant in the little garden on to which the sitting-room opened, and tea was served on the lawn, surrounded by trees and flowers. He sat in the midst of the guests for an hour or more, evidently enjoying the quiet, happy time, and after all had left one of the doctors remained with him for half an hour. Speaking of the privilege of bringing *everything* to God in prayer, Dr. Barrie said that he was sometimes hindered by the feeling that many things were too small, really, to pray about. Taylor's answer was that he did not know anything about it – about such a distinction, probably. Then he added:

There is nothing small, and there is nothing great: only God is great, and we should trust Him fully.

When the evening meal was ready Taylor did not feel inclined to go down, and a little later he was preparing to go to rest when his son brought him his supper. While waiting for him to be comfortably settled, his daughter-in-law spent a few minutes alone on the little roof-platform. Enjoying the cool and quietness under the starlit sky, she stood looking across at the distant mountains and river little realizing, as she wrote later,

... that in less than one half-hour our loved one would be with the Lord! Was the golden gate already swinging back on its hinges? Were the hosts of welcoming angels gathering to receive his spirit? What was happening, even then, over the sleeping city?

Knowing nothing, realizing nothing, I went down. Dear Father was in bed, the lamp burning on the chair beside him, and he was leaning over it with his pocket-book lying open and the home letters it contained spread out as he loved to have them. I drew the pillow up more comfortably under his head, and sat down on a low chair close beside him. As he said nothing, I began talking a little about the pictures in the *Missionary Review* lying open on the bed. Howard left the room to fetch something that had been forgotten for supper, and I was just in the middle of a sentence when Father turned his head quickly and gave a little gasp. I looked up, thinking he was going to sneeze. But another came, then another! He gave no cry and said no word. He was not choking or distressed for breath. He did not look at me or seem conscious of anything.

I ran to the door and called Howard, but before he could reach the bedside it was evident that the end had come. I ran back to call Dr. Keller, who was just at the foot of the stairs. In less time than it takes to write it he was with us, but only to see dear Father draw his last breath. It was not death – but the glad, swift entry upon life immortal.

'My father, my father, the chariots of Israel and the horsemen thereof!'

And oh, the look of rest and calm that came over the dear face was wonderful! The weight of years seemed to pass away in a few moments. The weary lines vanished. He looked like a child quietly sleeping, and the very room seemed full of unutterable peace.

Tenderly they laid him down, too surprised to realize for the moment their own great loss. There was nothing more to be done.

The precious service of months was ended. Chinese friends went out to make arrangements, but we could hardly bring ourselves to leave that quiet room. All the house was still, hallowed by a serenity and sweetness that hardly seemed of earth. Though he was gone, a wonderful love and tenderness seemed still to draw us to his side. Oh, the comfort of seeing him so utterly rested! Dear Father, all the weariness over, all the journeyings ended – safe home, safe home at last!

One by one or in little groups friends and Chinese Christians gathered round his bed. Even in those short days the sweetness and simplicity of his life had won their hearts.

'*O Sï-mu*,' whispered one woman as she left the room, '*ts'ien ts'ien wan-wan-tih t'ien-shi tsieh t'a liao!*' (thousands and myriads of angels have welcomed him).

Last of all a young evangelist and his wife, a bride of eighteen, came up. They had journeyed in from an out-station on purpose to meet Taylor, whose *Retrospect* they had been reading. Together they stood beside the bed in silence, until the young man said:

'Do you think that I might touch his hand?'

Then he bent over him, took one of Taylor's lifeless hands in his and, stroking it tenderly, began to talk to him just as if he could hear. He seemed to forget everything else in a great longing just to reach the one who still seemed near, and make him feel his love and gratitude.

> '*Lao Muh-sï, Lao Muh-sï*,' he said tenderly (dear and venerable Pastor), 'we truly love you. We have come today to see you. We longed to look into your face. We, too, are your little children, *Lao Muh-sï, Lao Muh-sï*. You opened for us the road, the road to Heaven. You loved us and prayed for us long years. We came today to look upon your face.
>
> 'You look so happy, so peaceful! You are smiling. Your face is quiet and pleased. You cannot speak to us tonight. We do not want to bring you back: but we will follow you. We shall come to you, *Lao Muh-sï*. You will welcome us by and by.'

And all the time he held his hand, bending over him and stroking it gently, his young wife standing by.

Downstairs, meanwhile, another touching scene was taking place. Those who had been out to make arrangements returned, bringing a coffin and bearers and everything necessary for the last journey. They had hoped when first they learned of Taylor's Home-call that he would be buried in Hunan, and had rejoiced to think that in this way they might keep him among them still. But when it was explained that his family grave was in Chinkiang and he had always wished to be laid beside his loved ones should he die in China, they set aside their own desire, and did all they could to forward the departure of the cortège.

They sent word to Taylor's son, asking if they might speak with him. He went at once and, gathering round him, they said that they had wished to obtain a more beautiful coffin, but had been obliged to be satisfied with the best they could find ready-made; that he need not ask the price, for it was their gift, the gift of the church; for if they could not be allowed to keep the Venerable Chief Pastor in Hunan, they must at any rate do everything for him at their own expense.

It was a great surprise, but they would take no denial. Had not the Lord brought their beloved father in the faith to Changsha, and permitted them to look upon his face? From their midst had he not been translated? Hunan Christians had been the last to hear his voice, to receive his blessing. Theirs must be the privilege of providing for his last needs.

So Hunan hands prepared his last resting-place, Hunan hearts planned all with loving care – one little company of the great multitude his life had blessed.

By the mighty river at Chinkiang they laid him, where it rolls its waters two miles wide toward the sea. Much might be said of the love and veneration shown to his memory; of memorial services in Shanghai, London and elsewhere; of eulogies in the public press; of sympathetic resolutions passed by missionary and other societies, and of personal letters from high and low in many lands. From the striking tribute of a High Church bishop in *The Guardian* to tender reminiscences of fellow-workers, many were the written and spoken words that showed him to have been not only 'the heart-beat felt throughout the Mission', but a vital force of life and love in almost every part, one might say, of the Body of Christ. But the voices that linger longest are those he would have loved the best – the voices of Chinese children singing sweet hymns of praise as they laid their little offerings of flowers upon his resting-place.

'Thus one by one the stars that are to shine for ever in God's firmament appear in their celestial places, and the children of the Kingdom enter upon the blessedness of their Father's house not made with hands.'